Profits
in the
Wilderness

John Frederick Martin

Profits

Entrepreneurship and the

in the

Founding of New England Towns

Wilderness

in the Seventeenth Century

Published for the Institute of Early American

History and Culture, Williamsburg, Virginia,

by the University of North Carolina Press,

Chapel Hill and London

The Institute of Early American History and Culture is sponsored
jointly by the College of William and Mary and the Colonial
Williamsburg Foundation.

Library of Congress Cataloging-in-Publication Data
Martin, John Frederick.

Profits in the wilderness : entrepreneurship and the founding of New
England towns in the seventeenth century / John Frederick Martin.

   p.   cm.

Includes bibliographical references and index.

   ISBN 0-8078-2001-6 (cloth : alk. paper). — ISBN 0-8078-4346-6
(pbk. : alk. paper)

   1. New England—Economic conditions.   2. Capitalism—New
England—History—17th century.   3. Entrepreneurship—New
England—History—17th century.   4. Cities and towns—New
England—History—17th century.   5. New England—Politics and
government—Colonial period, ca. 1660–1775.   I. Institute of Early
American History and Culture (Williamsburg, Va.)   II. Title.
HC107.A11M18   1991   91-2945
330.974'02—dc20   CIP

The paper in this book meets the guidelines for permanence and
durability of the Committee on Production Guidelines for Book
Longevity of the Council on Library Resources.

This volume received indirect support from an unrestricted book
publication grant awarded to the Institute by the L. J. Skaggs and
Mary C. Skaggs Foundation of Oakland, California.

Manufactured in the United States of America

95 94 93 92 91   5 4 3 2 1

TO DANIELA

Acknowledgments

In the course of a long project, one leans on many people. I owe a great debt of gratitude to the personnel of various libraries, archives, and the archival departments of several government offices—to Widener Library and Houghton Library at Harvard University, Massachusetts Historical Society, Massachusetts State Archives, New England Historic Genealogical Society, Boston Public Library, American Antiquarian Society, Library of Congress, Connecticut State Library, Rhode Island Historical Society, Pettaquamscut Historical Society, Bristol County Registry of Deeds and to keepers of probate records in Bristol, Suffolk, and Middlesex counties in Massachusetts.

Several people took precious time to read portions of the book in manuscript form and saved me from many, but not all, of my errors: Theodore Dwight Bozeman, Michael McGiffert, Drew R. McCoy, and James Henretta. Edwin J. Perkins took an interest in this project and gave me valuable advice and encouragement. Stephen Innes's comments on my paper (delivered at the American Historical Association meeting in December 1989) caused me to refine several arguments. I have learned from the writings and, even more, depended on the friendship for many years of Andrew Delbanco, Thomas Doerflinger, and Stephen Schuker. To all these scholars I am grateful.

Chances are I would never have embarked on this project nor for that matter have specialized in early American history if I had not taken Bernard Bailyn's seminar as a first-year graduate student. Bailyn as a teacher had two distinctive, admirable qualities. First, whenever a student finished a well-argued presentation, he would ask in a challenging tone, "So what's the news?" letting us know that mere competence was not what we should be after. Second, while badgering us with questions, he left us virtually alone to supply the answers. I am in his debt on both counts.

The editors of the Institute of Early American History and Culture, a patient lot if ever there were one, have stood by this book through multiple changes in its composition, in my availability, and in their own roster. Five editors—Philip Morgan, Steve Botein, Roger Ekirch, Thomas Purvis, and Fredrika Teute—have encouraged, criticized, and defended this book; I am indebted to each of them. I am especially grateful to the late Steve Botein, who saw the editor's role as not only critic but also partisan and friend. I am also indebted to Gil Kelly of the Institute for overseeing production and final editing of the book with care and skill, and to Linda Ray for proof-reading and casting her sharp editorial eye on the manuscript.

Every book has its costs; this one has been greedy in its demands on time and opportunity, missed paychecks, and frazzled emotions. Not only for patiently tolerating all this, and for reading, rereading, and improving this still-flawed work, but also, and mainly, for giving me her support, for seeing me through this book and through these years, Daniela Winkler is the one I really have to, want to, thank.

Contents

Abbreviations

AAS	American Antiquarian Society, Worcester, Mass.
BCPR	Bristol County Probate Registry, Taunton, Mass.
Cal. S.P., Col.	Great Britain, *Calendar of State Papers,* Colonial Series, 44 vols. (London, 1860–1969)
Conn. Archives	Towns and Lands Collection, microfilm, Connecticut Archives, Connecticut State Library, Hartford, Conn.
Conn. Records	J. Hammond Trumbull and Charles J. Hoadly, eds., *Public Records of the Colony of Connecticut . . . ,* 15 vols. (New Haven, Conn., 1818)
LC	Library of Congress, Washington, D.C.
Mass. Acts and Resolves	Massachusetts, General Court, *The Acts and Resolves, Public and Private, of the Province of the Massachusetts Bay . . . ,* 21 vols. (Boston, 1869–1922)
Mass. Archives	Massachusetts Archives, Boston
Mass. Records	Nathaniel B. Shurtleff, ed., *Records of the Governor and Company of the Massachusetts Bay in New England,* 5 vols. (Boston, 1853–1854)
MCPR	Middlesex County Probate Registry, Old Courthouse, Cambridge, Mass.
MHS	Massachusetts Historical Society, Boston
NHR	*Narragansett Historical Register*
RIHS	Rhode Island Historical Society, Providence, R.I.

SCPR   Suffolk County Probate Registry, Old Courthouse, Boston

York Deeds   York County, Maine, Register of Deeds, *York Deeds,* 1642 . . . , 17 vols. (Portland, Bethel, Maine, 1887–)

Profits
in the
Wilderness

Introduction

This book began as an investigation into land specula-
tion in seventeenth-century New England. Originally it focused on wilderness, not towns, but the more one studies speculators, the more one finds
them speculating in town lands; and so the focus turned to towns. This
book, then, has graduated from the somewhat contrarian task of demon-
strating speculative activity in Puritan New England to the more ambitious
one of interpreting an old, important institution, the New England town.
Still, the contrary-minded will not be disappointed.

[Since the turn of the century—since the works of Melville Egleston,
Herbert L. Osgood, Frederick Jackson Turner, Roy Hidemichi Akagi, and
Lois K. Mathews—the predominant interpretation has held that in the
early years of towns settlers were bound together in a community, sharing
power, the land, and a mutual fate.] Only during the second and third
generations of each town's life, so the interpretation goes, did the first land
grantees and their heirs draw a line between themselves and nonland-
holders and a landholding aristocracy emerge in New England towns.
Eventually the nonlandholding portion of the town meeting outgrew the
landholding portion, and conflict arose over control of the common lands.
While these changes were transforming older towns, toward the end of the
seventeenth century, land speculation began to play a role in the founding
of new towns. [Thus towns underwent an evolution similar to, and part of,
the general declension of New England culture, moving from community
to individualism, from Puritan to Yankee.[1]

1. Melville Egleston, *The Land System of the New England Colonies,* Johns Hopkins
University Studies in Historical and Political Science, 4th Ser., nos. 11–12 (Baltimore,
1886); Herbert L. Osgood, *The American Colonies in the Seventeenth Century,* 3 vols.
(New York, 1904–1907); Frederick Jackson Turner, "The First Official Frontier of the
Massachusetts Bay," in Turner, *The Frontier in American History* (New York, 1920), 39–

In recent decades, two schools of thought have reinforced this consensus: the school that has emphasized the peasantness of early New England village life, a life ordered by tradition, organic ties, and communal values; and the proliferating Puritanists. Very few scholars of Puritanism have commented on landholding patterns, let alone argued for one pattern as against another; but this renewed attention to Puritanism has served as a backdrop for social historians, enabling them better to argue that New England society started as one thing, pious and communal, and evolved into something else: materialistic and individualistic. Ironically, Perry Miller, who described a complex Puritan mind fully capable of reconciling itself to commerce, individualism, and worldliness, strengthened perhaps more

---

66; Roy Hidemichi Akagi, *The Town Proprietors of the New England Colonies: A Study of Their Development, Organization, Activities, and Controversies, 1620–1770* (Philadelphia, 1924); Lois K. Mathews, *Expansion of New England: The Spread of New England Settlements and Institutions to the Mississippi River, 1620–1865* (Boston, 1909). For a summary of the historiography of towns, see John Frederick Martin, "Entrepreneurship and the Founding of New England Towns: The Seventeenth Century" (Ph.D. diss., Harvard University, 1985), 1–28.

During the last couple of decades, several studies have departed significantly from the standard view. These works include Stephen Innes, "Land Tenancy and Social Order in Springfield, Massachusetts, 1652–1702," *William and Mary Quarterly*, 3d Ser., XXXV (1978), 33–56; Innes, *Labor in a New Land: Economy and Society in Seventeenth-Century Springfield* (Princeton, N.J., 1983); Christine Leigh Heyrman, *Commerce and Culture: The Maritime Communities of Colonial Massachusetts, 1690–1750* (New York, 1984); Paul R. Lucas, *Valley of Discord: Church and Society along the Connecticut River, 1636–1725* (Hanover, N.H., 1976). Other modern studies, though dealing more with the 18th century than with the 17th, shed new light on the rise of rural capitalism: Winifred B. Rothenberg, "The Market and Massachusetts Farmers, 1750–1855," *Journal of Economic History*, XLI (1981), 283–314; Allan Kulikoff, "The Transition to Capitalism in Rural America," *WMQ*, 3d Ser., XLVI (1989), 120–144; Daniel Vickers, "Competency and Competition: Economic Culture in Early America," *WMQ*, 3d Ser., XLVII (1990), 3–29. Edwin J. Perkins, *The Economy of Colonial America*, 2d ed. (New York, 1988), is also an important corrective to the standard interpretation. Still other studies, while not challenging the main premises of the standard interpretation, have recently added prodigiously to our knowledge of 17th-century local history. Among the most informative works are David Grayson Allen, *In English Ways: The Movement of Societies and the Transferal of English Local Law and Custom to Massachusetts Bay in the Seventeenth Century* (Chapel Hill, N.C., 1981); Bruce C. Daniels, *The Connecticut Town: Growth and Development, 1635–1790* (Middletown, Conn., 1979); Daniels, *Dissent and Conformity on Narragansett Bay: The Colonial Rhode Island Town* (Middletown, Conn., 1983).

than anyone else the grasp of the standard interpretation of town life (though Miller had nothing to say about the subject); for it was Miller who lent so much luster to the model of declension.

[Underlying the standard interpretation are three central assumptions, rarely stated as propositions: first, that commercial enterprise played at best a small part in town-founding during the seventeenth century; second, that in the first years of New England towns, a single class of individuals, the town residents, governed the town, shared the land, and formed a church; and, third, that the communal spirit was more powerful than individualism in seventeenth-century towns. This present study takes issue with each of these contentions and offers a different impression of early settlements.]

First, it concentrates on profits in town-planting. Part I describes the activities of roughly one hundred people who launched towns for money in the seventeenth century and attempts to recapture the complicated town-founding process. The entrepreneurs described here were chosen for study purely on empirical grounds: their names surfaced most frequently in connection with land ventures—in town records, town histories, land company records, and general court petitions regarding frontier settle-ments. Few men prominent in launching seventeenth-century towns have escaped notice here. But this sample is not scientific. It contains the same biases as the town sample (see Appendixes, Part II). On the other hand, the purpose of Part I is not to arrive at any specific calculation. It is instead descriptive: to describe the requirements of founding a town in the wil-derness, the organizations town promoters invented, the different profit schemes they devised, the general court policy, and the prevailing ideas (both secular and religious) about the frontier—all to give concreteness to the basic assertion that [entrepreneurship was a practical necessity, socially and culturally acceptable, at the heart of the effort to settle the wilderness in the seventeenth century.]

Part II is concerned with towns after they were founded; it takes issue with the second standard proposition, namely, that town residents shared land and power. This section is based on evidence from sixty-three towns, roughly half the number founded in the seventeenth century, includ-ing towns from every New England colony. [It argues that, having been launched by organizations possessing a strong business character, towns apportioned rights and responsibilities according to business principles.] In very few towns, if any, were all settlers owners of the undivided land—even at the outset of settlement. In very few towns, if any, were all adult male residents voters. In most towns, both the landholding body and the town meeting excluded a considerable portion of town residents.

The very exclusiveness of landholding and voting bodies brings into question the communalism of towns, the third leg of the standard interpretation. [Great unevenness in the distribution of economic and political rights separated the residents of seventeenth-century towns one from another and was the cause of much conflict.] On the other hand, communal spirit and harmony were not absent from towns. One is struck by the careful organization and orderliness of the land corporations that, in most towns, financed settlement, held title to the town land, and controlled the town meeting. As members of these corporations, people on the frontier did indeed work together, strive for consensus, live by carefully drafted rules, and subordinate their individual interests to the interests of the corporation. But not every resident was a member of the land corporation. [When historians attribute communal characteristics to the land system of New England towns, they are mistaking the fraternity of shareholders for the fraternity of town-dwellers. And when they attribute egalitarian characteristics to town meetings, they are calling "town democracy" what in many cases was really shareholder democracy.]

Historians have been no more confused than colonists were themselves, for a basic ambiguity existed about local institutions. If one's rights and duties in a town were fixed by one's shares, the question was inescapable: what was a town? Was it owned by shareholders or by all, was it private or public, a corporation or a community? Largely as the result of intervention from Whitehall toward the end of the seventeenth century, answers were supplied to these questions; they are the subject of Part III. [Threatened in their land rights by the crown, colonists drew a definite line between political and proprietary institutions, and the resulting separation of towns and proprietorships transformed the nature of rights in New England towns. Settlers won control over their own town meetings. Shareholder actions lost the color of public policy. Completely public institutions emerged for the first time in towns. Colonists began, at least on the local level in New England, to distinguish rights from privileges and separate them from the realm of property.]

[On the frontier, then, the turn of the seventeenth century to the eighteenth was not a hinge between two different spirits or two ethics, but a period when an ambiguous institution clarified its functions. It was a moment of institutional, not moral or social or cultural, significance; a time of change, yes: declension, no. The important decisions—to develop the wilderness, to rely on entrepreneurs toward that end, to organize towns upon business principles, to exclude nonshareholders from land divisions, and to encourage individuals to profit from landownership in return for their help in developing the frontier—had been made long before, at the start of the colonial period.

A word about the term "entrepreneurs." This term is employed, not to throw mud in the eye of the partisans of peasants and Puritans, but simply because there seems to be no alternative, no apter way of describing people who organized, managed, and assumed the risks of starting profit-making enterprises. Nothing more is meant by the use of this term. This author would not argue that the entrepreneurs of the seventeenth century were the same as the entrepreneurs of the twentieth, that John Pynchon was a Henry Ford on horseback. The differences in mind, in social and sumptuary restraints, in the scale of business, and in the range of economic activity all create insuperable barriers between the two ages and between easy comparison of their inhabitants. The main thing to bear in mind when studying the past, as Herbert Butterfield said, is that it was different from the present.

Nor are commercial terms used to imply that towns were nothing more than businesses. In fact, a single town had many facets—as home to a church, a military outpost, a community of neighbors, and a business corporation. This study focuses on only one of those facets, because entrepreneurship is the side to town-founding that has been inadequately reported and needs reporting in order to form a more complete understanding of the town-founding process. Also, whatever the differences between towns and incongruities within each town, all towns had to devise a means for holding and sharing land, and all towns resorted to a commercial model for this basic and initial activity in town life. Voluminous evidence contradicts the judgments reached in the following pages; much of it is noted. Still, some sense must be made of the past. I have tried to do justice to my own findings as well as to previous conclusions, which this study both contradicts and seeks to build upon and expand.

I | *Entrepreneurship*

1

Entrepreneurship
and Town-Founding

1. Varieties of Town Promoters

[Starting a town was an expensive, complicated affair] People did not simply move to the wilderness and build log cabins. Before that could happen, a great deal had to be done—the site chosen, the General Court's permission obtained, the land purchased from the Indians, and fellow settlers admitted to the group. Then the township had to be surveyed, the survey had to be accepted by the General Court, and the first lots had to be laid out—home lots, planting lots, wood lots, meadow, and swampland. Lots of poor quality had to be augmented by quantity, river frontage had to be rationed, rocky land shared. Roadbeds had to be found, rivers bridged. All of this had to be started before settlers could take up their lands and begin new lives. With good reason, Thomas Hooker called town-founding "hard work" after he founded his own.[1]

It was also expensive work. Indians, surveyors, and lot-layers all had to be paid. Trees could be had for the taking, but not lumber; that had to be bought. Nails, glass, wheels, livestock, and farm implements were not frontier products; they were purchased, sometimes in England, and hauled to the frontier. In theory, once the materials were purchased, settlers themselves could build the houses, pounds, bridges, roads, and meeting-houses and cultivate the fields. But often settlers were few, and then labor as well as materials had to be purchased. When the attempt to settle Lancaster failed (in the 1640s), John Winthrop explained: "The persons interested in

---

1. Lucius R. Paige, *History of Cambridge, Massachusetts, 1630–1877,* 2 vols. (Cambridge, Mass., 1877), I, 49.

this plantation, being most of them poor men . . . it went very slowly, so as that in two years they had not three houses built there."[2] It took individuals of means to pay the considerable costs of starting a new town.

It also took individuals with special talents to perform the multiple tasks—people who could deal with Indians to purchase the land, people who could win favor in the colonial courts to obtain the grant, and people who understood complex organizations to create a system for dividing land, assessing taxes, and managing the new town. It took colonists of renown, when associated with a new town, to attract the most important ingredient—the settlers. Individuals who could not provide the requisite expertise, money, or influence were not by themselves up to these tasks. The wealthy and the prominent, the politicians and the Indian fighters, the leaders of New England society were indispensable to town-founding.

Frontier settlers went to considerable lengths to attach such men to themselves. Ipswich tried to keep its founder, John Winthrop, Jr., from leaving by granting him extra-large portions of land and by petitioning the General Court. "This remote Corner," Ipswich settlers wrote, "would be left destitute and desolate" if Winthrop departed. It was "for his sake that many of us came to this place." Similarly, the settlement of Sherburn, in requesting town privileges in 1680, argued that the town was growing and that, just as important, the famous town founder and colonial official Daniel Gookin might move there, which event the settlers would "esteem an high favour from God."[3]

Every new town wanted a Gookin or a Winthrop to settle there, but prominent, wealthy men willing to live on the frontier were scarce. This scarcity hampered the founding of new towns. "All plantations find this a main wound," Thomas Hooker explained. "They want men of abilities and parts to manage their affairs, and men of estate, to bear charges."[4]

The solution to this shortage was to involve well-connected colonists in

2. John Winthrop, *History of New England from 1630 to 1649*, ed. James Savage, 2 vols. (Boston, 1825–1826; rpt., New York, 1972), II, 161.

3. Thomas Franklin Waters, *Ipswich in the Massachusetts Bay Colony . . .* , 2 vols. (Ipswich, Mass., 1905–1917), I, facsimile opp. pp. 50, 51; Sherburn Petition, Oct. 13, 1680, CXII, 317–320, Mass. Archives.

4. Paige, *History of Cambridge*, I, 49. The shortage of money in the colonial era was a related problem. It is covered in Andrew McFarland Davis, *Currency and Banking in the Province of the Massachusetts-Bay* (New York, 1901); and Charles J. Bullock, *Essays on the Monetary History of the United States* (New York, 1900; rpt., 1969).

town-founding as nonresidents. Sometimes towns formally acknowledged the nonresident status of a founder. Marlborough waived its prohibition on nonresident landholding when it granted land to Andrew Belcher, so important was his involvement with the town.[5] More often, there was no prohibition on nonresident landholding to be waived, and the involvement of nonresidents was common enough that it merited no mention. [Frontier settlers would have preferred prominent individuals to live among them, but if that was impossible, the next best thing was for a frontier venture to have prominent figures be affiliated as nonresidents. The involvement of nonresident town promoters was not a perfect solution, but it was the only solution at hand.]

There were several classes of nonresident town promoters.[6] First were the frontiersmen, men who moved from one frontier town to another, helping to begin two, three, or four settlements in their lifetime. Profit was not their sole (or perhaps principal) motive; the towns they began also served as home, albeit temporary, to these men. But as they moved to new towns, these town promoters kept their lands in the old towns; so profit, or land accumulation, whether or not a motive, was certainly one result of their repeated participation in town-foundings.

In Massachusetts, where more than half of New England's towns were established in the seventeenth century, these peripatetic frontiersmen were common. They were not famous colonists. (They come to our attention only because one discovers the repeated participation of the same individuals in several town-foundings.) One such individual was Cornelius Waldo, born in England in 1624. Waldo came to New England, moved to Ipswich, and in 1654 was one of the founders of Chelmsford, Massachusetts. By 1685, he was living in Dunstable, a new frontier town established in the late 1670s. This move did not, however, cost Waldo his Chelmsford tavern. Waldo also was one of the investors in the Wamesit Purchase in 1686, a venture launched with the idea of starting a settlement on the Merrimack River, which eventually became Lowell, Massachusetts. Waldo was typical of the professional frontiersman: not an owner of vast estates, he nonethe-

5. Franklin P. Rice, ed., "Colonial Records of Marlborough, Mass.," *New England Historical and Genealogical Register,* LXII (1908), 228.

6. Here, no more is attempted than to give a sense of the different types of town promoters and the qualities they brought to the task. Chapter 2 describes the major land entrepreneurs of the 17th century.

less held on to land in the towns he left behind him, helped start new towns, and engaged in small-scale business. His descendants, beginning with his son Cornelius, were prominent land speculators of the eighteenth century.[7]

Another Chelmsford founder was Solomon Keyes. Keyes lived, at different times, in the frontier towns of Billerica, Chelmsford, and Westford. He, too, was a purchaser of the Wamesit Purchase in 1686, when he was living in Chelmsford. Isaac Learned was another Billerica founder who moved to Chelmsford. He was first a resident of Woburn, then of Billerica, and then in 1653 was among the original petitioners and grantees of Chelmsford. Richard Blood was among the founders of Billerica, but then moved to Groton, where he was one of that town's first selectmen, later town clerk, and then largest shareholder in town. John Smedley was a shareholder in Concord, Massachusetts, but that fact did not prevent him from becoming a petitioner of Chelmsford, though he never lived there.[8]

James Parker lived in this same region of the Bay Colony. In 1652, while he was a resident of Woburn (a town begun ten years earlier), Parker bought land in Billerica, just then being launched. Later he joined the group petitioning the General Court for the grant of Chelmsford and moved there. Then Parker moved to Groton, even farther out, where he remained probably for the rest of his life, becoming a proprietor. But nonresidence did not stop him from becoming, in 1673, one of the petitioners and grantees of the new town of Dunstable. Throughout the 1670s, Parker was a nonresident proprietor of Dunstable and even served as selectman of Dunstable while he lived in Groton. His brother Joseph joined him in the petition for Chelmsford, the move to Groton, and the petition for Dunstable. Another brother, Jacob, also petitioned for Chelmsford, but moved from there to Malden. There were several Parkers also in the Wamesit Purchase.[9]

7. Ezra S. Stearns, *Early Generations of the Founders of Old Dunstable: Thirty Families* (Boston, 1911), 90; Wilson Waters, *History of Chelmsford, Massachusetts* . . . (Lowell, Mass., 1917), 511–524, 611; James Savage, *A Genealogical Dictionary of the First Settlers of New England, Showing Three Generations of Those Who Came before May, 1692, on the Basis of Farmer's Register,* 4 vols. (Boston, 1860–1862; rpt., 1965), IV, 389.

8. Waters, *History of Chelmsford,* 2–3, 511–524; Henry A. Hazen, *History of Billerica, Massachusetts* . . . (Boston, 1883), 10–11, 113; Samuel A. Green, ed., *The Town Records of Groton, Massachusetts, 1662–1678* (Groton, Mass., 1879 [rpt. in Green, ed., *Pamphlets on History of Groton* (n.p., n.d.)]), 23 (hereafter cited as *Groton Town Records*); Lemuel Shattuck, *A History of the Town of Concord* . . . (Boston, 1835), 34.

9. Hazen, *History of Billerica,* 10–11; Waters, *History of Chelmsford,* 2–3, 8–9; Elias

New England Towns in the Seventeenth Century

It cannot be known for sure why these and other individuals kept moving, remaining always on the edge of the frontier. In other cases, the cause of continual migration was plain. Samuel Gorton lived in Boston, Plymouth, Portsmouth, Providence, Warwick, and probably other towns because he was so independent in his thinking, so committed to his religious and political convictions, and, in the end, so difficult to get along with that towns kept throwing him out.[10] Gorton's migrations had nothing to do with profit schemes. Gorton did not even keep the lands he left· behind each time he moved. But these other individuals were not hounded from their homes, and they did not lose their old lands with each new purchase. If, like Gorton, they had forfeited their old lands each time they moved, these frontiersmen would be noteworthy for their uprootedness and nothing more. But Parker and Keyes and Waldo and others kept ownership of their old lands, even as they founded new towns. There may have been an element of profit seeking mixed in with other, unknowable elements in the motives of these roving town starters.

Interestingly, these frontiersmen did not disclose their landholdings when they petitioned the court for new grants. The Chelmsford petition of 1653 stated that some of the petitioners had never had "acomidationes," which meant land distributed to commoners, and that others had very little land. In fact, Isaac Learned, James Parker, John Smedley, Thomas Chamberlain, Joseph Parker, and Jacob Parker—all Chelmsford petitioners—already possessed farms and probably held shares in other towns at the time. The petitioners were indeed so content with their existing lands that fifteen of twenty-nine of them never even moved to Chelmsford, and another six petitioners moved to Chelmsford only briefly. Only nine of the twenty-nine petitioners who had asked for the Chelmsford grant because they allegedly needed land moved to and remained in that town. Avowals of land hunger cannot be taken at face value. Land accumulation for the sake of profit, among other things, probably propelled these experienced fron-

Nason, *A History of the Town of Dunstable, Massachusetts* . . . (Boston, 1877), 8–9, 22, 26–27; Samuel A. Green, ed., *An Account of the Early Land-Grants of Groton, Massachusetts* (Groton, Mass., 1879 [rpt. in Green, ed., *Pamphlets on History of Groton* (n.p., n.d.)]), 13–14.

10. Samuel Greene Arnold, *History of the State of Rhode Island and Providence Plantations,* 2 vols. (New York, 1859–1860), I, 164–176; Adelos Gorton, *The Life and Times of Samuel Gorton* . . . (Philadelphia, 1907), 32–44.

tiersmen to pick up and move, carrying their experience in town-launching to new wilderness settings.[11]

[Founding towns required more, however, than frontier experience. It also required action by the General Court—and therefore the involvement of political leaders, who, unlike frontiersmen, did not usually move to the towns they helped found. Political leaders contributed to town-planting in several ways.] Some sat on the committees of the General Court that examined petitions for grants, and some sat on the committees that oversaw the founding of new towns. In both cases, political leaders often gave themselves, or were given, shares in new towns. In still other cases, members of the General Court were among the petitioners themselves, asking their own legislative body for the grant of a township. However they first became involved, political leaders helped a town venture win favorable treatment by the General Court and, at the same time, won for themselves a landed interest in the new town.

Among this class of town promoters was Joshua Fisher. In 1639, when he joined the Dedham church, Fisher was still an indentured servant, but with time he became a blacksmith, carpenter, town selectman, deputy to the General Court, and lieutenant of the militia. Throughout his career in the General Court, Fisher sat on committees concerned with land matters. In 1659, he laid out a 250-acre court grant to his fellow Dedham resident Eleazer Lusher.[12] In 1665, he joined Daniel Gookin, Edward Johnson, and Thomas Noyes in examining a tract and recommending that the court make a grant of it; this became Worcester. In return for this kind of public service, the General Court rewarded Fisher with a grant of 300 acres near Medfield. But the principal means by which Fisher accumulated land was, not by receiving grants to himself, but by sharing in grants to Dedham, grants that as a leader of Dedham and as a deputy to the General Court Fisher helped arrange. In 1663, the General Court granted 8,000 wilderness acres to Dedham. In 1664, Fisher with others staked out this tract and began planning its division. In 1673, the court enlarged the tract, which then

11. Waters, *History of Chelmsford*, 2, 8, 9. Evidence of and arguments regarding profits are discussed in the next section of this chapter.

12. B. Katherine Brown, "Puritan Democracy in Dedham, Massachusetts: Another Case Study," *William and Mary Quarterly*, 3d Ser., XXIV (1967), 384; Court Order, Oct. 18, 1659, XLV, 81b, Mass. Archives.

became the town of Deerfield.[13] Fisher received several rights to the undivided land of Deerfield, which during the 1660s he sold to other men,
not residents of Dedham. Medfield was another town that Dedham started
with permission of the General Court and in which Fisher was granted
land. At his death, he left an estate of £1,145, of which more than half
(£585) was in real estate. Having started out as a servant, Fisher ended his
life as a rentier, owner of many common rights, sawmills, and some thirty
parcels of land scattered in at least four different settlements.[14]

Eleazer Lusher was another Dedham resident who rose to high office—
selectman, deputy, and assistant—and fostered colony land development.
In 1656, Lusher, Fisher, Thomas Danforth, and two others laid out the
new town of Marlborough. In 1664, Dedham chose Lusher and Ensign
Daniel Fisher (also of Dedham) to prevail upon John Pynchon to negotiate
with the Indians for the tract of land that became Deerfield. In 1665, the
General Court sent Lusher, Danforth, and John Leverett to Maine to bring
that rebelling province back under Massachusetts jurisdiction. Meanwhile,
Lusher acquired land for himself. At death, two-thirds of Lusher's wealth
lay in real estate: common rights and some fifteen parcels in three or four
locations.[15]

Andrew Belcher, Sr., the great-grandfather of the eighteenth-century
governor, lived in Cambridge, yet he was an original commoner of both

13. The court often granted remote tracts to older towns. How older towns created
new towns on these tracts is discussed in Chapter 6.

14. William Lincoln, *History of Worcester* . . . (Worcester, Mass., 1862), 10; General
Court Grant, Oct. 26, 1664, photostats, MHS; George Sheldon, *A History of Deer-
field* . . . , 2 vols. (Deerfield, Mass., 1895–1896), I, 4, 10; Medfield Grant to Fisher,
Feb. 6, 1659, Washburn Manuscripts, 1640–1795, MHS; Joshua Fisher Inventory,
Aug. 20, 1672, VII, 239–243, SCPR.

15. Kenneth A. Lockridge, *A New England Town, the First Hundred Years: Dedham,
Massachusetts, 1636–1736* (New York, 1970), 45, 62; William D. Williamson, *The
History of the State of Maine* . . . , 2 vols. (Hallowell, Maine, 1832), I, 404; Franklin P.
Rice, ed., "Colonial Records of Marlborough, Mass.," *NEHGR*, LXII (1908), 224;
Sheldon, *History of Deerfield*, I, 6; William Willis, "History of Portland . . . ," Maine
Historical Society, *Collections*, 1st Ser., I (1831), 111; Harry Andrew Wright, ed., *Indian
Deeds of Hampden County* (Springfield, Mass., 1905), 61–62; Eleazer Lusher Inventory,
Dec. 5, 1672, n.s., I, 107, SCPR. According to Lockridge, Lusher was not a land
speculator (*A New England Town*, 62). If indeed he was not—and certainly Lusher did
not accumulate so much land as others did—he nevertheless acquired numerous tracts of
land while performing official duties on the frontier.

Sudbury, in 1640, and Marlborough, in 1660. Belcher was a land expert. During the 1650s, the General Court frequently called upon him to lay out wilderness tracts. In 1667, the court appointed him along with others to report on the progress of Worcester. Belcher had probably helped procure the grants of Sudbury and Marlborough; his land rights in those towns were most likely given in compensation for his service in their foundings.[16]

Thomas Danforth, born in England in 1622, came to New England as a young man, lived in Cambridge, and was an assistant for twenty years, then deputy governor of Massachusetts in 1679. He served as president of the Board of Commissioners of the United Colonies and judge of the Supreme Court of Judicature. But Danforth's most influential work concerned the province of Maine. Having brought the wayward settlers there back under Bay Colony jurisdiction in the 1660s, Danforth was appointed president of Maine in 1680, an office he held until the revocation of the charter. Maine had been devastated by the Indian war of 1676–1678, and it was Danforth's job to resettle the area and also to improve its security. These goals required the reconstituting of towns such as North Yarmouth and Falmouth and the creation of new settlements. In pursuing these efforts, Danforth wielded the power of a virtual lord proprietor over Maine— granting townships to petitioners, confirming land titles, and admitting shareholders to land corporations. This work required familiarity with the needs of frontier settlement and with the complexities of organizing towns. (Such knowledge ran in the family, for Danforth's brother Jonathan had earlier drawn up the complicated land division and taxation scheme that was instrumental in launching the town of Billerica.) For his work in Maine, Thomas Danforth was rewarded by the grant of Shebiscodego Island in Casco Bay. In addition to owning property in Cambridge, Danforth bought one thousand acres in the Nipmuck country sometime around 1663, shared in the division of the Charlestown commons in 1681, and rented out a farm of three hundred acres south of Sudbury in 1693 for £4

16. "Original Proprietors of Sudbury, Mass.," *NEHGR,* XIII (1859), 261; Rice, ed., "Colonial Records of Marlborough," *NEHGR,* LXII (1908), 228; *Mass. Records,* IV, part 1, 353, 370, 376, 405; Lincoln, *History of Worcester,* 10. His son Andrew Junior continued his interest in wilderness lands, buying and selling tracts near Marlborough and north of the Merrimack. Deed of Sale, Mar. 13, 1671, Misc., MHS; George Augustus Gordon, *The Early Grants of Land in the Wilderness North of Merrimack* (Lowell, Mass., 1892), 21–23; Savage, *Genealogical Dictionary,* I, 155–156.

10s a year (the tenants paying all taxes). At death, Danforth's real estate was appraised at £400.[17]

Perhaps even more valuable to town-founding were not just officials, but officials who knew how to deal with Indians. There were two kinds of Indian experts: those who knew the Indians as traders and neighbors and were valuable in founding towns because they spoke the Indians' language and could negotiate with Indians for the purchase of land, and those who were military experts and were valuable in town-founding because, often without provocation, they attacked and exterminated Native Americans and then led the efforts to form new towns on the conquered lands.

In the first group fell such individuals as Joseph Parsons, Sr., John Prescott, and Simon Willard, among others. Joseph Parsons was one of the first settlers of Springfield, arriving there in time to witness the deed that William Pynchon executed with the Indians, in 1636. He apparently left for Windsor or Hartford soon thereafter and then returned to Springfield, becoming in the 1640s and 1650s a landowner there, selectman, and Indian trader. In that same decade, he was among the "venturers" of the new town of Northampton, where he received several lots of land and became a resident, selectman, and tavern owner. Through his Indian connections, Parsons bought a valuable piece of property that he turned around and sold for a profit to the town of Hadley. In 1671, Parsons was among the petitioners for the grant of Northfield. He also represented the petitioners, negotiating with the Indians for the tract of Northfield. Though he did not settle in Northfield, Parsons received several shares of land there and was required to place three inhabitants on his lots. By the time he died, in 1683 (having moved back to Springfield in 1679), this fur trader had helped start at least five Connecticut Valley towns. His estate was one of the larg-

17. Williamson, *History of Maine*, I, 558–559, 565; Willis, "History of Portland," Maine Hist. Soc., *Colls.*, 1st Ser., I (1831), 111; Edward Russell, "History of North Yarmouth," Maine Hist. Soc., *Colls.*, 1st Ser., II (1847), 172–173; Hazen, *History of Billerica*, 31; George Augustus Wheeler and Henry Warren Wheeler, *History of Brunswick, Topsham, and Harpswell, Maine . . .* (Boston, 1878), 17; Petition to the General Court, October 1663, photostats, MHS; Boston, Registry Dept., *Charlestown Land Records (Third Report of the Record Commissioners of the City of Boston)* (Boston, 1878), 194–195; Danforth Indenture, Mar. 25, 1693, Misc. Large, MHS; Thomas Danforth Inventory, Nov. 14, 1699, box 1629, docket 5915, MCPR. Like many sellers and renters of land, Danforth held back a parcel (150 acres) for himself, adjacent to the land assigned to tenants, in all likelihood expecting to benefit from the appreciation caused by improvements next door.

est probated in the seventeenth century in Hampshire County—£2,088. Roughly four-fifths of this amount (£1,609) was in houses and lands, scattered through Springfield, Northampton, Northfield, and Boston.[18]

John Prescott also was a fur trader. In the 1640s, he was one of the original undertakers of the Nashaway Company, a venture that sought to establish a trading and mining enterprise on the Nashua River. Several prominent colonists participated in this venture, but John Prescott was the only undertaker that actually settled there, on a site that eventually became the town of Lancaster. In 1645, Prescott built a trading post at Nashaway. Later, he built the first mill in town. Prescott also was among the founders of Groton, where he owned a share in the first mill and also a land share, which he left to his son in 1673. At death, Prescott owned nine parcels, amounting to two-thirds of his estate.[19]

Simon Willard, another fur trader, came to Massachusetts in 1634 and the next year helped found Concord, a suitable outpost for his fur-trading business. He was deputy from Concord for many years, assistant in 1654, and commander of the county militia. Throughout his career, Willard dealt with Indians. In 1647, he drew up a code of rules for the Indians at Concord. In 1654, the United Colonies (over Roger Williams's objection) sent Willard to reprimand the Indian sachem, Ninigret, for his alleged rough treatment of the Pequots. In 1652, the General Court sent Willard and Edward Johnson to explore the Merrimack River up to Lake Winnepesaukee. Five years later, Willard, Thomas Henchman, William Brenton, and another man owned the fur trade franchise on the Merrimack River.[20]

18. Henry M. Burt, *Cornet Joseph Parsons: One of the Founders of Springfield and Northampton, Massachusetts* . . . (Garden City, N.Y., 1898), 6, 7, 9, 11, 12, 13–15, 43–51, 57–60, 65–68; J. H. Temple and George Sheldon, *A History of the Town of Northfield, Massachusetts* . . . (Albany, N.Y., 1875), 51, 67–69; Wright, ed., *Indian Deeds,* 80–81, 105–107.

19. Alden T. Vaughan, *New England Frontier: Puritans and Indians, 1620–1675* (Boston, 1965), 215–216; Samuel Eliot Morison, "The Plantation of Nashaway—an Industrial Experiment," Colonial Society of Massachusetts, *Transactions,* XXVII (1927–1930), 207–210; Samuel A. Green, *Remarks on Nonacoicus, the Indian Name of Major Willard's Farm at Groton, Mass.* . . . (Cambridge, Mass., 1893), 2; John Prescott, Sr., Inventory, 1682, box 1814, docket 18076, MCPR.

20. John Gorham Palfrey, *History of New England during the Stuart Dynasty,* 3 vols. (Boston, 1865; rpt., 1966), II, 195, 329–330; Shattuck, *History of Concord,* 4–5; Williamson, *History of Maine,* I, 334–340; Vaughan, *New England Frontier,* 215–216, 250.

Willard was a town founder, too. After helping start Concord, he laid out the new township of Chelmsford and relayed that town's petition for town privileges. For a period of fifteen years, from 1657 on, Willard, Johnson, and Thomas Danforth supervised the settlement at Lancaster as that town struggled to get on its feet. As of 1659, Willard owned five hundred acres in the Pequot country and also a farm in the new town of Groton, where he was a shareholder and selectman. Around 1667 Willard bought fifteen hundred acres at Saco Falls, in Maine, from Edward Tyng (who himself had purchased the land from a Maine speculator, William Phillips). By the 1670s, if not sooner, Willard was living in Groton, though he had also become a shareholder in the new town of Dunstable. Fur trader, part-time missionary, explorer, military leader, political leader—Simon Willard helped establish at least five new towns in the wilderness and acquired considerable land along the way. At death, he owned some fourteen hundred acres in fourteen different parcels.[21]

Indian experts were necessary who not only could negotiate with Indians but also could protect the whites from Indians and seize new lands. One such man was Edward Tyng, Jr., the son of a prominent Boston merchant.[22] Tyng moved to Falmouth, Maine, in 1680, married the grand-

21. Waters, *History of Chelmsford*, 13, 75; Nason, *History of Dunstable*, 16, 22; Henry S. Nourse, ed., *The Early Records of Lancaster, Massachusetts, 1643–1725* (Lancaster, Mass., 1884), 50–52; *Mass. Records*, IV, part 1, 304; Green, *Remarks on Nonacoicus*, 2; Book of Eastern Claims, 3–4, Mass. Archives; Simon Willard Inventory, 1676, box 1878, docket 24955, MCPR. It is possible that only Willard's son, and not Willard as well, had a share in Dunstable.

22. The military leader most hostile to Native Americans was probably Humphrey Atherton, who was also among the most active land speculators. The ignoble connection between military conquest and land greed deserves a study by itself; it was apparent to Roger Williams, who was appalled by Atherton's depredations against the Narragansetts. Atherton is discussed below, in Chapter 2. Edward Tyng's father was a prominent Boston merchant, deputy, and assistant who accumulated considerable property himself. In 1639, Boston granted Tyng land in Mount Wollaston. In 1660, Tyng bought from James Parker of Chelmsford 3,000 acres in what became Dunstable and, later, Tyngsborough. That same year, he purchased with Thomas Brattle, John Winslow, and Artepas Bois the Kennebec Patent from Plymouth Colony; in the hands of their descendants this patent was the basis of an active land company in the 18th century. During the 1660s, Tyng bought and sold several tracts in Casco Bay and Saco Falls, including one sold to Simon Willard. In 1679, he moved to Dunstable, where he lived with his son Jonathan until his death two years later. Nason, *History of Dunstable*, 296; Stearns, *Early Genera-*

daughter of George Cleeves, the former agent of Ferdinando Gorges, and became one of the major figures in northern New England. In that year and the next, Tyng commanded Fort Loyal and was one of the magistrates advising Thomas Danforth on his administration of Maine. As part of his plan to resettle Maine, Danforth appointed a board of trustees for each town, which then distributed town land, ruling on questions of title and equity. The board he appointed for Falmouth included Tyng as well as Tyng's father-in-law, Thaddeus Clark. But that was just one of Tyng's many offices. In September 1684, a warrant listed Tyng as a justice of the peace for Maine. In 1686, he was a member of the council of Joseph Dudley, his brother-in-law. When Andros arrived, Tyng continued as a member of the Andros council.

Tyng's officeholding and landholding were mutually reinforcing activities. In 1687, he asked Andros for (and received) confirmation of his title to three houses and numerous lots in Falmouth and advised Andros on similar petitions by other Maine men. When Indians renewed hostilities in Maine in 1688, Tyng asked for more troops, and the Andros council complied, placing an Eastern expedition under the command of recently promoted Colonel Tyng. The troops were to "Assist in the Resettlement of the people" in the various towns of Maine, towns that Tyng and several others had responsibility for resettling and in which he also possessed interests. After the overthrow of Andros, the Council of Safety kept Tyng on as military commander of the Eastern expedition, but this appointment did not sit well with the residents of Falmouth. On May 24, 1689, sixty-eight inhabitants of Falmouth complained to Simon Bradstreet about Tyng's rule, accusing him of profiteering. However much he advanced the cause of resettlement by his military and political leadership, Tyng's profits along the way gave offense to some.[23]

Edward's older brother Jonathan had a similar career. In 1673, he was

tions of Dunstable, 82–83; Williamson, History of Maine, I, 365–370; Book of Eastern Claims, 3–4, Mass. Archives; York Deeds, II, 46.

23. Stearns, Early Generations of Dunstable, 84–85; Willis, "History of Portland," Maine Hist. Soc., Colls., 1st Ser., I (1831), 214; Williamson, History of Maine, I, 568; James Phinney Baxter, ed., Documentary History of the State of Maine, IV–VI, IX–XVI, The Baxter Manuscripts (Portland, Maine, 1889–1916), IV, 416–419, VI, 215–216, 240–241, 283–284, 346–347, 376–377, 388–389, 423–424, 427–428, 476–480, 481–483.

one of the original petitioners for the town of Dunstable, on the Merrimack River, where he built a house and lived with his father and family. Through the years, he was selectman, Dudley councillor, judge in Middlesex County, and supervisor of the Praying Indians on an island in the Merrimack. His most important public service was military. Jonathan Tyng built block-houses in Dunstable, Billerica, and Chelmsford to protect these frontier towns during the Indian war of 1676 and during the renewal of hostilities in 1696. On both occasions, when settlers fled the frontier, Tyng remained with a garrison to protect towns to the south. By the end of his career, he had risen to colonel of the upper, or northern, Middlesex regiment. His son, Captain John Tyng, gained similar renown when he led the famous snowshoe march against the Indians in 1703–1704, for which, years later, his men and their heirs were granted a township by the General Court.[24]

In the course of his years on the frontier, Jonathan Tyng did not neglect his own interests. He was the largest landholder in Dunstable, possessing more rights than any other single individual in the town's undivided lands. The Tyng estate formed the nucleus of later Tyngsborough. He and Thomas Henchman also purchased the Wamesit tract on the Merrimack River from the Indians in 1686; their sale to other men was the beginning of that land venture.[25]

Another political and military leader who helped himself as he advanced frontier settlement was Daniel Denison. Denison was among the early settlers of Ipswich, along with Simon Bradstreet, Thomas Dudley, John Winthrop, Jr., and others. He was at various times lot-layer, selectman, deputy, and head of the colony's militia. In 1651, the General Court appointed Major Denison along with Bradstreet and Captain William Hawthorne to be commissioners to compel the submission of Kittery. As major general, Denison led Massachusetts forces against Indians on several occasions. Probably the first sizable land tract Denison possessed was the twelve hundred acres Ipswich granted him, a holding that put him in the top bracket of town landowners. He owned another Ipswich tract with three other men, which they rented for £14 per year. In 1658, to reward Denison for his public service, the court granted him a farm of five hundred acres near Hadley, by similar grants laid out to Bradstreet, Samuel Symonds, and Humphrey Atherton. Denison's estate inventory listed an island

24. Nason, *History of Dunstable*, 8–9, 23, 31, 34; Gordon, *Grants in Merrimack*, 26–29; Stearns, *Early Generations of Dunstable*, 84–86.
25. Nason, *History of Dunstable*, 28; Waters, *History of Chelmsford*, 511–524.

in the Merrimack River as well as a tract in the Narragansett region of Rhode Island. Perhaps he came by his Merrimack land in 1675. In that year, he was appointed to a committee overseeing a new town on the Merrimack. (The war intervened, the settlement probably did not get started, and the proprietors sold their tract to others in 1682.) When he died, Denison left an estate of £612, roughly half of it in housing and land.[26]

One who acted on a larger scale than either Denison or the Tyngs was Daniel Gookin. During an active public career in the Bay Colony, Daniel Gookin was deputy, then speaker, then assistant, an office he held continuously for thirty-five years (except for 1676). Among his other offices were Cambridge selectman, superintendent of the Praying Indians, then superintendent of all Indians in 1656, a post he held with only one brief interruption until his death in 1687. John Eliot was his friend, in whose company he visited Indians in the Nipmuck country in 1673 and again in 1674 to "encourage and exhort them to procceed in the ways of God." But Gookin's dealings with the Indians were not confined to religious meetings. Early on, he was made head of the Cambridge militia. In 1677, the council appointed Gookin, now major, one of three commanders of an expedition against the Indians in Maine. Four years later, Gookin was chosen major general, or commander in chief, of the colony's forces. By the time Gookin died, he had risen to the top of colonial society, a social position reinforced by his marriage with the daughter of Edward Tyng and sister-in-law to Joseph Dudley.[27]

He had also accumulated a sizable estate, much of it in wilderness lands. Soon after he moved to Massachusetts in 1644, Cambridge voted to grant Gookin a farm in Shawshin, the new town that would be Billerica, on

26. Edward S. Perzel, "Landholding in Ipswich," Essex Institute, *Historical Collections*, CIV (1968), 309–310, 322–323; Baxter, ed., *DHM: Baxter MSS*, IV, 11, VI, 153–155; Savage, *Genealogical Dictionary*, II, 36; Indenture of Daniel Denison, Jan. 16, 1650/1, photostats, MHS; Williamson, *History of Maine*, I, 334–340; Sylvester Judd, *History of Hadley, Including the Early History of Hatfield, South Hadley, Amherst, and Granby, Massachusetts* (Springfield, Mass., 1905), 18–19; Grant to Daniel Denison, June 9, 1658, XLV, 66a, Mass. Archives; General Court Order, May 27, 1659, photostats, MHS; Township Grant on Merrimack, 1675, XLV, 215, Mass. Archives; Daniel Denison Estate Inventory, 1690, photostats, MHS.

27. Frederick William Gookin, *Daniel Gookin, 1612–1687* . . . (Chicago, 1912), 81ff, 114–116, 128ff, 177, 181; Vaughan, *New England Frontier*, 294; Baxter, ed., *DHM: Baxter MSS*, VI, 153–155.

condition that he purchase a house in Cambridge. He complied with the condition, buying a house on the site of the present Hasty Pudding Club, and shortly thereafter received a 500-acre farm in Shawshin. In 1657, the General Court granted Gookin 500 acres, which he requested be laid out in the Pequot country on the edge of the Narragansett. Gookin thereupon became one of the proprietors of Southertown (later Stonington, Connecticut), a township owned at first largely by absentee investors from Massachusetts. In 1665, the court granted him another 500 acres as reward for public service; this tract fell between Concord and Lancaster. In 1677 Gookin took advantage of his Indian contacts to purchase a tract of 130 acres from the "Indian plantation" just south of Marlborough. He also had a farm and proprietary right in Boggswon (later Sherburn), a struggling frontier community that hoped Gookin might someday move there. He owned considerable land in Worcester, whose founding he led, and retained ownership of distant lands in Virginia and Maryland long after he moved to Massachusetts.[28] In time, Gookin built himself a new "mansion house" in Cambridge on land extending from the corner of Bow and Arrow streets down to the Charles River. To pay for this dwelling, he sold his Shawshin property to the Englishman Robert Thompson, who joined several real estate ventures in New England during the 1680s. Gookin sold more of his tracts and rented still others, but in spite of sales, more than three-quarters of his estate lay in real property by the time he died.[29] Gookin was not fabulously rich, but he died a wealthy man, thanks to his lands.

28. Gookin, *Daniel Gookin*, 62–66, 70ff, 78ff, 114; Hazen, *History of Billerica*, 9; Gookin Grant, 1657, XLV, 60b, Mass. Archives; General Court Order, May 20, 1658, photostats, MHS; Southertown Proprietors Petition, 1663, II, 43, Mass. Archives; Gookin Indian Deed, May 2, 1677, and Court Confirmation, May 28, 1679, photostats, MHS. Sherburn was granted out initially in large farms to Gookin, Joseph Dudley, and other prominent individuals, and only later was a town formed there by the tenants or purchasers of the grants. Sherburn Division, 1686, XLI, 289 (mentioning Gookin's interest); Sherburn or Boggswon Settlers Petition, Oct. 7, 1674, CXII, 241; Proprietors Petition, Jan. 19, 1738/9, XLI, 276–280; Petition for Township Grant, 1679, XLI, 281–283, Mass. Archives.

29. Gookin, *Daniel Gookin*, 190; Daniel Gookin Inventory, Mar. 31, 1687, IX, 341–343, SCPR. Gookin's estate inventory overlooked several parcels of his land, which means that real estate accounted for even more than the 77% of his wealth reflected in the probate records. As for his renting and selling, see "Profits," below, this chapter.

Much of this real estate came to Gookin's attention while he oversaw new settlements in the wilderness on behalf of the colony government.[30] [As the example of Worcester makes clear, public officials charged with monitoring new towns functioned not only as supervisors but also, at the same time, as full-fledged settlement entrepreneurs.] In 1664, several individuals purchased a large tract of land on the site of what would become Worcester. The next year, they petitioned the General Court for the grant of a township. In response the court appointed Edward Johnson, Joshua Fisher, Thomas Noyes (who had been among the petitioners), and Captain Gookin to survey the site and report on its suitability for a town. Nothing happened until 1667, when a new committee, composed of Gookin, Andrew Belcher, Johnson, and Samuel Andrews viewed the land and recommended that the town be established. The General Court accepted this new report and appointed Gookin, Thomas Prentice, Daniel Henchman, and Richard Beers to be a committee to lay out the town, admit inhabitants, and order affairs in the new settlement.[31]

Gookin then took the lead in overseeing settlement. In 1669, he drew up "foundation principles and Rules concerning the affayres of that place." These orders provided that each inhabitant should receive at least one twenty-five-acre lot, that all should contribute to town rates "according to proport[ion] and division of house lots," that future land divisions be made according to number of house lots, and that all public expenses should be paid out of "a common Stock rraised upon the inhabitants in proportion according to their rrespective grants and house lotts." Under this plan, Gookin and his committee accepted thirty men as inhabitants and in 1675 laid out their lots in the new town. Of these thirty people, only seven eventually settled in the town, and they did so only briefly. The others never went to Worcester, and some of them never intended to go to Worcester. Dr. Leonard Hoar, then president of Harvard and resident of Cambridge, was a grantee of a twenty-five-acre right. Ephraim Curtis, a large landowner

30. Among his several assignments, Gookin served on a committee with Danforth to oversee settlement in Maine. Gookin, *Daniel Gookin*, 122ff; Baxter, ed., *DHM: Baxter MSS*, IV, 394.

31. Petition to the General Court, XLV, 145–146, Mass. Archives; Lincoln, *History of Worcester*, 10–11, 302; Report to the General Court, Oct. 20, 1668, CXII, 187, 189, Mass. Archives; Ellery Bicknell Crane, ed., *History of Worcester County, Massachusetts*, 3 vols. (New York, 1924), I, 37–38.

who lived in Sudbury, was another. So were Captain Thomas Prentice, Daniel Gookin, Phineas Upham, and other members of the committee—grantees by virtue of grants to themselves. These individuals were useful town founders, not as settlers, but as well-connected leaders and, too, as contributors able to raise the "common Stock" that financed early Worcester.[32]

That same year, war broke out with the Indians, and the settlement was destroyed. In March 1678/9, Gookin called a meeting of his committee along with people "Interes[ted] in the plantation" in Cambridge. This was a sort of proprietors' meeting, held under the supervision of the General Court committee members, who themselves were also proprietors. The proprietors agreed "to endeavor either in their persons, or by their Relations or by their purses to Setle the Said plantation" by the summer of 1680. But nothing came of this resolution, and in 1682 the General Court warned the committee that the grant would be forfeit if Worcester were not soon resettled. So Captain Daniel Henchman (who was also a committee member and fellow grantee) undertook responsibility for settling the town, in return for which Henchman and his "undertakers" would receive two hundred lots of land (some of which they would settle and some of which they would keep for themselves). Another two hundred lots would go to the old grantees, and additional lots to committee members and to Daniel Gookin "who procured the Said grant and hath laboured many yeares in that afffayre."[33]

Under this arrangement, the grantees in effect subcontracted the settlement obligation to a company of "undertakers." The scheme worked: during the late 1680s, settlement proceeded under the supervision of the nonresident committee. But then a renewal of Indian war interrupted settlement again, this time for more than two decades. The third and permanent settlement did not begin until after 1713, at which time it was yet another nonresident committee that granted lots, including grants to committee members who never settled. Nonresidence continued to be a

32. Franklin P. Rice, ed., *Records of the Proprietors of Worcester, Massachusetts* (Worcester Society of Antiquity, *Collections*, III [Worcester, Mass., 1881]), 14–19, 21–30 (hereafter cited as Rice, ed., *Records of Proprietors of Worcester*); Savage, *Genealogical Dictionary*, I, 484, II, 430–432, III, 479, IV, 360–361.

33. Rice, ed., *Records of Proprietors of Worcester*, 30–39.

feature of Worcester land ownership through at least half of the eighteenth century.[34]

Until his death, Gookin led the effort to settle Worcester. He convened the business meetings in Cambridge, where he lived, and recorded the minutes himself. It was Gookin who petitioned the court on several occasions for assistance, and it was probably Gookin who kept his colleagues in the General Court from revoking this grant, which, because its terms went unfulfilled for decades, was certainly ripe for revocation. These efforts repaid him, but not lavishly. Altogether Gookin's Worcester lands and land rights were valued at just £10 upon his death. He nevertheless profited from his Worcester tenants. Years later his heirs sold Gookin's holdings for £120.[35]

More striking than Gookin's profits was the mingling of public and private business in the Worcester venture. Gookin and his colleagues were first appointed by the General Court to examine the land in question, then appointed to draw up rules for its settlement and to admit inhabitants, and then reappointed as the supervisory committee several times. These appointments were official ones, and the mission was the public duty of launching and regulating a frontier town. Yet at the same time, the committee members acted as the directors of the proprietors of Worcester. They held rights to the undivided land (which they parceled out among themselves), they convened proprietors' meetings, and they rented and sold their lands there. In the covenant they drew up for inhabitants, the committee members stressed that the plantation had been "granted by" the General Court "unto" Gookin, Prentice, Henchman, and Beers, the committee to manage the new settlement.[36] Not only did this committee hold supervisory authority over the town; it also appeared to possess title to the town's land. In the founders of Worcester, personal interest was married to public duty.

Gookin also wore two hats while dealing with the Indians. On his trip to the Nipmuck country with John Eliot in 1674, Gookin not only helped

34. *Ibid.*, 46, 47, 77–78, 100ff, 149ff.

35. Gookin, *Daniel Gookin,* 167, 170; Petition to General Court, May 27, 1674, CXII, 236, Mass. Archives; Rice, ed., *Records of Proprietors of Worcester,* 38–39, 42; Daniel Gookin Inventory, Mar. 31, 1687, IX, 341–343, SCPR.

36. Rice, ed., *Records of Proprietors of Worcester,* 19, 48–49.

Eliot minister to the Indians' spiritual needs but also met with the two sachems who executed to Gookin and his committee the deed for the tract of Worcester.[37] A year after this purchase, when King Philip's War broke out, the founders of Worcester were those who prosecuted the war against the Nipmuck tribe. Two of those leading troops against the Indians served on the General Court committee that supervised the founding of Worcester and also had an interest in the proprietorship: Captain Henchman and Captain Prentice. Two others were Worcester proprietors: Lieutenant Phineas Upham and Lieutenant Ephraim Curtis. Their assaults effectively exterminated the Nipmuck tribe. Political leaders and nonresident investors led the founding of Worcester; the efforts of Indian fighters were also helpful.[38] An essential combination of assets—political connections, military leadership, familiarity with Indians, financial strength, and organizational ingenuity—was necessary to transform a distant, unsafe tract into the town of Worcester.

II. Profits

Not every town venture was led by individuals seeking a profit. The first settlers of Rowley, New Haven, Exeter, and Hartford were led by ministers seeking a religious refuge. Doubtless the aforementioned town promoters themselves engaged in town-planting for many dutiful reasons: to strengthen the colony militarily, give land to the landless, expand the economy, perhaps. Towns could serve different purposes; even in the founding of a single town could several motives be mixed. The same new town could provide land for the landless and speculation for an investor: such was Deerfield—or land for the landless and refuge for the religious: such was Hartford. No one motive, no one pattern prevailed. But many, probably a majority of towns were launched with the assistance of people who had no interest in settling on the frontier and who, instead, expected to make a profit. For them, profits were the reward for time-

37. Lincoln, *History of Worcester*, 16–17, 23; Gookin, *Daniel Gookin*, 132–134.

38. Lincoln, *History of Worcester*, 24–27, 31–32. It is not possible to state that extermination of the Nipmucks was caused by the land hunger of speculators, nor is it necessary. The important conclusion to draw from Worcester's early history is that the town was founded by men who were colony leaders, military leaders, Indian experts, and nonresident owners of the town they helped to develop.

consuming work, the necessary inducement to attract prominent individuals to the difficult enterprise of town-founding.

[Such individuals were nonresident landholders, whose absenteeism is perhaps the best proof of the profit motive operating in town-founding.] Nonresidents owned land rights in forty-three of the sixty-three towns covered in this study (see Appendix 7). Additional absentees owned land through other entities—primarily land companies and individual speculative ventures—not included in this list of towns. Not every absentee landowner was necessarily a land speculator. Some nonresident owners bought lands for their children. Others were prevented from settling by Indian hostilities. But the overwhelming evidence from these forty-three towns concerns landowners who did not settle in the wilderness, were not barred from settling, and failed to place relatives on the land. Their only motive for shouldering the burdens of town-founding was the expectation of profit from owning wilderness land.

Thus, sixty-six commoners of Dedham held the original tract of Deerfield, but none of them became a permanent resident of Deerfield. Of the 113 Cambridge grantees of the tract that became Billerica, only 1 or 2 settled there. Governor Winthrop, Governor Dudley, Daniel Gookin, Harvard President Henry Dunster, Jonathan Danforth, and other renowned colonists owned land which they did not settle—so many absentees that only two-fifths of the town's land was in the hands of residents in the early years. Only 9 of the 29 men who petitioned for Chelmsford in 1652 settled permanently in the town. The merchants Robert Keayne and John Hull as well as Joshua Fisher and others were absentee landowners in early Medfield. In Worcester, in 1732 the proprietors debated whether their clerk for the first time should be a town resident, some seventy years after the town venture was begun.[39] The same was true not only in Massachusetts but up and down the seacoast, in Maine, New Hampshire, Connecticut, Plymouth, and Rhode Island (see Appendix 7).

39. Dedham, Mass., *The Early Records of the Town* . . . , 6 vols. (Dedham, Mass., 1886–1936), IV, 136–137; Sheldon, *History of Deerfield*, I, 36; Hazen, *History of Billerica*, 14, 31, 113; Waters, *History of Chelmsford*, 2–3, 8, 9; Robert Keayne Estate Inventory, James Otis, Sr., Papers, 1642–1823, box 1, MHS; John Hull, "Diaries of John Hull, Mint-Master and Treasurer of the Colony of Massachusetts Bay," AAS, *Transactions, Collections*, III (1857), 149; Joshua Fisher Inventory, Aug. 20, 1672, VII, 239–243, SCPR; William S. Tilden, *History of the Town of Medfield, Massachusetts, 1650–1886* (Boston, 1887), 39, 64; Rice, ed., *Records of Proprietors of Worcester*, 217–218.

[Multiple landholding, as disclosed in probate records, is another measure of town promoters' interest in profits (see Appendix 1).] Real property constituted 73 percent of the value of town promoters' estates, on average, during the seventeenth century. It is likely that the actual figure is closer to 80 percent, for estate inventories of town promoters (unlike inventories of ordinary town settlers) undercounted the land worth of these men. No town promoter owned more personal property than real property at death. By contrast, among the general male population in Connecticut real property exceeded personal property only after King Philip's War. Among Rowley's residents, two-thirds of inventories before 1665 showed land equaling less than one-half of men's wealth; one-third showed land equaling less than a third.[40] Land was disproportionately the basis of wealth for town promoters.

Town promoters also owned far more acres than did the average New Englander. At any given time, the average Connecticut farmer in the seventeenth century had about 60 acres of land. The median holding for farmers just starting out was 40 acres, for a middle-aged farmer 100 acres. By the 1690s, the median acreage holding of Connecticut men at death was 88 acres. In Rowley, Massachusetts, the average landholding was 25.9 acres; in Hingham, it was 22.5; in Newbury, 13.8. Deerfield residents owned an average of 66 acres at the time of their death (up to 1704).[41] By contrast, town promoters left an average of 2,910 acres at death. Even though this figure is inflated by the few enormous landholdings, the median figure was still 950—more than ten times the average and median figures for the male population generally. The probate records of town

40. Jackson Turner Main, *Society and Economy in Colonial Connecticut* (Princeton, N.J., 1985), 68; David Grayson Allen, *In English Ways: The Movement of Societies and the Transferal of English Local Law and Custom to Massachusetts Bay in the Seventeenth Century* (Chapel Hill, N.C., 1981), 26. New England being overwhelmingly rural, it stands to reason that land accounted for a large share of mean wealth. But taking all 17th-century inventories, Main found that land equaled 60% of mean personal wealth, still well below that of town promoters. Moreover, town promoters consistently held more than half their property in land all through the century, not just after King Philip's War. In this study, three-fifths of the town promoters' estates were probated after King Philip's War, two-fifths before (or during) the war.

41. Main, *Society and Economy,* 68, 233–234; Allen, *In English Ways,* 23, 65, 100; Richard I. Melvoin, "Communalism in Frontier Deerfield," in Stephen C. Innes *et al., Early Settlement in the Connecticut Valley,* ed. John W. Ifkovic and Martin Kaufman (Deerfield, Mass., 1984), 49.

promoters, moreover, usually undercounted the acreage, since appraisers seldom inspected a decedent's lands in the wilderness, particularly if they fell in another colony. Median landholding likely exceeded 1,000 acres for town promoters (see Appendix 1).

Large landholdings do not by themselves constitute proof of profit seeking. Possibly some of these individuals accumulated vast quantities to assemble large baronial estates for themselves, in which case probate records do not reveal so much entrepreneurial activity as interesting social data. Or possibly individuals were buying land merely to provide farms for their children. But neither is likely, for the records disclose that town promoters held land, not in one location, but in an average (and a median) of four different towns or regions. Moreover, the holdings were not consolidated even within each region. Town promoters owned an average of 8.7 parcels of land. Would-be barons would have concentrated their land in one place, as Richard Wharton tried to do in Maine. Concerned fathers would have purchased lands together and probably near home or, at farthest, in one distant town. Certainly, New England had its barons and patriarchs, but the serial pattern of landholding adopted by town promoters—huge quantities, chopped into parcels, spread over far-flung places—is roundabout testimony to their entrepreneurial interest in land.

Absenteeism, sizable acreage, multiple landholding: these are signs of a profit interest. But they do not explain how speculators made their money from landownership. In fact, money was made by several different methods.

First, town promoters sold land rights, that is, rights to the undivided lands and pasturage. Of the original Deerfield owners (all of whom were nonresident), many sold their rights to other nonresidents, to men like John Pynchon and Governor Leverett—so many, indeed, that by the 1660s an active market in Deerfield land shares had sprung up.[42] Second, absentee

---

42. Sheldon, *History of Deerfield*, I, 10, 201–202, 207–209. In Essex County it was not always clear whether a purchaser of a commonage share also obtained the right to future allotments (David Thomas Konig, *Law and Society in Puritan Massachusetts: Essex County, 1628–1692* [Chapel Hill, N.C., 1979], 51). No comparable ambiguity existed in Deerfield, nor in Newbury, where a similar market in land rights opened up in the 1640s, although David Grayson Allen does not argue that the transactions involved nonresidents (*In English Ways*, 113). There was considerable variation from town to town on this important relationship between land ownership and the ownership of rights in repeated divisions and stinting of the commons. See Chapter 7, below.

owners sold, not rights, but town lots or large farms in towns. John Hull came by his farm in Medfield by purchasing it. Edward Collins bought most of the land in Medford from Mathew Cradock's estate in 1652 and then proceeded to sell parcels in later years (including one tract of four hundred acres for £404). He also received from Cambridge a large farm in Billerica; this, too, he sold. Of the fifty-one owners of home lots in Norwalk, Connecticut, during that town's first twenty years, fourteen bought their lots from original shareholders.[43]

Third, men sold tracts lying, not within a town, but in the wilderness, in a tradition begun by the agents of Sir Ferdinando Gorges and John Mason in Maine and New Hampshire and continued throughout New England. In the seventeenth century Massachusetts alone granted some 100,000 wilderness acres to individuals as reward for services rendered to the colony.[44] Usually the grantee asked that the land be laid out in some promising area just then being developed. Then he might sell it after holding it for several years. In 1672 Daniel Gookin sold to Boston's Simon Lynde a farm in the Pequot country for £206 sterling only a few years after receiving the grant for free.[45]

Before he sold that parcel, Gookin had tenants on it: renting was the fourth way that absentees made money from distant lands. In 1670 Gookin and his fellow absentee owners complained to the General Court that men from Rhode Island were "dispossessing our tennants" in the Pequot country. Gookin also had tenants on his Worcester lands.[46] Joshua Fisher rented

43. Charles Brooks, *History of the Town of Medford* . . . (Boston, 1855), 41, 43; Hazen, *History of Billerica*, 9; Edwin Hall, ed., *The Ancient Historical Records of Norwalk, Conn., with a Plan of the Ancient Settlement, and of the Town in 1847* (New York, 1865), 22–29. Allen found evidence of an active market in land lots in Watertown and Ipswich as early as the 1630s, though, again, he does not find that nonresidents played a role in these transactions (*In English Ways*, 121–131).

44. See Grants to Individuals, XLV, Mass. Archives; William Haller, Jr., *Puritan Frontier: Town-Planting in New England Colonial Development, 1630–1660* (New York, 1951), 33. As for Gorges and Mason, see Chapter 2, below.

45. Gookin, *Daniel Gookin*, 111ff; Gookin Grant, 1657, XLV, 60b, Mass. Archives. The following month, Lynde bought 150 acres in the wilderness near Marlborough from Andrew Belcher, Jr., who himself was a nonresident landowner in Marlborough as well as owner of lands north of the Merrimack. Deed of Sale, Belcher to Lynde, Mar. 13, 1671/2, Misc. MSS, MHS; Gordon, *Grants in Merrimack*, 21–23.

46. Petition of Stonington [Southertown] Proprietors, Apr. 25, 1670, photostats, MHS; Rice, ed., *Records of Proprietors of Worcester*, 42.

out several distant lots of land; so did William Tyng. Governor Simon Bradstreet rented his lands in Lynn, Topsfield, and Andover, with the last one bringing in five pounds a year. In his will Edward Hutchinson listed five different properties rented out in Massachusetts, Rhode Island, and the Narragansett. Francis Brinley of Boston, in his will, mentioned the "Rents Issues and profits" of his land in the Narragansett. Richard Bellingham bequeathed the rents from three different farms he owned. John Pynchon let out his lands at Deerfield during the 1670s, obligating his tenant to pay all rates, build fences, a house, and a barn, and pay rent to Pynchon besides. In an exceptional circumstance, more than one-third of the adult males in Springfield between 1652 and 1702 rented either land or livestock, most of them from John Pynchon. The settlers of Braintree complained about the nonresidents who, in the former's words, owned the bulk of the town's land and rented it at "dear rates." Shareholders of the land companies operating in Rhode Island, the Atherton and Pettaquamscut ventures, put tenants on their lands.[47]

These isolated examples of land renting point to a larger process that played a key role in peopling the seventeenth-century wilderness. When prominent individuals received a township, they usually accepted the obligation to recruit and place settlers in the frontier town. Sometimes these settlers were tenants of town promoters; on other occasions, the cash flowed in the other direction, and town promoters paid individuals to settle remote and undesirable lands. The precise transaction depended on the availability of settlers, the town's location, the quality of the land, and the risk of Indian hostilities. But whichever way the cash flowed in this relationship, the town promoter was not an accidental absentee; he was an intended absentee, contributing to the new town not only money, contacts,

---

47. Joshua Fisher Inventory, Aug. 20, 1672, VII, 239–243; William Tyng Inventory, 1653, II, 138–147; Simon Bradstreet Will, Dec. 23, 1689, XI, 276–282; Edward Hutchinson, Sr., Will, Aug. 19, 1675, VI, 95ff; Francis Brinley Will, Oct. 19, 1719, XXI, 526–529, SCPR; Richard Bellingham Will, Nov. 28, 1672, Misc. Bound, MHS; Sheldon, *History of Deerfield*, I, 179–180, 207–209; Stephen Innes, *Labor in a New Land: Economy and Society in Seventeenth-Century Springfield* (Princeton, N.J., 1983), 38; Braintree Petition, Oct. 11, 1666, photostats, MHS; Peleg Sanford, *The Letterbook of Peleg Sanford of Newport, Merchant . . .* , ed. Howard W. Preston *et al.* (Providence, R.I., 1928), 35–36, 52–54; Hull to Terry, Sept. 4, 27, 1672, Hull to Heifernan, 1673, John Hull Letterbook, AAS. Some of Hutchinson's tenants, mentioned above, were on lands he received by virtue of his membership in the Atherton Company.

and organizational talent but also, through his recruitment efforts, even the bodies.

Thus in Worcester, a group of "undertakers" shouldered the burden of finding settlers, reserving lots for themselves as compensation. In Dunstable, the grantees, who included prominent figures—Thomas Brattle, William Brenton, William Davis, Joseph Dudley, and the heirs of John Endicott—promised the General Court that they would "give encouragement to those that shall improve the said lands." During the first effort to settle Northfield, the thirty-three grantees agreed to put twenty families in the township; during the second, they agreed to "settle two inhabitants" for every sixty acres of meadow they received. Joseph Parsons, with ninety acres, was obliged to recruit three men.[48] The first proprietors of Marlborough pledged in 1656 that they would either settle the town themselves "or sett A man in that the Towne shall approve of, or els to loose theire Lotts." Westerly's nonresident owners, who included the most prominent men of Newport, were so eager to place settlers on their lands that they offered five pounds to each settler. In 1662 the company assessed each proprietor eight pounds per share to pay for this expense.[49] In the 1690s, the grantees of New Roxbury, Massachusetts, split themselves into two groups, the "goers" who were to settle in the new town and were exempt from taxation, and the "stayers" who enjoyed equal rights to the land and who contributed to the project, not by moving to the infant settlement, but by financing it.[50]

The practice of investors' contracting with settlers to people vacant land had its antecedents in the original colonization of New England. The agreement between the Pilgrims and their backers in London centered on the idea that the "adventurers" would remain in England and provide the

48. Nason, *History of Dunstable*, 6–10, 12, 16–17, 26–27; Dunstable Meeting, July 22, 1685, MSS Bound, MHS. Interestingly, the Northfield proprietors' obligations to recruit settlers became progressively more onerous over the three periods of settlement of 1672, 1683, and 1714. Temple and Sheldon, *History of Northfield*, 60–61, 67–69, 95, 103–107, 115ff, 132–134, 144–145.

49. Rice, ed., "Colonial Records of Marlborough," *NEHGR*, XLII (1908), 224; Elisha R. Potter, Jr., *Early History of Narragansett* (RIHS, *Collections*, III [Providence, R.I., 1835]), 251–253, 256–261, 263. Compare the free inhabitants' list (Frederick Denison, *Westerly [Rhode Island], and Its Witnesses . . . 1626–1876 . . .* [Providence, R.I., 1878], 51–52) with the purchasers' list (Thomas Barber, "Contributions to the History of Westerly," *NHR*, II [1883–1884], 36–37).

50. See discussion in "Towns Launched by Other Towns," below, Chapter 6.

money, the "planters" would go to New England and perform the labor, and both would see a return, one group from its investment, the other from its labor. The Massachusetts Bay Company was organized, financially, upon the same principle. Mathew Cradock was the largest investor in the company, in return for which he was granted most of Medford, Massachusetts, known in the 1630s as "Cradock's plantation," a place peopled by Cradock's employees and tenants and managed by Cradock's agent. Cradock himself never set foot in America.[51] Before the Bay Company was organized, Ferdinando Gorges, John Mason, and other English venturers spent considerable money recruiting settlers for their lands in Maine and New Hampshire. Elsewhere in the Atlantic world, the Cromwellian project to settle Ireland divided county lands between the London merchants who put up the money and the soldiers who presumably were to be settlers. New York under the Dutch was in part peopled by individuals whose settlement was financed by the investors of the Dutch West India Company.[52] So when the founders of New Roxbury or Worcester or Westerly employed the goer-stayer technique of peopling remote lands, they were using an established transatlantic settlement model in which the interests of settlers and financiers were combined in a single enterprise, both attracted by land as an incentive, land that was home to some but commodity to others.

In some instances, town promoters appear to have recruited settlers before they received a township grant. In requesting a grant of land, town promoters often told the court that men were "straitened" for land, when clearly the town promoters themselves were not. As the Chelmsford case demonstrates, men who already had land asserted to the court that they lacked "acomidationes," when in fact many of the twenty-nine petitioners were landed men, only nine of whom moved to and remained in Chelmsford. John Pynchon headed several groups of people asking for land on the

51. William Bradford, *Bradford's History "Of Plimoth Plantation"* (Boston, 1898), 56–58; Brooks, *History of Medford*, 30–35, 38–41, 59, 83, 87, 123, 451–452. Medford, established in 1630, had one of the smallest populations of Massachusetts towns. As late as 1707, it had only 46 ratable polls. Not until 1712 did enough people live there to warrant ordaining their own minister. Yet because of Cradock's fishing and shipbuilding enterprises, Medford was one of the wealthiest towns of the colony—superior in wealth to Newbury, Ipswich, Hingham, and Weymouth during the first decade of settlement. Winthrop, *History of New England*, ed. Savage, II, 161–162n.

52. Karl S. Bottigheimer, *English Money and Irish Land: The "Adventurers" in the Cromwellian Settlement of Ireland* (Oxford, 1971), 143; Jessica Kross, *The Evolution of an American Town: Newtown, New York, 1642–1775* (Philadelphia, 1983), 12.

grounds that they lacked accommodations—when Pynchon was one of the largest landowners in the colony. In 1670, Pynchon along with other Springfield leaders asked for a new township, stating that land between Springfield and Westfield was vacant and that people "amongst us" wanted land for improvement. The township would be "for the use" of those in Springfield wanting to settle this particular tract. The court granted the request, and thus yet another township grant included as grantees Pynchon, George Colton, Elizur Holyoke, Samuel Marshfield, Henry Chapin, and Benjamin Cooley, all landed men who had no intention of moving out of Springfield.[53]

The petitioners of Marlborough asked for that township, saying they and their sons had been denied land in Sudbury, when that could not have been the whole reason. Of the first thirty-six landowners of Marlborough, fourteen were granted large farms in Sudbury after the Marlborough grant had been made to them. Of these fourteen, eleven were shareholders in Sudbury's undivided land. Ten of these shareholders had been petitioners, in addition to being first landowners, of Marlborough. By 1660, two-thirds of the petitioners for Marlborough had been shareholders of Sudbury, and somewhat fewer than half of the Marlborough landowners still owned land in Sudbury. In other words, the founders of Marlborough who had come from Sudbury were not the poor and the landless of Sudbury; nor did they lose their land and shares in Sudbury upon their removal to Marlborough. On the contrary, many of them were the successful founders of two frontier towns, Sudbury and Marlborough, holding extensive lands in both.[54]

In these and other instances, it is impossible to know whether town promoters were creating the illusion of land shortage to justify a new grant and thereby acquire land for themselves (as the General Court suspected in one case discussed below), or whether they were motivated by the desire to help the landless and strengthen the country. Motives from this distance are

53. Springfield Petitions, May 1670, Oct. 7, 1670, CXII, 207–211, Mass. Archives.

54. These calculations are derived from figures given in the appendix to Sumner Chilton Powell, *Puritan Village: The Formation of a New England Town* (Middletown, Conn., 1963), 192–193. (Powell drew no such conclusions from these figures.) In the town of Saybrook, the term "straitened" appeared to mean "inconveniently laid out," for there the proprietors said they were "straitened" when they owned (in awkward divisions) more than 100 square miles. Christopher Collier, "Saybrook and Lyme: Secular Settlements in a Puritan Commonwealth," in George J. Willauer, Jr., ed., *A Lyme Miscellany, 1776–1976* (Middletown, Conn., 1977), 16.

not easily discerned. But it is likely that a mixture of motives prompted town promoters; certainly a mixture of interests was served. The cause of landless families justified many new grants, and the sponsorship of prominent individuals facilitated the grants, in which both classes of New Englanders shared. The landless and the prominent operated symbiotically in these petitions for wilderness grants, just as they did in the goer-stayer schemes after grants were made.

Nor is it possible to know in every case by which method town promoters hoped to make a profit: by selling rights, selling lots, selling tracts in the wilderness, renting land, or—by paying others to settle their lands—seeing their land values rise. It is likely that some ventures made little or no profit. Once the Worcester proprietors asked for special consideration from the court, saying that their township was "not So profittable to yor Petitioners as it might bee."[55] But one thing was clear: for town promoters to have any hope of making a profit, they needed settlers who would risk the dangers of the frontier for the sake of having land. Only by settlers' presence did town promoters make money and see their land appreciate. The profit incentive was necessary to involve prominent men in town-founding ventures, but profit, in turn, depended on the settlers.

III. Land Policies of the General Courts

The general courts, aware of this dualism, protected both interests, the entrepreneurial interest of town promoters and also the interest of settlers. It has been thought that colonial land policies of the seventeenth century prevented land speculation. But there is confusion between speculation on the one hand and the accumulation of idle land by absentees who did nothing to develop it on the other. The latter was steadfastly opposed by general courts. In 1634 the Massachusetts General Court ordered that "any man that hath any greate quan[tity] of land graunted him, and doeth not builde upon it or imp[rove it] within three yeares, it shalbe Free for the Court to disp[ose] of it to whome they please." Connecticut reserved the right to dispossess landowners who failed to cultivate their court grants. When the court of assistants granted John Winthrop land in 1632, it provided that the grant would be null if his heirs

55. Thomas Noyes Petition, Oct. 18, 1665, photostats, MHS.

allowed the land "to lye wast, and not improve the same." In his will, Edward Tyng, Sr., instructed that none of his money should be spent on farming except for "ten pounds in building to prevent the looseing or forfiting of any Lott of Land."[56] To maintain his title, a land speculator had to spend just enough to satisfy the requirement of improving his land. (In practice, speculators wished to do more than barely satisfy the minimum legal requirement, for improvements enhanced the value of their land.)

Improvement—building and planting—was the key, the goal of land policy, the condition of nearly every grant. The court wanted improvements that fortified the frontier, expanded the economy, and accommodated the growing population. Toward that end, it was against the continuous owning of unused, idle land. Land was meant to be settled, not merely owned.

But that same policy made room for absentee ownership. It was the Massachusetts General Court, after all, that bestowed 100,000 inland acres on seacoast-dwelling colonists; granted dozens of townships to groups, the principals of which never settled on the frontier; and gave English investors large tracts, never expecting them to move to America, let alone the wilderness. It was the court that granted lots in Sudbury in 1640 to two men explicitly "wthout condition of dwelling there, onely Mr Pelham promised to build a house there, and settle a family there, and to bee there as much as hee could in the sumer time." And it was the court's committees that ordered the absentee owners of Worcester, Simsbury, Northfield, and elsewhere, not to settle themselves necessarily, but to find other people to settle their lots.[57] Far from barring absentee owners, the court used absentee owners in the effort to develop the frontier, not by compelling them to move there, but by compelling them to spend their resources—Edward Tyng's ten pounds—to improve their lands.

Tax policy as well favored absentee ownership. In Connecticut, a 1641 order ruled that the charge for making ways or any common benefit "shall be paid by the land wthin the said liberty, as yt shall be taken uppe and possest." This last clause specifically exempted unimproved lands, of

56. *Mass. Records,* I, 114; *Conn. Records,* I, 58–59; Peter N. Carroll, *Puritanism and the Wilderness: The Intellectual Significance of the New England Frontier, 1629–1700* (New York, 1969), 183; Edward Tyng, Sr., Will, Aug. 5, 1677, VI, 380, SCPR.

57. *Mass. Records,* I, 292; Rice, ed., *Records of Proprietors of Worcester,* 30–39; Noah A. Phelps, *A History of Simsbury, Granby, and Canton, from 1642 to 1845* (Hartford, Conn., 1845), 28; Temple and Sheldon, *History of Northfield,* 95.

which nonresidents were often the owners. That colony's 1650 code of laws also exempted from assessment "common" land, dedicated "to the use of the Inhabitants in generall, whether belonging to the Townes or perticular persons." Again, unimproved lands were freed from charge. Then in 1676, in setting down rules for evaluating lands for the country rates, Connecticut ordered that improved land should pay at the high rate, house lots at the highest, and all other land, including fenced land, at the lowest rates.[58]

Massachusetts taxes were equally lenient on nonresident owners. In 1634, the court ordered that in "all rates and publique charges" towns should rate each man "according to his estate, and with consideracon of all other his abilityes . . . not according to the number of his persons." There was no mention of nonresident taxation. In 1636, the court ordered that all men should be rated "in all rates for their whole abilitie, wheresoever it lyes"; however, only those living outside the jurisdiction should be rated for goods, stock, and land within the jurisdiction. Nonresident owners living in Massachusetts could not be taxed for their polls, possessions, estates, and abilities, but taxed only for their lands (except of course where they lived).[59]

Massachusetts eventually got around to taxing nonresidents. In March 1643/4, the court ordered that the lands and estates of all men, wherever they lived, were liable to be rated for all town charges where the lands lay, though persons were to be rated for church and country rates only where they lived. In 1647, the court observed that the church was being neglected in certain towns when inhabitants moved and so it amended the 1644 order to allow all property to be rated for all common charges, "in the same place where the said estate is."[60]

These laws, though imposing a tax on nonresident lands, placed no

58. *Conn. Records*, I, 59, 547–548, II, 294–295. There is an apparent discrepancy between the general policy of improving the wilderness and these tax laws favoring unimproved lands. It is explained by observing that these tax laws concerned lands in towns already launched, whereas the policy mentioned above was concerned with the wilderness generally. The court did not mind having unimproved lands exist within a town, if a town was indeed established. In fact, it would have been difficult for the court to encourage entrepreneurs while requiring them to improve every parcel they owned or pay taxes on all unimproved land.

59. *Mass. Records*, I, 120, 166, 168.

60. *Ibid.*, II, 60, 209–210.

special burden on unimproved lands or nonresident lands. Regardless of what colony law stated, moreover, town authorities did not believe they had automatic power to tax nonresidents. In 1684, Mendon had to petition the court for permission to tax nonresidents' lands. Lancaster, in a slightly different case, also petitioned for taxation power when men moved off their home lots and onto outlying lots recently separated from the common land.[61] Apparently Lancaster authorities had power to tax only home lots; if so, the bulk of nonresident lands in Lancaster escaped taxation. In Wrentham, residents sent a petition to the court in 1673, complaining that the nonresident proprietors in Dedham were not living up to "what is ingaged" and that, as a result, the town could not support its minister. This petition made no mention of a tax law, no accusation that the nonresidents had not obeyed the law, no plea for assistance in enforcing the tax laws. Instead, the residents appealed to a sense of fairness in the legislators, alleging that the nonresidents had gone back on a promise.[62]

Wallingford raised taxes upon the "Distribution of accomdations of our Lands," not upon real or personal property generally. But the nonresidents objected to "this way of leving Rate for our towne conserns and the ministrey" and, apparently, refused to pay. To force the nonresidents to pay taxes, the residents asked the court in 1677 for exemption from the law that required town rates to be raised in the manner of country rates. Country rates fell upon polls, wealth (as in livestock, personal effects), faculty (as in ability to earn income from a trade), and real property, which bore a higher tax if improved than if unimproved. If a person did not live in town, had none of his livestock or effects in that town, and his land was unimproved, then the town could tax his unimproved land, perhaps, but nothing else. Large nonresident owners escaped most taxation by this means, and as a result the Wallingford settlers "canot see how we shall be able to carry on. for our Lands out of which must be Raised to maintaine ministrey and defray other towne charges, are in a great measure in the hands of such as in that way will contribute Little or nothing. for theyr persons they are absent[,] estate they have little or none amongst us. Theyr Land Little or not at all improved." According to the Wallingford settlers, nonresidents

61. Mendon Petition, Sept. 10, 1684, photostats, MHS. The issue at stake in Lancaster was the minister's rate, which initially fell upon home lots. When people began moving to their untaxed second division lots, the support of the minister was threatened. Nourse, ed., *Records of Lancaster,* 28, 140–141.

62. Wrentham Petition, Oct. 15, 1673, Misc. Bound, MHS.

who kept no assets in town and did not improve their lands had to pay little or no taxes at all under Connecticut law; so the settlers petitioned for special authority to tax nonresidents' lands.[63]

It was precisely this sort of tax loophole for nonresidents that Gershom Bulkeley of Connecticut had in mind when he attacked the large land-owners of New England. According to Bulkeley:

The landed men do save themselves and the burthen of the rates is cast upon the heads and personal estates, and so upon the poorer sort of the people. The reason is, because as they value and rate all not by the yearly value as in England, but by the (pretended) true value or purchase, so they value their lands and real estate below a quarter of the worth of them, for which they will buy or sell, but overvalue the personal estate generally. And for the poll-money, every man is every year, (and sometimes more than once,) as aforesaid, poll'd, and every man alike, the poorest and meanest as much as the richest and best, viz. 18d. for his head in every penny rate.

This, said Bulkeley, was an unfair system, imposed upon New England by those with great lands. When Sir Edmund Andros altered the tax system, people complained that Andros was taxing them without the consent of assemblies; but Bulkeley said that the hidden motive behind the outcry was objection by "landed men" at being taxed for the first time in accordance with their true wealth.[64]

From time to time, in these controversies over taxes and other disputes, the interests of nonresidents and settlers came into conflict. Sometimes nonresidents failed to pay their taxes, or they could not find settlers to take their lots, or they gouged settlers in rents and land prices. When this happened and the settlers sought redress from the colony government, the authorities' response put in sharpest relief the official attitude toward entre-preneurship in town-founding. In that response, the courts proved them-selves extraordinarily reluctant to interfere with property rights and to discipline nonresidents. Mindful that the pursuit of the supreme goal of improving the wilderness required the help of town promoters as well as

63. Wallingford, May 9, 1677, Towns and Lands, I, 170, microfilm, Conn. Archives.

64. Gershom Bulkeley, Will and Doom; or, The Miseries of Connecticut by and under an Usurped and Arbitrary Power (1692) (Connecticut Historical Society, Collections, III [1895]), 126–127, 194.

settlers, authorities handled land disputes by carefully balancing the interests of each. Only when absentees' behavior plainly hindered settlement of the land did courts take action, and even then the courts acted with a light hand.

When Dedham launched the town of Deerfield, not a single Dedham resident moved to this satellite in the wilderness. After King Philip's War devastated the town, the settlers complained to the General Court that nonresidents owned the best soil in town and would not relinquish their rights to settlers or move to the town, by which behavior the settlers had become "much discouraged." In response, the court unhelpfully referred the petitioners to the nonresident proprietors. Several Deerfield proprietors, however, did take action, agreeing to place every tenth acre in a common stock for the purpose of promoting settlement. But this concession was not enough, and three years later the residents asked the court's permission to expropriate the land of deceased proprietors and place it, too, in the common stock. Again, the court was unhelpful. It was not "sattisfied," the court responded, "that they may give away other proprieties wthout their consent." Instead the court "doe commend it to the rest of the proprietors to follow the good example of those that have give up every tenth acre" to the common stock.[65] In other words, the most vigorous remedy the court proposed was moral suasion. Even in a town where residents suffered from war and twice asked for relief, where nonresidents traded shares among themselves and never settled—even in Deerfield, the court would not act against nonresident proprietors.

In 1663 the Connecticut General Court bestowed the future site of Simsbury on certain Windsor residents, whose failure to settle their lands produced complaints by the new town's settlers. In response, the court ordered "that those who are proprietors of land in Simsbury might be compelled to com to their alottments and settle themselves, or [put] som other suitable persons on their accomodations there." The penalty for noncompliance was, not forfeiture, but a fine of forty shillings a year. Not choosing to punish or dispossess the absentee owners, the Connecticut government instead encouraged them to do what they were supposed to do: add settlers to the town.[66]

65. Deerfield Petition, May 8, 1678, XLIX, 200–201, Mass. Archives; Sheldon, *History of Deerfield*, I, 193–194.
66. Phelps, *History of Simsbury*, 28.

Braintree, Brookfield, Billerica, Mendon, Wrentham, Marlborough, Westfield, Deerfield, Simsbury, Wallingford, and Bristol all complained about nonresident owners who would not settle or sell or pay their taxes. All got some relief from general courts, but in their most active mood, courts merely ordered nonresidents to settle people on their lands—not themselves necessarily—and to pay their taxes.[67]

Only when individuals stood in the way of settlement did they risk forfeiting their land. Ephraim Curtis and others possessed extensive lands that, as it happened, fell precisely where Daniel Gookin decided to place the center of the new town of Worcester. Gookin tried to buy out Curtis but could not reach agreement with him, so he petitioned the court, asking the court to "remove these obstructions" and arguing that the "good of many may be preferred before one." After several petitions and five years of delay, the court in 1674 granted Curtis 250 acres outside Worcester, and Curtis surrendered his desirable tract (keeping 50 acres in the center of town).[68]

Simon Bradstreet also had a grant of wilderness land, given him for service to the colony, which stood in the way of a town. In 1658, Bradstreet asked the court to locate his grant on the Connecticut River, which was done. Shortly thereafter, in 1659, when the town of Hadley was begun across the river from Bradstreet's grant, the settlers discovered that Bradstreet's five hundred acres contained the best nearby meadowland. So Hadley asked the court to relocate Bradstreet's grant. The deputies, in turn, asked Bradstreet to exchange his grant for another, Bradstreet refused, and the magistrates backed him up. Hadley offered Bradstreet two hundred pounds for his land, and again he refused to give up his land. Only after the court gave Hadley one thousand acres of land, which Hadley then gave to Bradstreet, in addition to two hundred pounds, did Bradstreet relent and

67. For Mendon, Wrentham, Deerfield, Simsbury, and Wallingford, see the notes immediately foregoing. For the rest, see Braintree Petition, Oct. 11, 1666, photostats, MHS; Braintree Petition, May 13, 1670, CXII, 206, Mass. Archives; Brookfield Petition, Oct. 25, 1692, CXII, 425–427, Mass. Archives; Billerica Item, Sept. 20, 1658, XLV, 333; Billerica Petition, May 28, 1674, CXII, 239, Mass. Archives (also in photostats, MHS); Rice, ed., "Colonial Records of Marlborough," *NEHGR*, LXII (1908), 226, 342; General Court Order, Westfield, June 3, 1679, CXII, 272, Mass. Archives; Wilfred H. Munro, *The History of Bristol, R.I. . . . *(Providence, R.I., 1880), 60–61, 89–90, 122.

68. Gookin Petition, May 27, 1674, CXII, 236, Mass. Archives; Lincoln, *History of Worcester,* 12–16.

surrender his grant. The center of Hatfield was located on Bradstreet's former grant; his new land fell within the borders of what later became the town of Whately.[69]

What is interesting about the Bradstreet-Hadley dispute and the Curtis-Worcester dispute is, not that Bradstreet and Curtis were dispossessed of their land, but that it took so much time and effort to assert the interests of settlers above the interests of nonresident landholders. In both cases, settlers (or their representatives) succeeded only after appeals and several years' delay. In both cases, the solution lay in appeasing the individual landholders with even larger grants of land for them to hold as absentee landlords. In Curtis's case, settlement was held up during the controversy; in Bradstreet's, the magistrates did not want to accommodate the settlers at all. The interest of settlement prevailed in these cases, but only with difficulty; and the principle of nonresident landholding was upheld, not undermined.

Circumstances varied, but the principle was the same in a dispute involving John Pynchon. Pynchon and others of Springfield were proprietors of the land that split off from Springfield and became the town of Westfield. In 1679, the settlers at Westfield complained to the General Court that the nonresident proprietors of Westfield had refused to give them deeds to the land they lived on. The court ordered the proprietors to give deeds to the settlers, and the proprietors complied, but only after the court made a gift of twelve hundred acres to the proprietors as compensation for their loss. Notwithstanding this sequence of events, as much as five years later Pynchon referred to land he still owned in Westfield.[70]

In yet another case, when Pynchon and other Springfield leaders asked for a township near Westfield, saying that men "amongst us" wished to settle there, the magistrates agreed on condition that twenty families be settled in two years and that no one receive more than eighty acres. The deputies, however, withheld their consent, saying that the court should wait until such as wanted to improve the land appeared. The following session, Pynchon renewed the petition, this time assuring the court that

69. Bradstreet Petition, June 6, 1658, XLV, 67, Mass. Archives; General Court Order, May 27, 1659, photostats, MHS; General Court Grant, May 30, 1660, CXII, 125, Mass. Archives; Hadley Petition to General Court, May 1663, photostats, MHS; Judd, *History of Hadley*, 18–22.

70. General Court Order, Westfield, June 3, 1679, CXII, 272, Mass. Archives; Wright, ed., *Indian Deeds*, 97.

because of the shortage of "accomodations" the petitioners would move to the new township. Thus assured, the deputies went along, and the court granted the township.[71] In other words, although the deputies objected to giving yet another township to wealthy nonresident landowners who, in the absence of ready settlers, were apparently using the pretext of land shortage to acquire more land for themselves, and although even the magistrates insisted that the petitioners put twenty families on the site in two years, the final grant did include, yet again, Pynchon and his friends, who had no intention of moving out of Springfield. For the General Court relied upon precisely such nonresident land engrossers as Pynchon to start new towns, in this case insisting that he manage the new town as one of the grant's conditions. What the deputies had objected to was not Pynchon's nonresidency, speculation, or leasing of wilderness lands, but the fact that the first petition bore no relation to the advancement of settlement.

Pynchon's case raises another important point. Pynchon was a magistrate. Bradstreet was a magistrate, then governor. There were at least seven New England governors who as nonresidents profited from developing the wilderness: John Winthrop, Jr., William Brenton, Benedict Arnold, William Coddington, Peleg Sanford, Simon Bradstreet, and John Leverett. There were deputy governors, John Mason and William Stoughton, involved in land development. There were dozens of assistants involved. And there were dozens of deputies—developing, owning, and profiting from new towns. The official attitude was not hostile to nonresidency and multiple landholding: indeed, the absentees were often the officials.

71. Springfield Petitions, May, Oct. 7, 1670, CXII, 207–211, Mass. Archives.

2 | *The Leading Entrepreneurs*

There was tremendous variation in landholding patterns from town to town and from colony to colony. Some individuals owned a fraction of land in ten or twenty towns; others acquired huge tracts of land but participated in few or no town-foundings at all. Some towns had nearly all absentee landowners, others but one or two. But throughout New England, in spite of regional and local variation, whether absentees were few or many, certain individuals participated in land development on such a scale as to create a distinct group of leading entrepreneurs.

The leading entrepreneurs were set apart by several marks from the types of town founders just described. To most of these developers, land ventures were a side issue—one of several activities that returned a profit and contributed to the expansion of their colonies. (Other common activities engaging these men's attention were shipping and trade.) They were not frontiersmen, but wealthy, educated, mostly urban individuals; not fur traders and surveyors, but often governors, deputy governors, assistants, and military commanders. Some of them helped launch four or five towns, and sometimes ten or twenty, not just two or three. They operated, not just in one region, but in several regions; not in one colony, but in two or three colonies at once. In many instances, they were related to each other. A network of business and family relations bound most of these men together in an intercolonial commerce in land.[1]

These things made them alike. What distinguished the leading specula-

1. Bernard Bailyn demonstrated a similar oligarchical pattern of intermarriage among Boston merchants (*The New England Merchants in the Seventeenth Century* [Cambridge, Mass., 1955], 138–140).

tors one from another were the different methods of their entrepreneurship. Entrepreneurs used all methods in all regions, but circumstances in each region favored certain methods, including some precocious ones. ⌈Focusing here on that regional variation can demonstrate the complexity and precocity of seventeenth-century land development.⌉

1. The Connecticut Valley and Connecticut Colony

⌈The first region in New England to be developed outside the coastal strip was the Connecticut Valley, and the men who led the development there were perhaps the most successful and aggrandizing land developers of the century—the Pynchons.[2] William Pynchon demonstrated that one man (and his son) can make a difference, that the tasks of starting, provisioning, and defending remote towns in the Connecticut Valley required the leadership of well-connected, resourceful individuals with ready access to the centers of political, commercial, and military power back east.⌉

William Pynchon was one of the patentees and assistants named in the Massachusetts Bay Company charter. In 1634, he extended his fur-trading business, which he had started at Roxbury, to the Connecticut River. In 1635, he visited Agawam, a perfect site for a trading settlement, near the crossroads of a major Indian path and the Connecticut River, and the following May he returned and commenced the settlement of Springfield. On July 15, he and his son-in-law Henry Smith and others bought the site from the Indians.[3]

2. Bruce C. Daniels, in his very informative study, *The Connecticut Town: Growth and Development, 1635–1790* (Middletown, Conn., 1979), 119–127, counts 25 towns incorporated in Connecticut between 1635 and 1675. Of these he finds only 4 were begun by other than "communal means" and with the help of speculators. Though I have not attempted a survey of Connecticut town origins, I suspect that the role of entrepreneurship may have been somewhat larger than Daniels does (see John Frederick Martin, "Entrepreneurship and the Founding of New England Towns: The Seventeenth Century" [Ph.D. diss., Harvard University, 1985], Tables 4a, 5, 6, 7, 8a, and 9, wherein are discussed 8 Connecticut towns with absentee landowners and another 3 with business characteristics).

3. Samuel Eliot Morison, "William Pynchon, The Founder of Springfield," MHS, *Proceedings,* LXIV (1930–1932), 71, 74, 76; Alden T. Vaughan, *New England Frontier:*

This was the beginning of Pynchon enterprises in the Connecticut Valley; they would last a century. The first object of the empire was fur. William Pynchon began trading for pelts during the first spring of permanent settlement, even before he bought the land. (A minister did not arrive at Springfield until the following year, 1637.) He soon established trading posts at Woronoco (later Westfield) and elsewhere in the valley. During the 1650s and 1660s, Pynchon's son John exported twenty-five thousand pounds of beaver hides, not counting other skins, to England from the Connecticut Valley.[4]

William Pynchon also procured a contract to deliver corn to Connecticut towns, and he built the first gristmill in the valley. In addition to corn, the Pynchons supplied settlers with all manner of goods, imported and locally manufactured. They owned the only store in Springfield and the sawmills. A great many Springfield families had retail accounts with the Pynchons. Many borrowed from the Pynchons through their store. Many were also Pynchon tenants and laborers. From 1652 to 1702, more than two hundred men were either tenants, debtors, or wage laborers of the Pynchons: at any one time, approximately one-half of the adult male population of Springfield.[5]

The Pynchons also made money from landownership up and down the Connecticut Valley. The Pequot War may have slowed settlement at the end of that decade, and the drop in immigration during the 1640s probably also reduced the demand for land in the Connecticut Valley. But in the 1650s the land market improved. (By this time, William Pynchon had returned to England, leaving his lands and other business in the hands of his son John and his sons-in-law, Henry Smith and Elizur Holyoke.) Probably the most profitable of the family's lands lay in Springfield. As Stephen Innes has

Puritans and Indians, 1620–1675 (Boston, 1965), 216; Harry Andrew Wright, ed., *Indian Deeds of Hampden County* (Springfield, Mass., 1905), 11.

4. Morison, "William Pynchon," MHS, *Procs.*, LXIV (1930–1932), 78, 79, 83; William Haller, Jr., *The Puritan Frontier: Town-Planting in New England Colonial Development, 1630–1660* (New York, 1951), 99–103; Vaughan, *New England Frontier*, 216.

5. Morison, "William Pynchon," MHS, *Procs.*, LXIV (1930–1932), 83, 91; Stephen Innes, "Land Tenancy and Social Order in Springfield, Massachusetts, 1652 to 1702," *William and Mary Quarterly*, 3d Ser., XXXV (1978), 34–37; Stephen Innes, *Labor in a New Land: Economy and Society in Seventeenth-Century Springfield* (Princeton, N.J., 1983), 38.

shown, John Pynchon granted himself by far the largest single holding of Springfield's land. He could do so because he was the town meeting moderator, selectman, magistrate, and member of the land committee for Springfield during most years, and because most of the town was in his debt one way or another. In 1685, a total of 120 people held nine thousand acres of town land; more than eighteen hundred of those acres, or 20 percent, were owned by Pynchon. At this same time, there was a land shortage in town. There were many landless men in town, and the average holding of those that did have land (excluding Pynchon) was sixty acres.[6]

Many of the landless were Pynchon's tenants. A typical tenant might rent fifteen acres, some housing, and a yoke of oxen for twelve to sixteen years. By the terms of his lease, he would be obligated to improve and maintain the land or fences, perhaps construct a house, pay the taxes, and, sometimes, give up half the offspring of his livestock. The result of these arrangements, by which farmers surrendered their principal equity, was the impoverishment of Pynchon tenants.[7]

But Pynchon did not confine his renting arrangements to Springfield. In 1677, Pynchon made an indenture with Philip Mattoon, a newly married settler who agreed to take up some of Pynchon's Deerfield lands. Pynchon's account book recorded the transaction: "Let out to Philip Mattoon my 18 cow commons and 4 sheep commons at Pocumtuck, all the intervale land belonging to sd commons . . . for 11 years . . . to pay all rates, taxes and charges, make and leave good fences, to build on the land a good dwelling house, strong, substantial and well built, and compleatly finished. . . . Also a barn. . . . Also to pay thirty shillings a year for nine years, £3 the tenth, and £4 the last year."[8]

Pynchon came by his Deerfield lands in the same way that Gookin acquired his Worcester lands: he helped to launch new towns. Often Pynchon negotiated with the Indians for title to a new town's lands. Then, in return for purchasing the tract, Pynchon held title to the township until the town reimbursed him the purchase money. Towns also gave Pynchon land

6. Morison, "William Pynchon," MHS, *Procs.*, LXIV (1930–1932), 105; Haller, *Puritan Frontier*, 99–103; Innes, "Land Tenancy and Social Order in Springfield," *WMQ*, 3d Ser., XXXV (1978), 41; Innes, *Labor in a New Land*, 45–46.

7. Innes, "Land Tenancy and Social Order in Springfield," *WMQ*, 3d Ser., XXXV (1978), 43–44; Innes, *Labor in a New Land*, 48–51.

8. George Sheldon, *History of Deerfield, Mass.* . . . , 2 vols., (Deerfield, Mass., 1895–1896), I, 179–180.

rights as reward for serving as town financier. Northampton, Hadley, Westfield, Deerfield, Hatfield, Suffield, Brookfield, Enfield, and North-field—all were initially purchased by Pynchon.[9]

Often Pynchon did more than finance town-launchings. He was ap-pointed head of the General Court committees charged with supervising new Connecticut Valley towns. In 1653, a group of men petitioned the court for the grant of Nonotuck, above Springfield. The court appointed Pynchon, his brother-in-law Elizur Holyoke, and fellow Springfield land-owner Samuel Chapin to be a committee for overseeing the new settlement. In 1653, Pynchon bought the land from the Indians, laid out half of it to be a township, and then admitted the petitioners to the grant, surrendering the Indian deed to the grantees. This became Northampton. Six years later, Pynchon laid out the other half for the new town of Norwottuck, which soon took the name Hadley, and made over the Indian deed to the grantees. In 1667, the court charged Pynchon and several others with admitting inhabitants, granting lands, and managing the new town of Brookfield. In 1671, Pynchon and Holyoke laid out the new plantation of Suffield on orders from the General Court.[10]

Some of these towns Pynchon began simply by splitting land off the tract held by himself and the other proprietors of Springfield. For in-stance, Springfield began granting lots in Woronoco during the 1650s and 1660s to leading Springfield citizens, among them John Pynchon, Thomas Cooper, Samuel Chapin, and George Colton. (In effect, these men were granting lots to themselves, but formally it was the town of Springfield that made the grants.) In 1662, several men asked the court for the grant of a plantation in the area of these lots. The court granted the request and left the organizing of the new town to the town of Springfield. Springfield thereupon appointed Pynchon, Colton, Holyoke, and two other men to

9. Wright, ed., *Indian Deeds*, 24–27, 33–35, 37–39, 69–70, 74–75, 94–97, 99–101; Innes, *Labor in a New Land*, 26.

10. Josiah Gilbert Holland, *History of Western Massachusetts*, 2 vols. (Springfield, Mass., 1855), I, 45–48, II, 244–245; John Warner Barber, *Historical Collections . . . History and Antiquities of Every Town in Massachusetts . . .* (Worcester, Mass., 1848), 329; Wright, ed., *Indian Deeds*, 26–28; Pynchon Report on Norwottuck, Sept. 30, 1659, CXII, 115, Mass. Archives; Sylvester Judd, *History of Hadley, Including the Early History of Hatfield, South Hadley, Amherst, and Granby, Massachusetts* (Springfield, Mass., 1905), 3; Ellery Bicknell Crane, ed., *History of Worcester County, Massachusetts*, 3 vols. (New York, 1924), I, 32–35; Pynchon Report on Suffield, May 20, 1674, photostats, MHS.

admit inhabitants, grant lands at Woronoco, govern the settlement, and help the settlers win the court's approval to be a town. (A committee with only slightly different membership was at the same time in charge of distributing the undivided lands of Springfield.) Approval won, the town was officially named Westfield in 1669. In all, the proprietors of Springfield owned and controlled 729 square miles of land, from which were created, in addition to Westfield, the towns of Suffield, Southwick, West Springfield, Enfield, Somers, Wilbraham, Ludlow, and Longmeadow.[11]

In each of these cases, Pynchon acquired land. Sometimes when making the Indian purchase, Pynchon would specifically reserve a "Grant or right" for himself. On other occasions, he appears to have been admitted to the fraternity of purchasers after he bought the land and conveyed it to them. In 1666, he bought the Indian title to Deerfield for the proprietors of Dedham and, then, became one of the new proprietors of Deerfield. In 1670, he was with Eleazer Lusher, Joshua Fisher, and others helping to organize the proprietors into a governable association. Pynchon probably did not have to pay for admission to the Deerfield proprietors; his participation would have been welcomed by the other proprietors. But whether admitted for free or not, Pynchon soon was buying up the shares of other men. Governor John Leverett and Joshua Fisher both sold Pynchon Deerfield shares. By this means, Pynchon became one of the largest landowners of Deerfield—and one of only two proprietors to keep his rights from the 1660s to the 1680s.[12]

Pynchon repeated his Deerfield activity elsewhere. He owned land in every town of the valley, more than 2,000 acres in Groton, Connecticut, and part of Antigua in the West Indies and was granted more than 8,170 acres by the General Court. At his death in 1703, these lands exceeded eight thousand pounds in value.[13]

Pynchon had just the right talents for town-planting. He had wealth, political connections back east, knowledge of the frontier, the ability to

11. Holland, *Western Massachusetts*, I, 64–65; Henry M. Burt, *The First Century of the History of Springfield: The Official Records from 1636 to 1736*, 2 vols. (Springfield, Mass., 1898–1899), II, 80, 98–100, 107; Petition from Woronoco Settlers, 1662, CXII, 143–144, Mass. Archives; Barber, *Historical Collections: Massachusetts*, 291, 299–304.

12. Wright, ed., *Indian Deeds*, 74–75, 99–101; Sheldon, *History of Deerfield*, I, 10, 15, 93, 100–101, 115, 117, 179–180.

13. Innes, "Land Tenancy and Social Order in Springfield," *WMQ*, 3d Ser., XXXV (1978), 39; Innes, *Labor in a New Land*, 28–29.

provision frontier settlements. Of all the people in the Connecticut Valley, Pynchon was in the best position to organize landless men, be their voice, place petitions in their behalf before the authorities, find empty tracts, extinguish Indian titles, survey the lands, know who were the most promising men to admit as inhabitants, and regulate the affairs of infant settlements until town privileges were granted.[14] That he was a wealthy landholder, ever accumulating real estate by his involvement in town-founding, did not bar him from serving as an advocate for frontier settlers. When the refusal of nonresidents to settle Brookfield and pay their assessments crippled that struggling town and inhabitants of Brookfield appealed for help to the General Court, John Pynchon put the weight of his signature behind their appeal. When the new settlement of Suffield was barely getting off the ground, Pynchon and Holyoke asked on behalf of the settlers that Suffield's country rate be remitted for seven years. Pynchon was a reliable champion of frontier people because his fortunes were yoked to theirs. When they suffered, he did. When the Indian war broke out in 1675, it was Pynchon who led the English forces protecting the Connecticut Valley, and Pynchon's mills and rent-producing property were destroyed along with the homes and farms of settlers.[15] But when settlements prospered, Pynchon prospered. He expended tremendous energy and time dealing with Indians, debtors, tenants, surveyors, committees, and the General Court to advance white settlement—and his family's estate.

At the same time William Pynchon was opening up the Connecticut Valley, John Winthrop, Jr., was opening up the Pequot country, that corner of fertile land where southern Rhode Island and Connecticut come together. Winthrop was one of the most accomplished New Englanders of the seventeenth century: son of the Massachusetts Bay governor, governor in his own right (of Connecticut), scientist, celebrity on both sides of the ocean. Among his many endeavors, John Junior developed wilderness lands.

Soon after his arrival in New England in 1631, the Massachusetts authorities, fearing French claims to lands to their north, asked Winthrop to launch a town on the coast north of Boston. In March 1633, Winthrop

14. See above, Chapter 1, for the General Court's treatment of Pynchon's land engrossing.

15. Brookfield Petition, Oct. 25, 1692, CXII, 425–427, Mass. Archives; Pynchon Report, May 20, 1674, photostats, MHS; Sheldon, *History of Deerfield*, I, 101–104, 115.

went there and began building. He purchased land from the Indian sachem Masconomet for twenty pounds (and later argued with the town, as did his children, over proper reimbursement). In 1633 or early 1634, he moved his home there, and in 1634, the town was named Ipswich. It was the first new town authorized by any New England colony government—significantly, a town begun for defensive, not religious, reasons, by a peripatetic town founder, not a man looking for a new home.[16]

No sooner had Winthrop arrived than he left Ipswich, in 1634. Other prominent men also left Ipswich in its early years—William Hubbard, William Paine, William Bartholomew, Thomas Dudley, Simon Bradstreet, and William Symonds.[17] Their departure, with John Winthrop's, leads one to believe that these men went to Ipswich only to found it, not to make new homes. As prominent men they could attract other settlers to the new town, and as wealthy men they could finance the new town. Once the town was on its own feet, they departed. They did not, however, lose their land upon leaving. On the contrary, founding Ipswich added substantial land to Winthrop's estate. He was one of the largest landowners in town when he left, possessing at least two town lots, two large farms, and other meadow and upland. In 1638, he sold one tract of 320 acres to Ipswich resident Samuel Symonds. Ipswich tried to give Winthrop even more land as a lure to keep him from leaving the town, but Winthrop had other plans.[18]

When he left Ipswich, Winthrop went to England, the first of several trips there, and returned in 1635 holding a commission from Lord Say, Lord Brook, and others to start a town in their patent in Connecticut. These patentees hired Winthrop, paid the settlement costs, and sent over settlers, all in the hopes of realizing a profit either from land sales and fees or from agricultural production. Winthrop began the project in November 1635, and by the following spring was on the spot supervising construction of a fort and settlement at Saybrook. After Saybrook, Winthrop spent part of the next few years trying to establish a New England ironworks. This

16. Haller, *Puritan Frontier*, 93–99; Sidney Perley, *The Indian Land Titles of Essex County, Massachusetts* (Salem, Mass., 1912), 26–29; Melville Egleston, *Land System of the New England Colonies*, Johns Hopkins University Studies in Historical and Political Science, 4th Ser., nos. 11–12 (Baltimore, 1886), 30.

17. Edward S. Perzel, "Landholding in Ipswich," Essex Institute, *Historical Collections,* CIV (1968), 316–317.

18. Thomas Franklin Waters, *Ipswich in the Massachusetts Bay Colony . . .* , 2 vols. (Ipswich, Mass., 1905–1917), I, 9–10, 11, 12, 50; Haller, *Puritan Frontier,* 93–99.

project required the assistance of the General Court, which granted him an iron-making monopoly as well as land grants in Lynn and Braintree, and also brought Winthrop to the Pequot country, where he looked for minerals. In 1644, Massachusetts gave Winthrop permission to start a plantation in the Pequot country, whereupon he explored the region, chose a site, and laid out house lots in a settlement later called New London. Winthrop did not stay in New London any longer than he had anywhere else. He was offered money to start towns on Long Island and along the Delaware Bay, but declined and instead moved on to New Haven and then Hartford. In 1657, he was elected governor of Connecticut. By then, he had lived in Boston, Salem, Ipswich, Saybrook, New London, New Haven, and Hartford. Three of these towns he had founded himself. And they do not count the settlement efforts he was to take part in as governor.[19]

In 1659, John Winthrop, Jr., joined several prominent figures from Massachusetts in the purchase of land in Rhode Island which later became, with some additions, the principal assets of the Atherton Company (discussed below). The next year, Winthrop represented the United Colonies when that body received payment of a fine from the Atherton Company. This fine had been levied against the Narragansett Indians by the United Colonies for certain alleged Indian offenses. The Atherton Company agreed to pay the fine for the Indians in return for receiving a mortgage on the Narragansett lands. When the Indians did not redeem the mortgage, the Atherton Company took possession of the whole Narragansett. The central figure in this shady transaction was John Winthrop, Jr., who served as one of the United Colonies commissioners levying the fine at the same time he was holding stock in the company that directly benefited as a result of the Indians' fine.[20]

It appears that, as important as he was to this transaction, Winthrop was not the moving force behind the Atherton Company and that Humphrey

19. Benjamin Trumbull, *A Complete History of Connecticut* . . . , 2 vols. (New Haven, Conn., 1818), I, 167–169, 230–231, 497–498; Haller, *Puritan Frontier*, 93–99; Vaughan, *New England Frontier*, 117; Daniels, *Connecticut Town*, 97–99.

20. Elisha R. Potter, Jr., *The Early History of Narragansett* (RIHS, *Collections*, III [Providence, R.I., 1835]), 265–269 (hereafter cited as Potter, *Early History of Narragansett*); entries for Oct. 13, Nov. 16, 1660, Apr. 7, 1663, Narragansett Land Papers, microfilm reel 6, Winthrop Papers, MHS (hereafter cited as reel 6, Winthrop Papers, MHS); John Fones, *The Records of the Narragansett, Otherwise Called the Fones Record*, ed. James W. Arnold (Providence, R.I., 1894), 1–3, 15, 19–21, 24–25 (hereafter cited as *Fones Record*).

Atherton and others drew him into the venture. They did so because, being absentees, they feared that the Rhode Island authorities would not recognize their title to the Narragansett, and they hoped that by giving Winthrop a share in the venture he would work to bring the land under Connecticut jurisdiction and confirm the company title to it.[21] In these hopes they were not disappointed. In April 1663, John Winthrop accepted an arbitration in behalf of Connecticut by which "the proprietrs and Inhabitants of that Land about Mr Smiths trading house claimed or purchased by Major Atherton . . . shall have free Liberties to choose which of these colonies [Rhode Island or Connecticut] they will belong." Not taking long to make up their minds, the Atherton Company chose Connecticut on July 3, 1663. That was just the beginning, however, not the end, of the jurisdictional and proprietary disputes over the Narragansett, through all of which John Winthrop, Jr., ably represented the interests of his company and himself.[22]

John Winthrop, Jr., used his Rhode Island lands for one purpose only: he rented them out to farmers. He did so with the assistance of Richard Smith, Jr., a fellow Atherton stockholder who lived in the Narragansett. On January 8, 1681/2, Smith wrote to Winthrop's son, Fitz John, asking him to approve a tenant to whom he had rented Winthrop's property on Boston Neck. The following April, Smith again wrote to Fitz John Winthrop about the latter's land at Boston Neck, informing him that he had engaged a man to rent the property for ten years at eight pounds per year. For some twenty years, Richard Smith was the Winthrop family's agent, managing their Narragansett lands.[23]

Meanwhile, John Winthrop, Jr., acquired other lands within Connecticut's boundaries. While embarked upon his ironworks project, Winthrop bought from the Indians one hundred square miles near Sturbridge in the Nipmuck country, north of the Pequot country. In 1647, he claimed before the disbelieving United Colonies commissioners a great swath of eastern

21. Humphrey Atherton and Edward Hutchinson to John Winthrop, Jr., Oct. 23, 1660, Misc. Bound, MHS; Richard Smith, Jr., to John Winthrop, Jr., Feb. 13, 1667/8, May 1670, in Daniel Berkeley Updike, *Richard Smith: First English Settler of the Narragansett Country, Rhode Island* . . . (Boston, 1937), 30, 34–35.

22. Apr. 7, 1663, entry, reel 6, Winthrop Papers, MHS; Trumbull, *History of Connecticut*, I, 318–321.

23. Their correspondence spanned at least the years 1668–1684, and probably longer. Smith to John Winthrop, Jr., Feb. 13, 1667/8, Smith to Fitz John Winthrop, Jan. 8, 1681/2, Apr. 13, 1682, and 1684, in Updike, *Richard Smith*, 30, 34–35, 39, 62.

Connecticut. And in 1659, he purchased with the permission of the Connecticut General Court land at Quinebaug, in northeastern Connecticut, on which several settlers were already living. This last purchase was the source of a later controversy. In 1690, Winthrop's sons Fitz John and Wait Winthrop asked the Connecticut General Court to confirm their claim to the Quinebaug lands against the rival claim of Captain James Fitch. The fight between the Winthrops and Fitch divided the Connecticut political community for two decades. It also slowed settlement, since settlers were continually being evicted and sued by one claimant or another. In the end, the assembly resolved the dispute by awarding both the Winthrops and Fitch one thousand acres in each of the two contested towns, Plainfield and Canterbury.[24]

John Winthrop, Jr., died in the spring of 1676. By then he had accumulated land in four different colonies and owned absentee farming operations in the Narragansett, in the area of New London, on Fishers Island off Long Island, Charlestown, Massachusetts, and perhaps elsewhere.[25] He possessed vast stretches of empty land in the Nipmuck country that would begin to be developed in the lifetime of his sons. He had launched three or four towns himself and had purchased Indian land where many other towns went up. He had used high office to help himself and his friends start new towns and acquire considerable farmland, which he and they worked as absentee farmers and landlords.

The Winthrops' rival in the Quinebaug territory, James Fitch, was the chief Connecticut land speculator of the later seventeenth century. Fitch was born in 1649 in Saybrook, the son of the Reverend James Fitch, and was by turns land surveyor, land registrar, county treasurer of New London County, deputy, councillor, military captain, and Indian fighter. His business strategy centered upon suborning Indian sachems to obtain their deeds and gaining political office to register the deeds and confirm his

24. Wright, *Indian Deeds*, 15–23; Trumbull, *History of Connecticut*, I, 167, 400; Winthrop Petition, Oct. 13, 1698, Towns and Lands, 2d Ser., II, 69; General Court Committee Report, Sept. 12, 1706, Towns and Lands, II, 186–190, Conn. Archives; Dorothy Deming, *The Settlement of Connecticut Towns* (New Haven, Conn., 1933), 57–58.

25. Richard S. Dunn, *Puritans and Yankees: The Winthrop Dynasty of New England, 1630–1717* (Chapel Hill, N.C., 1971), 70, 186, 202; John Winthrop, Jr., Inventory, Nov. 3, 1676, XII, 109–110, SCPR. His Charlestown farm alone was appraised at £1,900.

titles.[26] But the skills of land management—surveying, apportioning land rights, finding buyers—not just the powers of office, were essential tools of his trade.

In 1680 and again in 1684, Fitch persuaded the Mohegan chief Owaneco to accept him as guardian and to vest in Fitch title to the Quinebaug country, containing more than one million acres. By the end of the decade, Fitch was settling tenants on the part of this tract that later became Canterbury. Fitch also moved to Canterbury himself, laid out the house lots, built the first house and barn there, attracted settlers from Norwich, served as representative to the General Court, and died there in 1727. The Owaneco tract eventually had six different towns on it. Fitch sold one piece to the proprietors of Roxbury, who started the town of Woodstock upon it. He sold another piece called the Mashamoquet Purchase to the same Roxbury men, who launched the town of Pomfret. He sold shares to men and with them launched the towns of Windham and Mansfield. Then in the mid-1690s, Fitch sold a tract to men from Ipswich, who started the town of Lebanon. After the turn of the century, he began selling lands north of Tolland—to the protests of Connecticut authorities.[27]

Fitch was not the most popular man in Connecticut. The settlers of Canterbury complained that he had lured them there with the promise of good land, only to keep the good land for himself, giving to settlers "pore rockey hills." The Winthrops called him Black James; others called him "a great land pirate." The Connecticut assembly repeatedly objected to Fitch's speculations and annulled his titles, and repeatedly Fitch resumed his speculative activities, usually after regaining political office. By the time Fitch died, he had either lived in or owned land in six different frontier towns, had sold land to the founders of many more towns, and had laid claim to the bulk of northeast Connecticut.[28]

26. James M. Poteet, "More Yankee than Puritan: James Fitch of Connecticut," *New England Historical and Genealogical Register*, CXXXIII (1979), 102; Frances Manwaring Caulkins, *History of Norwich, Connecticut* . . . (Hartford, Conn., 1874), 61–62, 95.

27. Poteet, "More Yankee than Puritan," *NEHGR*, CXXXIII (1978), 104–105, 108, 116; Deming, *Settlement of Connecticut Towns*, 54–55, 61; Caulkins, *History of Norwich*, 136–138, 257; Canterbury Town Meeting Order, May 5, 1707, Towns and Lands, III, 202, Conn. Archives. See below for discussion of Woodstock, Pomfret, and nearby towns.

28. Petition of Canterbury Settlers, Oct. 10, 1717, Towns and Lands, III, 136, Conn. Archives; Poteet, "More Yankee than Puritan," *NEHGR*, CXXXIII (1978), 102; Caul-

There were many other land entrepreneurs in Connecticut and the Connecticut Valley—the Masons, Thomas Stanton, George Denison, and more—but as to both scale of landownership and social prominence, Pynchon, Winthrop, and Fitch were in a class by themselves. Pynchon was a magistrate, Winthrop governor, and Fitch councillor. All three played large roles in the United Colonies' efforts to remove Indians from desirable lands upon which whites soon planted new towns. The remote and hostile lands of the Connecticut Valley and colony, lying several days' journey from Boston, presented obstacles to settlement that people of means and influence were uniquely suited to overcome.

11. Rhode Island

By 1700, Rhode Island still had only a handful of towns, probably no more than nine or ten.[29] The land upon which nearly all of these had been founded, with the dramatic exception of Warwick, had been owned by men who wished, among other things, to make a profit from land development. In some cases (the towns of Kingston and Wickford) the first landowners were men who lived in Massachusetts. In other cases (Westerly, Portsmouth, and Providence) the speculators were Rhode Islanders. The scene of great land commerce in the seventeenth century, Rhode Island had the distinction of being owned and developed by speculators from Massachusetts, Plymouth Colony, and Connecticut as well as by Rhode Island's indigenous active entrepreneurs.

Perhaps because of this great land commerce, or perhaps because the investors in this colony were nonresidents who needed structures to conduct business activities in their absence, Rhode Island speculators stood out for their use of corporate, business methods. There were, to be sure, land engrossers in Rhode Island who pursued their profits without elaborate corporate instruments, relying on the same skills that speculators relied on elsewhere. William Harris, Benedict Arnold, and William Coddington used political office to affirm their land titles. Humphrey Atherton played a key role in fighting and removing Indians from lands he later owned. John

kins, *History of Norwich,* 137–138. In 1698, the General Court became the General Assembly; hence the change in terms.

29. Evarts B. Greene and Virginia D. Harrington, *American Population before the Federal Census of 1790* (New York, 1932), 64–65.

Winthrop, Jr., William Harris, Richard Smith, and others tried for decades to have much of Rhode Island's territory transferred to another jurisdiction to protect the speculators' claims. In these ways Rhode Island entrepreneurs resembled land entrepreneurs everywhere; but in precociously using business corporations—with management delegated to committees, shares representing claims on company assets, and permanent corporate-run enterprises—the Rhode Island speculators created business entities in advance of those used in any other economic sector, entities that would become in later generations the basic organizational tools of American enterprise.

After Providence, Portsmouth, Newport, and Warwick—all except the last of which contained a number of land engrossers and considerable wrangling over land—the next large town established was Westerly, in the far southwest corner of the Narragansett country, near the Pequot country.[30] A group of Newport residents formed a company and bought the

30. The history of Rhode Island's first three towns demonstrates that land greed and great inequities accompanied the first efforts to settle Rhode Island. For early Providence land controversies, see Henry C. Dorr, "The Proprietors of Providence, and Their Controversies with the Freeholders," RIHS, *Publications*, n.s., III (1895), 143, 201–206, 209–215; Samuel Greene Arnold, *History of the State of Rhode Island and Providence Plantations*, 2 vols. (New York, 1859–1860), I, 101, 121; A. B. Patton, "The Early Land Titles of Providence," *NHR*, VIII (1890), 166–167; Sidney S. Rider, "The Forgeries Connected with the Deed Given by the Sachems Canonicus and Miantinomi to Roger Williams of the Land on Which the Town of Providence Was Planted," *Rhode Island Historical Tracts*, 2d Ser., no. 4 (Providence, R.I., 1896), 59–64. For Portsmouth, see Henry E. Turner, "William Coddington in Rhode Island Colonial Affairs," *R.I. Hist. Tracts*, 1st Ser., no. 4 (Providence, R.I., 1878), 9–22; Arnold, *History of Rhode Island*, I, 69–71, 124; John Callender, *An Historical Discourse, on the Civil and Religious Affairs of the Colony of Rhode-Island and Providence Plantations* . . . (Boston, 1739 [republished in RIHS, *Colls.*, IV (Providence, R.I., 1838)]), 84, 84n, 85, 212–215. For Newport, see Adelos Gorton, *The Life and Times of Samuel Gorton* . . . (Philadelphia, 1907), 23–24, 28–29, 32–33; Callender, *Historical Discourse*, 218–219; Turner, "Coddington," *R.I. Hist. Tracts*, 1st Ser., no. 4, 23–25. As to land engrossing, William Harris, leader of the Providence proprietors, owned land in Providence, Pawtuxet, and the Narragansett and left more than 1,100 acres at death (Providence, R.I., Record Commissioners, *The Early Records of the Town of Providence*, 21 vols. [Providence, R.I., 1892–1915], VI, 48–56). Governor Benedict Arnold owned land in Newport, Dutch Island, and Conanicut Island, was a shareholder in the Pettaquamscut and Misquamicut purchases, and left more than 5,000 acres at death (Benedict Arnold Will, 1677, in Elisha Stephen Arnold, comp., *The Arnold Memorial: William Arnold of Providence and Pawtuxet, 1587–1675, and a Genealogy of His Descendants* [Rutland, Vt., 1935], 54–56). Most 17th-century probate and land records of Newport are no longer extant, owing to their removal by the

tract of Misquamicut from the Narragansett Indians on June 29, 1660. They received from the General Assembly the grant of a township and drew up "articles of agreement" to govern the planting of this town, in which they ordered that charges would be assessed "according to the proportion of land they have" and men would forfeit their land if they did not pay their charges.[31] The vast majority of the seventy-six signatories never left the towns they lived in, never moved to Misquamicut. Some of them, living in Newport, invested in lands besides the Misquamicut Purchase. Benedict Arnold owned tracts and shares throughout Rhode Island. Philip Sherman purchased Aquidneck along with William Coddington in 1638 and at death owned land in Portsmouth, Dartmouth (Plymouth), and Westerly. John Coggeshall was also an original Aquidneck purchaser who owned land in at least three different places at his death. Jireh Bull owned land developed by the Pettaquamscut company, near Misquamicut, as well as property in Newport. John Fones began a separate land development venture in the Narragansett named after himself. Richard Smith was a prominent Narragansett resident and shareholder in the Atherton Company. George Denison lived in Stonington, Connecticut, across the river from Misquamicut, and acquired land throughout the Pequot region. Simon Lynde lived in Massachusetts and owned land in several colonies. Misquamicut, the rich land along the southern shore of Rhode Island, drew investors from all over New England.[32]

British in 1779 and subsequent loss at sea, including those of William Coddington and other land engrossers of that town (Darius Baker, "The Coddington Portrait," *Bulletin of the Newport Historical Society,* no. 25 [April 1918], 8). For nonprobate evidence of Coddington's land acquisitions, see Charles Francis Adams, *History of Braintree, Massachusetts . . .* (Cambridge, Mass., 1891), 3; Turner, "Coddington," *R.I. Hist. Tracts,* 1st Ser., no. 4, 23–25, 48–59; Potter, *Early History of Narragansett,* 54. Evidence of Newporters' land engrossing occurs in the Misquamicut and Pettaquamscut company records, discussed below.

31. Thomas Barber, "The Settlement of Westerly," *NHR,* I (1882–1883), 125–127; Potter, *Early History of Narragansett,* 241–252; Frederick Denison, *Westerly (Rhode Island), and Its Witnesses . . . 1626–1876 . . .* (Providence, R.I., 1878), 47–51; Barber, "Contributions to the History of Westerly," *NHR,* II (1883–1884), 36–37.

32. Arnold, *History of Rhode Island,* I, 124; Potter, *Early History of Narragansett,* 251–253; Barber, "Contributions to the History of Westerly," *NHR,* II (1883–1884), 36–37; Benedict Arnold Will, in Arnold, comp., *Arnold Memorial,* 54–56; Philip Sherman Will, July 31, 1681, in Roy V. Sherman, *Some of the Descendants of Philip Sherman, the First Secretary of Rhode Island* (Akron, Ohio, 1968), 26–28; "Copy of the Will of Major John Coggeshall," in Charles Pierce Coggeshall and Thellwell Russell Coggeshall,

But most of the purchasers lived in Newport, where company meetings were held. For these Newport residents, Westerly was an investment, not a new home, and it was not even an investment they wished to manage personally. Thus, in August 1661, the shareholders created a committee of "Trustees" to order "all the affairs of Misquamocuck." These trustees, in turn, appointed treasurers, surveyors, and company agents (who were to "act for us . . . managing our affairs at Misquamacuck") and, furthermore, contracted with men to go to Misquamicut and settle the town, offering five pounds to each settler and assessing the shareholders eight pounds per share to cover this expense. In Westerly, settlement was not only a consequence of land speculation; it was company policy, supported by shareholder subscriptions.[33]

---

comps., *The Coggeshalls in America* (Boston, 1930), 355–362; [re Jireh Bull], *NEHGR,* XXIV (1870), 326–327; Norman H. Isham, "Preliminary Report . . . on . . . Jireh Bull Garrison House . . . ," RIHS, *Colls.,* XI (1918), 3, 10–11; P. F. Pierce, "Descendants of Richard Smith," MS, RIHS. George Denison was an interesting figure, arriving in the Pequot country in 1654, becoming a member of the Atherton Company and the Misquamicut Company, leading forays against the Narragansett Indians in 1676 in the area of his company lands, and acquiring a share in Windham and then Voluntown, Conn. The base of his operations was Southertown (later Stonington, Conn.), in which several prominent Massachusetts men, such as Gookin, Thomas Prentice, Amos Richison, Thomas Danforth, Samuel Symonds, and Edward Rawson (the last named, Bay Colony secretary) also had land shares. Denison sought to place Southertown under first Massachusetts, then Connecticut, jurisdiction—anything but Rhode Island, whose men he accused of dispossessing the "tennants" of the nonresident, Massachusetts proprietors of Southertown. It appears that because this land was so far from Boston, the absentee landlords needed loyal agents on the spot to manage their affairs in the Pequot country, and Denison was one such loyal agent (Thomas Stanton another). A local landowner with both military and political connections, Denison operated across colony lines, helping one colony annex another's land, developing and defending new towns. Richard Anson Wheeler, *History of the Town of Stonington* . . . (New London, Conn., 1900), 5; Potter, *Early History of Narragansett,* 53, 68, 77, 95–97, 256; Southertown Petition, Oct. 25, 1658, photostats, MHS; Grants in XLV, 60b, 61a, 69, 105, Mass. Archives; General Court Order, May 20, 1658, photostats, MHS; Petition of Gookin *et al.,* 1663, II, 43, Mass. Archives; Petition of Denison *et al.,* Apr. 25, 1670, photostats, MHS.

33. Potter, *Early History of Narragansett,* 251–253, 256–261, 263; Denison, *Westerly,* 51, 52 (where the free inhabitants are listed, which can be compared with the purchasers' list given in Barber, "Contributions to the History of Westerly," *NHR,* II [1883–1884], 36–47). Not every purchaser looked upon the Westerly venture as a speculative enterprise. In 1669, 10 of those who had signed on as subscribers in 1661 were accounted "free inhabitants" of Westerly. On the other hand, that amounts to only 13% of the purchasers, which means some 87% were absentees.

Westerly was just one of the midcentury land companies in Rhode Island. The rich pasture lands of the Narragansett, close to good harbors and the open sea, attracted many investors. In 1687, Edward Randolph reported to an English friend: "I looke vpon R: Island to be the best land and for that quantity the most profitable part of New England."[34] Three decades before, the founders of the Atherton Company had come to the same conclusion.

In the summer of 1659, Humphrey Atherton and several partners bought from the Indians two large tracts of land in the Narragansett. One was called Quidnesset, south of Wickford, the other Namcook or Boston Neck, north of Wickford. These purchases, being so-called Indian purchases, violated Rhode Island law and gave no legal title to the purchasers. But the Atherton Company got around that law by concealing their payment and making the purchases appear as gifts from the Indians, given by the sachem Coginaquand out "of the greate love and Eaffection, I doe beare unto Englishmen, Especially mr. John Winthrop [Jr.]." In any event, their purchase did not violate Rhode Island law, the shareholders argued, because their land was not part of Rhode Island. The Atherton shareholders worked for many years to have jurisdiction over the Narragansett taken away from Rhode Island and assigned to either Massachusetts or Connecticut, and the principal reason for this prolonged campaign was to validate their Indian title. This goal became all the more important when, with the help of John Winthrop, Jr., and the United Colonies, the Atherton Company took possession of the mortgage lands. With that stroke, the Atherton Company then laid claim to most of Rhode Island south of Providence, including much land claimed by Rhode Island settlers and investors.[35]

The man behind this land scheme was Humphrey Atherton. Atherton lived in Dorchester, Massachusetts, which he represented in the General Court as deputy from 1639 to 1641. He represented Springfield at the time he was chosen speaker of the house, in 1653. The next year, he was

34. Randolph to John Povey, June 27, 1686, in Robert Noxon Toppan and Alfred Thomas Scrope Goodrick, eds., *Edward Randolph, Including His Letters and Official Papers* . . . , 7 vols., Prince Society, XXIV–XXVIII, XXX–XXXI (Boston, 1898–1909; rpt., 1967), VI, 178–182.

35. Arnold, *History of Rhode Island*, I, 272, 275; Potter, *Early History of Narragansett*, 58, 265–269; *Fones Record*, 1–4; William Davis Miller, "The Narragansett Planters," AAS, *Proceedings*, n.s., XLIII (1933), 57–58; entries for Oct. 13, 1660, Sept. 22, 1662, reel 6, Winthrop Papers, MHS; Quidnessett, "Notes on Quidnessett," *NHR*, I (1882–1883), 305–311.

assistant. Atherton was also a military leader, rising to major general in 1661. When Daniel Gookin was out of the country, Atherton served for three years as superintendent of the Praying Indians, from 1658 to 1661. This was not his first contact with Indians. In the 1640s, Atherton asked the Indian sachem Ninigret whether he would part with Block Island. He also approached Roger Williams, asking his advice about how to obtain land from the Indians. At the same time, during the 1640s, Massachusetts and the United Colonies sent Atherton on several missions to subdue the Indians of Rhode Island.[36]

Atherton's lands were extensive, not just in Rhode Island but elsewhere as well. He was a leading proprietor of Dorchester, which covered a great deal of land south of Boston.[37] By virtue of his Dorchester proprietary share, Atherton received a large lot in what later became the town of Milton.[38] In the 1650s, the General Court granted Atherton two tracts of five hundred acres as reward for public services. One of these was found to fall in the midst of Hadley, so the General Court relocated the grant, adding two hundred acres to it, in Woronoco, which soon became Westfield. By 1653, Atherton had also probably acquired an interest in the land of Springfield.[39] When Atherton died in 1661, falling from his horse on

36. John Gorham Palfrey, *History of New England during the Stuart Dynasty,* 3 vols. (Boston, 1865; rpt., 1966), II, 338–339n; John Winthrop, *The History of New England from 1630 to 1649,* ed. James Savage, 2 vols. (Boston, 1825–1826; rpt., New York, 1972), II, 137–139n; Potter, *Early History of Narragansett,* 58–59, 151–152; Frederick William Gookin, *Daniel Gookin, 1612–1687 . . .* (Chicago, 1912), 128ff; Vaughan, *New England Frontier,* 294; Roger Williams to John Winthrop, Jr., Nov. 7, 1648, in Roger Williams, *The Letters of Roger Williams . . . ,* ed. John Russell Bartlett (Narragansett Club, *Publications,* 1st Ser., VI [Providence, R.I., 1874]), 158–159. Atherton was not unique. Other land speculators who doubled as military commanders conquering Indian lands were Ephraim Curtis, Thomas Henchman, John Mason, James Fitch, John Pynchon, Edward Tyng, George and Daniel Denison, Thomas Willett, Benjamin Church, and Thomas Stanton.

37. Boston, Registry Dept., *Dorchester Town Records (Fourth Report of the Record Commissioners)* (Boston, 1880), 99. The Dorchester Proprietors met occasionally in Atherton's house when they considered dividing their common lands.

38. Albert Kendall Teele, *The History of Milton, Massachusetts, 1640 to 1887* (Boston, 1887), 17. This was in 1660.

39. Atherton petition, May 26, 1658, photostats, MHS; General Court Order re Atherton *et al.,* May 27, 1659, photostats, MHS; Atherton Petition, Oct. 18, 1659, photostats, MHS; Judd, *History of Hadley,* 18–19; Woronoco, CXII, 143–144, Mass. Archives; Winthrop, *History of New England,* ed. Savage, II, 137–138n. The supposition

Boston Common, he left an estate valued at nine hundred pounds, not counting most of his land.[40]

Atherton collected as partners in the Narragansett venture powerful men. There was his copurchaser John Winthrop, Jr., governor of Connecticut. William Hudson, another purchaser, lived in Boston, where he was a vintner (he sold his share in 1673). Amos Richison, also of Boston, was a merchant, tailor, and owner of shares in Stonington and Westerly, in addition to his Atherton share. He may have moved to Stonington. John Tinker lived first in New London, then Boston, and then was one of the adventurers of the Nashaway venture (later the town of Lancaster).[41] The only other first purchasers were Richard Smith, Sr., and his son, Richard Smith, Jr. They were also the only early owners of Atherton Company land to live in the Narragansett. Richard Smith built the first house in the Narragansett in the 1640s and began trading with the Indians in a place known as Wickford (later North Kingston), the early center of Atherton Company activities in the Narragansett. Smith had a daughter who married John Viall of Boston, himself an investor in Plymouth Colony lands, who became as the result of his marriage an Atherton Company shareholder. Richard Smith's son, Richard Junior, acquired land on Long Island (which later became part of what was known as Smithtown), a house at Wickford, a house and island at Bristol, a house in Newport, Atherton Company lands, many livestock, an interest in a sloop, and eight slaves—for a total

---

that Atherton acquired land in Springfield is based on Atherton's representation of Springfield to the General Court. For discussion of representation by absentee landlords, see "Voting," below, Chapter 5.

40. Probate records indicate that "a considerable part of the majors estate" lay in the Narragansett, where one inventory appraised his holdings at £461, three-quarters of which was land and a dwelling house. Administration of Humphrey Atherton Estate, 1661, n.s., I, 466; Inventory of same, Nov. 7, 1661, IV, 192–193, SCPR. See also Winthrop, *History of New England*, ed. Savage, II, 137–139n.

41. *Fones Record*, 1–3; William Davis Miller, *A Brief Account of the William Withington Plat of Boston Neck, with a Description of the Shares of the Proprietors* (Providence, R.I., 1924), 25 n. 14, 27 n. 26; Potter, *Early History of Narragansett*, 265–269. The Nashaway venture initially failed, and Tinker returned to New London sometime before he participated in the Atherton enterprise. He became assistant in the Connecticut government (Potter, *Early History of Narragansett*, 265–269; Miller, *Withington Plat*, 25 n. 13). Checking archives in Massachusetts, Rhode Island, and Connecticut, I have not found probate records for Hudson, Richison, or Tinker.

worth (not counting his land) of £1,159. Many settlers in the area, perhaps his tenants, were debtors to Richard Smith, Jr.[42]

All this wealth, especially the land wealth, was worth protecting, and in seeking to protect it Smith entered politics. In 1663, he (or his father) submitted Wickford to Connecticut jurisdiction. The next year, the Rhode Island assembly ordered the arrest of Richard Senior for holding a Connecticut commission as constable in the Narragansett. Through the 1660s, Richard Junior wrote to his friend Governor John Winthrop, Jr., complaining of the Rhode Island government and asking Connecticut to "take us under yor Government." Later Smith turned down a Connecticut commission and accepted a Rhode Island one because, as he put it, William Brenton was the new governor and the climate had turned more favorable to men like himself.[43] The one loyalty Smith maintained was, not political, but economic: Smith stuck by his company. Even when he would not serve Connecticut, he was writing Winthrop continually, managing the Winthrop family's Atherton Company lands. In 1682 he told Fitz John that a tenant procured by Smith would build a fence and rent the property for seven years, "by which time it will be worth more rent." In 1670, Richard Smith, Jr., went to England and saw Anthony Ashley Cooper about the Narragansett question; Cooper apparently helped bring the Atherton proprietors' problems before the king and council. In 1678, Smith renewed his petition to the crown for a Narragansett government, saying that in the war just ended Rhode Island had been ineffectual in defending the Narragansett and that only Massachusetts had come to their rescue. This petition conflicted directly with the mission of Rhode Island's agents, and because of it Rhode Island arrested Smith in 1679. Smith was for his whole life at the

42. Updike, *Richard Smith,* 3–19, 27, 65, 66, 108; J. Warren Gardiner, "Roger Williams, the Pioneer of Narragansett," *NHR,* II (1883–1884), 25–34; Arnold, *History of Rhode Island,* I, 195; Potter, *Early History of Narragansett,* 31–33, 388; Miller, "Narragansett Planters," AAS, *Procs.,* n.s., XLIII (1933), 54–55; Richard Smith Petition, Dec. 10, 1683, photostats, MHS.

43. In 1686, President Dudley made Smith justice of the peace, sergeant major, and chief commander of the militia in the Narragansett. Later, Smith was councillor in the Andros council. Richard Smith was an *insumergible,* in the vivid Spanish expression: unsinkable. He jumped from one jurisdiction to another, never to be caught going down with a foundering ally. Potter, *Early History of Narragansett,* 388–389; Arnold, *History of Rhode Island,* I, 312, 366; Updike, *Richard Smith,* 30, 36–39, 42, 64–65; Miller, "Narragansett Planters," AAS, *Procs.,* n.s., XLIII (1933), 61 n. 1.

center of the controversies between Rhode Island, Massachusetts, and Connecticut, and the loyalty he most consistently upheld was to his fellow proprietors, most of them nonresident, of Narragansett lands.⁴⁴

These were the initial owners of the Atherton tracts. Others followed, one of them Simon Bradstreet, who became a shareholder in 1660. Bradstreet, the future Massachusetts governor, was more than a political figurehead for the company; he served on the company committee charged with managing company business. In 1678, this committee circulated a broadside advertising the sale of Narragansett lands. Later the Atherton shareholders met in Bradstreet's house in Boston to dispose of company business.⁴⁵

Simon Bradstreet, sometimes described as head of the Whig, or country, party in Massachusetts, was not averse to acquiring country land. The Bay Colony appointed him to hear cases in a frontier town and, next, to bring the towns of Maine under Massachusetts jurisdiction. (Other Maine commissioners were Major General Daniel Denison of Ipswich, also an Atherton Company shareholder, and William Hawthorne, speaker of the house.) In 1653, the General Court rewarded Bradstreet and the other commissioners with grants of 500 acres each. Bradstreet received from the court an additional 500 acres, which he located on the Connecticut River and which later became the subject of the dispute between Bradstreet and the town of Hadley. Bradstreet was an active landlord, renting out farms, seizing the property of his debtors, and accumulating (in Massachusetts alone) by the end of his life more than 1,556 acres scattered through eighteen parcels in five different towns.⁴⁶

44. Updike, *Richard Smith*, 30–31, 35, 36, 43, 47, 57–59, 115, 116; Arnold, *History of Rhode Island*, I, 451, 456, 457.

45. Entry for Oct. 13, 1660, reel 6, Winthrop Papers, MHS; Worthington Chauncy Ford, ed., *Broadsides, Ballads, etc., Printed in Massachusetts, 1639–1800* (MHS, *Collections*, LXXV [Boston, 1922]), 11; *Fones Record*, 30–31, 39–40; *Conn. Records*, III, 267–269.

46. New Hampshire, *Town Charters Granted within the Present Limits of New Hampshire* (vol. II of Albert Stillman Batchellor, ed., *Town Charters*, vol. XXV of *State Papers* [Concord, N.H., 1895]), 706–707; William D. Williamson, *The History of the State of Maine . . .*, 2 vols. (Hallowell, Maine, 1832), I, 334–340; James Phinney Baxter, ed., *Documentary History of the State of Maine*, IV–VI, IX–XVI, *The Baxter Manuscripts* (Portland, Maine, 1889–1916), IV, 11; George Augustus Gordon, *The Early Grants of Land in the Wilderness North of Merrimack* (Lowell, Mass., 1892), 34–37; Simon Bradstreet Will, Dec. 23, 1689, XI, 276–282, SCPR. This summary of assets does not

Another early company member was Captain Edward Hutchinson, admitted at the company's first business meeting held in Hutchinson's house in Boston. From then on, Hutchinson played a key role in company business. It was he who gave Winthrop the money that paid the Indians' fine, he who received the payments by settlers taking up company land, and he who served with Atherton, John Brown, Sr., Richard Smith, Jr., Thomas Willett, and others on a committee to handle all company business—a sort of executive committee. He kept the company's records. Up until his death at the hands of Indians in 1675, Edward Hutchinson undertook the most important assignments for the Atherton Company.[47]

The Hutchinsons owned many lands. In 1654, Edward rented out a piece of land in Lynn for fifty shillings a year; he also seems to have been involved in the ironworks there. In the 1650s, he purchased shares in sawmills in Maine. He had land in Boston, an island, and a court grant not laid out. All told, Hutchinson's lands equaled two-thirds of his estate's value, not counting his farms in the Narragansett and Aquidneck, which paid him handsome rents of more than fifty pounds per annum.[48] Edward's son Elisha—captain, then colonel; deputy, then councillor—once improved land upon which was built Union, Connecticut. He received a farm in the environs of later Dunstable and in time was a proprietor of that town as well as selectman, though he never lived there. In the 1690s, Elisha and Samuel Sewall and others jointly owned a collection of tracts in Braintree, Muddy River (later Brookline), Rumney Marsh (later Chelsea), and part of Boston Neck. The shareholders met periodically to divide and sell their holdings. For many years Elisha bought up lands in Maine. His wife was the stepdaughter of William Phillips, of Saco, one of the premier land traders of Maine. From Phillips, Elisha received along with sixteen other

---

include his Narragansett property or any land in Ipswich. See above, Chapter 1, for Bradstreet's troubles with Hadley.

47. *Fones Record,* 4–5, 15, 17, 19–21, 21–23. Originally Edward Hutchinson's links to Rhode Island were nonbusiness. He had left Boston with his father and mother, William and Anne Hutchinson, during the Antinomian crisis and, with William Coddington and other dissidents, founded Portsmouth. But then Hutchinson returned to Boston and carried on a successful career as a merchant with the help of his sons Elisha and Eliakim. Thos. Lincoln Casey, "The Hutchinson Family," *NHR,* II (1883–1884), 177–179.

48. Edward Hutchinson Lease, 1657, photostats, MHS; *York Deeds,* 1642, I, 57; Edward Hutchinson Inventory, Aug. 24, 1675, V, 287–289; Will of same, Aug. 19, 1675, VI, 70–72, SCPR.

people shares in a nineteen-thousand-acre tract that later became Sanford, Maine. In 1683–1684, Elisha owned land at Scarborough, Small Point Neck, Sheepscot, and Damariscotta, all in Maine. In 1684, settlers at New Dartmouth appealed to Governor Dongan of New York for assistance against Elisha Hutchinson, who, they said, claimed the land they lived on and was trying to make them his tenants. Elisha claimed this disputed land by virtue of the Indian titles that Thomas Clarke and Thomas Lake purchased in the 1650s, which came to Elisha by marriage and which in the eighteenth century formed the basis of the Pejepscot Purchase. The Pejepscot Proprietors, of whom a later Hutchinson was one, were responsible for importing settlers and settling Bath, Georgetown, and several other towns along the Sagadahock River. In the later seventeenth century, Elisha Hutchinson managed this patent, rented out lands, visited the area often, and defended the title. In the opening years of the eighteenth century, Elisha bought and sold numerous tracts along the Maine coast.[49] The interest in developing Maine for profit was continuous from the seventeenth to the eighteenth centuries.

But of all the tracts the Hutchinsons owned, the Narragansett lands were the best, especially the lands fronting Narragansett Bay. Observers noted the rockiness of most Rhode Island ground, but the strip along the shore known as Boston Neck stood out as some of the best grazing land in New England, where snow was light, rain evenly distributed, and cold weather tempered by the ocean. It was this corner of their large tract that the Atherton shareholders selected, in 1659, to be laid out in farms for them-

49. Casey, "The Hutchinson Family," *NHR,* II (1883–1884), 177–179; Edward Hutchinson Petition, Towns and Lands, VI, 69, Conn. Archives; Elias Nason, *A History of the Town of Dunstable, Massachusetts* . . . (Boston, 1877), 26–27, 283; Proprietors of Commons of Braintree, etc., July 23, 1693, CXIII, 13, Mass. Archives; *York Deeds,* IV, 15, VII, 39, 56, 58–59, 83, 93; Elisha Hutchinson's Lands, XLV, 194b, Mass. Archives; Franklin B. Hough, "Pemaquid Papers," Maine Historical Society, *Collections,* V (1857), 95–100; Henry Wilson Owen, *The Edward Clarence Plummer History of Bath, Maine* (Bath, Maine, 1936), 34–35, 56–57, 58, 60–63. Edward's other son, Eliakim, bought 1,000 acres of land in Saco, Maine, in 1673. With John Viall, Eliakim purchased the lands of Thomas Willett in Rehoboth and Swansea, a total of 600 acres, in 1679 (Thomas W. Bicknell, *Sowams, with Ancient Records of Sowams and Parts Adjacent* [New Haven, Conn., 1908], 78–82). In 1687, he purchased 500 acres of Kittery, Maine, from Robert Tufton Mason (*York Deeds,* IV, 151–153). He paid Mason £60 for this land; 12 years later, he sold the same, plus another smaller tract, less what he had conveyed in the meantime, for £500 (*York Deeds,* VI, 102–103).

selves: 700 acres for Atherton, and for the other shareholders, 661.5 acres to each whole share. Next to these great farms, the company set aside a common, on Point Judith, for pasturing the cattle of shareholders. These decisions were among the earliest in company history.[50]

Upon these tracts, the shareholders (at least the ones who kept their lands) launched large-scale farming operations, raising horses and cattle and letting out pieces to tenants. Since Edward Hutchinson lived in Boston, he sent his brother-in-law, John Cole, to live in Rhode Island and manage his Boston Neck farm. Another local, Edward's nephew Peleg Sanford of Newport, handled the family's export business in Rhode Island. Peleg was the son-in-law, first, of William Brenton and, then, of William Coddington, both Rhode Island governors with multiple landholdings. Peleg himself sat in the governor's council, then was governor himself, and then member of the Andros council.[51] When he was not practicing politics, Peleg represented one corner of the triangle trade carried on by the Hutchinson family, exporting livestock and provisions to the West Indies, where his brothers (who lived there) exchanged them for sugar and cotton, which the Hutchinsons then sold for credit in London; meanwhile, Richard Hutchinson, Edward's brother in London, supplied the American Hutchinsons with manufactured goods for sale in New England. Sanford also helped manage the Hutchinsons' Atherton Company holdings, renting and selling lands, dealing with tenants. Along the way, he collected substantial real estate of his own, at one time owning seventeen parcels across New England, from Saco and the Merrimack to Newport and Portsmouth, amounting to more than three thousand acres.[52]

Over the years, other prominent New England merchants and leaders bought into the Atherton Company. Josias Winslow, governor of Plymouth Colony; Thomas Willett, first English mayor of New York; Cap-

50. Miller, "Narragansett Planters," AAS, *Procs.*, n.s., XLIII (1933), 50–52; Palfrey, *History of New England*, III, 37; Updike, *Richard Smith*, 20n; Miller, *Withington Plat*, 14–16; *Fones Record*, 23–24.

51. John B. Pierce, "A Sketch of the Cole Family," *NHR*, II (1883–1884), 181–182; Peleg Sanford, *The Letterbook of Peleg Sanford of Newport, Merchant* . . . , ed. Howard W. Preston *et al.* (Providence, R.I., 1928), iv–vi; Turner, "Coddington," *R.I. Hist. Tracts*, 1st Ser., no. 4, 52–53.

52. Sanford, *Letterbook*, ed. Preston *et al.*, iv–vi, 8–9, 35–36, 52–54; Bailyn, *New England Merchants*, 88–90; G. Andrews Moriarty, "President John Sanford of Portsmouth, R.I., and His Family," *NEHGR*, CIII (1949), 274.

tain George Denison and Thomas Stanton, founders of Stonington; John Paine, owner of lands in several colonies; Daniel Denison, major general of the Massachusetts militia; John Saffin, Boston resident, councillor, and landowner in several Plymouth towns (and son-in-law of Thomas Willett); John Brown, resident of Taunton and commissioner of the United Colonies (and father-in-law of Thomas Willett); John Viall, vintner of Boston and owner of Plymouth lands (and son-in-law of Richard Smith, Sr.); Richard Wharton, the Boston owner of extensive tracts in Maine and Andros councillor—these were some of the Atherton shareholders in addition to Atherton, Governor Winthrop, Governor Bradstreet, Richison, Tinker, Hudson, the Smiths, and the Hutchinsons. They came from every colony in New England but New Hampshire and Maine (and some of them owned land in those colonies, too).[53]

These men would meet every now and then, sometimes every few days, sometimes every few months, usually in Boston, in the house of Hutchinson or Bradstreet, and at least once in the Narragansett, in the house of Richard Smith, Jr. They first of all divided Boston Neck in the southern tract into farms, giving each shareholder a quantity proportional to the number of shares he held. (Confusingly, they also called their lots "shares" or "half shares" of land.) Owners either farmed these lands, rented them out, or sold them; there was considerable turnover in the southern tract during the 1660s–1680s. But the Atherton Company was more than merely a vehicle for grabbing and dividing land to tenants in severalty; it was a business, an organized land company, and its purpose was to return a profit to its investors.[54] This corporateness can be seen in several company functions. Just as the Atherton purchasers used the term "share" in the vague sense of a "piece" or "lot" of land, they also used the term in the modern, precise sense of a claim on the assets of the corporation. One could sell one's "share" in the southern tract yet still be possessed of a "share" in

53. Entry for Oct. 13, 1660, reel 6, Winthrop Papers, MHS; *Fones Record*, 1–3, 5–6, 12–13, 31, 39–40; Miller, *Withington Plat*, 16–17, 18, 25–27. See below for discussion of Willett, Paine, Viall, Saffin, and Wharton; above for George Denison, Stanton, Atherton, Winthrop, Richison, Tinker, Bradstreet, the Smiths, and the Hutchinsons.

54. *Fones Record*, 5, 25–27, 85–93, 122–125. The chief historian of early American land companies has said that "there were no organized land companies before 1745," and that the Atherton company in particular was a community, a town, assuming the powers of a corporation. In neither case was he correct. Shaw Livermore, *Early American Land Companies: Their Influence on Corporate Development* (New York, 1939), 14 n. 11, 55.

the company, which continued to incur for the holder both benefits and liabilities. These stock shares were had for the purchasing of them, just as in modern corporations. When Hutchinson was admitted in 1659, the company granted him "equal sheire and Interest with us . . . he paying his sheire as we doe." But it appears that after the first year or two, the company issued no new shares, the number of shares remained steady at twenty-two, and anyone wishing to invest in the company had to purchase a share or the fraction of a share from a current shareholder.[55]

Once admitted as a shareholder, an individual shouldered obligations proportional to the size of his holding. In 1660, the Atherton Company paid the Indians' fine to the United Colonies, the shareholders "paying there proportions of what shall be paid to the Commissioners." In later years, shareholders bore the burden of repeated subscriptions to meet company expenses rather than issue new stock. In 1676, when the company sent John Saffin to Connecticut to ask for protection against Rhode Island encroachment upon their lands, to pay for Saffin's journey the company raised ten shillings on each share. In 1683, the company carried its case to the crown and, the next year, voted a subscription of fifty pounds per share.[56]

Another clearly corporate feature of the Atherton Company was the proliferation of committees. Whenever a problem appeared, there was a committee to address it. The Atherton shareholders formed committees to manage company business during the year between shareholder meetings, to oversee the planting of a town, to defend their title, and to win Connecticut jurisdiction over Narragansett lands. There was nothing ingenious about creating these committees, but it said something about the intentions of shareholders, who delegated chores to committees because they did not want to occupy their own time, the time of all shareholders, in company business. Atherton was a military commander, Winthrop a governor, and Hutchinson a merchant, and others engaged in other activities. They did not have time to regulate company business; they did not have time even to manage their own lands. They wanted others to perform these tasks—fellow members, who rotated in and out of committees, and also tenants

55. *Fones Record*, 4–5. Shares were transferable property, frequently bought and sold; however, the company ruled that no one could sell a share except to those approved by the company. Richard A. Wheeler, "Major Atherton's Company," *NHR*, II (1883–1884), 106–107.

56. *Fones Record*, 29–30, 49–50.

and foremen, who operated their farms. For the shareholders of the Atherton Company, their investment was a side issue, a way to make money without devoting one's full attention to the business activity, the same goal of today's corporate stockholders.[57]

One of the ways the shareholders sought to make money (in addition to dividing to themselves the southern tract) was by settling the northern tract. This was the principal business conducted by the company (as opposed to the business conducted by each individual shareholder). At the company's very first meeting, just after the shareholders admitted Hutchinson and set aside farms for themselves in the southern tract, they voted to create "a Plantation wch we intende into sixty shaires And to give out of the same to such men as shall be aproved of by us, such proportions as shal orderly be granted them and that what proportions is granted to any shal pay to us, towards our greate charge we have been at, twelve pense for every Acker is Alotted to them and alsoe . . . contribute to the maintenance of an able goodly orthodox minister." To oversee the launching of this town, the company appointed a committee of Atherton, Hutchinson, and others with authority for "Admiting of Inhabitants and ordering all matters."[58] The following year, Hutchinson was appointed treasurer to receive "the Eighteen pence an acre of every man that have alotments" in the northern tract. (Apparently, the company increased the price of its town land by 50 percent.) The company at the same time ordered that those taking up lands "in the Town" must build upon them and settle either themselves or someone else in two years or else forfeit the lots; moreover, if purchasers wished to sell their lots, they could sell to none except as approved by the company.[59]

The company did its best to speed settlement; that was the means to greater profits. In 1678, John Saffin, Simon Bradstreet, and Elisha Hutch-

57. *Ibid.*, 18–19, 19–21, 24, 29–30.

58. *Ibid.*, 5. The profit to the company was probably not based on the price per acre, but, rather, on the expected appreciation of company and shareholder lands. Evidence for this profit theory appears in 1660, when the company revised its plan, voting to lay out the northern tract into 40 shares, not 60—12 for shareholders and 28 to be sold to settlers. Thus the profit was to accrue to the Atherton members not just from company sales of town land but also from individual sales of town land which shareholders would make once the value of their holdings had increased with the coming of settlers. *Fones Record,* 18–19.

59. *Ibid.*, 17.

inson distributed a handbill in Newport advertising company land on advantageous terms.[60] Then in 1686, Saffin, Hutchinson, and Richard Wharton, acting for the company, struck an agreement with Ezekiel Carre, Peter Le Breton, and others for the settlement of a plantation in the Narragansett by French Huguenot refugees. The plan called for conveying five thousand acres to the immigrants in the town of Kingston, each French family receiving one hundred acres of land and a one-hundredth part of a meadow. The price was fixed at four shillings per acre, cash, or five shillings per acre payable within three years (which amounted to 8 percent interest). Under this arrangement, forty-five families arrived and built houses and a church.[61]

Settlement on all these sites proceeded slowly at first, probably because of the cloud over titles. But it picked up in the mid-1670s, and in 1674 Rhode Island erected Kingston, where the Quidnesset Purchase was located; this was the seventh town of the colony.[62] In 1708, it had grown to become the third largest town in Rhode Island, with 1,200 residents, twice as large as Portsmouth. In 1730, even after Kingston had been divided in two, North Kingston had 1,875 whites, still the third largest town in the colony. (South Kingston had 965.) Moreover, only South Kingston and Newport had more slaves than North Kingston. It was not only a growing town but a prosperous one, too.[63]

To the south of Atherton Company lands operated yet a third Rhode Island land company, the Pettaquamscut Company. In January and March of 1657/8, several men from Rhode Island (Samuel Wilbore, John Porter, Samuel Wilson, and Thomas Mumford) and one from Boston (John Hull)

60. Ford, ed., *Broadsides, Ballads, etc.* (MHS, *Colls.*, LXXV [1922]), 11; Potter, *Early History of Narragansett*, 101; Arnold, *History of Rhode Island*, I, 445. For this broadside, which also said that the land fell in Connecticut, Saffin was jailed.

61. Elisha R. Potter, "Memoir concerning the French Settlements in the Colony of Rhode Island," *R.I. Hist. Tracts,* 1st Ser., no. 5 (Providence, R.I., 1879), 14–18, 31. Eventually this settlement broke up after a clash between the Huguenots and others over land claims.

62. In 1671, the Rhode Island assembly counted 23 adult male residents of both Wickford and Quidnesset (Miller, "Narragansett Planters," AAS, *Procs.,* n.s., XLIII [1933], 60; J. Warren Gardiner, "The Pioneers of Narragansett," *NHR,* II [1883–1884], 113; Arnold, *History of Rhode Island,* I, 368). In 1687, Kingston had 138 ratable men (Greene and Harrington, *American Population before the Federal Census of 1790,* 65).

63. Greene and Harrington, *American Population before the Federal Census of 1790,* 64–65; Potter, *Early History of Narragansett,* 144.

bought the Pettaquamscut Purchase from the Indians. This tract took in the southeastern corner of the Narragansett, including the point that juts out into the Atlantic between Block Island Sound and Narragansett Bay, Point Judith (named for John Hull's wife). It amounted to twelve miles square of choice land.[64] This company was different from the Atherton Company in one respect: most of the shareholders were Rhode Islanders. John Porter and his son-in-law Samuel Wilbore lived in Newport, having moved to Aquidneck with William Coddington in 1638. Samuel Wilson and Thomas Mumford also lived in Rhode Island, the latter moving to his Pettaquamscut lands sometime in the 1660s. These with Hull were the original purchasers in 1658. In 1668, at a meeting in Newport, the company accepted Benedict Arnold, governor of Rhode Island, as a shareholder, to have "one seventh part of all the lands and . . . to receive his seventh part of the payments for what land is formerly sold by us. Provided, the said Mr. Arnold do pay one seventh part of all disbursments relating to the said lands, both past and to come." The company created no new shares from this early date on. Other men held shares and fractions of shares over the years, but they did so only as the assigns and heirs of the shareholders existing in 1668. And even these assigns had to have the approval of the existing shareholders in order to join their ranks. The Pettaquamscut Company was a tightly controlled, small concern, with abundant land.[65]

Sometime before Arnold joined the company, William Brenton was admitted, another governor of Rhode Island. Brenton was one of the widest-ranging land developers of the seventeenth century. He had come from Hammersmith, England, to Boston, where he was admitted freeman in 1634 and served as selectman and deputy before moving to Newport in 1638. His removal to Rhode Island did not sever his northern connections. In 1657, Brenton, Simon Willard, Thomas Henchman, and another man

64. In succeeding years, new deeds may have augmented this tract. The purchasers paid cash, not more than £200 for all the various deeds. The Rhode Island assembly banned Indian purchases probably in reaction to the Pettaquamscut Purchase. Arnold, *History of Rhode Island*, I, 267; Miller, "Narragansett Planters," AAS, *Procs.*, n.s., XLII (1933), 55; Potter, *Early History of Narragansett*, 53, 58, 275–276.

65. "Pioneers of Narragansett," AAS, *Procs.*, n.s., XLII (1933), 114; Potter, *Early History of Narragansett*, 277–278, 292–299, 393–395; "Gentlemen and Partners in the Lands at Petaquomscot," 1677, John Hull Letterbook, AAS; "Narragansett Lands," 27–29, Prince Collection, BPL.

bought for twenty-five pounds from Massachusetts the fur trade franchise on the Merrimack River, just then beginning to be explored.[66] Around the same time, Brenton paid two hundred pounds to Billerica for eight thousand acres granted to that town. Billerica used the two hundred pounds to buy out the Cambridge nonresident owners of Billerica lands; Brenton used the eight thousand acres to speculate. This land was on the Merrimack; it later became the center of Dunstable, of which Brenton was a grantee in 1673. By the time he died in 1674, Brenton's Merrimack holdings had somehow mushroomed to ten thousand acres—so said his will, at least.[67]

Samuel Sewall was another large landowner interested in the Pettaquamscut Purchase, not as a purchaser, but as heir to one of the founders, his father-in-law, John Hull. Sewall inherited Hull's large farm on Point Judith as well as a share in the company entitling him to other divisions. Sewall was not an aggressive businessman; he gave away some of his Pettaquamscut land, including one piece as endowment for supporting the teaching of English to Indian children.[68] But one should not be led by the piety of his diaries to suppose him incapable of making a good deal. The lands Sewall inherited he managed well.[69] In addition, Sewall owned a farm

66. Potter, *Early History of Narragansett*, 295–299; Nason, *History of Dunstable*, 16.

67. Henry A. Hazen, *History of Billerica, Massachusetts* . . . (Boston, 1883), 44; Nason, *History of Dunstable*, 6; Potter, *Early History of Narragansett*, 298; Arnold, *History of Rhode Island*, I, 254; "Narragansett Lands," 38–42, Prince Collection, BPL; John Osborne Austin, *Genealogical Dictionary of Rhode Island* . . . (Albany, N.Y., 1887; rpt., 1969), 254. In that will, Brenton bequeathed additional lands he had acquired on Martha's Vineyard, Elizabeth Island, Canonicut Island, and his Pettaquamscut lands, the last valued at £300. Brenton toward the end of his life also "bought considerable Lands" in Taunton, according to a deposition of the 18th century.

68. Norman M. Isham *et al.*, eds., *Rhode Island Land Evidences*, I, 1648–1696: *Abstracts* (Providence, R.I., 1921), map facing frontispiece; Pettaquamscut Purchase: Sewall School Land, Feb. 10, 1695, MHS; Potter, *Early History of Narragansett*, 291. Even with these bequests, Sewall kept enough of his lands there so that his grandson in the 18th century was able to inherit 1,200 acres on Point Judith (Potter, *Early History of Narragansett*, 293).

69. In 1693, he asked the General Court to lay out 1,000 acres sold to Hull on Casco Bay—an area growing quickly in the 1680s and 1690s. In 1695, he petitioned the court to have a grant to Hull, which had never been laid out, located at Penicook on the Merrimack River. In 1701, he protested to the court the attempt by an Indian to sell 1,150 acres of meadow that Hull had purchased in 1683 for £115 and that Sewall had

at Sherburn, where Daniel Gookin, Joseph Dudley, and other nonresidents also had farms. In the 1690s, he divided with Elisha Hutchinson and others lands in Braintree, Rumney Marsh (Chelsea), Muddy River (Brookline), and Boston Neck. On June 11, 1705, Sewall sold for one hundred pounds a piece of land in the town of Newbury to one of its residents. Sometime before 1713, he purchased land in the wilderness at a place which became the town of Rutland; when the court made the grant of Rutland, it included Sewall among the grantees. And in 1736, the proprietors of Dunstable laid out two hundred acres to the heirs of Samuel Sewall on account of a right he must have bought in that town.[70] Sewall was not a leader of settlement ventures, but he knew how to profit from them.

His father-in-law, on the other hand, was such a leader. John Hull—mint-master, merchant, goldsmith, a king of Boston society—initiated the Pettaquamscut Purchase. He arrived in Boston in 1635, began his mint in 1652, became a wealthy man, and held a series of public offices: selectman, captain of the artillery company, deputy to the General Court for five different towns, colony treasurer during King Philip's War, and assistant from 1680 until his death in 1683. In addition to these activities, Hull was a leading merchant of New England and owner of ships, lumber mills, land (in Charlestown, Medfield, Braintree, Muddy River [Brookline], and Penicook), and several houses and warehouses in Boston. Hull's motives for buying the Pettaquamscut lands appear to have been similar to Hutchinson's in joining the Atherton Company. He wanted first of all to produce livestock for sale and export, and sometime before 1672 he was doing just that. In 1677, he got a new idea about the kind of livestock that Pettaquamscut might produce. As Hull explained in a letter to fellow purchaser Benedict Arnold: "I have sometimes thought if we, the partners of Point Judith Neck, did fence with a good stone-wall at the north end thereof . . . and procure a very good breed of large and fair mares and horses, and that no mongrel breed might come among them . . . we might have a very choice breed for coach-horses, some for the saddle, some for the draught,

been renting out. He requested a stop to "the further spreading of this Gangrene." Sewall Petition, 1693, XLV, 211, Mass. Archives; Sewall Petition, Nov. 20, 1695, photostats, MHS; Sewall Petition, June 5, 1701, photostats, MHS.

70. Sewall, July 14, 1704, XLV, 305; Proprietors of Commons of Braintree, etc., July 23, 1693, CXIII, 13, Mass. Archives; Sewall Sale, June 11, 1705, Misc. Bound, MHS; Crane, ed., *Worcester County*, I, 65; Dunstable Land Committee, Apr. 27, 1736, Misc. Bound, MHS.

and, in a few years, might draw off considerable numbers, and ship them for Barbadoes, Nevis, or such parts of the Indies where they would vend. We might have a vessel made for that service, accommodated on purpose to carry off horses to advantage." Hull and company acted upon his suggestion, and within a few years Narragansett horses were a principal Rhode Island export.[71]

Like other investors in vacant lands, Hull was a busy man. As goldsmith, merchant, and public official he did not have time to manage his Pettaquamscut business. Besides, Pettaquamscut was far from Boston. Even in summer, when travel was easy, Hull spent anywhere from six to ten days just going to his lands at Pettaquamscut and returning to Boston. Unable to oversee personally a farm at such a distance, even if he had had the time and inclination to do so, Hull hired men to do the job for him. Just as Thomas Broughton managed Hull's mills in Maine, just as the captain of the *Friendship* carried out Hull's instructions about what routes and products and markets to choose, so William Heifernan managed Hull's farm in Rhode Island according to Hull's direction.[72]

Large-scale farming was not the only way to turn a profit from the Pettaquamscut lands. Another way was by selling land. Through repeated division, the shareholders divided among themselves approximately 49,000 acres, of which each individual shareholder farmed part and sold part.[73] Another portion of their purchase, perhaps as much as 43,000 acres to the north of Point Judith, the shareholders jointly sold. In 1663, the company

71. John Hull, "The Diaries of John Hull, Mint-Master and Treasurer of the Colony of Massachusetts Bay," AAS, *Transactions, Collections,* III (1857), 117–125, 127, 128, 149, 152, 258–262; Samuel Sewall Petition, Nov. 20, 1695, photostats, MHS; Samuel Sewall Petition, June 5, 1701, photostats, MHS; Hull to Arnold, Apr. 16, 1677, John Hull Letterbook, AAS; Miller, "Narragansett Planters," AAS, *Procs.,* n.s., XLIII (1933), 72–83.

72. Hull, "Diaries of John Hull," AAS, *Trans., Colls.,* III (1857), 150–151, 154; Hull to Terry, Sept. 4, 27, 1672; Hull to Heifernan, 1673; John Hull Letterbook, AAS.

73. The divisions occurred once soon after the purchase, again in 1704, and again in 1727. Since the number of shares remained constant at seven—after the admission of Benedict Arnold in 1668—each share received approximately 7,000 acres of land in this part of the purchase. (Individuals divided their shares among heirs and assigns, so no single person received the full 7,000.) It was out of these large divisions that shareholders sold pieces to settlers, saving other pieces for farms for themselves. Potter, *Early History of Narragansett,* 275ff, 290; Miller, "Narragansett Planters," AAS, *Procs.,* n.s., XLIII (1933), 56–57, 61–66.

sold 1,000 acres to George Gardiner, who built a house there and whose family became one of the wealthiest Rhode Island families. In 1671, it sold 500 acres to William Knowles and 500 to Robert Hazard and other parcels to others. The Pettaquamscut Purchase, like the Atherton Company, was a business, not just a means of acquiring and dividing land. Also like the Atherton Company, the Pettaquamscut shareholders wished to create a town and make a profit doing so. Meeting in Newport on June 4, 1668, the shareholders William Brenton, John Hull, Samuel Wilbore, Samuel Wilson, and Thomas Mumford agreed that all settlers must pay for their lands forthwith, with the revenue distributed "unto each particular Person his equal part."[74] Over the next eleven years, the company sold 7,630 acres of land to twenty-four men in parcels of 200, 300, and 500 acres.[75]

In 1679 the Atherton and Pettaquamscut companies pooled their efforts specially to settle the Narragansett, and it was because of this collaboration that only one town, instead of two, emerged from their settlement efforts. But this town, Kingston, was such a prosperous and growing town that in the first quarter of the eighteenth century it divided in two. This development would have been received with applause by the Pettaquamscut shareholders, one of whom, Samuel Sewall, declared himself in 1685 "so desirous of the countryes being Peopled."[76]

Rhode Island attracted so many outside speculators for several reasons.[77]

74. Miller, "Narragansett Planters," AAS, *Procs.*, n.s., XLIII (1933), 64–66; Potter, *Early History of Narragansett*, 291–292; John B. Pierce, "One Line of the Haszard Family," *NHR*, II (1883–1884), 45; Pettaquamscut Purchasers' Meeting, June 4, 1668, "Narragansett Lands," 27–29, Prince Collection, BPL. At the same meeting it was agreed to set aside 300 acres for a preacher.

75. Award of Refereees re Narragansett lands, Dec. 5, 1679, "Narragansett Lands," 29–34, Prince Collection, BPL; 1679 entry, reel 6, Winthrop Papers, MHS; Potter, *Early History of Narragansett*, 286–288, 390–391.

76. Hull to Peleg Sanford, 1679, John Hull Letterbook, AAS; Award of Referees, Dec. 5, 1679, "Narragansett Lands," 29–34, Prince Collection, BPL; Sewall to Josiah Arnold, Aug. 8, 1685, John Hull Letterbook, AAS. South Kingston, formerly Pettaquamscut Company land, had in 1730 the highest proportion of slaves to free men in New England—roughly one of every three residents. By 1780, South Kingston had become the wealthiest town in Rhode Island, paying more tax than either Providence or Newport. Edward Channing, *The Narragansett Planters: A Study of Causes,* Johns Hopkins University Studies in Historical and Political Science, 4th Ser., no. 3 (Baltimore, 1886), 2, 10.

77. By the beginning of the 18th century, there were 10 towns in Rhode Island. Only 1 of them, Warwick, was largely free of land disputes and nonresident owners, and even

Because Rhode Island was small and began without a charter, it was vulnerable to annexation; and because it was tolerant of religious diversity, it offended its neighbors. Rhode Island also had a more temperate climate than northern New England, good lands, and ready harbors. But, as the cases of Westerly and Pettaquamscut make clear (to which one could easily add Providence, Pawtuxet, and Jamestown), not all the speculators came from outside Rhode Island; most lived within the colony, though not on the wilderness lands they bought. Not only Massachusetts entrepreneurs but Rhode Island entrepreneurs as well joined the land rush in the 1630s and were fully capable of buying up and selling the Narragansett without the help of outsiders. They did, however, often need the help of business corporations, which provided a means of organizing widely dispersed and otherwise engaged individuals intent on making a profit from the land.

III. Plymouth Colony

Nearly one-third of all Plymouth Colony towns established in the seventeenth century were launched by individuals who did not settle in them. Only a handful of ventures, however, produced these settlements, and an even smaller handful of entrepreneurs controlled these ventures. In this little colony, a tightly knit group of individuals, political and military leaders of Plymouth, many related by marriage, were responsible for launching many towns.[78]

Warwick had some nonresident shareholders and some residents without shares. (See Warwick discussed below, in Part II.) The foregoing treatment of leading figures does not exhaust the numerous cases of entrepreneurship in town-founding in 17th-century Rhode Island. There were, for example, the purchase of Conanicut Island by 100 Newport men in 1657, many of whom never lived in the subsequent settlement of Jamestown, and the grant of East Greenwich to 50 men, one-quarter of whom settled there, the remainder selling their shares. Bruce C. Daniels, *Dissent and Conformity on Narragansett Bay: The Colonial Rhode Island Town* (Middletown, Conn., 1983), 30–32; Sydney V. James, *Colonial Rhode Island: A History* (New York, 1975), 82–83, 104.

78. Some 17 towns were established in Plymouth during the 17th century, including several that later fell under Rhode Island jurisdiction (Palfrey, *History of New England,* IV, 135–136). I have not investigated the origins of all 17; the chances are likely that more than one-third were launched by nonresidents. Five certainly were: Bristol, Swansea, Attleborough, Marshfield, and Scituate, the first 3 of which are discussed in the following pages. As to the last 2, see William Bradford, *Bradford's History "Of Plimoth Plantation"* (Boston, 1898), 362–363, 439; Palfrey, *History of New England,* I, 336–337.

No one was more prominent than Thomas Willett. Willett was a merchant who met the English Separatists while on business in Holland. He came over in 1630, went to Maine to manage Plymouth's Indian trade, and returned to Plymouth in 1636, where eventually he succeeded Miles Standish as captain of the militia and served as an assistant. Willett boosted his rise in Plymouth society by marrying the daughter of John Brown, an early assistant; he later married his own daughter to John Saffin, himself an owner of Boston, Plymouth, and Rhode Island properties. In 1665 Willett became the first English mayor of New York, where he died in 1674.[79]

Willett helped begin several Plymouth towns. In 1661, on behalf of the colony, he purchased from the Indians the great tract north of Rehoboth and Taunton, which the court then divided into the Rehoboth North and Taunton North purchases. He subsequently became a shareholder in both these purchases, out of which were formed the towns of Attleborough, Cumberland, Norton, Easton, and Mansfield. Willett was also a proprietor of Rehoboth as of 1655, if not earlier. He owned land in the town of Plymouth. And, finally, outside Plymouth Colony, Willett bought from John Tinker half of his share in the Atherton Company, which gave him a large farm on Boston Neck as well as an interest in the company's other lands.[80] Altogether, leaving aside his activities on the Kennebec and in the conquest of New York, Willett owned land in as many as seven towns and directly contributed to the launching of perhaps three new towns.

Probably the most important of his Plymouth land ventures was the Sowams purchase, a tract Miles Standish once described as the "garden of the patent." Sowams was granted to Plymouth Colony's most illustrious leaders—William Bradford, Thomas Prince, Edward Winslow, John Adams, Thomas Cushman, John Winslow, Thomas Clarke, Experience Mitchell, Thomas Willett, William White, and Miles Standish—probably as reward for their assuming the colony's debt to the London financial backers. The grant was in September 1652; already by April 1653/4, the grantees were dividing their tract, though none of them needed new

79. Potter, *Early History of Narragansett*, 313; Bicknell, *Sowams*, 133–134, 141, 146; Bicknell, *A History of Barrington, Rhode Island* (Providence, R.I., 1898), 69–71; John Daggett, *Sketch of the History of Attleborough* . . . (Dedham, Mass., 1834), 127–131.

80. Mortimer Blake, "Taunton North Purchase," Old Colony Historical Society, *Collections* (1885), 36–38; Daggett, *Sketch of Attleborough*, 127–131; Bicknell, *Sowams*, 133–134, 140–141. See discussion above of Atherton Company.

homesteads. The grantees had houses in Plymouth, Rehoboth, and other settled towns. They held their proprietors' meetings in Plymouth.[81]

In its corporate features, the Sowams land proprietorship resembled the Atherton and Pettaquamscut companies. It began with a "first originall agreement of the proprietors," stating each investor's share and binding each to pay his portion of common charges. (The initial common charge was thirty-five pounds owed to Massasoit, chief of the Wampanoags, for the land.) The Sowams venture divided land according to shares, sold lands to pay for common charges, appointed committees to handle company business, and placed some two hundred settlers on the Sowams tract by 1667. In that same year, the General Court gathered these settlers into the town of Swansea.[82] Eventually the Sowams tract would contain the towns of Swansea, Barrington, East Providence, Warren, and Bristol in Rhode Island and Massachusetts.

Between 1654 and 1660, all the original shareholders either died or sold their shares, except for Thomas Willett. It was Willett who led the effort to develop this tract—who sat on the committee charged with dividing the tract, who bought many lots distributed to his fellow proprietors, and who drafted the rules for admitting inhabitants when the General Court granted the proprietors the right to create a township. These rules became the "foundation orders" of Swansea. In 1671, the town listed Willett among its nine largest landowners.[83]

Willett's father-in-law, John Brown, also helped start several towns. Arriving in New England in 1636, Brown was assistant for seventeen years and commissioner of the United Colonies for twelve years; he died in 1662. Living first in Duxbury, Brown with others purchased the tract that became Taunton, and he moved there. In 1641, Brown (with Edward Winslow) bought Seekonk, or Rehoboth, from Massasoit, apparently on behalf of Plymouth Colony, and soon became a proprietor and resident of that

81. Deed of Sale, Mar. 20, 1653/4, Rehoboth Lands, James Otis, Sr., Papers, 1642–1823, box 1, MHS (hereafter cited as Otis Papers, box 1, MHS); Bicknell, *History of Barrington*, 58–59, 64–65, 75, 135; Bicknell, *Sowams*, 34–36; Indian Deed to Thomas Prince *et al.*, Mar. 20, 1653/4, Rehoboth Lands, Otis Papers, box 1, MHS.

82. Parts of this town later became Barrington and Warren, Rhode Island. Bicknell, *Sowams*, 34–36, 37–40, 44–45, 49, 186; Bicknell, *History of Barrington*, 58–59, 64–65, 100–102, 135.

83. Bicknell, *Sowams*, 34, 35; Bicknell, *History of Barrington*, 80ff, 139, 141–142, 157–158.

settlement. In 1645, he purchased the tract of Wannamoisett from Massasoit, near Rehoboth, and moved there. In 1653, Brown bought into the Sowams proprietorship and sometime thereafter became clerk of the proprietorship. Then in 1661, the year before he died, Brown acquired a portion of a share in the Atherton Company. Brown's union with the Atherton Company was not by chance. He had earlier purchased land in the Narragansett and was, moreover, a United Colonies commissioner at a time when the Atherton Company was counting on the United Colonies to back its claim to Rhode Island land. All these holdings brought Brown considerable wealth; his Rehoboth land alone was worth six hundred pounds by the 1660s.[84]

Willett's son-in-law was John Saffin, born in England in 1632, raised in New England. Saffin's commonplace book reveals a well-read man, amateur astronomer, merchant, friend of the powerful (he was married by Joseph Dudley; he mourned the death of John Hull), and a Puritan torn by the contradictory commands of his faith. He went to considerable lengths to acquire wealth, yet privately he condemned money, "the Universall Mistriss that all sorts of men doe Court." He was deputy, speaker, councillor in the Andros council, then judge of the Supreme Court; yet he told his diary he would be happy to "Change the whole life I have liv'd in the Palace, for one hours Enjoyment of God in the Chappell."[85] But whatever his private misgivings, outwardly Saffin exhibited no ambivalence about land accumulation. He owned property in Boston, either inherited Willett's rights or purchased rights in the Sowam's proprietorship, bought a right in the new town of Bristol (a Plymouth Colony town developed by Boston speculators), and purchased several Atherton Company shares and fractions of shares from the heirs of Humphrey Atherton, which together with the Willett interest he inherited in the Atherton Company entitled Saffin to play a large role in company proceedings and own a large farm on Boston Neck.[86] The late 1670s were troubled years for the Atherton

84. Miller, *Withington Plat*, 15, 25 n. 14; Bicknell, *Sowams*, 140–142; Plymouth Court Order, June 1683, Rehoboth Lands, Otis Papers, box 1, MHS.

85. John Saffin Note-Book, 1665–1708, 13, 15, 41, 82ff, 104, transcribed MS, MHS.

86. In 1676, the Sowams shareholders appointed Saffin to the committee laying out lands. In 1683, Saffin was one of several Sowams proprietors asking the court for permission to choose their own proprietors' clerk. In 1680, the town of Swansea admitted Saffin to the first rank of "inhabitants"—though he still lived in Boston at the time. (The three ranks of inhabitants in Swansea determined the share of land that each

Company. The Rhode Island assembly was asserting its jurisdiction over the Narragansett, and Rhode Island emissaries went to England to plead the colony's case against Connecticut, the Atherton Company, and other speculators. The Atherton Company sent its own agent to England, William Harris, who was taken captive by Barbary pirates. In this climate, in 1678, Saffin, Hutchinson, and Bradstreet circulated a handbill in Rhode Island, advertising Atherton lands and stating that the patent fell under Connecticut jurisdiction. For this defiance, the assembly ordered Saffin's arrest. Saffin fled, but was caught and jailed, tried and fined; and his estate in Rhode Island was forfeited. Saffin was not only a large landowner in New England; he was one who paid a higher price than most for his land investments.[87]

John Viall was another Bostonian who invested in both Rhode Island and Plymouth lands. Born in 1619, he came to America and was admitted a freeman in Boston in 1641. During the 1650s and 1660s, Viall was something of a land trader in Boston, buying and selling lots in town. Viall married Elizabeth Smith, daughter of Richard Smith, Sr., and later bought and inherited lands at Wickford, Rhode Island, the settlement begun by Smith. It appears that he became an Atherton shareholder, and he may also have represented the Smith shares, since he lived in Boston and company meetings were convened in Boston. Sometime in the 1670s, Viall also bought into the Sowams land company and, in 1679, left Boston and moved to Swansea. There, with Eliakim Hutchinson, he bought the lands of Thomas Willett in Swansea and Rehoboth, totaling six hundred acres. (He also bought two slaves from John Saffin.) In 1683, he and Saffin and others asked the court for authority to appoint a clerk for the Sowams

---

shareholder was entitled to draw.) At about the same time, he began paying taxes on his land in Bristol, though he did not move to Bristol for another eight years. Once he did move there, Saffin became an active member of the Bristol community, representing the town to the General Court and leading a protest of settlers against the four speculators who developed the town. Bicknell, *Sowams*, 44–45; Plymouth Court Order, June 1683, Rehoboth Lands, Otis Papers, box 1, MHS; Bicknell, *History of Barrington*, 157–158, 160; Wilfred H. Munro, *History of Bristol, Rhode Island: The Story of the Mount Hope Lands* . . . (Providence, R.I., 1880), 87–90, 115, 122.

87. Potter, *Early History of Narragansett*, 270; Arnold, *History of Rhode Island*, I, 447, 456, 457, 464; Ford, ed., *Broadsides, Ballads, etc.* (MHS, *Colls.*, LXXV [1922]), 11; Miller, *Withington Plat*, 20n, 26. Saffin's probate records were not found. His widow Elizabeth left an estate worth £4,891, 41% of which was lands and chattels (Elizabeth Saffin Inventory, 1688, n.s., I, 231–232, SCPR).

proprietorship. When Viall died in 1686, he left an estate valued at £388, not counting his lands in Rhode Island, Massachusetts, and Plymouth.[88]

The Paine family, like Willett, Saffin, and Viall, also invested across colony lines. William Paine came to America in 1635, went to Watertown and then to Ipswich, just then being launched by John Winthrop, Jr. He invested in the iron mines of Lynn and Braintree and lead mines of Sturbridge, all of them Winthrop enterprises. William also wished to open the Hudson River to English traffic, then controlled by the Dutch, but he did not accomplish this task, leaving it instead to his son, John Paine, to carry out. John inherited wealth from his father and used it to invest in the Atherton Company, receiving as a partial dividend a 661-acre farm on Boston Neck. He also owned Prudence Island in Narragansett Bay. Paine bought and sold several large tracts in Maine during the 1660s and 1670s and bought into the Sowams proprietorship.[89] But John Paine's largest undertaking was to carry forward the work begun by his father on the Hudson River. In May and June 1672, Paine explored the far western parts of Massachusetts on an eight-day expedition. Taking a sloop from New York to Albany, he switched to horseback and struck out heading east from the Hudson, accompanied by Indian guides. He took careful note of the terrain, the rivers, the soil, the vegetation and forests, always keeping a lookout for "valuable Lands." Then he returned to Boston, made his report to the General Court, and asked for the grant of a township and the grant of the trading privilege in that region. In his petition, Paine told the court that this would be a good "Towneship for husbandrie" and also, when settled, would improve defenses against Indians and encourage the "Settling other Plantacions" in the area. Paine promised to "Produce persons Qualifyed" to be settlers, whom he would transport at his own expense.[90] The General Court acted favorably on this petition, granting Paine a tract twice the size

88. David Jillson, "John Viall, of Swansey, Mass., and Some of His Descendants," *NHR*, III (1884–1885), 97–112; Miller, *Withington Plat*, 16–17; Plymouth Court Order, June 1683, Rehoboth Lands, Otis Papers, box 1, MHS; Bicknell, *History of Barrington*, 60–61; John Viall Inventory, May 18, 1686, X, 13–16, SCPR. Viall also owned the Ship's Tavern in Boston in the 1660s and 1670s.

89. Potter, *Early History of Narragansett*, 274–275, 320–323; entry for Nov. 28, 1664, reel 6, Winthrop Papers, MHS; Miller, *Withington Plat*, 18; *York Deeds*, I, 148, 158, III, 28; Bicknell, *Sowams*, 54; Bicknell, *History of Barrington*, 60–61.

90. John Paine's Journal of a "Short discoverye up Albany for a Plantacion," May 31, 1672, photostats, MHS; John Paine Petition, 1672, photostats, MHS. The same items, with different dates, can be found in CXII, 221–224, Mass. Archives.

of most townships, twelve miles square, as well as the trading franchise, on the condition he settle families and a minister there. Over the next several years, Paine ran the lines between New York and Massachusetts and received other large tracts from Massachusetts in the area. Whether settlement ever occurred is not known; probably the Indian war prevented it.[91]

Paine had a brother, Stephen, who was an original grantee (with Henry Smith, Joseph Peck, and others) of the Rehoboth Patent in 1641.[92] Stephen bought into the Rehoboth North Purchase when that grant was made to Rehoboth, in 1666. He and a handful of shareholders (Willett was another) owned two shares in that purchase; most shareholders owned but one share each. Like the Atherton and Sowams investors, the owners of the Rehoboth North Purchase assumed various corporate powers. They kept their own records, hired their own surveyors, held their own meetings, and elected (as of 1682) their own clerk. Settlement proceeded slowly. By 1699, there were 133 proprietors but fewer than sixteen families on the tract. Eventually the settlement filled up and became the town of Attleborough. Meanwhile, Stephen Paine owned a share of the Sowams company, too.[93]

Stephen's son, Nathaniel, also participated in these same ventures. He purchased a right in the Sowams proprietorship and held it at the same time his father held his right. Nathaniel was also in the first rank of proprietors of the town of Swansea, with Willett, James Brown, John Allen, and other leading proprietors. In the early 1670s, Nathaniel owned a full share in the Rehoboth North Purchase, having bought it in halves from two different shareholders. Ten years later, Nathaniel purchased a thirty-second part in

91. General Court Order, Oct. 23, 1672, CXII, 227, Mass. Archives; Potter, *Early History of Narragansett*, 320–323.

92. Plymouth Court Order re Rehoboth, Mar. 6, 1685–1686, photostats, MHS; Bicknell, *Sowams*, 140–141.

93. Daggett, *Sketch of Attleborough*, 5–6, 9–13, 18, 20, 22, 39–41, 46, 52, 54. Other towns also claimed pieces of land that formerly had belonged to the Rehoboth North Purchase. The figure of "fewer than 16" is derived from there being only 16 families in town in 1708, and therefore probably fewer than that nine years previous.

Stephen Paine was one of 10 Sowams proprietors in 1660, was still a proprietor in 1673 and in 1676, when he served on a committee to divide lands among the shareholders, and remained a proprietor at least until 1682. In 1668, the court appointed him to the committee for admitting inhabitants to the new town of Swansea, created out of Sowams Company lands. Bicknell, *History of Barrington*, 60–61, 66, 81, 140; Bicknell, *Sowams*, 41–44, 54.

the town of Bristol, developed by Boston speculators. Bristol listed Nathaniel as an inhabitant in 1681, but the chances are that he still lived in Rehoboth. By the time he died, Nathaniel owned shares in at least four land corporations, not counting his hometown of Rehoboth.[94]

Some of these same Plymouth investors—the Paines, John Saffin, and others—joined the effort to exploit the conquered Indian lands after King Philip's War, the most desirable of which was called Mount Hope, a site Massachusetts, Rhode Island, and Plymouth each claimed for itself. In 1680, the crown awarded Mount Hope to Plymouth, and immediately the General Court sold the tract to four men for eleven hundred pounds. All four lived in Boston. Two or three may have moved to Bristol, the new town they launched, but at least one of them never did; instead, he sold his quarter-interest. Soon the Boston investors admitted others to their venture, not all of whom settled in Bristol. Nathaniel Paine, John Saffin, and Robert Thompson (an Englishman who speculated in various New England lands) all took up rights. John Saffin eventually moved to Bristol, but not until 1688.[95] Benjamin Church, another Bristol investor, may well have settled there, but it is hard to tell. Just returned from King Philip's War, in which he had become a military hero, Church was busy launching several towns, all in this region, and each listed him as a settler. The four purchasers of Bristol gave Church a one-sixteenth interest in their tract, perhaps in the hope that a war hero would attract settlers to their venture. Colonel Church joined other speculators from Portsmouth in purchasing the tract that became the town of Tiverton, and he also owned a large interest in the town of Little Compton, which after the war rapidly filled up with settlers.[96]

94. Bicknell, *Sowams*, 44–45; Bicknell, *History of Barrington*, 157–158; Daggett, *Sketch of Attleborough*, 10–12; Munro, *History of Bristol*, 97. Stephen Paine, whose estate was inventoried in 1710 (and was perhaps brother to Nathaniel and son of Stephen), left real estate appraised at £264 in Rehoboth and Attleborough, which amounted to roughly two-thirds of his estate (Stephen Paine Inventory, Mar. 18, 1709/10, BCPR). The probate records of the more active members of this active, landed family were not found.

95. Munro, *History of Bristol*, 53, 60–61, 79, 87–88; Daggett, *Sketch of Attleborough*, 10–12. For more on Paine and Saffin, see above; for Thompson, see below.

96. Munro, *History of Bristol*, 77–79; Arnold, *History of Rhode Island*, II, 163–165. One of Church's partners in the Tiverton purchase, Christopher Almy of Portsmouth, also had invested in the Misquamicut, or Westerly, venture in Rhode Island. Compare the purchasers of Tiverton (Arnold, *History of Rhode Island*, II, 164–165) with those of

Wilderness landownership in Plymouth Colony was such that all the Sowams proprietors except one were also proprietors of Rehoboth.[97] Some of these same men later launched the town of Attleborough. And some were proprietors of the towns of Swansea and Bristol when they were founded.[98] In view of this overlapping ownership, one has the sense that several Plymouth proprietary associations (those of Rehoboth, Sowams, and Rehoboth North Purchase, at least) were like interlocking directorates—different business boards run by the same small group of individuals. One is also struck by the out-of-colony investments made by several men prominent in Plymouth land matters. John Brown, Thomas Willett, John Saffin, John Viall, Benjamin Church, and John Paine all invested in Rhode Island lands. Some also invested in wilderness tracts in Massachusetts, Maine, and New York, in addition to their Plymouth Colony holdings. These individuals engaged in both an inter- and an intracolonial commerce in land, buying and selling both to one another and to settlers, linked together by their common enterprise, their interlocking directorates, and their family ties.

iv. The Nipmuck and the Merrimack

During the seventeenth century's last quarter, several events forced Massachusetts land investors away from Rhode Island and Plymouth. The Rhode Island government became more protective of its jurisdiction than it had previously been, Connecticut replaced Massachusetts as the colony most interested in taking the Narragansett away from Rhode Island, and the extirpation of the Indians in the 1670s made it less risky to start new towns than it had been in the vast expanse between the

Westerly (Barber, "Contributions to the History of Westerly," *NHR*, II [1883–1884], 36–37) for additional examples of multiple landholding.

97. In 1641, John Brown and Edward Winslow bought Rehoboth from Massasoit, and soon Henry Smith, Joseph Peck, Stephen Paine, and Samuel Newman associated with them. In 1643, Peter Hunt and John Allen also owned Rehoboth land. In 1655, two others appeared as Rehoboth proprietors, including Thomas Willett. All these were also Sowams proprietors (after the original Sowams men sold out to new proprietors). See above discussion; also Bicknell, *Sowams*, 140–142.

98. Among the shareholders of the Rehoboth North Purchase were Willett, Stephen Paine, and Nathaniel Paine. Nathaniel Paine was a proprietor of Swansea and Bristol, Willett of Swansea.

coast and the Connecticut River. Prodded by these developments, leading Boston entrepreneurs turned their attention to the Massachusetts frontier in the years following King Philip's War. They were drawn to two areas in particular, on the southern and northern borders of the colony: the Nipmuck and the Merrimack.

The Nipmuck country, named after the Indians who inhabited it, was the region where Massachusetts, Connecticut, and Rhode Island came together. It eventually came to include towns in south-central Massachusetts and northeast Connecticut. One of the first ventures there began in 1659, when Braintree petitioned the General Court for a Nipmuck tract. The court granted a township of eight miles square and appointed a committee of Eleazer Lusher, Roger Clap, Humphrey Atherton, and others to make rules for land division, admit the grantees, and supervise the planting of a town. Joshua Fisher surveyed the town. And, in 1667, the court granted to the inhabitants of Mendon town liberties (the power to elect town officers, levy town rates, convene town meetings, and the other political powers of a town). At least half the town's proprietors lived outside Mendon in the 1680s. Nonresidence was such a problem that the town selectmen petitioned the court for assistance in 1684, arguing that the nonresidents' "lands Regaine considerable advantage" and that the least the nonresidents could do was pay their share of public expenses.[99]

But large-scale development of the Nipmuck did not occur until the 1680s. And it was led in that decade, not by men from Braintree, but by one of the most ambitious land speculators in New England, Joseph Dudley.

By blood and marriage, Dudley was connected to the most important families in Massachusetts.[100] Born in Roxbury, Massachusetts, in 1647, he served as deputy, then commissioner of the United Colonies, assistant, then president of the Dominion of New England, and later governor of the province. No one had a more distinguished career in New England than Joseph Dudley. Nor did anyone profit from politics so much as Dudley did.

---

99. Mendon, Mass., *The Proprietors' Records of the Town of Mendon, Massachusetts* (Boston, 1899), 5–6, 11–12; Mendon Petition, Sept. 10, 1684, photostats, MHS; Crane, ed., *Worcester County,* I, 26–29. The court granted the town the right to tax nonresidents' lands, bringing an end to tax-free land speculation in Mendon.

100. His father was Thomas Dudley, once governor of the Bay Colony. His older sister Anne, the poet, married Simon Bradstreet, governor in his day. Another sister married Major General Daniel Denison, who had helped Bradstreet and Thomas Dudley and John Winthrop, Jr., settle Ipswich and who owned land from the Merrimack to the Narragansett. Dudley himself married a daughter of Edward Tyng.

The single most important goal of the General Court in the 1670s and 1680s was the retention of the Massachusetts Bay charter. The court chose Dudley, among others, to represent Massachusetts before royal authorities and to fight for the charter. Dudley pretended to do so. But at the same time, in 1683, he was meeting privately with Edward Randolph and drawing up plans for vacating the charter and establishing a royal government over New England. Just after the crown vacated the charter, Randolph wrote to Dudley, "I am not wanting to press for . . . all your rights and possessions, and have nominated, according to what was agreed betwixt you and myselfe, persons for the councill."[101] When the crown replaced the charter government with a new government, it named Joseph Dudley president until Andros could be sent over as governor general.

Most of the men in Dudley's council speculated in land. Several councillors were also related to each other by marriage—Dudley, Richard Wharton, John Usher, Wait Winthrop, and Edward Tyng. These were also the most active members of the Dudley council (when William Stoughton and Bartholomew Gedney are added to the list). Government for the six months of the Dudley council was rule by a closely knit group sharing common interests, one of which was land.[102]

The Dudley council helped nonresident speculators in several ways. Not more than a month after Dudley took office, he convened a court in the Narragansett to settle title disputes. Present were Dudley, related to several Atherton shareholders; John Winthrop, Jr., Richard Wharton, Elisha Hutchinson, Richard Smith, Francis Brinley, and John Saffin, all Atherton shareholders; John Fones, the Atherton clerk; John Blackwell, a shareholder in numerous other land ventures; two other men; and Edward Randolph. Of these, at least Dudley, Winthrop, Wharton, and Randolph were sitting as justices; probably the others were, too (since they were councillors), except Fones, who was clerk of the court. Hutchinson pre-

101. Everett Kimball, *The Public Life of Joseph Dudley: A Study of the Colonial Policy of the Stuarts in New England, 1660–1715,* Harvard Historical Studies, XV (New York, 1911), 2–3; Michael G. Hall, "Randolph, Dudley, and the Massachusetts Moderates in 1683," *New England Quarterly,* XXIX (1956), 513–516; Toppan and Goodrick, eds., *Randolph Letters,* IV, 13.

102. Theodore B. Lewis, "Land Speculation and the Dudley Council of 1686," *WMQ,* 3d Ser., XXXI (1974), 255–272; Robert N. Toppan, ed., "Records of the Council of Massachusetts, under Joseph Dudley," MHS, *Procs.,* 2d Ser., XIII (1899–1900), 222–286. Those who attended most frequently are described here as the "most active."

sented the Atherton Company book of records, which the court declared the "Authenticke Records of this Province." Then the court ordered that all squatters upon the mortgage lands should come to some understanding with the proprietors of those lands, "Either upon Purchase Rents or other good Agreem'ts." It would not have been surprising if the settlers in attendance did not automatically rely upon the court's declaration that it was acting "for the Impartiall Issue of Titles of land within this Province"— assuming any settlers were admitted to the court, which was held in Richard Smith's house.[103]

This was not the first time these same individuals had helped that company. In 1683, Dudley had served as one of the "uninterested persons, fit to be Commissioners in the Narragansett affair." The other commissioners at the time—Fitz John Winthrop, Samuel Shrimpton, William Stoughton, and others—had also been speculators and friends of speculators. Together they had ruled in favor of their relatives and friends and found the Atherton deeds to be good. Now, in 1686, Dudley had a second opportunity to help out the Atherton Company. He would get yet a third opportunity, when he was governor, in 1705. At that time, as part of their appeal, the Atherton shareholders thanked Dudley for his previous assistance while president of Massachusetts and New Hampshire.[104]

The most significant of the Dudley council's actions regarding land was the confirmation of titles. On June 2, the council awarded Councillor Wharton possession of the Pejepscot Purchase in Maine. Two weeks later, the councillors validated the deeds and transactions recorded in the Atherton Company records. On July 12, 1686, the Dudley council confirmed the title of the Million Purchase, a speculative venture claiming a large swath of the Merrimack River valley. Several councillors were among the Million Purchase proprietors.[105] A month before Andros arrived and replaced the Dudley government, the council confirmed Jonathan Tyng's Indian purchase near the Merrimack River and ruled that his claim did not conflict with another by Wait Winthrop in the same area. Both Winthrop and Tyng were among those who made up the quorum of seven that voted this

103. *Fones Record*, 175–179.

104. Toppan and Goodrick, eds., *Randolph Letters*, III, 59; *Cal. S.P.*, Col., XI, 34; *Fones Record*, 38–39, 64–74; Arnold, *History of Rhode Island*, II, 22–23.

105. *Cal. S.P.*, Col., XII, 653 (see below for more on the Pejepscot Purchase); *Fones Record*, 50–51; Toppan, ed., "Records under Dudley," MHS, *Procs.*, 2d Ser., XIII (1899–1900), 255–256. See below for more on the Million Purchase.

confirmation. In six busy months, the Dudley council boosted the land fortunes of its members, then expired. Randolph was therefore not far off the mark when, turning for his own reasons against Dudley and his councillors, he complained to officials in England that it was impossible to "bring titles of land to Tryall before them where in his Ma[jes]ties's right is concernd, the Judges being also partyes."[106]

Both Dudley's career and his land accumulation were interrupted when the colonists overthrew Sir Edmund Andros, for the rebels threw Dudley in jail for ten months, then shipped him off to England.[107] But Dudley bounced back. In 1702, appointed royal governor of Massachusetts, Dudley took up where he had left off. He served on a commission to arbitrate a dispute over Mohegan lands between James Fitch and Connecticut while holding a stake in the Mohegan venture with Fitch and others. Not surprisingly, the commission ruled in favor of the speculators. Then in 1705, Dudley recommended to the Board of Trade that the Atherton Company claims to the Narragansett be honored against the wishes of Rhode Island.[108]

Public ethics did not condemn bribery, but Dudley exceeded even his own age's tolerance of corruption. Nevertheless, as Joseph Dudley profited

106. Toppan, ed., "Records under Dudley," MHS, *Procs.*, 2d Ser., XIII (1899–1900), 274. For this and other Randolph allegations of land greed by Dudley and his friends, see Toppan and Goodrick, eds., *Randolph Letters,* IV, 153, 218, 221–222.

107. During the rebellion, Dudley even more than Andros was, as Thomas Danforth put it, "in a peculiar manner the object of the people's displeasure." One man said of him, "Oh the poison of the serpent is deadly." Kimball, *Dudley,* 52; XXXV, 262–264, Mass. Archives.

108. Kimball, *Dudley,* 146–147; Trumbull, *History of Connecticut,* I, 403, 410–427; Arnold, *History of Rhode Island,* II, 7, 22–23. Dudley denied to the Board of Trade that he had interest in the Mohegan venture, but Trumbull was sure that he did, and a document in the Massachusetts Historical Society appears to bear Trumbull out. This is an indenture giving Dudley a 13th interest in a land venture located in the Nipmuck (Indenture between William Stoughton *et al.,* and Joseph Dudley *et al.,* May 23, 1686, photostats, MHS). Parties to this indenture were Samuel Shrimpton, William Stoughton, John Blackwell, Richard Wharton, John Nelson, John Allen, Edward Palmes, and James Fitch (among others)—the last one mentioned having sold this same tract to Stoughton, Shrimpton, and Blackwell on May 7. Some of these individuals were members of the newly formed Dudley council. The indenture provided that the signatories would appoint a committee for "the managing disposing and improveing the same by Conveying granting Leasing out or Selling any parts or parcells" of their grant, reserving 5,000 acres for each shareholder before any sales or rents.

from public office, he also did much to advance the line of settlement on the New England frontier. As president in 1686, he organized towns, counties, and courts in the Narragansett, Maine, and elsewhere. As governor in the 1700s, he pushed harder than anyone else for building forts and protecting vulnerable New Hampshire and Maine against the French and Indians.[109] And as a proprietor, he helped launch many inland towns. The lands Dudley owned were scattered. Having owned a farm in the area of the Merrimack River for some years, Dudley was one of the proprietors of the new town of Dunstable after that grant was made in 1673. He was one of the many Boston-area men who owned a farm in the town of Sherburn, near Medfield. By the end of his life, Dudley held more than seven thousand acres in six frontier towns, in addition to his house and lands in Roxbury.[110]

His most extensive holdings were in the Nipmuck. King Philip's War decimated the Nipmuck tribe, and soon after the war white squatters moved onto the abandoned Indian lands. When a few straggling Nipmucks returned to the region, fights broke out between them and the whites. To compose these differences, in May 1681 the court empowered Joseph Dudley and William Stoughton to investigate the title claims of the Indians and make a report. Dudley and Stoughton met with the Indians in Cambridge; John Eliot served as interpreter. Dudley and Stoughton persuaded the Indians to accept a twenty-five-square-mile tract in the region of their former domain and to sell the rest to the whites. Dudley and Stoughton thereupon purchased on behalf of the colony about one thousand square miles near the junction of the Quinebaug and French rivers, paying the Indians fifty pounds and a coat. Dudley and Stoughton reserved for themselves two thousand acres. The surveyor they hired, who returned the plat to the General Court, was John Gore, the same man who surveyed the Atherton Company lands.[111]

After obtaining the Nipmuck country for Massachusetts in 1682, Dudley and Stoughton received a township grant eight miles square, which they

109. Toppan, ed., "Records under Dudley," MHS, *Procs.*, 2d Ser., XIII (1899–1900), 226–286; Kimball, *Dudley*, 86, 98, 138.

110. Nason, *History of Dunstable*, 12; Deed of Sale, Sherburn, XLI, 307, Mass. Archives; Joseph Dudley Will, Oct. 27, 1719, XXI, 708–710, SCPR.

111. Crane, ed., *Worcester County*, I, 11; *Fones Record*, 85–86.

promised to settle with recruits brought over from England.[112] This grant included land covered by the present towns of Oxford and Charlton and parts of Dudley, Auburn, and Southbridge. Dudley and Stoughton's partners in this venture were all Englishmen. Major Robert Thompson, a London merchant (and president of the Society for the Propagation of the Gospel in New England), invested in Bristol (the Plymouth venture launched by Boston speculators in 1680), owned 500 acres in Woodstock, and held the largest single interest in Guilford, Connecticut. Another associate was Dr. Daniel Cox of London, a friend of Dudley and one of the proprietors of West Jersey.[113] The fifth associate was John Blackwell. Having been a member of Parliament under Cromwell and a treasurer in Cromwell's army, Blackwell went into exile during the Restoration and eventually came to New England, seeking to build a refuge for English and Irish dissenters. In three busy years, Blackwell became involved in perhaps as many as four different Nipmuck ventures. He petitioned for (and received) a Nipmuck grant eight miles square, vowing that he had Englishmen ready to come over and settle. He joined Dudley in the Oxford enterprise. He held a one-thirteenth interest in another Nipmuck venture with Dudley, Stoughton, and others. And he acquired a parcel near the future Pomfret, Connecticut, which Blackwell sold upon his return to England after the Revolution of 1688.[114]

112. General Court Grant to Dudley *et al.,* May 18, 1683, CXII, 341, Mass. Archives. The grant was made in 1683.

113. George F. Daniels, *The Huguenots in the Nipmuck Country; or, Oxford Prior to 1713* (Boston, 1880), 38–39, 40n, 41; Munro, *History of Bristol,* 79; Holmes Ammidown, *Historical Collections* . . . , 2d ed., 2 vols. (New York, 1877), I, 114; Kimball, *Dudley,* 58.

114. Indenture between William Stoughton *et al.,* and Joseph Dudley *et al.,* May 23, 1686, photostats, MHS; Blackwell Petition and Grant, Jan. 28, 1684/5, CXII, 376–380, Mass. Archives; George F. Daniels, *History of the Town of Oxford, Massachusetts* . . . (Oxford, Mass., 1892), 283–287; Daniels, *Huguenots in the Nipmuck,* 40–41; Ammidown, *Historical Collections,* I, 117–119. This last piece of land, near Pomfret, amounted to 5,750 acres that Blackwell had bought from Fitch in 1686 and named Mortlake. (Fitch was active that year, selling the tracts of New Roxbury, Pomfret, the unnamed tract with 13 investors, as well as developing Plainfield and Canterbury—all in the Nipmuck.) Back in London, Blackwell sold Mortlake to his attorney in America, Jonathan Belcher, who by virtue of this ownership sought to represent Pomfret to the General Court, although he was not "Actually Resident In Said Township." Belcher also asked that the occupants of

The five grantees divided their sixty-four-square-mile tract, setting aside 11,250 acres for settlers and 30,000 acres for themselves (which in 1688 they divided into five equal parts, 6,000 acres per grantee). John Gore performed the survey. They also reserved for themselves several hundred acres in the heart of the land set aside for settlers, probably in the belief that this land would appreciate even more quickly than their outlying 30,000 acres once settlement commenced. Then they looked for settlers. In 1685, Robert Thompson in London happened to meet Gabriel Bernon, a merchant of Rochelle who had fled to England after the Revocation of the Edict of Nantes. The two made an agreement providing that Bernon would settle the Oxford township with thirty Huguenot families and that Bernon himself would receive a tract of 1,750 acres there. In 1686, the French arrived in Boston, their transportation paid for by Bernon, and immediately went to Oxford. As of November 1687, there were fifty-two people at Oxford.[115]

For the next several years, Oxford prospered. In 1688, Andros confirmed the grant of Oxford to Dudley and his four associates. Andros confirmed several tracts to Dudley in this same year: 1,786 acres in the Nipmuck country, his house and land in Roxbury, and his farm at Sherburn. Then in 1696, Indians attacked Oxford, and the French fled, never to return. Bernon attempted to keep up the settlement by sending tenants to his land there, but he himself resettled in Newport, Rhode Island, and the other French scattered. Not without cause, Dudley held that the French forfeited their land, since settlement had been a condition of the grant. So in 1712, Dudley and the heirs of the other grantees advertised for new settlers for Oxford, offering the same 11,000 acres. By 1713, thirty families had

---

his "Mannors"—he had divided Mortlake into the manors of Kingwood and Wiltshire—should "have a Right or Interest of Voting According to the proortion the Said Mannors bear to and With the Said Town in Quantity of Land, the petitioner having So Paid his proportion of Charge towards the Settlement of Said town of Pomfret." Although the inhabitants of Pomfret gave their consent to this petition, and the upper house accepted its main provisions, the lower house vetoed the bill. Years later the Connecticut assembly associated Mortlake first with Pomfret, then with Brooklyn. Belcher Petition re Mortlake, Oct. 14, 1714, Towns and Lands, III, 30; Mortlake, 1747–52, Towns and Lands, VIII, 101–105; Brooklyn Petition, 1786, Towns and Lands, IX, 345–355, Conn. Archives.

115. Daniels, *Huguenots in the Nipmuck,* 46, 48, 65–73; Ammidown, *Historical Collections,* I, 128–135; Crane, ed., *Worcester County,* I, 53; A. Holmes, "Memoir of the French Protestants, Who Settled at Oxford, Massachusetts, *A.D.* 1686," MHS, *Colls.,* 3d Ser., II (Boston, 1830), 59.

appeared and received a deed from the grantees. This was the beginning of the permanent settlement of Oxford, carried on by English, not French, settlers.[116]

Oxford was not the only land venture Dudley launched in 1682. After he and Stoughton purchased the Nipmuck for Massachusetts and deeded a twenty-five-square-mile reservation to the Indians, they turned around and, in the same year, bought back half of that reservation from the Indians. In 1707, William Dudley bought the remaining half of this tract, allowing the Indians hunting rights within it. In 1724, William took away the hunting rights and crowded the Indians onto a one-square-mile piece of land. In the 1750s, the Dudley heirs further reduced this square-mile reservation to a plot of land of 440 acres. Settlers began arriving on the former Indian reservation in 1714, when Joseph was still alive. In 1723, Joseph's children began deeding the property to whites. And by February 1731/2, the court incorporated the town as Dudley, Massachusetts.[117]

In the early 1680s, other towns nearby—Worcester, Brookfield, Lancaster, and Mendon—were trying to reestablish themselves in the wake of the war, and there was very likely a shortage of settlers in the region. It was not

116. Andros Grant to Dudley, Jan. 11, 1687/8, Misc. Large; Andros Patents and Confirmations, July 5, 20, 1688, Misc. Large, MHS; Daniels, *Huguenots in the Nipmuck,* 83, 88–89, 97–98, 138, 142. Bernon himself was allowed to keep his land in return for providing the French settlers, and he profited from this holding once the English settled the town. Dudley and the heirs of Stoughton also profited from their large lots. Dudley's 6,000 acres fell in the south of the township, which was settled in the 1720s and 1730s as Dudley's heirs, mainly his daughters and his son Paul, sold the land piece by piece to settlers. Blackwell's heirs sold his 6,000 acres in 1720 to Peter Papillon of Boston, whose heirs in turn sold the land to settlers. These settlers were the first inhabitants of Southbridge. Stoughton's heirs sold most of his 6,000-acre share to Samuel Brown in 1717 or 1718, and Brown made no conveyances. Sold for taxes, the land ended up in the hands of a loyalist and remained off the market until after the Revolution. Cox's share passed to his son Daniel, who sold part to Thomas Freak of England and part to John Blackwell. Freak's heirs sold the land to settlers in the 1730s, and the rest either was sold to Papillon or became tied up in litigation until the 1780s. The final share, belonging to Thompson, passed to his children, who sold a third of it to an Oxford settler; the remaining two-thirds did not pass to settlers until 1786. Holmes, "Memoir of the French Protestants," MHS, *Colls.,* 3d Ser., II (1830), 66, 67; Daniels, *History of the Town of Oxford,* 283–287.

117. Crane, ed., *Worcester County,* I, 12, 131–133. The following deeds given by William Dudley were probably to land that fell within the town of Dudley: Deed to Thomas Child, Apr. 16, 1726, Misc. Bound; Deed from William Dudley, Dec. 29, 1727, Misc. Bound, MHS.

until the 1710s, thirty years after Dudley first asked for the grant, that Oxford began on a permanent footing. But settlement would have been even slower without Dudley and his partners, for they secured the grant, negotiated with the Indians, bought the tract, hired the surveyor, found the Huguenots, and organized the resettlement when the first settlement collapsed. It was the connections, the wealth, the influence, as well as the greed, of Dudley, Stoughton, and his associates that launched Oxford and its satellites, even if it did take a while to get these towns off the ground.

Still others focused on the Nipmuck during the 1680s. In 1683, the court granted to Roxbury a township to be located in the Nipmuck.[118] Roxbury then formed an organization of all those Roxbury residents who did not wish to move to the new town but who nonetheless wished to own land there. This society paid one hundred pounds to the actual settlers of New Roxbury, and in return the nonresidents received the northern half of the township to divide among themselves. By this ingenious arrangement, the very different aims of the "goers" and the "stayers," as they were called, were served. The landless Roxbury residents received land, and the investors earned a chance to speculate in the increasingly popular Nipmuck lands. The fruit of this collaboration was the town of Woodstock, which Connecticut later claimed.[119]

It was not by chance that Roxbury should be the town to develop one of the Nipmuck settlements, for Joseph Dudley was the leading Roxbury resident. He undoubtedly helped Roxbury secure the General Court grant, which, coming five months after the Oxford grant, explicitly provided that New Roxbury should not encroach upon Oxford. It was also Dudley who on behalf of Roxbury purchased from James Fitch title to the township and whom, in October 1684, Roxbury appointed to draft proposals for settling the new township.[120]

On the committee with Dudley was Samuel Ruggles. Ruggles owned four shares in the northern half of New Roxbury, one of the largest holdings, and was with Paul and William Dudley among the most active nonresident proprietors of the town. Joshua Lamb, Benjamin Gamblin, John Grosvernor, and John Pierpont were other Roxbury residents who invested in New Roxbury. John Chandler also was active in New Roxbury, but as one who moved from Roxbury to New Roxbury and became one of

118. Court Grant, Oct. 10, 1683, CXII, 342–343, Mass. Archives.

119. Ammidown, *Historical Collections,* I, 257–262.

120. Daniels, *Huguenots in the Nipmuck,* 56; Ammidown, *Historical Collections,* I, 261.

its leading residents.[121] These Roxbury men are worth mentioning, because they helped found not just New Roxbury but surrounding Nipmuck towns as well. Chandler bought shares in Oxford after the French left that unfortunate settlement.[122] In 1686, Chandler, John Gore, John Pierpont, John Grosvernor, Samuel Ruggles, John Ruggles, and six other Roxbury residents purchased the Mashamoquet Purchase, soon to be settled as Pomfret, from the Connecticut speculator James Fitch.[123] In December of that same year, several of these same people—Joshua Lamb, Nathaniel Paige, Andrew Gardiner, Benjamin Gamblin, John Curtis, and Samuel Ruggles—bought a tract twelve by eight miles in the Nipmuck. For this land, they paid twenty pounds to the same Indians who had sold Dudley his Nipmuck lands. (The deed was registered before the ubiquitous William Stoughton.) Massachusetts incorporated the settlement that resulted as Hardwick.[124] Again, a group including roughly the same Roxbury individuals—Joshua Lamb, Nathaniel Paige, Andrew Gardiner, Benjamin Gamblin, Benjamin Tucker, John Curtis, Richard Draper, Samuel Ruggles, and Ralph Bradhurst—made an Indian purchase in the Nipmuck, this one on January 27, 1686/7. Several Indian wars interrupted this venture, but eventually it succeeded in peopling the town of Leicester.[125]

121. Ammidown, *Historical Collections*, I, 260–261, 279; Boston, Registry Dept., *Roxbury Land Records (A Report of the Record Commissioners . . . [Sixth Report])*, 2d ed. (Boston, 1884), 51–56, 68–70 (hereafter cited as *Roxbury Land Records*). Ruggles also served on the town committee that examined the tract in 1684, along with John Ruggles and John Curtis.

122. Daniels, *Huguenots in the Nipmuck,* 57n. This may have been Chandler's son, or perhaps both were involved in Oxford.

123. Trumbull, *History of Connecticut,* I, 445–446; John Warner Barber, *Connecticut Historical Collections . . . History and Antiquities of Every Town in Connecticut . . .* (New Haven, 1846), 437–440; Deming, *Settlement of Connecticut Towns,* 61. Fitch charged the Roxbury men £30 and also insisted that they give him two shares in the proprietorship they formed. The Roxbury men complied, the Connecticut assembly confirmed the purchase, and in 1713 the settlement was granted privileges as the town of Pomfret.

124. Wright, *Indian Deeds,* 111–113. Owing most likely to warfare, this town did not get off the ground for many years. After Lovewell's war, however, the heirs of the purchasers hired a surveyor, petitioned the court for confirmation, and received a township grant in 1732. Enough settlers arrived by 1736 that the court incorporated the place as the District of Lambstown. In 1739, the court made the district a town by the name of Hardwick. Crane, ed., *Worcester County,* I, 140–142.

125. Crane, ed., *Worcester County,* I, 61–64. In 1713, the surviving original purchasers and heirs petitioned the court to confirm their title, and the court did so on condition that they settle 50 families there in 7 years. The proprietors probably met these

As might be expected, these Roxbury men acquired considerable land through these activities. Samuel Ruggles died owning twelve parcels in five towns, worth 79 percent of his estate. His son, also Samuel, died with nine parcels in five towns, worth 88 percent of his estate. John Chandler ended up with ten pieces in Pomfret and Woodstock, worth 70 percent. Andrew Gardiner's estate was 86 percent in land; Joshua Lamb's, 70 percent. Benjamin Tucker owned seven parcels in four towns, constituting 73 percent of his estate.[126]

Such were the ventures launched in the Nipmuck by Dudley, his friends, and his fellow Roxbury townsmen. Altogether this small group of individuals initiated half a dozen ventures in the mid-1680s, resulting in the eventual establishment of at least ten new towns—Oxford, Charlton, Dudley, Thompson, Southbridge, Webster, Auburn, Pomfret, Woodstock, and Brooklyn—all in the Nipmuck region. (And that does not count the towns of Canterbury, Plainfield, and others in the region established at this same time by Fitch and the Winthrop brothers.) They developed various kinds of grants: township grants, additions to older towns, and vast tracts. In at least one instance, Mortlake, the proprietor had the idea of creating baronial manors, occupied by tenants and endowed with political rights commensurate with economic power. But whatever the method, all these Nipmuck towns were started by a small group of investors who were nonresidents, who knew each other, and who used their money and their considerable influence to acquire wilderness land and seek a profit. The boom in Nip-

---

conditions—though not by becoming settlers themselves. They offered lots in the eastern half of the tract at low prices and kept the western half for themselves (just as, 30 years before, the Roxbury proprietors, including some who also participated in this venture, had set aside the southern half of New Roxbury for settlers, keeping the northern half for themselves). The committee for laying out the lots was composed of Roxbury residents William Dudley, Joshua Lamb, Samuel Ruggles, and one other—veterans of Nipmuck town-launching ventures. John Chandler surveyed the bounds, another veteran. On Jan. 11, 1724/5, the proprietors executed deeds to 37 lot owners who were also settlers.

126. Samuel Ruggles Inventory, Nov. 11, 1692, XIII, 103–104; Samuel Ruggles Inventory, Apr. 1716, XIX, 149–150; John Chandler Inventory, Apr. 15, 1703, XV, 152–153; Andrew Gardiner Inventory, Apr. 16, 1694, XIII, 584–585; Joshua Lamb Inventory, Mar. 13, 1700, XIV, 316–317; Benjamin Tucker Inventory, Aug. 9, 1714, XVIII, 351; Appraisal of same, Jan. 31, 1714/5, n.s., VIII, 52, SCPR. Not all the land in these estates lay in frontier towns; on the contrary, the most valuable single item was invariably the decedent's house, which in most cases was located in an older community. Still, the frontier properties were impressive in numbers, acreage, and value.

muck lands led by Dudley represented a full development of the entrepreneurship that had been stimulating frontier expansion for several decades.

The only region rivaling the Nipmuck during the 1680s as a magnet for investment was the Merrimack River valley. As early as the 1650s, backwoodsmen had explored the Merrimack region, hoping to expand the fur trade with new Indians. Frontiersmen like Simon Willard, Thomas Henchman, and the Parkers established the first white settlements in this area during that decade.[127] But it was not until the 1680s that the Merrimack boom occurred. Again, Dudley and his friends helped to lead it. On May 13, 1686, John Blackwell, Samuel Shrimpton, Charles Lidgett, Joseph Dudley, William Stoughton, Richard Wharton, Peter Bulkeley, John Usher, Daniel Cox, William Blathwayt (of the colonial office in Whitehall), Edward Randolph, Jonathan Tyng, Thomas Henchman, and others made an agreement for dividing a large tract of Merrimack country land.[128] Several of these partners sat on the Dudley council when, the following July, the council confirmed their title and included this territory in the new county of Merrimack. This act of confirmation gave to twenty men title to one million acres along the Merrimack River in both New Hampshire and Massachusetts, a venture that came to be known as the Million Purchase. The owners intended to divide the tract among themselves and to settle towns within it, but three decades of continual Indian war prevented them, and the claim lapsed. Individuals like William Brenton, Jonathan Tyng, and Samuel Shrimpton salvaged something of their claims, selling and renting land there. Smaller ventures succeeded: the Wamesit Purchase, owned by

127. For discussion of Groton, Chelmsford, and Dunstable, see above, Chapter 1.

128. By this indenture, the principals agreed to divide 5,000 acres to each shareholder and to admit others to their ranks until they reached the number of 20 adventurers. They made this indenture 10 days before many of these same individuals made a similar indenture concerning Nipmuck lands (Merrimack Country Division, May 13, 1686, photostats, MHS). For the many other purchases made during the early 1680s by these same people in the Merrimack region, see, among others, in photostats collection, MHS, the following documents: Indian Deed to Jonathan Tyng, Merrimack River, Dec. 22, 1683; Indian Deed to Tyng, Jan. 3, 1683/4; Indian Deed to Tyng, Oct. 10, 1685; Indian Deed to Dudley, Shrimpton, and Wharton, Nov. 5, 1685; Tyng to Hubbard, May 21, 1684; Tyng to Stoughton, Dudley, Bulkeley, Wharton, Henchman, and Maccarty, May 21, 1684; Stoughton and Dudley to Tyng and Wharton, Oct. 2, 1684; Mason to Usher et al., Apr. 15, 1686; Dudley, Shrimpton, Wharton, et al. to Wharton, Shrimpton, et al., May 12, 1686; Tyng, Bulkeley, Wharton, et al., to Blackwell, Shrimpton, and Lidgett, May 13, 1686.

Tyng, Henchman, the Parkers, and others from towns near Dunstable, developed the land that turned into Lowell.[129] But this enormous venture, the Million Purchase, apparently failed.

Exactly why it did, when others succeeded, is not clear. Andros probably rejected the Million Purchase title, just as he rejected most claims by large land speculators. But a brief cloud on their titles did not stop the Atherton, Pejepscot, and other ventures, and there is no reason to believe that a similar cloud was enough to stop the Million Purchase.[130] Perhaps the Million Purchase was too large to develop. Or perhaps the owners concentrated their attention on the Narragansett and Nipmuck, where their other holdings were located, and left the Merrimack to local developers, like the Tyngs, to plant and profit from. For whatever reason, the Million Purchase did not endure. And settlement did not pick up in that region until the mid-eighteenth century. But for a while the biggest speculators in New England—not counting Fitch, the Winthrops, the Hutchinsons, and the Pynchons—had turned to the Merrimack Valley with the same expectation of profit and the same designs with which they had already launched new towns in the southerly parts of New England.

v. Maine and New Hampshire

The problem of sparse settlement was even greater in Maine and New Hampshire than in the Merrimack Valley. There the military vulnerability of isolated towns, thin soil, harsh climate, and con-

129. Dudley Council Action on Merrimack Claim, July 12, 1686, photostats, MHS. The new county included other recent purchases by Jonathan Tyng, Dudley, Stoughton, Wharton, Shrimpton, and others in the Merrimack Valley. For Wamesit Purchase, see Waters, *History of Chelmsford,* 511–524. For the dormancy of the Million Purchase, see Dr. William Clarke to John Yeamans (Shrimpton heir), Dec. 23, 1749, Million Purchase, photostats, MHS.

130. On Oct. 31, 1687, Andros rejected Wharton's Pejepscot claim, saying it was "a great hindrance to settlement." He also rejected the Atherton title to the mortgage lands, saying that the "grant was extorted by a troop of horse . . . the debt was fictitious." Yet both claims survived the assault by Andros. For these and other Andros actions against large landholders in Maine and the Narragansett, see *Cal. S.P., Col.,* XII, 422–423, XIII, 255; Andros Item concerning King's Province [Narragansett], CXXVI, 203, Mass. Archives; Toppan and Goodrick, eds., *Randolph Letters,* IV, 224.

flicting, clouded titles made the far north an undesirable place to live. It was not, therefore, until the eighteenth century that New Hampshire and Maine were the scenes of the same kind of speculative activity that had peopled much of southern New England in the seventeenth century. Nonetheless, entrepreneurs did speculate in northern lands in the seventeenth century.

Indeed, the search for profits in the New England wilderness began with the first English adventurers who launched an assortment of enterprises in northern New England during the 1610s and 1620s. These entrepreneurs were not town founders, and the industries they erected on the North American seacoast—fisheries, timber harvesting, and specialized agriculture—bore little relation to the enterprise of land speculation. On the other hand, the English adventurers of the early years prefigured the town founders of later decades in two important respects. First, they invested in the North American wilderness with the expectation of profit, among other goals. Sir Ferdinando Gorges, in writing a narrative of his effort to colonize northern New England from 1606 to 1620, declared that he lost some of his investors in colonization projects precisely because profits were not forthcoming. Christopher Levett, another member of the Council of New England, argued for the establishment of North American colonies as a way to increase fishing profits.[131]

Second, English entrepreneurs employed certain methods for conducting their business that later town founders also employed, including the recruiting of farmers to cultivate their American lands and of fishermen to run their fisheries. In 1622, Captain John Mason and others obtained from the Plymouth council a grant of all the land between the Merrimack and Kennebec rivers. This tract became known as Laconia, after the name of the company of merchants that Mason put together to develop the land. In 1623 and in later years, the Laconia Company sent settlers to several places on the Piscataqua River with the object of establishing a fishing enterprise there. Once there, the settlers were Mason's tenants and his employees. Mason never made money on New Hampshire (so he said), but by the time

131. Sir Ferdinando Gorges, *A Briefe Narration of the Originall Undertakings of the Advancement of Plantations* . . . (London, 1658 [rpt. Maine Hist. Soc., *Colls.*, 1st Ser., II (1847)]), 15–34 (hereafter cited as Gorges, *Briefe Narration*); Christopher Levett, *A Voyage into New England, Begun in 1623, and Ended in 1624* (London, 1628 [rpt. Maine Hist. Soc., *Colls.*, 1st Ser., II (1847)]), 100–105.

he died in 1635, he had spent twenty-two thousand pounds trying—
sending supplies, livestock, tradesmen, and more than seventy settlers to
the Piscataqua.[132]

The Laconia Company was not the only entity recruiting settlers for that
part of New England. In the late 1620s, Edward Hilton, the man sent out
by the Laconia Company to supervise the Piscataqua River plantation,
received from the Plymouth council a patent for lands on the river. In 1630,
he sold this patent to several Bristol merchants. Two years later, these
merchants sold the land to other wealthy Englishmen, who were friendly to
the newly established Massachusetts Bay Colony, and during the 1630s this
group recruited settlers from the West of England and sent them to the
Piscataqua. These settlers were the founders of Dover. When the English
owners of Dover deeded the land to the settlers in 1641, the merchants
made sure to keep one-third of the patent in their own hands and thus be in
a position to benefit from the expected appreciation in the land's value.[133]

There were many such settler recruitment schemes. In the 1630s, Sir
Ferdinando Gorges (who had also participated in the Laconia venture)
advertised for settlers to "plant in any part of his limits" in Maine, promising them as much land as they needed for a rent of two shillings per
hundred acres every year. In 1630, another group of London entrepreneurs, the Lygonia Company, sent a shipload of farmers to begin an
agricultural plantation at Casco Bay. (The farmers gave up the next year,
complaining that the land was not fit for agriculture.) A Bristol merchant,
Gyles Elbridge, obtained the patent of Pemaquid from the Plymouth council and sent over an agent to manage a fishing and fur trade business. In
1639, Elbridge secured permission to export eighty people to carry on his
enterprise. In February 1629/30, the Plymouth council granted Thomas
Lewis and Richard Bonython a tract of land four miles along the sea and
eight miles inland just east of the Saco River, because these two "with their
associates and Company have undertaken at their own proper Costs and
Charges to transport fifty persons thither within seven yeares next Ensue-
ing." This venture was the beginning of Saco and Scarborough, Maine. It

132. Jeremy Belknap, *The History of New Hampshire* (Dover, N.H., 1831), 3–4, 428;
Otis Grant Hammond, "The Mason Title and Its Relations to New Hampshire and
Massachusetts," AAS, *Procs.*, n.s., XXVI (1916), 248.

133. New Hampshire, *Town Charters Granted within New Hampshire*, ed. Batchellor
(vol. II of *Town Charters*, vol. XXV of *State Papers*), 698–703, 707–709; Belknap,
History of New Hampshire, 17–18.

would not be the last time a governing authority encouraged the recruitment of settlers with the gift of land.[134]

It was not always to procure labor, however, that entrepreneurs engaged in the recruitment of settlers. Sometimes, foreshadowing settler agents of the eighteenth and nineteenth centuries, English merchants of the seventeenth century recruited settlers purely to make a profit from the steerage. By the 1640s, William Bradford was writing that "some begane to make a trade of it, to transeport passengers and their goods, and hired ships for that end. . . . And by this means the cuntrie became pestered with many unworthy persons." Whether making money from the passenger trade or from industries requiring labor, English-based merchants of the 1620s and 1630s began a transatlantic tradition of shipping humans for profit that in future generations would become a lucrative enterprise and play a substantial, if often ignominious role, in the peopling of America.[135]

English colonizers also rented out land for profit. All of Gorges's grants were accompanied by a charge of anywhere from two shillings to five shillings per hundred acres of land. These rents were quitrents, vestiges of feudal tenure, not modern lease arrangements. But not all rental income of the English proprietors came from quitrents; some of it came from a form of sharecropping. Samuel Allen, the Englishman who bought the province of New Hampshire in 1691, explained the system to a fellow proprietor: "I intend to goe there to take order about settling some servants to improve my Land there," Allen wrote, "Eyther by granting deeds to them and their heires for ever Reserveing a quitt Rent, which is my waye I take in this province, or putting in Servants of my owne to manage it with a stock, allowing them ½ the increase for their paynes, which is the coustoms of these partes." Either way, the landlord made money, both in the 1630s and in the 1690s.[136]

134. Gorges, *Briefe Narration,* 70–71; Williamson, *History of Maine,* I, 238–240; J. Wingate Thornton, "Ancient Pemaquid," Maine Hist. Soc., *Colls.,* 1st Ser., V (1857), 222; Baxter, ed., *DHM: Baxter MSS,* IV, 1–4; William S. Southegate, "The History of Scarborough, from 1633 to 1783," Maine Hist. Soc., *Colls.,* 1st Ser., III (1853), 17; William Willis, "The History of Portland . . . ," Maine Hist. Soc., *Colls.,* 1st Ser., I (1831), 16.

135. Bradford, *Bradford's History,* 477. For the definitive account of the recruitment of nonslave labor on the eve of the Revolution, see Bernard Bailyn, *Voyagers to the West: A Passage in the Peopling of America on the Eve of the Revolution* (New York, 1986), 296–352.

136. *York Deeds,* I, 57–58; James Phinney Baxter, ed., *Documentary History of the State of Maine,* III, *The Trelawny Papers* (Portland, Maine, 1884), 394–397. On account of

In these early ventures, English entrepreneurs pioneered the techniques of settler recruitment and land renting, later used by town founders. But they were, by and large, not successful, in part because of the industries they chose to build: silkworms and vineyards did not thrive in the northern climate. Another likely problem was the absence of the investors, three thousand miles away from the enterprises they owned. Their agents, on the spot, no doubt did better than they, just by virtue of their proximity to the enterprise. The most prominent of these agents worked for Gorges and Mason.

In 1637, Sir Ferdinando Gorges gave a commission to George Cleeves for "letting and settling all or any part of his lands or islands lying between Cape-Elizabeth and the entrance of Sagadahock River." Immediately, Cleeves and his associate Richard Tucker began selling lands, continuing until 1662, by which time their deeds had become the chief source of titles in the town of Falmouth, Maine. Thomas Cammock also got his start as an agent for Mason and Gorges on the Piscataqua. Receiving grants from them and from the Plymouth council, he began a fishing settlement at Black Point in the early 1630s. In 1635, another agent for Gorges and Mason, Henry Jocelyn, joined him. After Cammock died, Jocelyn acquired Cammock's lands (and his widow), and for thirty years he sold and rented lands at Black Point, becoming a large landowner and source of many people's titles.[137]

Edward Godfrey was another factor, first employed by the Laconia Company, then by Mason, then by Gorges. He settled on the York River in 1632, received along with several associates a grant of 12,000 acres, became an officer in the government Gorges established, and sold a great deal of land to settlers at Agamenticus (sometimes called Gorgeana, now the town of York). Godfrey did not, however, always please the residents of York. In 1654, settlers there petitioned the Massachusetts General Court, protesting the "great praejudice [that] must redowne to the well being of a Towne, w[here] considerable quantitys of Land are dispos'd of to particu-

---

their large expenses, it is unlikely that the largest English landlords—Gorges, Mason, and Allen—made a profit.

137. Willis, "History of Portland," Maine Hist. Soc., *Colls.,* 1st Ser., I (1831), 30–31, 37–38, 65–74; Southgate, "History of Scarborough," Maine Hist. Soc., *Colls.,* 1st Ser., III (1853), 12, 16, 26, 33–35, 77.

lar persons in convenient places for the settling thereof," and specifically protesting Godfrey's claims.[138]

There were many other land traders (Joshua Scottow, Thomas Wiggin, Robert Jordan, Walter Barefoote, Richard Waldron, Nicholas Shapleigh, and, later, William Phillips, Silvanus Davis, and Walter Gendall) who derived their titles from the first English proprietors of Maine and New Hampshire. The absence of continuous political authority in northern New England provided a hospitable business environment for these entrepreneurs. In Maine especially, where land titles conflicted, different jurisdictions competed, and organized government was absent, conditions were just right for individuals, outside strong town or colony authority, to amass large tracts and sell them off in pieces to settlers. Organized towns were late in starting; independent speculators thrived.[139]

By midcentury the agents of the English proprietors were joined by colonists from lower New England who bought northern lands (just as they bought lands in the Narragansett, Nipmuck, and elsewhere) purely as a speculative investment. One of these was Simon Lynde, who lived in Massachusetts and was judge of the Suffolk County Court of Pleas. Lynde owned stock in the Atherton Company and a share in Westerly in Rhode Island. In 1671, Lynde bought a house in Kittery, and five years later took possession of several farms and mills in Wells in a debt recovery. Another Boston-based entrepreneur was Thomas Brattle. Brattle bought a large farm (1,650 acres) near the Merrimack in 1671 and was a founder of Dunstable, where his farm lay and of which he was a selectman, though he continued to live in Boston.[140] In the early 1660s, with two others, Brattle

138. Willis, "History of Portland," Maine Hist. Soc., *Colls.*, 1st Ser., I (1831), 18, 18n; William M. Sargent, "The Division of the 12,000 Acres among the Patentees at Agamenticus," Maine Hist. Soc., *Colls.*, 2d Ser., II (1891), 319–327; *York Deeds*, I, Index of Grantors; Baxter, ed., *DHM: Baxter MSS*, IV, 124–126.

139. For the land activities of these other traders, see Williamson, *History of Maine*, I, 570–571; Baxter, ed., *DHM: Baxter MSS*, VI, 16–17, 232–237, 297–300, 335, 481–483; *York Deeds*, I, Index to Grantors; and Charles E. Clark, *The Eastern Frontier: The Settlement of Northern New England, 1610–1763* (New York, 1970), 16–25, 47–51, 55–58. For Phillips, see below.

140. *Fones Record*, 30, 39–40, 64–66; Potter, *Early History of Narragansett*, 77; *York Deeds*, II, 146; Dunstable Meeting, July 22, 1685, MSS Bound, MHS; Nason, *History of Dunstable*, 7, 22, 26–27. At the outbreak of Indian hostilities in 1675, the court ordered Brattle and Henchman to draft men for garrisons in Dunstable, Groton, and Lancaster.

bought more than 10,000 acres at Saco, Maine, and an interest in several mills and mines from William Phillips. Around this same time, in 1661, he joined Edward Tyng, John Winslow, and Antipas Boyes in purchasing from Plymouth Colony what was known as the Kennebec Purchase. All the purchasers were Boston merchants. They paid four hundred pounds for a tract described as extending fifteen miles into the wilderness on both sides of the Kennebec River, all the way to the "Western ocean." This transaction terminated Plymouth Colony's thirty-year attempt to make a profit from the fur trade in Maine and began a proprietorship that in the eighteenth century developed the Kennebec Valley and launched several frontier towns. Brattle left an estate of seventy-six hundred pounds, including lands in Boston, Concord, Quebaug, Maine, and the Narragansett.[141]

Another Maine investor was John Leverett, governor of Massachusetts. Leverett received rights in the new town of Deerfield, which he sold to John Pynchon in 1667; owned land in Hartford, managed for him by an agent on the spot; and received a sixteenth-interest in eight thousand acres that William Brenton owned on the Merrimack (the same eight thousand acres that Brenton had bought from Billerica).[142] But probably Leverett's largest holdings lay in Maine. During the 1660s, the General Court sent Leverett more than once to assert Bay Colony control over Maine communities, and during these trips, in the course of his public work, Leverett became interested in several Maine tracts. In 1673, he acquired as mortgagee an interest in a sawmill, gristmill, six hundred acres, and other property in York. For £190, Leverett also purchased nine thousand acres near Saco Bay from the local Maine speculator, William Phillips. Like Lynde, Leverett lent money to local Maine people (one of whom had to mortgage his mills and land to John Hull and Roger Plaisted in order to repay the loan). The provision of capital to local individuals appears to have been an important activity of Bostonians with interests in Maine during the latter half of the seventeenth century, and it was also one way that the Bostonians came to acquire holdings in Maine lands and mills.[143]

141. *York Deeds,* I, 112, IX, 226–228; Thomas Brattle Division, Mar. 13, 1683/4, n.s., II, 393–395, SCPR.

142. Sheldon, *History of Deerfield,* I, 10; Jonathan Gibbons to John Leverett, 1664, LVII, 7, Mass. Archives; John Leverett Will, Mar. 15, 1678/9, William H. Prescott Legal and Business Papers, 1665–1863, 15, MHS (hereafter cited as Prescott Papers, MHS). This will is also found in SCPR, VI, 259–261.

143. Willis, "History of Portland," Maine Hist. Soc., *Colls.,* 1st Ser., I (1831), 111; Williamson, *History of Maine,* I, chap. 16; *York Deeds,* II, 65, 168, III, 39, IV, 8–9, VI,

The man from whom Leverett bought land, William Phillips, sold Maine lands to a great many Boston men in the seventeenth century. A relative of both Peleg Sanford and Elisha Hutchinson, Phillips lived in Boston, then moved to Saco, Maine, sometime before 1661 and helped assert Massachusetts authority in Maine as an officer in the Maine militia. He carried on a mining business, built sawmills, and bought lands from Indians. And, of course, he sold lands. During the early 1660s, he made numerous sales in the area of Saco, both to Boston men and to local tenants of his own. From 1664 to 1674, he made an additional ten or twelve land conveyances to Richard Russell of Charlestown, John Leverett, William Hutchinson, and others.[144] In 1676, Phillips sold a Maine township eight miles square to a group of Boston and Rhode Island merchants, including Peleg Sanford, John Jolliffe, Elisha Hutchinson, William Hudson, and Theodore Atkinson, who intended to receive one thousand acres each and hold the remaining twenty-two thousand acres together, as a proprietorship, with "the Intent of settleing a Town." But like so many Maine projects of the seventeenth century, this one failed to materialize until the 1720s, when the heirs of the purchasers met, surveyed the land, divided some of it, and began a town. Individuals interested in Maine were not without speculative plans in the seventeenth century; what they lacked was the settlers, and peace, to make their plans work out.[145]

22; John Leverett Will, Mar. 15, 1678/9, Prescott Papers, 15, MHS; Book of Eastern Claims, 3, Mass. Archives. Leverett's will places this tract near Casco, not Saco, Bay.

144. Baxter, ed., *DHM: Baxter MSS,* VI, 14–16; Williamson, *History of Maine,* I, chap. 14; *York Deeds,* I, 112, 122, 138, II, 23, 47, 49, 135, 172, 181, III, 74. Even after all this selling, Phillips's will counted six tracts and mentioned others unenumerated. Land represented the entirety of his estate. William Phillips's Will, Feb. 1682, VI, 526, SCPR.

145. *York Deeds,* III, 5, XI, 16–17. New Hampshire also had its local speculators who developed close ties to Boston merchants. Roger Plaisted was Hull's New Hampshire agent for purchasing land, timber, and mills; he also helped start several New Hampshire towns, including Concord. Sampson Sheafe was a New Hampshire councillor with mercantile interests in Boston, Maine, and Strawberry Bank (forerunner of Portsmouth), who owned with others 6,000 acres on Saco River, upon which he constructed mills, houses, and fencing and settled 14 families. In 1687, Sheafe sold his interest in this tract for £80. Sheafe was also among the petitioners and original grantees of Dunstable in 1673. Hull, "Diaries of John Hull," AAS, *Trans., Colls.,* III (1857), 117–125; Petition for Grant, May 18, 1659, photostats, MHS; Baxter, ed., *DHM: Baxter MSS,* VI, 330–331; Clark, *Eastern Frontier,* 101; *York Deeds,* VI, 11; Nason, *History of Dunstable,* 8–9. Other Plaisted land purchases and sales are found in *York Deeds,* III, 1, 125, IV, 8–9.

Perhaps the most ambitious speculator who invested in northern lands in the seventeenth century was Richard Wharton. Wharton owned land in Rhode Island by virtue of his Atherton Company stock, joined Dudley in several ventures to develop the Merrimack and the Nipmuck regions during the 1680s, and was a nonresident proprietor of Dunstable. He served on the Dudley and Andros councils, then lobbied for the removal of Andros as governor of New England. Even though Andros had confirmed Wharton's Narragansett lands, Wharton objected to Andros's annual quitrents, his money policy, and his stringent land policy. It was while seeking Andros's removal in England that Wharton died in 1689, leaving a wealthy estate.[146]

The accumulation of a vast estate in Maine was Wharton's largest project. What he intended to do with it is not clear. But some sort of industry and shipping must have been included among his goals, for the place he chose was Pejepscot, a tract of land on both sides of the Androscoggin River, on Casco Bay and Merrymeeting Bay, where the Androscoggin, Kennebec, and other rivers come together. This tract also included at its inmost point what was later called Brunswick Falls, one of the strongest water powers on the Atlantic coast.[147] The actual size of the tract was the subject of extensive litigation in the eighteenth century, when the Kennebec proprietors (holding title based on Brattle's purchase of 1661) fought the Pejepscot proprietors (holding Wharton's title) over the boundary between them. Eventually Wharton's deeds were construed as having conveyed to him a tract of roughly 500,000 acres.[148] Having acquired this immense tract at consider-

146. Dunstable Meeting, July 22, 1685, MSS Bound, MHS; Andrew McFarland Davis, *Currency and Banking in the Province of the Massachusetts Bay* (New York, 1901), I, 34–35; Arnold, *History of Rhode Island*, I, 503; Samuel Sewall, *Diary of Samuel Sewall, 1674–1700* (MHS, *Colls.*, 5th Ser., V [Boston, 1878], 255; Inventory of Wharton's House in Boston, June 30, 1691, Otis Papers, box 1, MHS.

147. George Augustus Wheeler and Henry Wheeler, *History of Brunswick, Topsham, and Harpswell, Maine* . . . (Boston, 1878), 75–76. Wharton went about collecting all the possible titles to this tract he could find. In 1683, he bought the English title from the heirs of those who had the grant from the Plymouth Council. In 1684, he bought the Indian title to the same lands with additions. Wharton also received a grant from the General Court in the area of his intended "manor." Wheeler and Wheeler, *History of Brunswick, Topsham, and Harpswell, Maine*, 11–16; *York Deeds*, III, 127–128.

148. Wheeler and Wheeler, *History of Brunswick, Topsham, and Harpswell, Maine*, 24–26; Baxter, ed., *DHM: Baxter MSS*, IV, 412–413. Williamson states that the tract

able expense, Wharton next sought confirmation of it; and he almost got it. On June 10, 1686, several weeks after his friend Dudley was installed as president, a draft of a royal order was made granting Pejepscot to Wharton, creating "one entire Mannor," and bestowing upon Wharton authority to hold courts leet and baron. Blathwayt and the attorney general approved this draft, the latter noting that he could see no harm in it since it "amounts only to a confirmation of such Lands as he is already seized of by purchase." But apparently Whitehall decided to delay final issuance of this confirmation until Andros could come to America and review the entire landholding system. This delay was unfortunate for Wharton, for Andros denied confirmation and rejected his claim to Pejepscot.[149] Wharton then went to England to seek Andros's removal, Andros was overthrown, and Wharton died—all before Wharton had the chance to develop Pejepscot.

Others did get the chance. To liquidate Wharton's debts, his executor, Ephraim Savage, sold Pejepscot in 1714 for £140 to a group of investors who became known as the Pejepscot Company. This company settled some eight to ten towns on the coastline by giving land away, insisting only that the grantees build houses and place settlers upon the land within three years. The Kennebec, Lincolnshire, Pemaquid, and other land companies of the eighteenth century used similar methods to attract settlers, whose very presence in the empty wilderness attracted others to the frontier and pushed up the value of company lands.[150]

The colonists of the seventeenth century certainly differed from their eighteenth-century heirs, but not because the latter chased after land profits. Simon Lynde, Daniel Denison, Thomas Brattle, John Leverett, John Hull, Richard Wharton, Sampson Sheafe, John Paine, Samuel Sewall, John Alcock, William Brenton, Richard Russell, Peleg Sanford, John Jolliffe, William Hudson, Samuel Shrimpton, the Hutchinsons—none of these individuals lived in northern New England, but they bought property

contained 200,000 acres (*History of Maine*, I, 573–574). But Wheeler gives 500,000, and so does Viola F. Barnes ("Richard Wharton, a Seventeenth-Century New England Colonial," Colonial Society of Massachusetts, *Publications, Transactions*, XXVI [1924–1926], 247).

149. "Grant to Richard Wharton, June 10, 1686," Maine Hist. Soc., *Colls.*, III (1853), 325–329; *Cal. S.P.*, Col., XII, 422–423.

150. *York Deeds*, VIII, 56–59, 163, 167–168, 178, XVI, 150; Wheeler and Wheeler, *History of Brunswick, Topsham, and Harpswell, Maine*, 24–26.

there, because as investors they expected to profit from the increase in land values.[151] Nor did the presence of land companies distinguish the later age. To the south, the Atherton, the Pettaquamscut, the Sowams companies were different in no significant way from the eighteenth-century Kennebec and Pejepscot companies. Seventeenth-century investors tried to form companies in northern New England, too. That was the purpose of Dudley and others when they formed the Million Purchase to develop the Merrimack, and of William Phillips and others when they created an enterprise to settle the Saco River valley. Land companies were not new to New England in 1700.

What made frontier development different from one age to another, at least in northern New England, was not profit-mindedness and not corporate forms, but rather the matter of success. In the seventeenth century in Maine and New Hampshire, settlers were too few, warfare too common, and the land too poor for large-scale ventures to be successful. In 1708, there were one thousand white men in all of New Hampshire—and "daily lessening," according to one observer. In 1690, Maine had a total population of perhaps two thousand white people living in just eight towns.[152] What good did it do to buy up large tracts, form companies, and open business as a land speculator when there were all of two thousand people and eight towns in the province of Maine? It made more sense to buy and saw timber, export lumber, and speculate in lands on a small-scale, individual basis; so that is what entrepreneurially minded people did, resorting to the kind of extractive industry and agriculture that the first English companies in America—the Dorchester, the Laconia, and the Lygonia companies—had built back at the start of the century, as the means of profiting from the American wilderness. The cycle of developing wild lands, which in southern New England had advanced far by late in the century, was still just beginning in the north. A few individuals, such as Wharton and Brattle, did indeed amass large holdings, but it would be left to their descendants, when conditions had changed, to make a success of land speculation on the grand scale. And when those eighteenth-century companies finally did get off the ground, they were not a departure from—they were a continuation and culmination of—the ambitions and activities of seventeenth-century colonists.

151. See above for mention of all but one of these men; for Alcock, see *York Deeds*, I, 63.

152. Greene and Harrington, *American Population before the Federal Census of 1790*, 70–73; Clark, *Eastern Frontier*, 336–337.

3

Commerce
and
Culture

1. Frontier Expansion and Puritanism

How did this commercial use and expansion of the wilderness fit in with—conflict and coincide with—the commands of Puritan culture? Certainly, expansion dispersed the population and threatened to disrupt the sense of a unitary community, which was the essence of John Winthrop's model of Christian charity. For reasons of defense and population growth, to be sure, new settlements were inevitable, but they were not to spring up willy-nilly. In Massachusetts, no settlements could begin without approval from the authorities. And no person was to erect a dwelling place more than one-half mile removed from a meetinghouse, according to a colony order of 1635. Nearby, Plymouth leaders registered the same concern. Already by 1632, people sought out large tracts of land as pasture for their cattle, causing William Bradford to foretell the disintegration of Plymouth's "Christian and comfortable fellowship" and "the ruine of New-England." Bradford further noted that "it was not for wante or necessitie so much that they removed, as for the enriching of them selves." Enriching himself was not the reason Bradford had come to New England.[1]

On the other hand, there were powerful forces operating in favor of expansion. As early as the 1630s the authorities of the colony acted to

1. *Mass. Records*, I, 157, 167; William Bradford, *Bradford's History "Of Plimoth Plantation"* (Boston, 1898), 361–363, 507.

develop natural resources and expand the economy in a way that suggests the influence of a prodevelopment ethos. Franchises for fur trading and ironworks were speedily issued by Connecticut, Massachusetts, and Plymouth colonies. Land was given out on condition that the owners cultivate it. Commercial fishing, long an industry on the American coast, was encouraged. And immigration was invited, for strength lay in numbers.[2]

[To attract immigrants, Puritans employed a promotional, expansionist rhetoric not in contradiction with but nevertheless different in tone from the Christian fellowship rhetoric Bradford and others used to describe their compact communities.] Winthrop boasted of "the good land," this "fat black earth," as Francis Higginson called it, and others published a variety of tracts to lure people to America with pictures of abundance.[3] The promotional campaign was a success: between ten thousand and twenty thousand immigrants arrived during the first ten years of the Puritan migration. As new towns sprang up to accommodate these immigrants, Edward Johnson spoke with pride of the expanding Puritan civilization. He boasted how the Puritans' "constant penetrating farther into ths Wilderness, hath caused the wild and uncouth woods to be fil'd with frequented wayes, and the large rivers to be over-laid with Bridges," how they were converting this "remote, rocky, barren, bushy, wild-woody wilderness" into "a second England for fertilness in so short a space." Their work was, "indeed the wonder of the world." New Englanders had mixed thoughts about expansion: it threatened their first communities. But their

2. Perry Miller's description of the Puritans' mission to the New World gives a doctrinal explanation of this prodevelopment ethos, for in this view the Puritans came to New England on a world-transforming mission, which required them to prepare to do battle with the unregenerate and therefore to build a strong, fortresslike New England. See Miller, *The New England Mind: The Seventeenth Century* (Cambridge, Mass., 1939), 469–470. Others have challenged this interpretation: Theodore Dwight Bozeman, *To Live Ancient Lives: The Primitivist Dimension in Puritanism* (Chapel Hill, N.C., 1988); Andrew Delbanco, *The Puritan Ordeal* (Cambridge, Mass., 1989). Whatever was the Puritans' conception of their mission—a subject beyond the bounds of this study—the Puritans acted quickly to develop natural resources, including vacant lands, and wrote glowingly about their achievements.

3. John Winthrop, *A Model of Christian Charity / Christian Charitie: A Model Hereof,* in Edmund S. Morgan, ed., *Puritan Political Ideas, 1558–1794* (Indianapolis, Ind., 1965), 93; Peter N. Carroll, *Puritanism and the Wilderness: The Intellectual Significance of the New England Frontier, 1629–1700* (New York, 1969), 7–13, 48–49, 52, 55.

rhetoric also betrayed a sense of pride in the onward march of Puritan civilization.[4]

The Puritans' self-comparison to the ancient Jews reinforced the expansionist impulse. As the elect people, Puritans saw themselves as the moral descendants of the Jews. They believed that Abraham's children's covenant was theirs: to "encrease and multiply and replenish the earth and subdue it," as Genesis instructed them in a passage cited often by the Puritans.[5] With this appropriation of the biblical injunction, Puritans elevated the settling of the wilderness to a religious duty. They were "latter-day Israelites . . . summoned from the English Egypt to take possession of a second Promised Land." Speaking of the Israelites in their journey to the Promised Land, but having in mind his fellow colonists, Thomas Hooker said, "They must come into, and go through a vast and a roaring Wilderness, where they must be bruised with many pressures, humbled under many overbearing difficulties . . . before they could possess that good Land which abounded with all prosperity, flowed with milk and honey."[6] Nathaniel Ward wrote that by obeying God's command to go into the wilderness, Puritans had reaped "his large beneficence to us here beyond expectation."[7]

Hooker and Ward were speaking metaphorically, likening wilderness travails to the taxing preparation that one must go through before redemption. But Puritans also invested with spiritual significance the literal act of taking possession of the wilderness. John Winthrop, Jr., compared starting a town—"buildings, fencings, cleeringe and breakinge up of ground, lands to be attended, orchards to be planted, highways and bridges and fortifica-

4. Edward Johnson, *Johnson's Wonder-Working Providence, 1628–1651*, ed. J. Franklin Jameson (New York, 1910), 210, 234; Miller, *New England Mind: Seventeenth Century*, 470. Like other Puritans, Johnson, while praising the frontiersmen, simultaneously questioned the motives of those who would sunder older communities, and on this account hinted his disapproval of Hooker's migration to Connecticut (pp. 105–106).

5. Carroll, *Puritanism and the Wilderness*, 8–9, 14; Alan Heimert, "Puritanism, the Wilderness, and the Frontier," *New England Quarterly*, XXVI (1953), 361–362, 376–377.

6. Michael T. Gilmore, introduction, *Early American Literature: A Collection of Critical Essays* (Englewood Cliffs, N.J., 1980), 1–3; Thomas Hooker, *The Application of Redemption . . . The Ninth and Tenth Books*, 2d ed. (London, 1659), 5.

7. Nathaniel Ward, *The Simple Cobbler of Aggawam* (1646), in Alan Heimert and Andrew Delbanco, eds., *The Puritans in America: A Narrative Anthology* (Cambridge, Mass., 1985), 183.

tions to be made"—to "the beginninge of the world." [Others spoke of winning piety and godliness by the hard labor it would take to transform the wilderness.[8] The resourceful Puritan mind seized upon the difficult work of settling the wilderness, inevitable in any case to accommodate the growing population, as an activity worthy of moral improvement, as yet another spiritual waypoint on the path to godliness.

Godliness, whatever form it took, never triumphed without a struggle. Edward Johnson praised the courage and hard work of Simon Willard in establishing Concord: "Thus this poore people populate this howling Desart, marching manfully on . . . through the greatest difficulties, and forest labours that ever any with such weak means have done." Shepard spoke of all New England as "a place of tryall." Bradford called the wilderness "hidious and desolate."[9] Nearly everyone called it "howling" and "vast." The sense of evil was unmistakable. (As was the sense of contradiction: Puritans alternately described New England as the promised land and as an evil land, just as they condemned dispersal while promoting expansion.) The reality of the wilderness was doubtlessly uninviting. As Bradford said, there was no one to greet them on arrival except Indians who "were readier to fill their sid full of arrows then otherwise." But the extraordinary uniformity with which seventeenth-century New Englanders described the wilderness, the formulaic use of pejoratives, suggests that the designation of the wilderness as evil satisfied some intense and broadly felt psychological need: the harder the struggle, the greater their eventual, saintly triumph. Perhaps, too, Puritans were taking an adversarial stance that long habit had trained them to take. Puritanism was a movement born in persecution. Suddenly a people inured to combat found themselves with no enemies—no Laud, no church, no Star Chamber. The minority was now the majority; the once-persecuted, now in charge; the exiled, at home. This change was perplexing. In the remarkable words of Thomas Shepard, "New England's peace and plenty of means breeds strange security. . . . There are no enemies to hunt you to heaven . . . Here are not sour herbs to make the lamb sweet." [The wilderness may have served as a substitute enemy, the trial to undergo, sufficient in difficulty and terror to meet the psychological needs of a people whose movement was formed in opposition, who themselves depended on "enemies to hunt you to heaven." [For these and perhaps

8. Carroll, *Puritanism and the Wilderness*, 15, 70.

9. *Ibid.*, 65; Johnson, *Wonder-Working Providence*, ed. Jameson, 115; Bradford, *Bradford's History*, 95.

still other reasons, Puritans keenly felt the need to picture the wilderness as a place of struggle, hardship, and evil, which needed to be transformed by them into something good.[10]

Whatever the psychological pressures, the wilderness as evil satisfied a specific theological requirement as well. The wilderness was evil because it was empty, idle wasteland, and idleness occupied a high place in the Puritan hierarchy of sins. Wilderness was nature run wild—untamed, uncontrolled, unregenerate. A garden, on the other hand, was planted, cultivated, and improved, the result of industry. John Cotton spoke of sins as being like weeds. Hooker likewise said sinners were "like wildernesses overgrown with weeds." Conversely, planting signified regeneration. Cotton asked the question, "What is it for God to plant a people?" His answer was both allegorical and literal: God will place us where "he gives us roote in Christ," but also where we will be "sufficiently provided for."[11] In the next generation, Thomas Shepard, Jr., developed the simile more fully, asking in the voice of God, "Have I been a wilderness to Israel? i.e., have I been that to my people which a wilderness is unto men that are made to wilder therein, where they meet with nothing but wants, and terror, and woe. . . ." He goes on to list the five things that make up a wilderness: desolation and confusion; a condition of uncultivation and poverty; a place where men "are in danger to be lost"; a place of "many positive evils" and "temptations"; and, finally, a wilderness is "not hedged in, nor fenced about," thus

10. Thomas Shepard, *The Parable of the Ten Virgins,* chap. 12, sect. 5, in Thomas Shepard, *The Works,* ed. John Adams Albro, 3 vols. (Boston, 1853; rpt., 1971), II, 170. Alan Heimert has said that Puritans did not start off demonizing the wilderness, that it was the judaizing disposition of the Puritan mind (combined with a "realistic" appraisal of their needs) that accelerated the process by which New Englanders came to regard the wilderness as a "permanent and hideous wilderness," the subduing of which "quickly became an exalted calling for the Puritan" ("Puritanism, the Wilderness, and the Frontier," *NEQ,* XXVI [1953], 370, 382). It also is possible that this change in attitude was required by the very activity of expanding settlement (and there were many reasons, both spiritual and secular, for expanding settlement). For different views of the Puritans' conception of their purpose in the wilderness, see Andrew Delbanco, "The Puritan Errand Re-Viewed," *Journal of American Studies,* XVIII (1984), 351–353; Sacvan Bercovitch, "The Image of America: From Hermeneutics to Symbolism," in Gilmore, ed., *Early American Literature,* 158–167; Carroll, *Puritanism and the Wilderness,* 62. I have focused on some, not covered all, of the various Puritan conceptions of the wilderness that these authors so well describe and debate.

11. Carroll, *Puritanism and the Wilderness,* 112–113; John Cotton, *God's Promise to His Plantations* (London, 1634), 14–15.

being a place of darkness and ignorance. The opposite of this "wilderness condition," Shepard, Jr., said, was the "beauty of order" imposed by the Puritan way of worship. Happily, the Lord had "turned a wilderness into a fruitful field," nourishing to both body and soul. In large part, that transformation occurred because "the Lord sowed this land at first with such precious seed-corn"—the ministers of the first generation.[12]

Wilderness and garden thus were powerful symbols in Puritan cosmology, standing for the danger posed by idleness, the hope offered by improvement. But they were more than symbols. In the minds of seventeenth-century Englishmen, the wilderness was not only a metaphor for waste; it *was* a wasteland—without cultivation, fences, property lines, laws, morality, and all the other trappings of civilization—badly in need of improvement. Puritan divines spoke so often of the evil of wasting land and the good of improvement that these propositions acquired a unique cultural stature as self-evident truths. Francis Higginson found it sad "to see so much good ground . . . lie altogether unoccupied." In 1640 Ezekiel Rogers, the minister-leader of Rowley, defended the large grants of land there by declaring that "neither doe we purpose to keepe this lande unimployed." The danger in land speculation was, not the enterprise itself, but the possibility that land engrossment would discourage new settlers, "and then [in the words of Edward Johnson] . . . you shall have wast Land enough." Why should people suffer privation in England, asked John Winthrop, whilst allowing "a whole continent, as fruitful and convenient for the use of man, to lie waste without any improvement"?[13] The great emphasis that land policies of the general courts placed upon improvement probably had its roots not only in the desire to build up the frontier, find land for landless people, and strengthen the economy but also in a deeply held, theologically based loathing of empty, wasted space.

Unsurprisingly, the Indians' nonuse of the land vexed the first colonists.

12. Thomas Shepard, Jr., *Eye-Salve* (1672), in Heimert and Delbanco, eds., *Puritans in America,* 250–254. For more on wilderness versus garden, see Carroll, *Puritanism and the Wilderness,* 112–113, 119; Heimert, "Puritanism, the Wilderness, and the Frontier," *NEQ,* XXVI (1953), 370. Heimert places this emphasis on making a garden of the wilderness only after 1640.

13. Carroll, *Puritanism and the Wilderness,* 181, 184–185; Johnson, *Wonder-Working Providence,* ed. Jameson, 35; John Winthrop, *Reasons to Be Considered . . .* (1629), in Heimert and Delbanco, eds., *Puritans in America,* 72.

Winthrop proposed that the natives should "learn of us to improve" the land.[14] Robert Cushman (in a Separatist work composed in 1622) justified the taking of the Indians' "empty" land on the grounds that "their land is spacious and void. . . . They are not industrious, neither have art, science, skill or faculty to use either the land or the commodities of it, but all spoils, rots, and is marred for want of manuring, gathering, ordering, etc." Because the Indians let the land lie "idle and waste . . . it is lawful now to take a land which none useth, and make use of it." Calling the wilderness "a vast and empty chaos," Cushman argued that settling the wilderness would eradicate a moral chaos as well as a physical one, that the spiritual emptiness would be filled *because* the physical emptiness would be filled.[15]

Prompted by this assortment of emotions and doctrinal requirements, Puritans busied themselves settling the wilderness. They had set out expecting to keep a tight rein on town-founding; but during the first decade town-planting became a routine matter, as the Bay Colony authorized some twenty towns. Far from being condemned, the proliferation of towns won applause. With the help of God, New Englanders were turning "an howling wildernes . . . into a fruitfull paradeis."[16] In 1640 the General Court in Massachusetts repealed the law requiring houses to be built not more than half a mile from a meetinghouse—only five years after enacting it. Puritans were of two minds: they feared the dismemberment of community, yet they believed deeply in tearing down the empty wilderness and building up their own civilization. For many reasons, some practical, some psychological, and some theological, by 1640 the impulse to expand was stronger than the impulse not to.

14. William Cronon, *Changes in the Land: Indians, Colonists, and the Ecology of New England* (New York, 1983), 55; Winthrop, *Reasons,* in Heimert and Delbanco, eds., *Puritans in America,* 73.

15. Robert Cushman, *Reasons and Considerations* . . . (1622), in Heimert and Delbanco, eds., *Puritans in America,* 43–44. Cotton made the same argument, citing "a Principle of Nature, That in a vacant soyle, hee that taketh possession of it, and bestoweth culture and husbandry upon it, his Right it is" (*God's Promise to His Plantations,* 5).

Plymouth Colony would soon have tangible proof of Cushman's proposition in the defiant community Merrymount, led by Thomas Morton, whose libertinism could only have found sanctuary in the uncontrolled wilderness.

16. *Mass. Records,* I, 136, 146, 147, 149, 157, 210, 236, 238, 291. The words are Michael Wigglesworth's (Carroll, *Puritanism and the Wilderness,* 194).

II. Land as a Commodity

⌈Several elements of Puritan thinking, then, encouraged expansion of the frontier. The commercial use of land, however, was another matter. What in the Puritans' intellectual and cultural background made the connection between land and commerce possible, reasonable, or perhaps even natural?⌉

To some colonists, including the most prominent leaders, the connection was anything but natural. William Bradford worried that greed might sunder the Plymouth community. John Winthrop favored a land policy in Boston that guarded the interests of future generations, but he lost out to the faction urging rapid distribution of town lands. Roger Williams lost a similar battle in Providence and throughout his life opposed the individuals, many of them Bostonians, who preyed on his colony's land. Toward the end of his life, Williams feared that "God Land will be (as now it is) as great a God with us English as God Gold was with the Spaniards." This passion for wealth, in Williams's eyes, subverted the very purpose of land in Rhode Island. God had "provided this country and this corner as a shelter for the poor and persecuted," but now it was reduced to the rank of "children's toys."[17] Denunciations like these stand as testaments to the existence of land greed early in the colonies' lives. But they also give voice to the leaders' conception of land as a communal asset, not as a commodity. How, then, did Puritans reconcile themselves to assigning to entrepreneurship a major role in land development?

⌈By far the most important factor was the pragmatic emphasis of the Puritan mind. To the Puritan mind, the natural world was the revelation of God's will.⌉ Whatever nature required was therefore justified on the grounds that God had done the requiring. This theory lay behind a great many Puritan convictions—such as the idea that the godly individual must live in this world (while not being of it), that he obey moral laws, that he provide for himself and see to his own comfort.[18] It also accounted

17. John Winthrop, *The History of New England from 1630 to 1649*, ed. James Savage, 2 vols. (Boston, 1825–1826; rpt., 1972), I, 151–152; Roger Williams, *The Letters of Roger Williams . . .* , ed. John Russell Bartlett (Narragansett Club, *Publications*, 1st Ser., VI [Providence, R.I., 1874]), 319–320, 344 (hereafter cited as *Letters of Roger Williams*).

18. Miller, *New England Mind: Seventeenth Century*, 214. Beyond the scope of this study are the several features of New England Puritanism—the contractualism, volunta-

for the scavenging, heterodox character of the Puritan mind, its adoption of humanism and contractualism, of science and rationalism, its all-encompassing embrace of complex reality. Whatever history or nature presented, the Puritan mind made use of.

This practical bent especially characterized the Puritans in New England. The greatest difference between old and New England was that in the former they had stood "apart from the world" and in the latter they were "entangled with it."[19] Being entangled with it, Puritans, soon after arriving in Boston, began a series of accommodations with the world that continued for the rest of the century. When Winthrop left England, he carried with him ideals conceived in England that he hoped would be realized in the Puritans' new home: the ideals of fraternal love, community, and harmony; of a society dedicated to God's glory; of people weaned of worldly affections; of churches composed solely of saints. But these were ideals only and not a description of actuality. They were articulated, moreover, in an environment in which Puritans were reacting against an oppressive government, not seeking to create their own. No one could predict what change the transfer to America would effect upon the Puritans' ability to live up to these ideals. In crossing the ocean, Puritans went from being persecuted to being unopposed, from sketching ideals to leading a new polity. Instead of enemies to oppose, they had a government to form, churches to assemble, a society to build. These activities by themselves acquainted the first colonists with practical exigencies never encountered in England. Believers had to deal with the world around them, not just attack it.

In adjusting to their new role, Puritans resorted to improvisation and compromise. In church-building, they diverted their sights from a number

---

rism, stress on diligence, and the chosen-ness of New Englanders—that reconciled the colonists to entrepreneurship generally (with no reference to land matters), that both spurred the Puritans to greater industry and absolved them of the sin of worldliness if their industriousness profited them materially. The Puritans' faith and commerce certainly posed countervailing "insupportable pressures," as Bernard Bailyn put it (*The New England Merchants in the Seventeenth Century* [Cambridge, Mass., 1955], 44). But, just as certainly, elements of Puritan doctrine and psychology justified and perhaps even fostered the entrepreneurship of believers. Still today the one who has best captured the complexity of Puritan creeds is Perry Miller, *New England Mind: Seventeenth Century,* and *The New England Mind: From Colony to Province* (Cambridge, Mass., 1956).

19. David D. Hall, *The Faithful Shepherd: A History of the New England Ministry in the Seventeenth Century* (Chapel Hill, N.C., 1972), 271.

of high goals. First congregationalism, the ecclesiastical expression of Puritanism, was amended in the aftermath of the Antinomian crisis in recognition that even the commonwealth of saints needed a presbyterian structure to prevent heresy. Then there was the matter of church membership. Initially New England churches had instituted rigorous personal tests for church membership, but church population growth soon fell behind the population growth generally, and so steadily through the midcentury decades the clergy lowered the standards for church membership. The rise of the county magistracy was tacit admission that, however much colonists worshiped the communal ideal, communities themselves were not capable of shouldering the full tasks of local government.[20] On issue after important issue, New England Puritans accommodated their social and religious doctrines to the practical exigencies of building a godly commonwealth here on earth.

Especially in frontier matters were the exigencies pressing. Town-founding was hard work, as Thomas Hooker said, requiring money, contacts, and a range of expertises. Without individuals to supply these essential ingredients, it was harder still. The practical remedy to the shortage of such individuals was to involve prominent colonists in town-founding by giving them a financial incentive. Commerce in land could not have fitted any Puritan theory of proper land use, but the pragmatic bent of Puritanism disposed New Englanders to let the entrepreneurs do the work that, circumstances being what they were, only they could do to advance town-planting.

When Puritan goals came into conflict, the more remote ones gave way to the more pressing. An immediate problem for William Bradford was maintaining Plymouth's church, which was threatened by parishioners being drawn away in pursuit of distant, desirable lands. To preserve his church, Bradford's remedy was—not to forbid land accumulation by non-

20. Miller, *New England Mind: From Colony to Province*, 80. What precisely was the significance of changing tests for church membership is the subject of some dispute. This author agrees with David D. Hall that the model of declension is an inadequate tool for attacking the problem; see his "On Common Ground: The Coherence of American Puritan Studies," *William and Mary Quarterly*, 3d Ser., XLIV (1987), 223–225. Judged by the practices of the 1630s, the methods of accepting members and partial members after the 1660s were nevertheless a compromise with original goals.

On the county magistracy: David Thomas Konig, *Law and Society in Puritan Massachusetts: Essex County, 1628–1692* (Chapel Hill, N.C., 1979), 188. A more extensive treatment of communalism appears below, in Chapter 7.

residents—but to promote it; for by allowing people to own faraway lands, Plymouth might sate their appetite for land and thereby avoid losing them as residents. By granting "good farms to spetiall persons . . . [where] they might keepe their catle and tillage by some servants, and retaine their dwellings here" in Plymouth town, Bradford hoped to keep parishioners in town. In other words, the exploitation of lands by absentee owners was for Bradford, not the cause of, but the way to prevent the breakup of his church.[21] Bradford did not look fondly upon his fellows in the grip of greed. But absentee landownership was a necessary price to be paid to save his church. Such was the pragmatic New England mind. Compromise in the name of a higher goal was not contemptible: it was imperative. The good Puritan (or Pilgrim) not only lived in this world but negotiated with its vanities to achieve the most godly result.

Compromise with land greed was undoubtedly made more palatable by Puritan social theory. "Some must be rich some poore," explained John Winthrop on the *Arbella,* "some highe and eminent in power and dignitie; others meane and in subjeccion." Hierarchy was no accident: "It is not then the result of time or chance," as one writer put it, "that some are mounted on horse-back, while others are left to travell on foot. . . . The Almighty hath appointed her that sits behind the mill, as well as him that ruleth on the throne." If the higher ranks were thought the only ones qualified to rule, it followed that they were the same ones to lead an effort as large and important as expansion into the wilderness. That people made money from the enterprise did not violate social theory, but, rather, was justified by the same hierarchical thoughts. Said a London Puritan at midcentury, "A nobleman hath need of a large allowance to maintain him according to his nobility."[22]

These, then, were intellectual habits—of pragmatism and of hierarchy—that made it possible for Puritans to reconcile themselves to land commerce. What made it more than possible, even natural, to so reconcile themselves was the contemporary economic revolution in Europe and its transforming effect on ideas about business, trade, and land. This revolution, too, was a part of the New Englanders' intellectual world. The ideas it generated were secular, and they did not affect Puritan religious doctrine in

21. Bradford, *Bradford's History,* 362–363.

22. Winthrop, *Model of Christian Charity,* in Morgan, ed., *Puritan Political Ideas,* 76; Miller, *New England Mind: Seventeenth Century,* 423, 428; Paul Seaver, "The Puritan Work Ethic Revisited," *Journal of British Studies,* XIX, no. 2 (Spring 1980), 51.

the way that, say, the idea of contract did. But as a vital, changing part of the English culture that produced Puritanism, they helped constitute the intellectual background that predisposed Puritans to the commercial treatment of land.

In the economic change sweeping Europe during the late sixteenth and early seventeenth centuries, new patterns of trade linked together distant peoples. Local consumption no longer represented virtually the entire market. In England, output increased of coal, salt, iron, steel, lead, ships, and glass. Guilds declined, and capitalist employers emerged. Striking social change accompanied these economic changes. By 1600, the order was passing in which one's status was prescribed, one's duties fixed. The Statute of Artificers and the poor laws—Elizabethan attempts to reknit a social fabric unraveled by rapid economic change—were obsolete by the time they were passed.[23] Another by-product of this expansion was a new commercialism, a spirit infecting farmers and tradesmen alike.

Long-held attitudes toward land began to change. The expansion of both population and trade created new markets for food and put pressure on land. Landlords responded by raising rents, land values rose, and during the seventeenth century, for the first time in English history, land became commercially important, not just necessary for subsistence and status, but commonly sought as an object of speculation and investment for profit. By the late seventeenth century, the habit of thinking of land as commodity had become so imbedded in English economic thinking that this was not merely one aspect but the only aspect of land that John Locke addressed in his *Two Treatises of Government*.[24]

Nowhere was the commercial use of land advanced so forthrightly as in

23. Joyce Oldham Appleby, *Economic Thought and Ideology in Seventeenth-Century England* (Princeton, N.J., 1978), 3; Wallace Notestein, *The English People on the Eve of Colonization* (New York, 1954), 21; Godfrey Davies, *The Early Stuarts, 1603–1660*, 2d ed. (Oxford, 1959), 285, 286.

24. Christopher Hill, *The Century of Revolution, 1603–1714* (New York, 1966), 31; Notestein, *English People*, 23; Mildred Campbell, *The English Yeoman under Elizabeth and the Early Stuarts* (New Haven, Conn., 1942), 66–68, 104; Appleby, *Economic Thought and Ideology*, 53–59; John Locke, *The Second Treatise of Government* (1690), ed. Thomas P. Peardon (New York, 1952), 23–25, 28. Locke held that "improvement" increases land's value and that only when one takes more property than one can use and lets it go to waste does one offend nature. Once again, in Locke, we come across that all-important social goal—improvement—and its evil twin, waste, perhaps the most influential intellectual duality in the Atlantic world during the early modern period.

the various ventures to colonize and trade with distant lands. These ventures—first the East India Company and the Russia Company, later the Plymouth Company and the Massachusetts Bay Company—were foliations of the extraordinary commercialism that characterized late Elizabethan and early Stuart England. They broke new ground in business history, being the first British enterprises to adopt certain techniques that have come to be associated with modern corporations. Among these were the use of a perpetual stock, creation of management committees, payment of dividends, and more. Particularly, the plantation companies employed land commercially, doling it out as a return on investment. Far from being limited, therefore, by a medieval, communal view of land, the English coming to America arrived with the help of corporate entities that markedly advanced the commercial use of land and were themselves the product of England's new, expansive commercialism.

But even if colonists closed their eyes to the example of the plantation companies, local circumstances forced them to see the need for commerce in land; for the need was greater than it had ever been in England. Although in England their wealth had consisted of many things, now it lay largely in land. In New England there were little money, capital, and labor; but land and its products abounded. By default land was the principal capital of seventeenth-century America.[25] This fact alone, irrespective of any commercial mentalité imported from England, committed the colonists to land development. For there were only two ways to expand this, the only plentiful source of capital: first, to convert more wilderness from public to private ownership; and, second, to improve land and thereby (as Locke would later say) increase its value. Both means led to the same result: development of the wilderness. Combine these local economic conditions with the entrepreneurial spirit of early Stuart England and, too, with the plantation companies' tradition of using land as a means to generate profit from new plantations, and one can see how, when the Puritans confronted the difficult task of settling wilderness, they resorted to models of entrepreneurship ready at hand.

So Puritans did not have to shed their religion before they could don their acquisitiveness. They could wear the two hats simultaneously, and they did. Land developers of the seventeenth century came from the mainstream of

25. Cronon, *Changes in the Land,* 77–78, 168.

colonial society, not its margins, and were its leaders not just in politics, not just in wealth, but sometimes in religion as well. Examples abound.[26]

For John Hull, godly living was particularly important. He charged the captains of his ships to see that "god bee worshipped dayly . . . and the Sabothe Sanctifyed and all prophannete Suppressed," wrote down more than two hundred summaries of sermons and lectures he heard delivered at the First Church between 1655 and 1661, and was perhaps responsible for the decision of the Pettaquamscut partners in 1668 to set aside three hundred acres for the maintenance of a preacher on their Rhode Island tract.[27] Soon preachers arrived and began preaching to the settlers, not only those on Pettaquamscut lands but also those on Atherton Company

---

26. One who ably makes the same point about religion and acquisitiveness is Christine Leigh Heyrman in *Commerce and Culture: The Maritime Communities of Colonial Massachusetts, 1690–1750* (New York, 1984), according to which Gloucester underwent economic growth without diminishing the founding Puritan social values, and Marblehead saw the rise of a market economy that, far from destroying social harmony, helped produce for the first time a communal, ordered society (pp. 17–19, 407). Her work suggests that the relationship of commerce and culture is less susceptible to easy reduction than some have supposed. Rather than assume that economic activity necessarily must have been at odds with religious values, one may find it more promising to look for the ways in which the two were mingled and supported each other—the way, say, Marblehead's prosperity helped that town achieve Puritan ideals, and the way Puritan emphases on expansion and improvement helped to foster and justify land development. As David Hall has pointed out, the social historian's usual effort to divorce the ministry from the people of New England, an effort apparently attempted with the hope of diminishing the importance of the former, is coming into conflict with mounting evidence to the contrary; and in any event, this effort does nothing to advance the historian's task of sorting out the complex relationship between culture and behavior ("On Common Ground," *WMQ*, 3d Ser., XLIV [1987], 225).

The findings about land developers are consistent with the conclusion of Richard C. Simmons, namely, that "the godly and the politically privileged seemed also to include a large percentage of the propertied class and, to some extent, to exclude a varying but sometimes large percentage of the poor sort" ("Godliness, Property, and the Franchise in Puritan Massachusetts: An Interpretation," *Journal of American History,* LV [1968–1969], 508).

27. Hull to John Harris, Dec. 10, 1672, John Hull Letterbook, Manuscript, microfilm, AAS; John Hull, "The Diaries of John Hull, Mint-Master and Treasurer of the Colony of Massachusetts Bay," AAS, *Transactions, Collections,* III (Boston, 1857), 123; Documents in the Case of Torrey vs. Gardner, 1734, concerning the "Narragansett Lands," etc., 27–29, MS Am. 1505, Prince Collection, BPL (hereafter cited as "Narragansett Lands," Prince Collection, BPL).

lands. It appears that as interested as speculators were in obtaining settlers' money, they also wanted to save their souls.[28] But if Hull advocated the provision of religion by the Pettaquamscut Purchase, his partners in that venture did not need much persuading; for they, too, were devout men. William Brenton was admitted to Boston's First Church in 1633, and Samuel Wilbore in the same year (John Hull in 1648). John Porter was a member of the First Church of Roxbury. These were the principal founders and shareholders of the Pettaquamscut Company in the late 1650s and 1660s. Two of them, Wilbore and Porter, along with others were banished as Antinomians in the spring of 1638. Other Antinomians, like Philip Sherman and John Coggeshall, were leading investors in the Misquamicut Purchase. And yet another religious exile, William Coddington, earned the dislike of Roger Williams and Samuel Gorton partly because of his campaign to monopolize the political power and land of Rhode Island.[29]

The Atherton Company had its own share of devout stockholders. Its principal founder, Humphrey Atherton, signed the church covenant of the Dorchester church in 1636. The Hutchinsons, also shareholders, had been banished during the Antinomian crisis. Richard Smith, an Atherton shareholder who owned land at Misquamicut, had left England "for his conscience toward God," according to Roger Williams.[30] Whether from outside or inside the colony, the investors in Rhode Island lands were committed to their faith. In Massachusetts, Daniel Gookin, who was one of the most active town promoters in the midcentury years, was just as devout. As soon as he arrived in New England in 1644, Gookin joined the First

28. Richard Knight, "The Six Principle Baptists in the Narragansett Country," *NHR*, I (1882–1883), 203–206; Edward Channing, *The Narragansett Planters: A Study of Causes*, Johns Hopkins University Studies in Historical and Political Science, 4th Ser., no. 3 (Baltimore, 1886), 20–21.

29. John Callender, *An Historical Discourse on the Civil and Religious Affairs of the Colony of Rhode-Island and Providence Plantations* . . . (Boston, 1739 [republished in RIHS, *Collections*, IV (Providence, R.I., 1838)]), 73, 84n; Elisha R. Potter, Jr., *The Early History of Narragansett*, RIHS, *Colls.*, III (Providence, R.I., 1835), 125, 393–395; David Sherman, "The Sherman Family," *NHR*, II (1883–1884), 230.

30. Winthrop, *History of New England*, II, 137–139n; Daniel Berkeley Updike, *Richard Smith: First English Settler of the Narragansett Country, Rhode Island* . . . (Boston, 1937), 3–15; Potter, *Early History of Narragansett*, 115–135, 166–167; Channing, *Narragansett Planters*, 19–20. Williams frequently preached in Smith's house in the Narragansett. Smith's son, Richard, Jr., also an active developer, fought in Cromwell's army and was devout.

Church of Boston. Gookin thought, along with the principal divines, that to permit toleration in New England "would offend God," and in service of this theory he helped his colony carry out its persecution of Quakers. As superintendent of the Praying Indians, Gookin spent considerable time with John Eliot, teaching and preaching to Indians. While conducting his missionary work Gookin probably first saw some of the many tracts he helped develop into towns.[31]

On the Connecticut River, John Pynchon inherited his father's lands and enterprises earlier than he would have if William had not been so committed to his religious beliefs. In 1650, William Pynchon published a theological essay called "The Meritorious Price of Men's Redemption, Justification, etc.," a work the General Court condemned as heretical. When the court invited Pynchon to recant, Pynchon would not retract all his assertions, and returned to England rather than face punishment.[32] Major John Mason of Connecticut, who participated in several settlement ventures, saw the English victory in a Pequot battle as a divine judgment in favor of the Puritan nation: "And was not the finger of God in all this?" Mason asked. "What shall I say, God was pleased to hide us in the hollow of his hand." Mason's partner in several town ventures was James Fitch, himself the son of a minister. There were several other father-son relationships involving speculators and ministers. Humphrey Atherton's son, Hope, was the first minister of Hatfield. Simon Willard's son was the first minister of Groton, Massachusetts, and leading divine of his day.[33]

Bradford worried about greed's effects on the community, but others of the firstcomers, like Wilbore and Gookin, engaged in land speculation. Even Bradford himself owned an interest in the Sowams venture, a syndicate of absentee owners that, after Bradford conveyed his right, developed

31. Frederick William Gookin, *Daniel Gookin, 1612–1687* . . . (Chicago, 1912), 67, 72, 80ff, 172–176, 193.

32. Henry M. Burt, *The First Century of the History of Springfield: The Official Records from 1636 to 1736*, 2 vols. (Springfield, Mass., 1898–1899), I, 79–125 (hereafter cited as Burt, *Official Records of Springfield*).

33. Major John Mason, "History of the Pequot War, 1637," *NHR*, VIII (1890), 153; Sylvester Judd, *History of Hadley, Including the Early History of Hatfield, South Hadley, Amherst, and Granby, Massachusetts* (Springfield, Mass., 1905), 84; Samuel A. Green, ed., *An Account of the Early Land-Grants of Groton, Massachusetts* (Groton, Mass., 1879 [rpt. in Green, ed., *Pamphlets on History of Groton* (n.p., n.d.)]), 54–56.

the town of Swansea.[34] In Puritan New England, speculators were not outcasts. ⌈On the contrary, the cream of New England society, governors and assistants, military commanders and merchants—many of them devout Puritans—engaged in wilderness development for profit.⌉

Nor is it helpful to see land development by absentees as a sign of increasing secularism and declining piety. Rather, it represented the triumph of one half of the pious mind over the other. Against the Puritans' desire for compactness and otherworldliness was posed an array of counterarguments: Puritan social theory, giving wide berth to great men; the dominating Puritan obsessions with waste and idleness and improvement, which compelled the attack on wild lands; the Judaic parallel, generating pressures to elevate land development to a divinely appointed task; and the command of pragmatism. Prompted by these beliefs and instructed by the new commercialism that characterized the late Elizabethan and early Stuart

34. See discussion of Sowams above, Chapter 2. Other early ministers, although not involved in land speculation, were not indifferent to the quality and extent of wilderness holdings. The minister Ezekiel Rogers arrived in New England with his flock and planned to settle in the area around New Haven, but then heard of desirable lands in Massachusetts, and so went there and founded Rowley. Once in Rowley, Rogers complained to the court in 1640 that he and others had come to Massachusetts "upon some promises of large accomodation," and that these promises had not been kept. So the court granted an enlargement to Rowley. Although just 20 families arrived with Rogers in 1638, 59 lots were distributed in 1643 because, in addition to an enlargement of the settling party, some families received more than one lot (Winthrop, *History of New England*, ed. Savage, II, 17; William Haller, Jr., *The Puritan Frontier: Town-Planting in New England Colonial Development, 1630–1660* [New York, 1951], 90–91).

Thomas Hooker said that his flock wanted more land and better land than they could get in Cambridge; this was one of the reasons they moved and founded Hartford (William DeLoss Love, *The Colonial History of Hartford* . . . [Hartford, Conn., 1935; rpt., 1974], 116).

When the Pilgrims were about to set sail for America, they got into an argument with their London financial backers, objecting, among other things, to a clause in the articles of agreement calling for a division of land and other assets at the conclusion of seven years. The Pilgrims did not want to split these assets with their financial backers. They said that the arrangement presented "a greate discouragemente to the planters." The prospect of accumulating property "was one spetiall motive, amongst many other, to provoke us to goe." Their complaints about the contractual terms led their backers to wonder at how "worldly and covetous" the Separatists had become (Bradford, *Bradford's History*, 58–66, 75–77; William T. Davis, *History of the Town of Plymouth* . . . [Philadelphia, 1885], 29).

age, including the new treatment of land as commodity, the Puritans swallowed their loathing of greed, which was significant; overcame their fear of dispersal, which was even more formidable; and harnessed self-interest to the daunting task of transforming New England from wilderness to garden. Economics did not replace ethics in some slowly unfolding declension of values. Rather, the ethical demands to develop the wilderness (boosted by practical arguments) prevailed over the ethical demands to leave it alone. Fears of declension, falling off from certain standards, were present from the beginning; so was entrepreneurship. On making money and expanding settlement, the Puritan mind was ambivalent from the outset. The battle within New England culture was not principally chronological, but intellectual and psychological; nor was it waged so much between people of commerce and people of the cloth as between competing halves of the same New England mind.[35]

35. In the last couple of decades, seminary historians and historians of religion have questioned the theory of declension on different, albeit complementary, grounds: they have found it an inadequate description of religion, church membership, and the ministry during the course of the 17th century, just as this author finds it a wanting description of social and economic change. See Hall, "On Common Ground," *WMQ*, 3d Ser., XLIV (1987), 221–226.

II | *Towns*

4 *The Creation of Land Corporations in Towns*

[That launching towns was difficult and expensive work, that some people engaged in this work for profit, that nonresidents played a role in starting new towns—these elements of the town-planting process had a decisive influence on the character of the towns that emerged. For they called into being certain business practices that shaped town institutions long after each town had been planted. The most important of these practices was the formation of societies to hold and dispose of town land.]

Towns began in different ways. Sometimes individuals organized town proprietorships, like the one owning Westerly, and settled single townships. Sometimes they organized land companies, like the Atherton or Sowams companies, and developed great tracts of vacant land. Sometimes older towns launched new towns, like New Roxbury, by developing land granted by the court or by splitting apart and forming offshoots. [The circumstances of town-founding varied widely; but, in each instance, a society of named individuals owned the land, organized the settlement effort, and financed the cost of development.]

These societies are called corporations here even though they lacked corporate charters. For some time in England, the law had allowed enterprises to acquire a corporate character by long usage of corporate powers. In New England, certain enterprises holding court-granted monopolies acted like corporations, although the colonies (reluctant to exercise powers not granted in their charters) did not formally incorporate these entities. The adventurers of the Lynn ironworks, the vintners of Boston, and the undertakers of glassworks all enjoyed the powers of corporations during the 1640s without being incorporated. Harvard College was the only Massachusetts institution that received a charter of incorporation before the provincial period.[1] It was not a bar to corporateness, therefore, that towns lacked formal incorporation. Towns governed themselves, made their own laws, and, most important, owned land. The ownership of common property gave to any entity in England or America the fictitious nature of acting as a single individual, gave to towns on both sides of the ocean a strong corporate identity.[2]

But to say this much is to suggest no more than that towns resembled in their structure the vintner's or an almshouse, that is, were merely capable of corporate behavior without possessing corporate charters. In fact, towns sorted out the economic rights of their members, an undertaking that was vastly more complicated than anything shouldered by a college or a philanthropy. Towns were more complicated, too, than medieval villages. Villages did not need the organizational advantages of corporations, because, as F. W. Maitland put it, "simple arithmetic reigns over the village." Villages were "too automatic to be autonomous, too homogeneous to be highly organized, too deeply immersed in commonness to be clearly corporate." Only when Cambridge, England, became a military and market center did it require a corporate status. Complexity called into being

1. F. W. Maitland, *Township and Borough* (Cambridge, 1898; rpt., 1964), 19–20; Harold J. Berman, *Law and Revolution: The Formation of the Western Legal Tradition* (Cambridge, Mass., 1983), 219; Shaw Livermore, *Early American Land Companies: Their Influence on Corporate Development* (New York, 1939), 17–18, 43; Andrew McFarland Davis, "Corporations in the Days of the Colony," in *American Colonial History* (Cambridge, Mass., 1894), 10–15, 16–34.

2. Historians have long noted the corporate attributes of towns. John Gorham Palfrey, *History of New England during the Stuart Dynasty,* 3 vols. (Boston, 1865; rpt., 1966), II, 14; Herbert L. Osgood, *American Colonies in the Seventeenth Century,* 3 vols. (New York, 1904–1907), I, 461; Livermore, *Early American Land Companies,* 30; Davis, "Corporations in the Days of the Colony," in *American Colonial History,* 13–14; Hendrik Hartog, *Public Property and Private Power: The Corporation of the City of New York in American Law, 1730–1870* (Chapel Hill, N.C., 1983), 179–180; Maitland, *Township and Borough,* 83–84.

corporate structure.[3] In New England the challenges facing town founders were even more daunting than those facing the burgesses of Cambridge, England. Colonists were starting new towns, not just managing older ones suddenly grown urban. A host of organizational tools had to be created: a mechanism to pool the efforts of many people, a principle for raising the money to buy the land and commission the survey, a system for holding and then sharing the land. Above all, founding new towns (unlike governing Cambridge borough) required risk, expense, and travail. In some cases, nonresidents risked their capital and gave their name and time to the enterprise; in others, residents risked their lives and their labor. Whatever their differing commitments, town founders had a special stake, an interest to protect, an investment from which they expected a return. Some system for rewarding town founders had to be created. A means had to be put in place for yoking people's interest to the task—measuring that interest and rewarding and assessing people in proportion to it.

The task of founding towns, so different from the "automatism of village life" on the one hand and the noneconomic duties of a college or charitable organization on the other, called for a complex organization, such as Maitland's borough, but with the additional capacity for harnessing people's initiative and activism and for apportioning a myriad of new rights and duties. It called for combining in a single entity the different features of borough and business corporations. The model for the former existed in the cities of England, and for the latter in the English joint-stock company just then playing such a large role in the commercial expansion of early Stuart England.[4]

3. Maitland, *Township and Borough*, 27, 36, 83–84.

4. It was not until the 18th century, according to Shaw Livermore, that colonists formed land companies with a business motive. In those "truly corporate bodies" of the 18th century, Livermore found the origins of the American corporation. In town proprietorships of the century before, Livermore and others found merely a corporate shell, with the business content—the pursuit of profits—not yet formed (*Early American Land Companies*, 2 n. 2, 6, 7, 8). Only Charles Francis Adams bolted from his colleagues and declared that towns were essentially commercial organizations. But Adams offered only an idea, not an analysis. One later town historian accounted his "charter theory" the "least important" of all the late 19th-century theories about town origins. See Charles Francis Adams et al., *The Genesis of the Massachusetts Town, and the Development of Town-Meeting Government* (Cambridge, Mass., 1892), 7–41; John Fairfield Sly, *Town Government in Massachusetts (1620–1930)* (Cambridge, Mass., 1930), 66.

The principal trouble with Adams's argument was that he portrayed towns as purely

1. English Corporations

Until the fifteenth century, English merchants had conducted enterprise with the help of two common business organizations, guilds and partnerships. Then new mining ventures and foreign trade called for larger quantities of capital than partnerships could provide, and merchants designed the regulated company, an association governed by rules and capable of joint, or corporate, action. Notwithstanding these corporate features, regulated companies did not carry on business activities or pay a return on shares; and their members still acted individually, as merchants always had, in the manner of guild members and partners. Corporate investment and management of business, which so distinguish modern corporate enterprises from medieval ones and whose coming enabled merchants to raise even larger sums of capital, did not appear until 1553, when the first major English joint-stock company was formed, the Russia Company.[5]

Thereafter, joint-stock companies proliferated rapidly. The chief reason for their success was that they provided an investment opportunity to people who had not the inclination or ability to conduct an enterprise (or more than one enterprise) themselves; these companies were thus able to raise, as partnerships and regulated companies had not been, the huge capital in demand during the commercial expansion of the sixteenth and seventeenth centuries. Elizabethan joint-stock ventures were primitive. They kept the number of shares fixed; thus, to raise money companies levied new assessments upon existing shares rather than issued additional shares. These repeated subscriptions so burdened shareholders that men divided their shares into fractions and sold these portions to others. Companies did not, in Elizabethan times, distinguish between capital and dividends. Often they paid for capital expenditures out of revenue that, in a

---

commercial enterprises, ignoring the communal, religious, and other nonbusiness aspects of towns. Moreover, his argument rested upon technical similarities between towns and the Massachusetts Bay Company and did not explore several important town activities, such as the use of shares, the land division system, the taxation system, and the pursuit of profit—the last of which, if anything does, distinguishes businesses from other kinds of organizations. Adams confined himself to a static comparison of towns to the Bay Company, without attempting to distinguish classes, find conflict, or detect change through time.

5. William Robert Scott, *The Constitution and Finance of English, Scottish, and Irish Joint-Stock Companies to 1720*, 3 vols. (New York, 1951), I, 2–14, 17.

modern company, would have gone to dividends, and often they paid dividends out of capital assets. Legal incorporation was rare. Voting was by hands, not shares, in nearly all the sixteenth- and early seventeenth-century joint-stock companies.[6]

But as time went by, merchants refined certain of these features. In the seventeenth century, they assigned management to a governor and his assistants. They began keeping a permanent stock, instead of raising new capital for each new voyage or venture. This tendency toward permanent stocks was hastened by the plantation companies, the members of which, speculating in the gradual rise of land values and agricultural return from the colonies, took a long-term attitude toward investment. During the Restoration, major companies ceased voting by hands and voted by shares. In the 1690s, joint-stock companies had so proliferated that an open market in shares sprang up in London.[7]

It was a long distance from the joint-stock companies of England to the wilderness of New England. But the plantation companies, those corporations created in the early seventeenth century to colonize America, spanned the distance, carrying English business experience to the New World. They also brought a special view of land, which to them was not so much a time-honored place as a transferable asset: a dividend to be paid to shareholders, a commodity to be sold to settlers. Two of these companies, well known to New England colonists, were the Plymouth Company and the Massachusetts Bay Company.

Several months before the Separatists left Leiden, they drafted an agreement just as important as the more famous Mayflower Compact that followed. This was a business covenant, establishing financial arrangements between the Pilgrims and their backers in London. According to its terms, the "planters," as the Pilgrims were called, were to contribute their labor toward building a profitable venture in the New World, and the "adventurers," as the backers were called, were to contribute their capital. Each planter received one share for venturing himself and an additional share for every ten pounds he ventured; the adventurers remaining in London bought stock at the rate of ten pounds a share. At the end of seven years, the capital assets belonging to the company—lands, buildings, and livestock—

6. Theodore K. Rabb, *Enterprise and Empire: Merchant and Gentry Investment in the Expansion of England, 1575–1630* (Cambridge, Mass., 1967), 26–31; Scott, *Constitution of Joint-Stock Companies*, I, 44–46, 60–61, 163, 227.

7. Scott, *Constitution of Joint-Stock Companies*, I, 150–154, 246–247, 440–443.

as well as the profits that had accumulated in the company "treasury" were to be "equally" divided among the "whole company" of planters and adventurers. "Equally" meant here, as it later meant in many town covenants, "equal to the number of shares one possessed," not "equal to one another's portion."[8] (Four years before, the Virginia company, whose experience was known to the Plymouth adventurers, had pegged shares at £12 10s. and ordered land distributed at one hundred acres per share. Other plantation companies, even before the Virginia company, also paid out "dividends" in land.)[9]

The founders of the Massachusetts Bay Company, some of whom had invested in the Plymouth Company, devised similar financial arrangements.[10] They, too, pledged land as a dividend, in their case at the rate of two hundred acres for every fifty pounds subscribed. When the colonists went to America, the joint stock was dissolved, but business functions did not all cease. For many years, as late as the 1650s, the General Court was still granting parcels of land as "dividents" to adventurers on account of their stock subscriptions. This is not to say that the Massachusetts Bay Company was more a business than a commonwealth; it was not. Nonetheless, a joint-stock company launched the Bay Colony, and for a generation after its founding the colony continued to grant land as a dividend to shareholders, effortlessly merging colony and company business.[11]

8. William Bradford, *Bradford's History "Of Plimoth Plantation"* (Boston, 1898), 56–58 (where the financial agreement is reprinted). Scott is the authority for saying that "equally" meant division by shares; many towns, discussed later, assigned the same meaning to this term (Scott, *Constitution of Joint-Stock Companies,* II, 306–309).

9. Scott, *Constitution of Joint-Stock Companies,* II, 242–243, 255–256.

10. Frances Rose-Troup, *The Massachusetts Bay Company and Its Predecessors* (New York, 1930), 1–9.

11. Scott, *Constitution of Joint-Stock Companies,* II, 312–315, 315n; Rose-Troup, *Massachusetts Bay Company,* 98, 102–103; Massachusetts, *Records of the Company of the Massachusetts Bay, to the Embarkation of Winthrop and His Associates for New England as Contained in the First Volume of the Archives of the Commonwealth of Massachusetts* (AAS, *Transactions, Collections,* III [Boston, 1857]), cxxiii, 41–42; Melville Egleston, *The Land System of the New England Colonies,* Johns Hopkins University Studies in Historical and Political Science, 4th Ser., nos. 11–12 (Baltimore, 1886), 18–19. Another example of the overlap of company and colony was the offices of governor and assistants. The men holding these jobs functioned as mayor and assistants of a borough, but the offices themselves were vestiges of the joint-stock company that preceded the Bay Colony. See David Thomas Konig, "English Legal Change and the Origins of Local Government in Northern Massachusetts," in Bruce C. Daniels, ed., *Town and County: Essays on the*

Some of the early colonists, having been shareholders and even officers of the Plymouth Company, the Dorchester Company, the Massachusetts Bay Company, and other plantation companies, were familiar with these corporate practices. The leading founder of New Haven, Theophilus Eaton, had been deputy governor of the East India Company. New England's first leaders needed no coaching in how to put together a business corporation. Nor was it a great logical leap to apply the principles for settling a colony to settling a town. Many problems, particularly the question of holding and dividing land, were identical. The very first towns of New England, which were founded, not by colonial legislatures, but directly by the plantation companies, were governed by the same business principles governing plantation companies.[12]

Plymouth was such a town. The Plymouth Company covenant called for the distribution of capital assets according to shares at the conclusion of seven years. But before the seven years elapsed, the joint stock dissolved, and the planters in Plymouth bought out their partners in London and took ownership of the lands, buildings, livestock, and other assets. Breaking their connections with the adventurers, however, did not require the Pilgrims to break with the principles that had governed the former joint-stock company. Though they expanded the number of shareholders, the Pilgrims still limited the body of men with land rights to those possessing shares. Though they divided land among many people, they divided it according to shares: twenty acres per share. Though they eventually terminated this share-based land system (in 1640), Plymouth town continued for many years to restrict participants in its land divisions to those with an "interest" in undivided lands.[13]

Salem, the next town founded as the outpost of an English company, had a similar beginning. The Dorchester Company started this village in 1624,

---

Structure of Local Government in the American Colonies (Middletown, Conn., 1978), 30–31.

12. Bradford, *Bradford's History,* 52–71; Rose-Troup, *Massachusetts Bay Company,* 40–41; Edmund S. Morgan, *The Puritan Dilemma: The Story of John Winthrop* (Boston, 1958), 36, 50–51; Benjamin Trumbull, *A Complete History of Connecticut . . . ,* 2 vols. (New Haven, Conn., 1818), I, 99–100. The first English settlements in New England were fishing villages erected on the Maine coast by English ventures. But their records are not extant, most of them were not organized towns, and few of them endured.

13. Bradford, *Bradford's History,* 240–244, 254–259, 273, 444–446; Plymouth, Mass., *Records of the Town of Plymouth,* 3 vols. (Plymouth, Mass., 1889–1903), I, 4–6, 36–37, 54, 62–70. It is not clear how one came by an interest in later years.

then conveyed it to the Massachusetts Bay Company when the Dorchester Company dissolved. In 1629, Governor Endicott divided land at Salem among adventurers according to the capital they had subscribed. Once the town emerged with its own identity, separate from the company and colony, Salem began dividing land according to the number of people belonging to each family. Still, Salem, like Plymouth, began as a company town (as did Dover, New Hampshire, another of New England's first towns), its land divided as dividends among shareholders. These were the first examples colonists had of holding wilderness land in town-sized tracts in America.[14]

When the colonists set about owning, settling, and dividing vacant lands, therefore, they had before their eyes the unavoidable example of the plantation companies. They followed that example, even in nonspeculative settlement ventures. Town founders might not be seeking profit in every case— certainly that was not the primary motive of the founders of Warwick, Rhode Island—but they nevertheless, even in Warwick, apportioned rights and responsibilities according to people's interest and acted through a corporate structure resembling the English joint-stock company. Whether it was a large land company, such as the Million Purchase, or a single town proprietorship, such as Mendon, the parallels between New England land associations and the English joint-stock company were striking. Like the stock company, land corporations limited their beneficiaries to those with shares, held the number of shares fairly constant, fixed the value of shares proportional to investment, and distributed land, raised revenue, and sometimes even counted votes according to shares. Like English plantation companies, both land companies and towns merged public and private affairs, the community and the corporation. Both served public interests while producing private profits. Both treated land as a reward for investment. Both provided an investment opportunity to individuals who could not devote their full attention to the enterprise of town-founding. Just as English joint-stocks attracted gentry investment in mercantile ventures, so did the corporate structure of New England towns enable city-dwellers to invest in wilderness settlements without becoming pioneers.

14. Sidney Perley, *The History of Salem, Massachusetts,* 3 vols. (Salem, Mass., 1924–1928), I, 310, 460–465; Joseph B. Felt, *Annals of Salem,* 2 vols. (Salem, Mass., 1845–1849), I, 94–95, 177, 182–183; Jeremy Belknap, *The History of New-Hampshire* (Dover, N.H., 1831), 3–4, 428; Charles E. Clark, *The Eastern Frontier: The Settlement of Northern New England, 1610–1763* (New York, 1970), 16–20.

No two towns were the same. But every group of town founders had to face the problems of organizing individuals, financing costs, dividing land, and attracting participants. The business corporation, patterned after the plantation companies and the first company towns, answered these needs. Towns had other institutions and other means of regulating people's behavior, from churches to the common customs of settlers who, in some cases, all hailed from the same English shire. The sum of town life cannot be added up in the business characteristics of New England towns, but neither will that sum be total without adding those characteristics. For it was through the land corporation that town founders pooled the efforts of many individuals, held the land in trust for participants, raised capital, attracted participants with the promise of reward for their risk, and, by restricting corporate membership, limited the number of people entitled to have land and have a say in the management of the town. Creating a town was an arduous endeavor, but people united by a network of obligations and rewards were equal to the task.

11. Town Covenants

The first event in the life of a town corporation was the agreement that created it. Of the sixty-some towns surveyed here, about half had agreements that have survived or are conclusively evidenced (see Appendix 4). If all early town records were extant, however, they might well include a founding agreement for every town established.

These agreements took many forms. Sometimes they appeared in town covenants, as in the case of Lancaster. Other times, when there was no town covenant, they appeared in what were called "articles of association," as in Springfield's case. And on other occasions, they appeared in initial "town orders," as in Warwick's case. But whatever they were called, these agreements had the effect of organizing a group of individuals into a society for the purpose of holding, dividing, and developing a tract of land.

In most cases, agreements bound subscribers to perform certain common tasks: dividing the land, settling their lots, paying rates, and so forth. In the Hadley covenant, the founders agreed to settle the town within a year, to sell their land only to such as the town might approve, and to divide their common land according to the contribution that each founder made to the purchase of the Indian title and other expenses. In the Andover covenant, subscribers pledged to give to "every Inhabitant whome they received as a Townsman" a house lot with rights to undivided lands. In the Woodstock case, the proprietors agreed to split the town in two, giving half to people who wanted to move there and the other half to those who bound themselves to support the "goers."[15]

In other towns, agreements bound a small group of landowners on the one hand and settlers on the other. In 1640, Roger Ludlow bought a tract of land in Connecticut. Ten years later, he entered into "articles" of agreement with Nathaniel Eli, acting as agent for those wishing to settle the tract. By the terms of this agreement, the settlers agreed to start a town, procure a minister, and settle thirty families; and Ludlow agreed to surrender his title, reserving for himself a share of the town's land "to the vallue of 200 lb." This was the founding agreement of Norwalk, Connecticut. Similarly, in 1680, four men bought a tract of land from Plymouth Colony and drew up "Grand Articles" between themselves and those proposing to settle, spelling out how to share the tract and finance the town. This agreement was the beginning of Bristol, Rhode Island.[16]

In many cases, the covenant or agreement was drafted and subscribed by people who lived in the town or were about to move to the town. Such was the case with the Hadley, Dedham, Andover, Warwick, and many other agreements. But in other cases, nonresidents made these agreements. In 1669, a committee sitting in Cambridge drafted the "orrderrs and Agrreements . . . which arre laid as foundation principles and Rules concerning the affayres of" Worcester. Cambridge was where these orders were drafted because that was where Daniel Gookin, head of the Worcester committee, happened to live. Other towns—Northfield and Sudbury in Massachusetts, Waterbury in Connecticut—were launched when committees of the General Court framed initial orders and admitted individuals to the group entitled to town privileges, even though members of such committees never moved to the town.[17]

15. Sylvester Judd, *History of Hadley, Including the Early History of Hatfield, South Hadley, Amherst, and Granby, Massachusetts* (Springfield, Mass., 1905), 3, 6, 12–13; Philip J. Greven, *Four Generations: Population, Land, and Family in Colonial Andover, Massachusetts* (Ithaca, N.Y., 1970), 45; General Court Grant to Roxbury [which owned Woodstock], Oct. 10, 1683, CXII, 342–343, Mass. Archives; Holmes Ammidown, *Historical Collections . . .* , 2d ed., 2 vols. (New York, 1877), I, 259–281.

16. Edwin Hall, ed., *The Ancient Historical Records of Norwalk, Conn., with a Plan of the Ancient Settlement, and of the Town in 1847* (New York, 1865), 13, 32–33; Wilfred H. Munro, *History of Bristol, Rhode Island: The Story of the Mount Hope Lands . . .* (Providence, R.I., 1880), 53, 60–61, 94–96.

17. Judd, *History of Hadley*, 3, 6, 12–13; Dedham, Mass., *The Early Records of the*

Sometimes the people making the founding rules were nonresidents, not because they were members of a General Court committee, but because the township grant was bestowed upon an older town and it was a committee of the town meeting of the older town that drafted rules for the new town. Such was the case with Deerfield and Medfield, which were owned and launched by Dedham, and Woodstock, which was launched by Roxbury.[18]

In still other cases, the authors of agreements were nonresidents because they were businessmen with no intention of becoming pioneers. In the early 1660s, the Newport "adventurers" who launched Westerly drew up "articles of agreement" bestowing "the same privileges with ourselves, unto all those names are underwritten, according to their proportion of land in the aforesaid purchase" and requiring all subscribers to pay common charges "according to the proportion of land they have." Swansea, in Plymouth Colony, was also started by nonresident proprietors, who in 1652 framed "the first originall agreement of the proprietors . . . concerning each one's part in the lands at Sowams."[19]

In all these examples, the framers of an agreement were owners of a single tract. In other cases, the agreement was framed by the owners of several tracts. Those who claimed the land of Billerica, Massachusetts, derived their titles from several sources: from grants made by the church of Cambridge, the town of Cambridge, and the General Court. After settlement

Town . . . , 6 vols. (Dedham, Mass., 1886–1936), III, 2–5, 18, 24 (hereafter cited as *Dedham Town Records*); Greven, *Four Generations,* 45; Warwick, R.I., Town Records: First Book, 1647–1667 (typescript of original, 1911), 63–70, LC (hereafter cited as Warwick Town Records, LC); Petition to the General Court, 1665, XLV, 145–146, Mass. Archives; Franklin P. Rice, ed., *Records of the Proprietors of Worcester, Massachusetts* (Worcester Society of Antiquity, *Collections,* III [Worcester, Mass., 1881]), 11–19; J. H. Temple and George Sheldon, *A History of the Town of Northfield, Massachusetts . . .* (Albany, N.Y., 1875), 62–65; Sumner Chilton Powell, *Puritan Village: The Formation of a New England Town* (Middletown, Conn., 1963), 79–87; Mattatuck Petition, Oct. 9, 1673, Town and Lands, I, 162–164, Conn. Archives; Henry Bronson, *The History of Waterbury, Connecticut . . .* (Waterbury, Conn., 1858), 4–9.

18. George Sheldon, *A History of Deerfield, Mass. . . .* 2 vols., (Deerfield, Mass., 1895–1896), I, 2–3, 7, 14, 39–40; William S. Tilden, *History of the Town of Medfield, Massachusetts, 1650–1886 . . .* (Boston, 1887), 37–40; Court Grant to Roxbury, Oct. 10, 1683, CXII, 342–343; Court Confirmation of Woodstock, CXIII, 14–17, Mass. Archives; Ammidown, *Historical Collections,* I, 257–262.

19. Elisha R. Potter, Jr., *Early History of Narragansett* (RIHS, *Collections,* III [Providence, R.I., 1835]), 250–254; Frederick Denison, *Westerly (Rhode Island), and Its Witnesses . . . 1626–1876 . . .* (Providence, R.I., 1878), 47–51; Thomas William Bicknell, *A History of Barrington, Rhode Island* (Providence, R.I., 1898), 58–59.

began, the various owners pooled their holdings and established rules for admitting new owners, taxing inhabitants, and dividing their land. With this agreement (of 1658), they terminated their status as tenants in severalty, began their careers as tenants in common, and formed a de facto land corporation to hold the land of Billerica. The same combining of tracts through formal agreement led to the establishment of Dunstable.[20]

In Dunstable, as in most towns, agreements followed the General Court grant but preceded actual settlement. But elsewhere it was after settlement had commenced that towns passed bylaws with the same effect as covenants and articles of association. In Warwick, Rhode Island, four years after settlement (in 1647), the "purchasers of the plantation" made "Towne Orders" that kept disposal of lands in their own hands, set land prices, erected an admissions procedure for "inhabitants," and erected an even more rigorous admissions procedure for purchasers. In Cambridge, Massachusetts, where there probably had never been a town covenant, the town passed an order in 1636 restricting the undivided lands to those householders formally approved by the town and also naming the privileged householders. In Salisbury, in 1655, a group of settlers separated from the rest and "agreed and concluded that these men here after mentioned are accounted present Inhabitants and Commoners here in the new Town," which acquired the name of Amesbury.[21]

But whether agreements preceded or followed settlement, whether they appeared in covenants or town orders, they all accomplished the same purpose: to organize subscribers into a society and to lay down rules for owning, dividing, and developing the tract people owned together.

III. The Separation of Church and Corporation

Since historians have often emphasized the importance of religion in town-founding, it is worth adding here that these corporations were secular organizations; they were not churches or church con-

20. Henry A. Hazen, *History of Billerica, Massachusetts* . . . (Boston, 1883), 31–32; Elias Nason, *A History of the Town of Dunstable, Massachusetts* . . . (Boston, 1877), 6–10, 16.

21. Warwick Town Records, 63–70, LC; Cambridge, Mass., *The Records of the Town of Cambridge (Formerly Newtowne) Massachusetts, 1630–1703* . . . (Cambridge, Mass.,

gregations. [Of all the towns studied here, in only one did a person have to be a church member in order to be admitted to the land corporation; everywhere else, land corporations imposed no religious tests on their members.[22] That is, the memberships of the land corporation and of the church congregation, while overlapping, were not coterminous.]

The Dedham church had 171 members and had, moreover, baptized 199 children of members by 1653; in that year, 76 people participated in a land division. Already by 1635 one-quarter of those dividing land in Boston were non–church members. Ninety-four Springfield residents had church seats in 1663; the next year only 74 people appeared on an "inhabitants" list entitling men to town privileges. Of those pledging to support the town of Sudbury in return for their land grants, 60 percent were not church members in 1640.[23] These numerical discrepancies followed from the different principles upon which church and land corporation were founded.

1901), 17–19; Joseph Merrill, *History of Amesbury and Merrimac* (Haverhill, Mass., 1880; rpt., 1978), 53–55.

22. The town was Milford, Conn., where the town "Voted, that the earth is the Lord's and the fulness thereof; voted, that the earth is given to the Saints; voted, that we are the Saints" (Charles Thornton Davis, "Some Thoughts on Early Colonial Development," MHS, *Proceedings*, LXIV [1930–1932], 509). Although some authors take Milford to be more or less typical of New England towns founded in the 17th century, I have not found that to be the case. Nowhere else have I found a religious qualification for members of the land corporation. (It is also possible that the tale of the Milford vote is apocryphal.) The most thorough discussion of Milford is Leonard W. Labaree, *Milford, Connecticut: The Early Development of a Town as Shown in Its Land Records*, Connecticut Tercentenary Commission, no. 13 (New Haven, Conn., 1933). William Haller, Jr., also discusses this unusual town (*The Puritan Frontier: Town-Planting in New England Colonial Development, 1630–1660* [New York, 1951], 89–90).

23. *Dedham Town Records*, II, 13–43, III, 211–212; Darrett B. Rutman, *Winthrop's Boston: Portrait of a Puritan Town, 1630–1640* (Chapel Hill, N.C., 1965), 142–143; Henry M. Burt, *The First Century of the History of Springfield: The Official Records from 1636 to 1736*, 2 vols. (Springfield, Mass., 1898–1899), I, 126–129, II, 77; Powell, *Puritan Village*, 85–87. Other examples are Roxbury (Boston, Registry Dept., *Roxbury Land Records [A Report of the Record Commissioners . . . (Sixth Report)]*, 2d ed. [Boston, 1884], 4–5; Charles Mayo Ellis, *The History of Roxbury Town* [Boston, 1847], 16); Haverhill (George Wingate Chase, *The History of Haverhill, Massachusetts, from Its First Settlement, in 1640, to the Year 1860* [Haverhill, Mass., 1861], 60); Lancaster (Samuel Eliot Morison, "The Plantation of Nashaway—an Industrial Experiment," Colonial Society of Massachusetts, *Transactions*, XXVII [1927–1930], 213); and New Haven (Charles J. Hoadly, ed., *Records of the Colony and Plantation of New Haven, from 1638 to 1649* [Hartford, Conn., 1857], 13–14, 49–51, 112).

Land corporations were formed to develop the town and to repay in land shares those who contributed their money, labor, and time toward that end. Often land shares were owned by nonresidents, and where this happened— in two-thirds of the towns—the incidence of nonresident ownership precluded the possibility that land corporations and church congregations could have had identical memberships (see Appendix 7). The high incidence of residents without land shares also made it unlikely that congregations and corporations would have identical memberships in the many towns (three-quarters) where nonshareholders appeared (see Appendix 6). The universal exclusion of servants and slaves from land corporations and their frequent inclusion in congregations created yet more differences in the composition of the two bodies.[24]

This separateness of proprietors does not mean that town founders formed land corporations without any regard for religious considerations. On the contrary, while town covenants dwelt on organizational matters, some of them also mentioned "promulgation of the Gospell" as the goal of settlement and asserted the founders' wish to receive only "godly men" and men "of peaceable conversation" in their midst. Some town covenants mentioned religious goals while others—the agreements of Woodstock, Swansea, Waterbury, Attleborough, Westerly, and other towns—neglected religion altogether.[25] [Some covenants had both religious and business clauses, though historians have tended to emphasize the purely religious and communal meanings of town covenants.] For example, in Dedham's

24. One can also surmise a difference in composition in those towns where the minister's rate was levied in a different manner from town rates that fell exclusively upon shareholders. See Samuel A. Green, ed., *The Town Records of Groton, Massachusetts: 1662–1678* (Groton, Mass., 1879 [rpt. in Green, ed., *Pamphlets on History of Groton* (n.p., n.d.)]), 28; Henry S. Nourse, ed., *The Early Records of Lancaster, Massachusetts, 1643–1725* (Lancaster, Mass., 1884), 27–28, 140–141. For more on this numerical issue, see below, Chapter 7, n. 40.

25. The Lancaster, Medfield, and Northfield covenants contained clauses expressing religious and communal intentions of founders. Others omitted such clauses. There is little point debating whether the provenance of town covenants was religious or civil; function matters more than origins. It bears pointing out, nonetheless, that in drawing up town covenants, town promoters had not only the example of plantation companies, which used covenants and agreements as founding constitutions, but also of longstanding urban law. The medieval urban covenant (whether implied or expressed) formed a community that was, like the land societies formed by these New England covenants, a legal, corporate, secular body—not a religious body. Berman, *Law and Revolution*, 393, 395.

covenant, the subscribers bound themselves to practice Christian love, to accept only those of "peaceable conversation," and to arbitrate all differences. From these provisions, some have logically deduced that Dedham's founders were devoted to building a Christian community.[26] These provisions were followed, however, by a practical-minded passage outlining the relationships between land ownership and ratepaying that established Dedham's land corporation. The covenant provided, "That every man that now or at any time heerafter shall have Lotts in our said Towne shall paye his share in all such Rates of money and charges as shall be imposed upon him Rateably in proportion with other men" as well as become subject to such "orders and constitutions" as are made. Dedham's founders elaborated these relationships by passing a series of orders obligating landowners to pay town rates, giving the town permission to veto a lot purchaser for both financial and sumptuary reasons, regulating valuable water rights, and establishing detailed rules for apportioning upland, swamp lots, and meadow lots. These orders physically preceded the covenant in their placement in the town records and may have preceded it chronologically. Dedham's founders certainly wished to establish a Christian community, and perhaps even a peasant utopia; but the subject they lavished detail upon in their founding documents was Dedham's financial arrangements, and the first organization they formed in town was the land corporation, which preceded the forming of a church by two years.[27]

To found a town, people needed a secular, business organization for the purpose of holding, managing, and developing wilderness land, and this organization was distinct from the church and congregation. Not only was it distinct, in the vast majority of cases the land organization also preceded the formation of the church. In only twelve of fifty-three towns—fewer than one-quarter—was the church formed simultaneously with the commencement of settlement. In the other forty-one towns, churches followed town launchings by at least a year. In some cases, settlers did not get around

26. Kenneth A. Lockridge, *A New England Town, the First Hundred Years: Dedham, Massachusetts, 1636–1736* (New York, 1970), 1–78 (and 4–7 for his discussion of the covenant itself). Haller also discusses the religious significance of covenants (*Puritan Frontier,* 55).

27. *Dedham Town Records,* III, 2–5, 20–24. Dedham's first eight orders were found stitched in the town records between the petition for the township grant and the covenant, according to the records' editor (III, 4n). For more on the founding of this town, see Conclusion, below.

to gathering a church for five, ten, or twenty years after a town was settled.[28]

In some towns, founders formed their land corporation before the church was formed; in others, they settled or placed settlers in the town before the church was formed; and in the majority of cases, they both formed their land corporation and settled the town before the church was gathered. Though the incompleteness of records bars certainty, probably in none of the forty-one towns did founders even procure a part-time minister to preach to the churchless settlers during the first year of settlement.

To be sure, pastors founded some well-known towns—Boston, Hartford, New Haven, Hadley, Rowley, Andover, Exeter, and Milford. But to concentrate on these towns is to warp understanding of the founding circumstances of most seventeenth-century towns. Westerly, Rhode Island, had an association of resident and nonresident landowners in 1661, but it did not have its first church until 1708. The founders of Dunstable formed a land corporation in 1673 but did not organize a church until 1685 (and then it only had six members). Settlement began in Northfield in 1673, was suspended in 1675 on account of the Indian war, resumed in 1685, was suspended again in 1690, and resumed on a permanent footing in 1714. Yet not till 1718 did Northfield organize a church and ordain a minister. Connecticut granted the township of Middletown in 1651, settlers arrived there in the 1650s, and the first church was organized in 1668. The list of such towns goes on: four times longer than the list of towns with churches at their outset (see Appendix 2).

[Nor is it accurate to suppose that towns were founded by churches in the first two decades of colonial history and by other means in later decades, that the chronological relationship of land corporations and churches underwent its own declension.] For even in the 1630s and 1640s, settlement preceded the establishment of churches more often than churches preceded settlement. Fur traders established a trading post at Westfield in the 1630s, grantees took up land there in the 1650s and 1660s, the General Court granted a township there in 1662, the town was named and began to govern itself in 1669, and yet the settlers of Westfield went without the

28. See Appendix 2, also Chapter 7, wherein is discussed the Puritan propensity to compartmentalize reality, to pursue widely differing, even conflicting, goals at the same time. This intellectual habit was probably a precondition of the Puritans' ability to create several separate organizations with overlapping but different memberships, all existing in the same, small New England towns.

services of a preacher until 1669 and did not gather a church until 1679—more than forty years after first settlement. In Braintree, individuals received grants in the early 1630s, but the first church was not formed until 1639. In the 1630s, Dorchester granted land in the tract that became Milton, but the latter community did not have a church until 1678. Fur traders arrived in the Pequot country in the 1630s, Stonington's town charter was drafted in 1654, and yet a church was not formed until 1674. Settlers or land corporations preceded churches in a total of nineteen towns during the 1630s and 1640s, more places than had churches from the very beginning. Settlers arrived in Medford when John Winthrop arrived in America, yet that town did not gather a church until 1712.

Even when town founders required voters to be church members, still they created a separate land corporation, membership in which was saddled with no such requirement. It was a group of Puritans under the pastor John Davenport who founded New Haven in 1639. Their commitment to orthodoxy was so deep that they made church membership a condition of voting, an unusual requirement outside Massachusetts, was so stern that they reprimanded Milford, no nest of heretics, for relaxing a similar voting condition there. Yet even in religious New Haven an organization of "planters" separate from the church held the colony (later town) land, and this organization called the meeting to frame the political constitution of New Haven in 1639. During that meeting, one of the planters opposed to creating a religious test for voting declared that the "free planters ought nott to give this [political] power out of their hands." His motion was defeated, the religiously based franchise was passed, and the political constitution completed. Only then did John Davenport take over the meeting and gather a church. In other words, before the settlers organized a church, before they organized a political system, they had already organized an association of planters: landholders who, as years went by, closely regulated their membership and held exclusive title to New Haven's land.[29] That this was true of New Haven, peopled by thoroughly religious colonists, attests to the priority of land corporations in even the earliest, most Puritan communities.

Several different theories might explain the delay in church-gathering.

29. Hoadly, ed., *Records of the Colony of New Haven*, 11–15, 27. See "Voting," Chapter 5, for discussion of the relationship between the land corporation and the franchise. For evidence of the exclusivity of New Haven's planter class, see Hoadly, ed., *Records of the Colony of New Haven*, 49–51, 91–93, 112, 115, 200, 213, 222.

One historian has suggested that church formations were slowed by the lack of money with which to hire ministers.[30] Another has suggested that the delay in church-forming was a symptom, not of its secondary importance, but, on the contrary, of the greater care that town founders bestowed on religious as opposed to secular matters; they took longer on forming churches than on anything else, because churches mattered more than anything else.[31] A more obvious explanation is that although some things could wait, forming the land corporation could not. Founders could do without churches, meetinghouses, and ministers, but they could not live on the land without purchasing it, organizing themselves as tenants in common, and creating a system for sharing costs and dividing the property—without, that is, joining together in an association whose first purpose was, not to promote religion or realize communal ideals, but to perform the practical work of starting a wilderness settlement.

30. Bruce C. Daniels, *The Connecticut Town: Growth and Development, 1635–1700* (Middletown, Conn., 1979), 95. Daniels concluded that in the Connecticut towns started between 1650 and 1734 there was an average lag of 6.3 years between town incorporation and creation of ecclesiastical societies, and that in the colony's first 11 towns the two events were virtually simultaneous.

31. Communication from T. D. Bozeman, Nov. 25, 1985. I am indebted to Professor Bozeman for his careful reading of my MS and his numerous helpful suggestions.

5

The Use
of Shares

1. Dividing Land

After creating corporations, perhaps the most important activity that occupied founders was distributing the land. Towns could divide land many ways. They could distribute it according to an individual's wealth, prestige, usefulness, family size, or ability to use the land. Or they could distribute land equally. Rather than divide land in any of these manners, most towns apportioned it according to shares.[1]

All towns differentiated between rights to the undivided land and simple land grants. The former entitled one to share in repeated land divisions, and the latter entitled one merely to receive a single, usually small, piece of property. Sometimes the land divided to a person on account of his shares was called his "accommodation." In other towns, this land was called his "allotment." The land bestowed in a once-in-a-lifetime grant was called a "grant," "gift," or land granted "at the town's courtesy." As Lancaster's

---

1. In this study, the term "shares" often appears. It is here employed in a business sense, meaning proportions of interest in a commercial undertaking. "Share" can also mean "portions" or "parts," but that is not the sense intended here. The distinction is important. In a business, shares are fixed by investment. They are unchangeable proportions (unchangeable, that is, unless investment is either increased or withdrawn), signifying claims on company assets. Liabilities are measured in proportion to them. In the looser sense of the term, shares are merely portions that can be determined by any number of methods. Changeable, unrelated to investment, they measure whatever people decide they should measure. They are not fixed by one's interest and are not necessarily connected to any notion of liability. In towns, colonists thought of shares in the stricter sense. They apportioned land and raised revenue according to the fixed proportions of interest that each inhabitant held in the land corporation. This business use of shares defined inhabitants' financial relation to towns, made inhabitants akin to shareholders, and accented the commercial character of town institutions.

founders explained in that town's division rules, "We doe not heereby prejudice or Barr the Plantation from Accomodateing any man by Gifft of Land (which proply are not Allottme*ts:*)."[2] Confusion seldom arose over whether towns were dividing land among shareholders or were granting land to nonshareholders.

The method of distributing land was in each town the subject of carefully drawn rules, often called the "rules of division," which varied from town to town. Many towns drew up these procedures at the time of the first division of pasturage rights. Cambridge, for example, apportioned future land divisions according to "cow commons," the number of cows each individual could place on the common. Rowley allocated land according to one's "cow gates," perhaps derived from the length of common fence each person was responsible for maintaining. Woburn allotted land by "herbidge."[3]

Elsewhere the size of the first land grants determined the proportions of all future land divisions. Haverhill, Andover, and other towns set future allotments according to the size of house lots, usually the first lands granted. Henceforth a person in these towns with a two-acre house lot might draw six acres of upland, one with a three-acre house lot would draw nine acres of upland, and so on. In Sudbury, the size of the first meadow lots determined the size of other lots. In Groton, the first land grants gave rise to "acre-rights," the unit that measured all future allotments.[4] Whether

2. Henry S. Nourse, ed., *The Early Records of Lancaster, Massachusetts, 1643–1725* (Lancaster, Mass., 1884), 29.

3. Cambridge, Mass., *The Register Book of the Lands and Houses in the "New Towne" and the Town of Cambridge, with the Records of the Proprietors of the Common Lands . . .* (Cambridge, Mass., 1896), 144–148, 160–165 (cited hereafter as *Cambridge Proprietors' Records*); Rowley, Mass., *The Early Records of the Town of Rowley, Massachusetts, 1639–1672* (Rowley, Mass., 1894), 54, 75, 119–127; Samuel Sewall, *The History of Woburn, Middlesex County, Mass. . . .* (Boston, 1868), 36–37.

4. George Wingate Chase, *The History of Haverhill, Massachusetts, from Its First Settlement, in 1640, to the Year 1860* (Haverhill, Mass., 1861), 62; Philip J. Greven, *Four Generations: Population, Land, and Family in Colonial Andover, Massachusetts* (Ithaca, N.Y., 1970), 46, 52n; Sumner Chilton Powell, *Puritan Village: The Formation of a New England Town* (Middletown, Conn., 1963), 85, 121; Sudbury Petitions, 1708, CXIII, 441–449, Mass. Archives; Samuel A. Green, ed., *An Account of the Early Land-Grants of Groton, Massachusetts* (Groton, Mass., 1879 [rpt. in Green, ed., *Pamphlets on History of Groton* (n.p., n.d.)]), 5–6. Variety is the most striking thing about New England towns, reducing the value of any generalization about nearly every aspect of town life. See Commentary for Table 6, in John Frederick Martin, "Entrepreneurship and the Founding of New England Towns: The Seventeenth Century" (Ph.D. diss., Harvard University, 1985).

house lots or meadow lots or acre-rights, in these towns the number of acres contained in each person's first lot, in proportion to all acres granted at that time, became one's share of the total, undivided land.

These were only some of the yardsticks used by towns to apportion land; there were many others. Upon what principles did towns design these yardsticks? How did inhabitants determine the size of each person's first lots or pasturage, which, in turn, fixed people's shares? Of the towns covered in this survey, three-quarters leave evidence about their land division systems. In two-fifths (nineteen) of those, the size of each inhabitant's initial investment in the town determined the size of his land share. In other words, individuals literally purchased shares in the town, which then repaid them in dividends of land.[5]

The largest initial expense in founding towns was usually the purchase of the land from the Indians; so in many of these nineteen towns, the proportion of purchase money that one contributed determined one's share size. Land division according to purchase contribution was most common in Connecticut. Hartford, Lebanon, Waterbury, Wethersfield, and Windsor all divided land in this way. Wethersfield settlers subscribed to a common fund, out of which they purchased the land from Indians. They then apportioned allotments in the Great Meadow according to the size of their subscriptions. Later, when the town divided the Great West Field, each shareholder received three times whatever he had received in the Great Meadow. When the town divided the Naubuc Farms tract, each one received twice what he had received in the Great West Field, and so on. In this way, one's initial purchase contribution had the effect of purchasing shares that ever after determined the size of one's land draw. Other towns devised similar schemes.[6]

5. Those last towns (19) were Dunstable, Hadley, Lancaster, Northfield, Rowley, Salem, Woodstock, Hartford, Lebanon, Waterbury, Wethersfield, Windsor, Attleborough, Bristol, Plymouth, Swansea, Providence, Warwick, Westerly. See these towns in Commentary for Table 6, Martin, "Entrepreneurship."

If one imagines the town land system as egalitarian or even utilitarian, this evidence is surprising. But if one observes that the Massachusetts General Court as late as 1650 was still granting land as a "proportn for four hundred pounds Adventured, and layd out in the Comon Stocke" of the Bay Company, it is not so surprising. Petition of Thomas Dudley and Increase Nowell in behalf of Isaac Johnson's estate, c. 1650, XLV, esp. 16, Mass. Archives.

6. Dorothy Deming, *The Settlement of Connecticut Towns* (New Haven, Conn., 1933), 8–9; Charles M. Andrews, *The River Towns of Connecticut: A Study of Wethersfield, Hartford, and Windsor,* Johns Hopkins University Studies in Historical and Political

In towns launched by other towns, town founders also divided land according to investment, but in a roundabout way. In 1686, the town of Roxbury voted to apportion the north half of Woodstock "according to each man's assessment per head and estate, in the country rates." This scheme would seem to be land division by persons and estate, not by share. Roxbury had, however, already assessed the shareholders of Woodstock by persons and estate for the payment of a lump sum to the settlers of Woodstock. In other words, one drew land in Woodstock in proportion to one's contribution to the development fund, and it so happened that the easiest way to set each owner's contribution was by the town list of persons and estate.[7]

Even towns founded not primarily as speculative enterprises distributed land as a dividend. The town of Hadley was founded by religious dissidents, not land speculators, but Hadley did not advance any religious or social program by its land division system. In the agreement of 1659, the town founders pledged to divide land according to the contribution each one made toward the purchase of the Indian title and the cost of settlement. Lancaster was founded on the second attempt by people at least partly interested in leading godly lives in the wilderness. In 1653, those proposing to settle Lancaster subscribed to a covenant that bound them to lay out land for a church, build a meetinghouse, build a minister's house, provide for a minister, receive into the plantation only godly men, and submit disputes to arbitration so as to preserve "peace and love"—the most pious goals of New England colonists. Yet Lancaster had a corporation that excluded some residents from land rights, had many nonresident shareholders of town land, prohibited nonshareholders from voting in town meetings, and divided land partly according to the size of people's investment. Lancaster's religious founders put their land system upon a business basis.[8]

Science, 7th Ser., nos. 7–9 (Baltimore, 1889), 42–47. Not only in New England but also in Newtown, New York, founded in the 1650s, the founders determined share size according to money paid toward the Indian purchase. Jessica Kross, *The Evolution of an American Town: Newtown, New York, 1642–1775* (Philadelphia, 1983), 62–63.

7. Holmes Ammidown, *Historical Collections . . .* , 2d ed., 2 vols. (New York, 1877), I, 265–266. For an explanation of the founding of Woodstock by Roxbury, see Chapter 6, "Towns Launched by Other Towns."

8. Sylvester Judd, *History of Hadley, Including the Early History of Hatfield, South Hadley, Amherst, and Granby, Massachusetts* (Springfield, Mass., 1905), 3, 6, 12–13; Nourse, ed., *Early Records of Lancaster,* 15, 27–29, 41–44, 52; Lancaster, May 28, 1684, photostats, MHS; CXII, 366–366a, Mass. Archives; Samuel Eliot Morison, "The

Rowley was founded by members of a congregation who came over from England in 1638, led by their minister, Ezekiel Rogers. Rowley nevertheless distributed land to individuals according to the investment they had made in the purchase of the town, and the town excluded nonshareholders from the undivided land, denying land rights to more than one-fourth of the town's taxpayers by 1662. Neither the wealthiest settler nor the town minister had the largest land share in Rowley: instead, the largest investor did.[9]

These nineteen towns were the only ones in which it is established positively that investment formed the basis of land shares. But in many other towns, investment may well have played a part in determining land shares. This possibility lies in the intriguing way seventeenth-century colonists used the term "estates."

Most of the thirty other towns (about which we have information concerning land division) took into account the inhabitants' "estates" when apportioning land. Some took into account "persons and estates." This term "estates" did not necessarily mean the taxable or evident assets of town-dwellers. Consider the case of Roxbury. Sometime between 1638 and 1640, Roxbury drew up a list with the names of seventy individuals, including one woman. It was called a "note of the estates and persons of the inhabitants of Roxbury."[10] One would think from this heading that the list recorded the householders, the number of people in each family, and the value of each householder's estate. But that was not the case, apparently. The list had four columns: "Acres," "Persons," "Estate," and an unnamed column of numerical values ranging from one to twenty-six. This list reveals no statistical relationship between the size of estate and the number of acres each person received. The individual with the largest "estate" did not receive the most acres. Nor even did the estate figure represent each person's total wealth. No one on the list was accounted as having an estate of more than eighteen pounds. Thomas Dudley had a recorded estate of ten pounds.

The only statistical relationship between the numbers under one heading and the numbers under another was between the numeral set beside each

---

Plantation of Nashaway—an Industrial Experiment," Colonial Society of Massachusetts, *Transactions*, XXVII (1927–1930), 217–218.

9. *Early Records of Rowley*, v–x, 54, 60, 119–129, 132–133.

10. Boston, Registry Dept., *Roxbury Land Records (A Report of the Record Commissioners . . . [Sixth Report])*, 2d ed. (Boston, 1884), 4–5.

person's name (from one to twenty-six) and the number of acres each person received, in a ratio of one to three. Those with a four next to their names had twelve acres, those with seven had twenty-one acres, and so on. Land draws in Roxbury were apparently measured by some unit or share, the basis of which cannot be discerned. Nor can it be discerned what the figure given as "estate" represented.[11]

The use of the term "estate" in Norwalk, Connecticut, is also worth comment. Norwalk drew up a list in 1655 of "lands and accommodations," setting down the names of shareholders with an "estate" figure beside each name, given in pounds. Thus the minister was accounted as having £300, Nathaniel Eli £293, Thomas Fitch £314, and so on. In Norwalk, unlike the situation in Roxbury, the estate figure was related to the size of one's land draw. When, for instance, Roger Ludlow conveyed the town tract to the founders, he reserved for himself a lot "to the vallue of 200 lb. in the proportion of Rates." In 1669, the town meeting voted to divide lands "according to estate given in." This intriguing phrase "estate given in" sounds less like a description of assets than a summary of each person's contribution to a town fund. Moreover, the figures for 1669 had not changed since 1655, so the phrase "estate given in" could not have referred to one's current assets. It may well have meant "contribution."

In 1671, Norwalk voted that "every one of our inhabitants that have not as yet had any estate for their childring, shall have five pounds for every childe now in being; to be added to their father's estate, and this is to take place in the land that is now to be layed ut in the Indian feild." Here "estate" meant either land or an interest in land, measured in pounds. It is not known how Norwalk originally determined the size of one's interest, but certainly "estates" did not refer to the net worth of inhabitants.[12]

Norwich, in 1694, also apportioned shares among "first purchasers" according to "what estate each of them put in." New Haven likewise ordered in 1640 that every "planter" should have "a proportio of land according to the proportio of estate wch he hath given in, and number of heads in his famyly, (viz) in the first divisio of upland and meadow 5 acres for every hundred pound, [an]d 5 acres for every two heads, of upland, butt

11. *Ibid.*

12. Edwin Hall, ed., *The Ancient Historical Records of Norwalk, Conn., with a Plan of the Ancient Settlement, and of the Town in 1847* (New York, 1865), 17, 32–33, 56, 60–61. This definition of "estate" is the first given in *Black's Law Dictionary,* 4th ed., rev. (St. Paul, Minn., 1968).

halfe an acre of meadow to a head [and] in the necke an acre to every hundred pound, and halfe an acre to every head." It is not clear in New Haven what was meant by "estate given in," but in 1640 two people were allowed to increase their estate "formerly given in" if they paid all rates levied up to that time. In this light, "estate given in" probably did not refer to one's net worth.[13]

These examples are not taken from the nineteen towns that clearly used investment to determine share size, but from the thirty towns that determined shares by some other or by some unknown method. Returning for a moment to examples drawn from the nineteen towns, one learns that "estate" referred, at least sometimes, to an individual's investment or contribution and not to his total assets.

In Waterbury, the founding Articles of Association provided that meadow lands should be distributed according to each inhabitant's "estate." These articles did not explain how one's estate was to be constituted or measured, but later entries in town records provide two clues. First, one's stake in undivided lands was measured in pounds (as in Norwalk, above). The minister, for instance, was "invested with one hundred and fifty Pound propriety." By 1722, the sum of the town's land shares came to £8,637, owned by thirty-six full proprietors and fifty-seven bachelor proprietors. Second, these pound figures were described by one original proprietor as representing the financial contribution that each admitted inhabitant made to the town. In 1715, John Standley protested a division that included bachelor rights by arguing that "the first purchesurs of the land within the township did thereby aquire aright according to the propotion of what payments they made by order of the comity for the setling of the place." It would appear that Waterbury followed the Connecticut tradition of dividing land according to people's venture in a common stock, and that "estate" here referred to the size of their ventures.[14]

In Lancaster, the "undertakers" of 1645 also laid out their lots according to people's "estates." Then in 1653, when the court reorganized the town,

13. Frances Manwaring Caulkins, *History of Norwich, Connecticut* . . . (Hartford, Conn., 1874), 60; Charles J. Hoadly, ed., *Records of the Colony and Plantation of New Haven, from 1638 to 1649* (Hartford, Conn., 1857), 27, 43.

14. Henry Bronson, *The History of Waterbury, Connecticut* . . . (Waterbury, Conn., 1858), 8–10, 34, 35, 38, 123; Katharine A. Prichard, *Proprietors' Records of the Town of Waterbury, Connecticut: 1677–1761*, Publications of the Mattatuck Historical Society, I (Waterbury, Conn., 1911), viii, 90–91.

it permitted each undertaker to have allotments "in proportion to charges expended by him and such others" during the years of the venture. In the same year, the covenant subscribed by new town founders provided for land division according to "mens estates," counting "ten pounds a head for every person and all other good by due vallue, and to proportion to every ten pounds three acords of Land two of upland and one of Entervale and we give a years Libertie to Every man to bringe in his estate." The following year, the town divided meadow at the rate of four acres for every one hundred pounds of estate. This division caused some unhappiness, and the town revised the list of estates. Those who said they had spent much on the founding were set down as having larger estates than had been previously done; thus John Johnson, who had had a thirty pound estate, was raised to a "fowertie pound estate." Ten years later, the town voted to accept Mordechai Mukeload, giving him liberty "to bring in 50 lb estate to enter into the towne booke to draw Land and meddow by in a second devision And to have Comon Right suitable."[15]

These various measures—the apportioning of land by each man's contribution, the division of acreage according to pounds, the ability of one to raise one's estate according to what one paid toward the founding, and the setting of a certain time limit for "bringing in" one's estate—all suggest that in Lancaster "estate" meant contribution or investment. And the cases of Lancaster and Waterbury suggest that not only in these towns, where we know investment determined shares, but elsewhere, in New Haven, Norwich, and Norwalk, where "estates" were also the key to land division, as well as in the many other towns that proportioned land by "persons and estate," people may have divided land according to the investment each made in founding the town. Inhabitants did not divide land according to the ratable assets of the inhabitants just because they took "estates" into account. Sometimes their "estates" were their investments, and land was their dividend.[16]

15. Petition from Undertakers at Nashaway, 1645, CXII, 16, Mass. Archives; Nourse, ed., *Early Records of Lancaster,* 23–24, 29, 39, 43–44, 78.

16. Interpreting "estates" as meaning ratable assets, Melville Egleston said that land was almost always allotted according to men's assets; and others have followed his lead (*The Land System of the New England Colonies,* Johns Hopkins University Studies in Historical and Political Science, 4th Ser., nos. 11–12 [Baltimore, 1886], 44–46; Bruce C. Daniels, *The Connecticut Town: Growth and Development, 1635–1790* [Middletown, Conn., 1979], 120–121). Some writers have grasped the sense of "division by

Nor did a spirit of equality characterize the land system of New England towns in the seventeenth century.[17] That some historians have thought so may be owing to the misreading of a different seventeenth-century term: "equally."

In certain English joint-stock companies, when the shareholders divided profits or assets "equally," they in fact made the division "equal to each person's share." The Plymouth Company was one. New England towns used the term "equally" in precisely the same manner. The 1653 agreement binding together the founders of Nashaway provided this condition for land division:

> That Equallitie (which is the Rule of God) may be observed, we Covenant and Agree, That in a second Devision and so thrugh all other Devitions of Land the mater shall be drawne as neere to equallitie according to mens estates as wee are able to doe, That he which hath now more then his estate Deserveth in home Lotts and entervale Lotts shall have so much Less: and he that hath now Less then his estate Deserveth shall have so much more.

Here the founders were doing no more than insisting that the land division be faithful to the share structure, that each should receive land equal to his share.[18]

Similarly, in Rowley, so that every "man may have an equall sharre in the Commons According to purchase[,] it is agreed that every Acre and halfe Lot shall have one gate and halfe a gate." When colonists were founding

---

estates." When the proprietors of Lyme divided "according to the lists of each man's estate," noted Christopher Collier, they did so according to what each man initially put up toward purchasing or founding the town ("Saybrook and Lyme: Secular Settlements in a Puritan Commonwealth," in George J. Willauer, Jr., ed., *A Lyme Miscellany, 1776–1976* [Middletown, Conn., 1977], 19).

17. The notion of equality in land matters permeates the older literature. See Roy Hidemichi Akagi, *The Town Proprietors of the New England Colonies: A Study of Their Development, Organization, Activities, and Controversies, 1620–1770* (Philadelphia, 1924), 107–109; Herbert L. Osgood, *The American Colonies in the Seventeenth Century*, 3 vols. (New York, 1904–1907), I, 460–461. Edward Johnson was perhaps the first to express this belief (*Johnson's Wonder-Working Providence, 1628–1651*, ed. J. Franklin Jameson [New York, 1910], 114–115, 213).

18. William Robert Scott, *The Constitution and Finance of English, Scottish, and Irish Joint-Stock Companies to 1720*, 3 vols. (New York, 1951), II, 306–309; Nourse, ed., *Early Records of Lancaster*, 29.

Dedham, they agreed to "beare all equall charges with other men according to his proportion." When the Roxbury residents launched Woodstock, they agreed that it should "be equally and proportionably divided to them"; however, this did not mean that the town's land was shared equally. In Woodstock, nonresidents owned shares according to the amount they contributed to developing the town.[19] Thus did seventeenth-century individuals understand equality in land matters: they tried as well as they could, contending with the variety of terrains, to give land to each person equal to his share.

At least nineteen towns, therefore, and perhaps many more (including those where "estate" stood for investment) distributed land as a return on investment. They did not divide land equally, and they probably did not divide land according to ratable assets. Instead, in perhaps as many as half the towns surveyed here, land was divided according to purchased shares.

In many more than half the towns, the land system contained an additional business element. After shares were apportioned, most towns did not alter share size. Individuals divided land by fixed shares both in the nineteen towns just discussed and in another twenty-two towns that employed what might be called a modified share system. In these latter towns, the founders fixed the size of shares by some method—whether by assessing estates, counting persons, judging usefulness, or some unknown means—and then ever after divided land according to these shares.[20] (On the one hand, the modified share system was distinguished from the full share system in that towns may not have used investment as the basis for land distribution; and on the other hand, these towns fixed men's proportions and repeatedly divided land according to these proportions: hence the label "modified" share system.)

Only a handful of towns varied the proportions (as opposed to the actual lots, which varied everywhere) from division to division. Wherever individ-

19. *Early Records of Rowley,* 54; Dedham, Mass., *The Early Records of the Town* . . . , 6 vols. (Dedham, Mass., 1886–1936), III, 4 (hereafter cited as *Dedham Town Records*); Ammidown, *Historical Collections,* I, 261.

20. The 22 towns were Amesbury, Andover, Billerica, Cambridge, Charlestown, Dedham, Deerfield, Dorchester, Groton, Haverhill, Ipswich, Manchester, Marlborough, Mendon, Oxford, Roxbury, Salisbury, Sudbury, Worcester, New Haven, Norwich, and Norwalk. For evidence of fixed share systems in these towns, see Commentary for Table 6, Martin, "Entrepreneurship." Note that 5 of these towns also appear in Appendix 8b, below, that is, among those that divided land according to persons and estates. The reason is that these towns used two systems at the same time.

uals divided land according to "persons" and no other evidence indicates the repeated use of shares, it may be assumed that land proportions varied and that, in effect, perpetual shares did not exist. Such was the case with Dedham, Medfield, Northampton, and Woburn, which distributed land according to their lists of "persons and estates." (The above discussion relating to "estates" should be borne in mind, however, before ruling out the possibility that these towns used fixed shares.) Salem divided land according to number of persons in each family, Watertown according to persons and cattle, Exeter according to persons, cattle, and rates; and still other towns established peculiar, fluctuating ranks. Worcester called for land distribution according "to the quality, estate, usefulnes and otherr considerations [of] the persons and family, unto whome these lotts arre granted." A total of thirteen towns appeared to use fluctuating standards to determine share size—appeared, because, on occasion, these same towns also used fixed shares (see Appendix 8b).[21]

But in the vast majority of towns, forty-one of forty-eight, the commoners' proportions of undivided land were unchanging (see Appendix 8a).[22] This use of fixed shares was significant for several reasons. Since land distribution was regulated by fixed proportions of interest, the land system was unresponsive to the changing needs of landholders. Families would grow, their wealth would fluctuate, but year after year they drew land according to shares that had been determined by their size, wealth, or investment at the outset of the town. A shareholder's usefulness might earn him a large share in the first year of the town, and then in later years he might be incapacitated, yet his land draw would remain the same, even after his death. An individual would contribute a certain amount to the purchase of the township, and ever after, that individual would share the common land in proportion to this initial contribution. In 1675, New Haven was still dividing land according to "estates" measured in 1638. In 1672, Hartford was still dividing land according to a list of 1640.[23] No matter

21. The 13 were Dedham, Dorchester, Groton, Medfield, Northampton, Salem, Springfield, Worcester, Woburn, Watertown, New Haven, Wallingford, and Exeter. Some of these towns also appear in Appendix 8a because some towns used more than one land division system. See these towns in Commentary for Tables 6 and 6a, Martin, "Entrepreneurship."

22. Appendix 8a lists those towns that employed fixed share systems for land division.

23. *New Haven Town Records*, 333–335; Hartford, Conn., *Original Distribution of the Lands in Hartford among the Settlers: 1639* (Connecticut Historical Society, *Collections*, XIV [Hartford, Conn., 1912]), 549–551.

what changes time brought, shares were fixed in most seventeenth-century towns.

If shares had changed size according to inhabitants' changing needs or status, then the land system would have been a communal instrument, regulating relations within the community according to whatever standards the town devised at that moment. But the land system did not have a primarily public or communal function. When inhabitants gathered to distribute land every few years, they did not make community decisions about the best allocation of town resources; they conducted automatic distributions based upon predetermined shares.

The repetitive use of fixed shares involved a kind of return on investment even in those towns where financial contributions did not form the basis of shares. A person could contribute in many ways to the founding of a town. His prestige, if he was renowned, attracted other settlers or investors. His trade, if he was a miller or tanner or smith, helped provide for settlers' needs. His preaching, if he was a minister, helped attract other settlers and also helped win the court's approval for town liberties. His family, if it was large, helped populate the town. His money, if he was rich, helped purchase the land and pay public expenses. Each one of these contributions to the founding of a town was valuable; each was a form of investment. When towns repeatedly distributed land according to an individual's initial contributions to the founding, whether that contribution took the form of renown or wealth or skills, towns were in effect providing a return on investment. The sense in which these distributions were investment returns is all the more definite when one considers that these distributions continued even though family size changed and wealth fluctuated, and even after men died.

Because shares were fixed, they were transferable, and because they were transferable, a market in land shares sprang up in the seventeenth century. Nearly all the several score shares of the Deerfield proprietorship changed hands in the 1660s and 1670s. Nearly all the shares of Sowams changed hands in the 1650s. Billerica's commoners conveyed land rights more often than they conveyed land parcels. Northfield, Oxford, Worcester, Norwalk, Rowley, Bristol, Swansea, and Warwick—all had proprietors who not only sold land but also sold their rights to undivided land. (Towns enacted restraints upon alienation in the seventeenth century precisely because people sold land that also conveyed rights in the land corporation.)[24] As the

24. George Sheldon, *A History of Deerfield, Mass. . . .* , 2 vols. (Deerfield, Mass., 1895–

result of being transferable, shares were also divisible, just like the shares in Elizabethan joint-stock companies. Cambridge had 238.5 "cow commons" by 1665, Manchester had 29.25 "shares" by 1678. In Rehoboth North Purchase (later Attleborough) in the 1660s, there were 79.5 shares. In Ipswich and elsewhere people frequently had double shares, or two shares, and sometimes more than that. Owners sold land shares to escape assessments and to realize gains, and in so doing they sold fractions sometimes rather than whole shares.[25]

Thus did fixed shares lend a business character to town land systems. Because shares were perpetual, they were divisible, transferable, traded on an embryonic land-share market, and unconnected to the shifting circumstances of town-dwellers. Even where financial investment did not determine shares, it is difficult to detect a social or religious ideal behind the land system. Rather, nearly everywhere the land system centered on the principle of shares, fixed to proportional interests, unchanging through time, and held by shareholders only. And in many cases, financial investment alone determined shares, and the land system functioned as a business enterprise, distributing dividends to shareholders.

11. Financing Town Affairs

In many towns, not only did individuals divide land by shares, but for the first few years of settlement assessments upon shares

---

1896), I, 10, 36, 207–209; J. H. Temple and George Sheldon, *A History of the Town of Northfield, Massachusetts* . . . (Albany, N.Y., 1875), 135; George F. Daniels, *History of the Town of Oxford, Massachusetts* . . . (Oxford, Mass., 1892), 283–287; Franklin P. Rice, ed., *Records of the Proprietors of Worcester, Massachusetts* (Worcester Society of Antiquity, *Collections,* III [Worcester, Mass., 1881]), 60–63; Hall, ed., *Ancient Records of Norwalk,* 13, 17, 32–33, 55; Wilfred H. Munro, *History of Bristol, Rhode Island: The Story of the Mount Hope Lands* . . . (Providence, R.I., 1880), 94–96; Thomas Williams Bicknell, *A History of Barrington, Rhode Island* (Providence, R.I., 1898), 58–59, 64–65, 157–158; Warwick Town Records, 65, 311–312, LC; Billerica Petitions, 1705, XLV, 315–318, 325–340, Mass. Archives; *Early Records of Rowley,* 128–129. In some towns, land sales conveyed proprietary rights; in other towns, they did not. See also Chapter 7, below, for more about restraints upon alienation.

25. *Cambridge Proprietors' Records,* 144–148; Manchester, Mass., *Town Records of Manchester* . . . , 2 vols. (Salem, Mass., 1889–1891), I, 16–17; John Daggett, *Sketch of the History of Attleborough* . . . (Dedham, Mass., 1834), 10–12; Thomas Franklin Waters, *Ipswich in the Massachusetts Bay Colony* . . . , 2 vols. (Ipswich, Mass., 1905–1917), I, 70.

were the principal means of financing public affairs.[26] Records yield too little information to form an understanding of taxation in many towns, but in at least twenty-one of sixty-three towns, town affairs were financed solely by assessments upon shares during the early years of town life (see Appendix 9).[27] Towns achieved this result in several different ways, but the most common method was by levying a tax upon the house lot or some other lot of land that was given to individuals on account of their shares or that formed the basis for measuring their shares.

If these levies had been targeted merely on the land of shareholders, it would be easy to see them as a species of land tax. A land tax would be a practical revenue device in agricultural communities of the preindustrial age, but it was not the land of shareholders, nor their property, nor their wealth that was taxed in the first years of these twenty-one towns. It was their "proportions," or shares, as measured by their house lots or some other means.[28]

26. Town tax policy has never received the scrutiny it deserves. Some have said that the taxation of unimproved land discouraged nonresident landholding and land speculation, but this opinion is rebutted by evidence presented in Chapter 1. Others have suggested that town rates were a general tax assessed upon the wealth or property of all residents, falling upon both real and personal property. See Anne Bush MacLear, *Early New England Towns: A Comparative Study of Their Development* (New York, 1908), 60–61; Ruth Crandall, comp., *Tax and Valuation Lists of Massachusetts Towns before 1776: Finding List for the Microfilm Edition* (Cambridge, Mass., 1971), xiii; Daniels, *Connecticut Town*, 68. It is true that colony laws made all residents, including sojourners, liable for town rates. But towns did not always do what the general courts said they should, neither in tax policy nor in franchise restrictions. During the Wallingford tax dispute mentioned in Chapter 1, the town admitted that it had violated colony law by continuing to raise revenue solely upon proprietors' land shares.

27. Some towns, like Watertown, always rated men's real and personal property in town taxation. Historical Society of Watertown, *Watertown Records, Comprising the First and Second Books of Town Proceedings with the Lands, Grants, and Possessions*, 5 vols. (Watertown, Mass., 1894), I, 2, 3. In Newtown, New York, taxes in the early years were also raised upon shares, with men holding more shares paying proportionally more taxes (Kross, *Evolution of an American Town*, 63).

28. Hence Hingham was distinct from the towns herein mentioned, for there the opening act of the town merely stated that "everie man, that is admyted to be Townes man, and have Lots graunted them shall beare charges both to Church and Commonwealth proportionable to their abilities"—distinct because though taxation was linked to land privileges, the principle of shares seems to have been missing in Hingham. David Grayson Allen, *In English Ways: The Movement of Societies and the Transferal of English*

The founders of Billerica stated that public charges should be paid "acordinge to or severall proportions of land and meadowes." Dedham's founders agreed to pay taxes each "according to his proportion of Lotts. vizt for evry 12. [acre] lot 18.*d* and for eury 8. acre Lott 12*d*." They earlier had pledged in their covenant that whoever received land "shall paye his share in all such Rates of money . . . in proportion with other men." The owners of Westerly, Rhode Island, ordered that "every man that have a whole share is to make up his purchase money the full sum of seven pounds . . . and they that have but half a share are to do the like according to their proportion of land."[29]

Where shares were measured, not by house lots, but by some other commodity, this other commodity was the item subject to tax. In Exeter, where staves were the town staple and their making an important right of inhabitancy, the freemen ordered that every inhabitant must support the ministry in proportion to the number of pipe staves he made (at the rate of two shillings per thousand staves). In Swansea, where men were assigned to one of three ranks for the purpose of land divisions, the town taxed men according to the rank to which they belonged.[30] Whether one was assessed by his rank, his pipe staves, or his house lot, taxes fell upon a unit measured by shares.

This method of raising money resembled a stock transaction. When people in these twenty-one towns paid their taxes, called "rates" or "proportions," they were fulfilling a promise they had made in their initial articles of agreement, namely, to bear charges in "proportion" to their interest in the land corporation. Also in those articles, often in the same clause, town founders had agreed to divide the land "and all other priviledges," as the Billerica agreement put it, "acordinge to or publique charges."[31] In other words, shareholders agreed to pay assessments upon their shares and

Local Law and Custom to Massachusetts Bay in the Seventeenth Century (Chapel Hill, N.C., 1981), 74.

29. Henry A. Hazen, *History of Billerica, Massachusetts* . . . (Boston, 1883), 54–55; *Dedham Town Records*, III, 2–3, 23; Elisha R. Potter, Jr., *The Early History of Narragansett*, (RIHS, *Collections*, III [Providence, R.I., 1835]), 252–253 (hereafter cited as Potter, *Early History of Narragansett*).

30. Charles H. Bell, *History of the Town of Exeter, New Hampshire* (Exeter, N.H., 1889), 52; Bicknell, *History of Barrington*, 157–159.

31. Hazen, *History of Billerica*, 54–55.

in return to receive, in precisely the same proportions, dividends in land. This exchange put revenue raising more in the nature of subscriptions upon shares than levies upon assets.

In 1640, New Haven raised half the rate upon estates and half upon land; "estates" in New Haven possibly meant "shares." In the same year, two men who wanted larger land rights were granted their wish and had their "estates" increased—simply by agreeing to pay additional rates. In this arrangement, rates had the character of being stock purchases, with which one bought shares, called "estates"; and these shares in turn entitled the owner to dividends of land. In Lancaster, also, one could increase one's "estate," pay larger rates, and receive more land. To pay rates in these towns was to purchase rights; it was to engage in a stock transaction.[32]

In being financed in this manner, these twenty-one towns, and perhaps others, were no different from the Atherton Company, the Pettaquamscut Company, the various Dudley ventures, or, for that matter, any seventeenth-century joint-stock company. Like them, towns in their early years raised revenue irregularly, not on an annual schedule.[33] Like them, towns had investors who split up their shares under the pressure of repeated subscriptions. Like them, they used shares to award benefits in the same proportions as liabilities were assessed. And like company shareholders, town inhabitants paid rates as the necessary price of purchasing and keeping stock and receiving dividends. If one wanted land, one had to pay proportional rates; in stressing that connection, town covenants were emphatic.

The financial burden rested upon shareholders for the simple reason that they were the ones capable of bearing it. Uniquely able to finance town activities, shareholders routinely shouldered expenses that went beyond the purchase, surveying, and dividing of their land. In Woodstock, the town voted to engage a man to build a gristmill, "each planter to bear his proportion of the cost, according to the value of his home lot." When Medfield required people to work on highways, the labor contribution of each individual was calculated in proportion to the size of his house lot. Those with six-acre lots were to come with their hands, and twelve-acre

32. Hoadly, ed., *Records of the Colony of New Haven*, 40, 43; Nourse, ed., *Early Records of Lancaster*, 43–44.

33. This point, made by Anne Bush MacLear, is borne out by the records of many towns (*Early New England Towns*, 55).

men were to come with teams.[34] In Amesbury, Lancaster, Wrentham, and sporadically in Groton, shareholders by themselves supported the ministry. Springfield rated all residents for the minister's salary. Groton switched back and forth between assessing shares and taxing all people for the ministry. Although colony laws specifically required "every mann" to contribute to the ministry, in several towns the burden of supporting the minister, who served the whole community, fell exclusively upon members of the land corporation.[35]

The shareholders' burden was meant to be temporary, not permanent. As the Deerfield proprietors put it, they agreed to rate themselves only "for the present till the said towne be in a capasitye to manage their own affairs." The founders of Waterbury agreed that all revenue be raised on meadow allotments only for the first five years and thereafter upon persons and estates "acording to the law or custom of the country."[36] In 1641, the Connecticut General Court ruled that the charge of making ways or supplying any common benefit "shall be paid by the land wthin the said liberty, as yt shall be taken uppe and possest"—in other words, that divided land and not persons or estates should be the tax base of towns—and, further, that this rule should cease having effect once a settlement became a plantation with its own officers.[37]

Once towns got on their feet, shareholders ceased bearing the sole

34. Ammidown, *Historical Collections*, I, 280; William S. Tilden, ed., *History of the Town of Medfield, Massachusetts, 1650–1886 . . .* (Boston, 1887), 40–41, 58.

35. Joseph Merrill, *History of Amesbury and Merrimac, Massachusetts* (Haverhill, Mass., 1880; rpt., 1978), 85; Nourse, ed., *Early Records of Lancaster,* 22–23, 27; Jordan D. Fiore, *Wrentham, 1783–1973: A History* (Wrentham, Mass., 1973), 10; Samuel A. Green, ed., *The Town Records of Groton, Massachusetts: 1662–1678* (Groton, Mass., 1879 [rpt. in Green, ed., *Pamphlets on History of Groton* (n.p., n.d.)]), 11, 28, 39; Henry M. Burt, *The First Century of the History of Springfield: The Official Records from 1636 to 1736,* 2 vols. (Springfield, Mass., 1898–1899), I, 156–158, 160–161, 178, 185, 192, 245 (hereafter cited as Burt, *Official Records of Springfield*). Connecticut ordered as part of the 1650 code of laws that for the maintenance of ministers, "every mann" should "voluntarily sett downe what hee is willing to allowe," and if any "man" refused to pay a "meet proportion" he would be rated (*Conn. Records,* I, 545).

36. Sheldon, *History of Deerfield,* I, 39. As things turned out, the Waterbury proprietors probably paid for the town's public affairs during the first 16 years of settlement, until 1689. Bronson, *History of Waterbury,* 8–9, 36; Prichard, ed., *Proprietors' Records of Waterbury,* 33.

37. *Conn. Records,* I, 59.

financial burden, as towns began taxing other forms of property, not just land shares, and other residents, not just shareholders. In 1673, the proprietors of Deerfield, many of whom were nonresidents, voted to raise all taxes upon lands, each paying according to his proportion. Then, in 1687, the town meeting changed the tax base from proprietors' land to lands, heads, and flocks; in addition, Deerfield began taxing land by its quality, not by the number of land rights a person possessed. Haverhill initially taxed "all landholders . . . according to their number of acres that they hold to their houselotts," but fourteen years later voted to rate the landless as well according to their "visible estate."[38]

The shareholders of Springfield began by assessing themselves for all expenses (except those expenses connected with the ministry) "upon lands accordinge to every ones proportion aker for aker of house lotts and aker for aker of meddowe." In 1645, the town assessed merely house lots, exempting all other lots. Then in 1646, it voted to pay for the meetinghouse and the minister's salary by rates on all uplands and livestock. In 1655, it voted for the first time to raise the minister's salary by rating, among others, landless men. That same year, for all other public charges, the town voted to count, not land acres, but land value and to include houses and livestock in the assessment. Thus over twenty years Springfield gradually moved away from financial dependence upon the shareholders. Billerica at the outset (in 1654) raised revenue "acordinge to or severall proportions of land and meadowes," and then in 1685 voted "that from this day forward all priviledges shall cease to pay Towne charges."[39]

This shift in the tax burden from shareholders to residents instigated controversy in several towns. The land corporation, naturally, wished to shift the burden, and the nonproprietors wished to keep it where it rested. Groton, Wallingford, New Haven, Wrentham, and other towns had disputes about tax policy, prefiguring the numerous fights on this same subject in eighteenth-century towns.[40] In some cases, it appears that the shareholders were made to pay for town affairs longer than they wanted to; but

38. Sheldon, *History of Deerfield*, I, 39, 206, 274–276; Chase, *History of Haverhill*, 57, 87, 115–116.

39. Burt, *Official Records of Springfield*, I, 156–158, 160–161, 178, 185, 192, 244–245; Hazen, *History of Billerica*, 54–55, 187–188.

40. Green, *Town Records of Groton*, 11, 28, 36–37, 39, 45; Wallingford Petition, May 9, 1677, Towns and Lands, I, 170, Conn. Archives; Hoadly, ed., *Records of the Colony of New Haven*, 448; Wrentham Petition, Oct. 15, 1673, Misc. Bound, MHS.

eventually time brought an end to the town-launching stage in each town, and the town grew and released shareholders from their duty to finance the town.

III. Voting

After dividing land and raising money, the third most important public activity in towns was voting. Here, too, the land corporation played a special role.

The question at issue is, and has always been, the representativeness of town meetings. B. Katherine Brown has produced extensive evidence from the towns of Dedham, Cambridge, and elsewhere that points to voting by "inhabitants"; she has argued that the town franchise was broadly distributed. Other scholars have said, on the contrary, that Brown undercounted town residents in those towns; they in turn have argued that the town franchise was narrowly distributed.[41] It is likely that to some extent both sides of this debate are right: that all "inhabitants" voted in most towns and that many adult males in most towns did not vote. The solution to this apparent paradox lies in the definition of inhabitancy.[42]

41. B. Katherine Brown, "Puritan Democracy in Dedham, Massachusetts: Another Case Study," *William and Mary Quarterly,* 3d Ser., XXIV (1967), 378–396. Her opponents include Kenneth Lockridge, Arlin Ginsburg, Richard C. Simmons, Stephen Foster, and Robert E. Wall. See, in particular, Robert E. Wall, "The Franchise in Seventeenth-Century Massachusetts: Dedham and Cambridge," *WMQ,* 3d Ser., XXXIV (1977), 453–458; Arlin I. Ginsburg, "The Franchise in Seventeenth-Century Massachusetts: Ipswich," *WMQ,* 3d Ser., XXXIV (1977), 446–452. There are still, of course, a great number of other writers who have expressed opinions on this subject. For a summary of these opinions, see Brown, "The Controversy over the Franchise in Puritan Massachusetts, 1954 to 1974," *WMQ,* 3d Ser., XXXIII (1976), 212–241. More recent writers arguing democracy in 17th-century town meetings include Bruce C. Daniels (*Connecticut Town,* 66; *Dissent and Conformity on Narragansett Bay: The Colonial Rhode Island Town* [Middletown, Conn., 1983], 9–10, 47, 101, 111) and Richard I. Melvoin ("Communalism in Frontier Deerfield," in Stephen C. Innes *et al., Early Settlement in the Connecticut Valley,* ed. John W. Ifkovic and Martin Kaufman [Deerfield, Mass., 1984], 45).

42. Timothy H. Breen suspected that closer examination of the term and function of inhabitants might shed light on the franchise controversy ("Who Governs: The Town Franchise in Seventeenth-Century Massachusetts," *WMQ,* 3d Ser., XXVII [1970], 464–465).

Massachusetts, upon which the franchise controversy has centered, passed unequivocal laws defining the franchise. In 1631, Massachusetts ordered that "noe man shalbe admitted to the freedome of this body polliticke, but such as are members of some of the churches withn the lymitts of the same." In 1634, the court ordered that the freemen of every "plantacon" shall choose deputies to represent them. In 1635, it enacted that "none but freemen shall have any vote in any towne, in any accon of aucthoritie, or necessity, or that which belongs to them by vertue of their freedome, as receaveing inhabitants, and layeing out of lotts." And then on March 3, 1635/6, the court ordered that the freemen of every town "shall onely have power to dispose of their owne lands, and woods, with all the previlidges and appurtenances of the said townes, to graunt lotts, and make such orders as may concerne the well ordering of their owne townes."[43]

Some historians have assumed that towns followed these laws and restricted political participation to freemen.[44] Towns, however, frequently ignored colony statutes when it came to regulating the town meeting, as Brown points out.[45] And even if they had not ignored the laws of the court, those laws changed with great frequency. By 1641, only five years after Massachusetts required town voters to be freemen, the colony relaxed this standard and let anyone come to town meetings, though only freemen might vote. By 1647, the court allowed nonfreemen to vote in town meetings. Meanwhile, Connecticut had never imposed such a requirement on its town voters. Nor had Rhode Island. The freemanship standard was never a widespread qualification for town voters, nor did it last long, nor was it obeyed.

There was, however, another standard that was common to many colonial franchise laws and that was obeyed. All seventeenth-century town franchise laws (except the first Massachusetts orders of the 1630s) required that voters be inhabitants.[46] In 1647, the court undercut the freeman base

43. *Mass. Records*, I, 87, 118–119, 161, 172.

44. MacLear, *Early New England Towns*, 110. Breen also argued that it was likely that towns adhered to the freemen requirement ("Who Governs," *WMQ*, 3d Ser., XXVII [1970], 462–464). Wall, on the other hand, pointed out that several towns violated the law restricting selectmen to freemen ("Massachusetts Franchise in 1647," *WMQ*, 3d Ser., XXVII [1970], 143).

45. Brown, "Controversy over the Franchise," *WMQ*, 3d Ser., XXXIII (1976), 228–229; "Puritan Democracy in Dedham," *WMQ*, 3d Ser., XXIV (1967), 384.

46. This proposition does not count the 1641 *Body of Liberties*, which provided that nonfreemen could come to any public court or town meeting and move any lawful

of the town franchise: "Taking into consideration the usefull partes and abilities of divers inhabitants amongst us, which are not freemen, which if improved to publike use the affaires of this commonwealth may be the easier carried an end, in the severall townes," the court ordered that "henceforth it shall and may be lawfull for the freemen within any of the said townes to make choyce of the such inhabitants, though non freemen . . . to have their vote in the choyce of the select men for towne affaires, assessment of rates, and other prudentials."[47]

In 1648, the *Lawes and Liberties of Massachusetts* held that "the Freemen of everie town or *Township*, with such other inhabitants as have taken the Oath of fidelitie shall have full power" to choose selectmen. In 1658, the court further confirmed the voting power of "inhabitants" when it allowed as voters all Englishmen over the age of twenty-four who were among the "setled inhabitants and house holders" of towns (and took the oath of fidelity, were of good and honest conversation, and possessed an estate assessed at twenty pounds or more in a single country rate). A 1664 law reforming the colony franchise restricted it to "settled inhabitants" who met certain other qualifications. In the 1672 edition of Massachusetts laws, the editors changed the language of the 1636 law, the only one that century to restrict the town franchise to freemen, so that it encompassed freemen "with such others as are allowed." And in 1681, the court ruled that "any inhabitant" could be chosen constable, selectman, or juror, even though he did not meet the property qualification established for voters.[48]

In Connecticut, from the very beginning inhabitancy was the principal requirement of both the town and the colony franchise. The first order of

---

question. See *The Massachusetts Body of Liberties,* / *A Coppie of the Liberties of the Massachusetts Colonie in New England,* in Edmund S. Morgan, ed., *Puritan Political Ideas, 1558–1794* (New York, 1965), 181. (The full text of the *Body* is reprinted here, pp. 178–203.)

47. Breen argues that this modification did not open the floodgates, as Brown, Morison, and others have said. The position taken here is that Breen is probably right, but for different reasons than he advances. If one interprets "inhabitants" as land shareholders who were already voting in many towns, then the 1647 act was more a confirmation of established practice than it was a new departure. Floodgates were not suddenly opened, because they were already open—to inhabitants, that is. Breen, "Who Governs," *WMQ,* 3d Ser., XXVII (1970), 466–467.

48. *Ibid.,* 468–469, 471; *Mass. Records,* IV, part 1, 336; Brown, "Controversy over the Franchise," *WMQ,* 3d Ser., XXXIII (1976), 233–234, 238; John Fairfield Sly, *Town Government in Massachusetts (1620–1930)* (Cambridge, Mass., 1930), 75.

the Fundamental Orders of January 14, 1638/9, provided for the election of governor and magistrates by "admitted freemen" who had taken the oath of fidelity, who lived within the jurisdiction, and who had "beene admitted Inhabitants by the major part of the Towne wherein they live." The seventh order provided for the election of deputies "by all that are admitted Inhabitants in the sevrall Townes." In 1657, the court tightened the qualification for the colony franchise by adding a property requirement for young men who had not held office; but inhabitancy was still the basis of the franchise, and in any case, this revision applied to the colony, not the town, franchise.[49] Referring to the town franchise, in 1679 the Connecticut court ordered that only "admitted inhabitants" who were householders and men of sober conversation and had at least fifty shillings freehold estate could vote in town meetings.[50]

Thus for most of the seventeenth century, laws in the two largest colonies connected the town franchise to inhabitancy. In Massachusetts, laws permitted inhabitants to vote in town affairs by the second decade of the colony's founding. In Connecticut, laws made inhabitancy the essential condition of voting from the founding days onward. What is more telling than this legal consistency—considering how often towns defied colony standards—is voting behavior itself, for in a majority of towns inhabitants were the town voters.

In thirty-two of sixty-three towns, "inhabitants" were those who gathered in town meetings to decide town affairs (see Appendix 10). In some of these towns, inhabitants voted before the 1641 and 1647 revisions of the colony law, thus clearly defying the Massachusetts requirement that voters be freemen. Such was the case in Cambridge, Charlestown, Dedham, Dorchester, Springfield, Salem, and even Boston, where the law was made. In other towns, "inhabitants" participated in political affairs in the century's middle decades. Such was the case in Sudbury, Marlborough, Woburn, and Medfield. In still other towns, inhabitants were voting at the end of the century. Such was the case in Bristol, Lebanon, Northfield, and Simsbury. Colonies changed their laws defining the town franchise as time went on, but in spite of these changes, from the 1630s to the 1690s those

49. *Conn. Records*, I, 21, 23; Andrews, *River Towns*, 84–87. Andrews interpreted the inhabitancy requirement principally as a way for towns to keep out drunks and those who would become a burden to towns; the definition of inhabitancy offered here is a different one. See below, Chapter 7.

50. *Conn. Records*, III, 34.

who voted in most New England town meetings were the "inhabitants" of the towns.[51]

Although it has been possible to document voting by inhabitants throughout the seventeenth century, it does not follow that in these thirty-two towns the town meeting was composed of "inhabitants" during every decade of the century. Voting habits changed. Some towns convened several different kinds of meetings; other towns did not even hold town meetings, letting seven or ten men conduct town affairs for a time. In a very few towns, the freemen ruled, as early Massachusetts law provided. In some cases, a General Court committee supervised the town for years; in others, nonresident proprietors did the supervising. Political systems varied tremendously, both with the passage of time and from town to town. But amid this variety, one of the few elements common to many towns was the political participation of inhabitants. In most of these thirty-two towns, inhabitants did not just vote in one meeting or another but were the clearly designated voting class, constituting town meetings year after year.

This is what Brown argued: that all inhabitants voted. But Brown assumed that all people in town were inhabitants, when it appears that towns did not use "inhabitants" as a casual synonym for residents (see Chapter 7). Inhabitants were those people admitted by the existing inhabitants to a form of town citizenship. This citizenship gave to its beneficiaries shares in the land corporation and, so it appears (Appendix 10), the right to vote in town meetings. But not all residents were inhabitants. The inhabitants of each town formed a tightly controlled, exclusive group, so the very condition that voters be inhabitants virtually guaranteed the opposite result from the one Brown has depicted. Since many towns restricted the franchise to members of the exclusive land corporation, logic demands that the franchise was narrow, not broad.

Evidence confirms this logical conclusion. In twenty-one of the thirty-two towns where "inhabitants" voted in the town meeting, inhabitants also owned the undivided land and denied some residents land shares.[52] At one

51. The proportion was probably higher than half of all towns. Information was not obtainable for all 63 towns, yet in 32 towns inhabitants voted in town meetings. In some of these 32 towns, "townsmen" played the role that "inhabitants" did in most towns—that is, those who divided the land and voted were called townsmen, not inhabitants.

52. The 21 towns were Amesbury, Boston, Cambridge, Dedham, Dunstable, Groton, Haverhill, Ipswich, Lancaster, Manchester, Marlborough, Medfield, Northfield, Springfield, Sudbury, Watertown, Woburn, Lebanon, Norwalk, Warwick, and Exeter. These 21

time or another during the seventeenth-century lives of Boston, Cambridge, Ipswich, Dedham, Springfield, Haverhill, Marlborough, Warwick, Norwalk, Lebanon, and other towns, the inhabitants voted in town meetings, owned rights to the undivided land, and did not admit all residents to the enjoyment of these two essential privileges. The inhabitants of these towns enjoyed a monopoly of power and land.

In 1645, Dedham had 83 commoners; and in following years, 75 and then 79 men divided land. These proprietor totals nearly matched the town voter totals during the same period. In 1651, the town had 84 voters; and in 1666, it had 83 voters. Yet in 1647, the town had either 102 or 107 taxpayers. From one-sixth to one-third of the taxpayers were disfranchised and excluded from land divisions during the seventeenth century on the grounds that those excluded had not been admitted to "Towne privilidges."

That it was not precisely the same eighty people who shared Dedham's land and voted over the twenty-year period does not greatly diminish the importance of this numerical correlation. For shares often changed hands, and it is also possible that a man cast a vote for a woman, mother or sister, who owned a land share. (Women owned land shares in Dedham, as in many towns.) However often shares may have changed hands, the number of land shares stayed the same over a twenty-year period, the number of voters stayed the same, the two totals were similar, and a sizable part of the adult male population was excluded from sharing both the undivided land and political power.[53]

In Springfield, the town restricted town meeting voters to those who had been admitted as "inhabitants." It also denied rights in the undivided land to all but admitted inhabitants. It was no surprise, then, that the number of voters and the number of commoners were roughly the same. In 1665, there were 74 male inhabitants sharing in land divisions. In 1672, there

---

were towns in which inhabitants voted and also in which land shareholders were the sole voters (Appendix 10). It was the nature of inhabitancy, conferring both land and political rights upon inhabitants, that probably explains the correlation between property and the franchise that Richard C. Simmons discussed ("Godliness, Property, and the Franchise in Puritan Massachusetts," *Journal of American History*, LV [1968–1969], 495–511) and that Ronald K. Snell found in Springfield (see below). Simmons, however, was focusing on the colony, not the town, franchise.

53. Brown, "Puritan Democracy in Dedham," *WMQ*, 3d Ser., XXIV (1967), 387–389, 393; *Dedham Town Records*, III, 211–214; Wall, "Franchise in Seventeenth-Century Massachusetts," *WMQ*, 3d Ser., XXXIV (1977), 453–455.

were 76 people qualified to vote in the town meeting. At this same time the town contained well more than 100 adult males, assuming that the 132 figure of 1679 was matched and probably exceeded before King Philip's War.[54]

In Ipswich, the exclusion of nonshareholders from the franchise was just as great, though the numerical correlation between voters and commoners was somewhat less precise than in Springfield and Dedham. A voting list of 1679 shows 130 men voting in town affairs. At this time, from 440 to 474 males lived in town. The question is, How did the town justify denying the town franchise to some 300 men? The answer cannot be known for sure, but the town closely regulated the admission of "inhabitants," inhabitants held rights to the town's land, more than half the residents did not possess land rights, and inhabitants were voters in town meetings. In all likelihood the town restricted the franchise to admitted inhabitants who shared the town's land. A comparison of the commoners' and voters' lists strengthens this possibility. Of the 172 males owning commonage rights in 1679, 113 were voters. In other words, at least 66 percent of the commoners voted in the town meeting. The proportion was surely higher than that, for some of those commoners were undoubtedly nonresidents, which means that the proportion of resident commoners who voted reached perhaps 70 or 80 percent. By contrast, the proportion of adult residents who voted was only 15–40 percent. To take a different ratio, consider that, of 130 voters, 113 were commoners—or 87 percent—and the other 17 voters could well have been noncommoner freemen, entitled to vote by colony law.[55]

Voting depended upon shareholding in a linkage often forged in founding covenants or articles of association, which provided that admitted "inhabitants" should own the common land and have a voice in town affairs. After settlement, some towns also enacted laws reinforcing this

54. Burt, *Official Records of Springfield,* I, 8, II, 115–117. Ronald K. Snell has ably demonstrated the gradual decrease in the number of men allowed to vote in Springfield affairs. He does not, however, propose an explanation for this decrease, or link inhabitancy, land shares, and the town franchise (though he does identify the inhabitants as those residents owning real estate). See his "Freemanship, Officeholding, and the Town Franchise in Seventeenth-Century Springfield, Massachusetts," *New England Historical and Genealogical Register,* CXXXIII (1979), 163–179.

55. Waters, *Ipswich in the Massachusetts Bay Colony,* I, 91–106; Ginsburg, "Franchise in Ipswich," *WMQ,* 3d Ser., XXXIV (1977), 447–451. The numbers are Waters's and Ginsburg's, the analysis the author's.

linkage and strictly forbidding nonshareholders from voting in town meetings. In 1656, Cambridge ordered that any person "within the limitts of this Towne, not haveing Towne prviledges eyther by gift or purchase, or otherwise by consent of the select men for the time being, every such person shall have no power to give either vote or suffrage in any Eleccon of any Towne officr Deputy or reprsentative nor yet in ordering or disposeing any of the Comon interest of the Towne, nor making of Towne orders, nor yet be allowed wood or comonage from of or upon the Towne Comons," except as the General Court allowed.[56]

In other towns, it was the General Court that stepped in and resolved a dispute about land and voting rights by affirming the political monopoly of shareholders. In Lancaster, in 1657, the court ordered that "noe other person or persones whatsoever shalbe admited to the Injoyment of the privaledges of the place and towneshipp, either in accomodaccions vots elections or disposalles of any of the Comon privaledges and interests theirof, save only such as have beene first orderly admited and accepted . . . to the enjoyment theirof." In Sudbury, at roughly the same time, the court backed up the "allowed inhabitants" in their refusal to let noninhabitants vote on common land matters, and it also may be that noninhabitants were excluded from voting in the Sudbury town meeting.[57]

In all these towns the "admitted inhabitants" (occasionally called "townsmen") controlled both the town meeting and the land corporation and excluded residents from participation in either. In towns where "purchasers" or "proprietors" constituted the privileged class, instead of "inhabitants," the same allocation of power existed: land shareholders controlled the political power to the exclusion of some residents, only in these cases inhabitants were among the disfranchised. In 1679 the Norwich town meeting ordered "that the power and privilege of voting in town meetings in ordering any town affairs shall only belong to those who are the purchasers of the said plantation and consequently to their lawful heirs and not to any others who have been or shall be admitted to be inhabitants upon other considerations." (Church members in full communion were exempted from this

56. Cambridge, Mass., *The Records of the Town of Cambridge (Formerly Newtowne) Massachusetts, 1630–1703* . . . (Cambridge, Mass., 1901), 112.

57. Nourse, ed., *Early Records of Lancaster,* 52. It is possible that this order referred only to the ownership of land and commonage rights, but the inclusion of "vots [and] elections" suggests that the order also referred to town meeting participation. On Sudbury, see Powell, *Puritan Village,* 129.

order.) Stratford must have passed a similar order in the 1670s, for in February 1684/5, seventy-one men who had been denied shares in the common land petitioned the Connecticut court, alleging that the town would continue mistreating them "unless speedily by you stopt in their unrighteous career, and contradictory transactions at their Town-meetings, to the great detriment and abuse of us, that cannot well brook or bear such unequall dealing and unjust ways." The wording of this petition, especially the phrase "their Town-meetings," implies that the Stratford town meeting was a meeting of the proprietors of Stratford, from which these seventy-one people were excluded.[58]

Earlier in the century, the purchasers of Providence, Rhode Island, let no one else vote in the town meeting during the first ten years or more of the town. In 1646, the proprietors granted fractional rights to some residents but barred these quarter-right owners from voting in town meetings. Even after 1658, when Providence allowed all freeholders to vote on town affairs (though not on land matters), town orders favorable to the twelve original purchasers and their heirs demonstrated that the town meeting remained in the purchasers' hands for many years thereafter. Coddington and the proprietors of Portsmouth also denied newcomers the right to vote in town meetings, which was one of the reasons Samuel Gorton left that town for Providence, where he ran into the same combination of land and political monopoly.[59]

Other towns restricted the chief decision-making body to members of the land corporation—twenty-eight such towns in all, of sixty-three (see

58. Caulkins, *History of Norwich*, 101. In these towns, inhabitancy was a lesser status, discussed below in Chapter 7, "The Social Community." On Stratford: Stratford Petitions, Feb. 1684/5, Towns and Lands, I, 216, 218, 221, Conn. Archives.

59. Adelos Gorton, *The Life and Times of Samuel Gorton* . . . (Philadelphia, 1907), 23. Indeed, through much of the century, the Providence town meeting, in the hands of the proprietors, passed economic measures for the proprietors' sole benefit, exempting their common land from taxation and forbidding the felling of timber so as to forestall the rise of a competitive shipbuilding and commercial industry. Henry C. Dorr, "The Proprietors of Providence, and Their Controversies with the Freeholders," RIHS, *Publications*, n.s., III (1985), 203–206, 214–218, 222, 224–225; Evarts B. Greene and Virginia D. Harrington, *American Population before the Federal Census of 1790* (New York, 1932), 64; Sidney S. Rider, "The Forgeries Connected with the Deed Given by the Sachems Canonicus and Miantinomi to Roger Williams of the Land on Which the Town of Providence Was Planted," *Rhode Island Historical Tracts*, 2d Ser., no. 4 (Providence, R.I., 1896), 59–64.

Appendix 10).[60] Whether they called themselves "inhabitants," "proprie-tors," or "purchasers," these individuals formed an exclusive group in each town, wielding political power, owning the town land, and denying these same political and economic benefits to other residents of the community.

In these towns, voters followed several practices natural to a meeting of company stockholders but otherwise inexplicable in a meeting of commu-nity settlers. Towns sometimes convened meetings outside town. During King Philip's War, Dunstable's town meeting was convened in Woburn. Also during the war, Groton called "a generall town metting of the inhabit-ants of groaton" and held it in Concord. Thirteen men attended, all of them shareholders in the Groton undivided lands. One of the measures passed at this meeting was an order to raise all public charges purely on the lands of shareholders.[61]

In other cases, nonresident proprietors held de facto town meetings outside the town being launched—de facto in the sense that these meetings disposed of all town business, though they were not called "town meet-ings." Thus the proprietors of Deerfield and Woodstock disposed of town business in meetings convened in Dedham and Roxbury for several years; in the case of Deerfield, this nonresident management of town business continued probably beyond the first decade of the town's life. For the first five to ten years of Westerly's existence, proprietors living in Newport handled all town business. In August 1661, these men appointed a govern-ing board of trustees and ordered that "all the affairs of Misquamocuck be left to a committee of Trustees." The following February, the trustees ordered that any people engaged by the company to settle at Misquamicut should "be observant to the orders to be given by the trustees and their deputies." In March, the trustees appointed deputies to "act for us—managing our affairs at Misquamacuck."[62]

There were, of course, differences between these various meetings. In Groton and Dunstable, a "town meeting," attended by inhabitants, met outside the town. In Deerfield, Woodstock, and Westerly, a nonresident proprietary organization met outside the town. But these were surface

60. Appendix 10 lists those towns where land proprietors, whether "inhabitants" or others, had sole exercise of political power.

61. Elias Nason, *A History of the Town of Dunstable, Massachusetts* . . . (Boston, 1877), 26–27; Green, ed., *Town Records of Groton,* 45.

62. Ammidown, *Historical Collections,* I, 259–268; Sheldon, *History of Deerfield,* 6–40; Potter, *Early History of Narragansett,* 250–252, 256, 259–263.

differences. In each case, those who voted, passed rates, and decided all town business were shareholders in the land corporation. In each case, the town's decision-making body met outside the confines of the town. In Westerly and Deerfield, settlers lived on the spot who could have disposed of town business if they had been called upon to do so. But they were not called upon, for the decision-making body in these cases was not a meeting of community settlers.

Regardless of venue, selectmen of some towns did not resemble attorneys or leaders of settlers so much as directors of a business corporation. This study does not set out to scrutinize the relationship between commoners and selectmen, but it appears likely that in most towns only shareholders were elected selectmen. During the first ten years of Springfield's existence, only thirteen men served as town selectmen, although election rules made it theoretically possible for fifty different men to have served as selectmen during that period. As late as 1700, in the sixth decade of Manchester's existence, all town selectmen and all but three of the lowest town officers (of a total of nine) were shareholders. At this time, shareholders made up, at most, 38 percent (and probably not more than 25 percent) of Manchester taxpayers.[63]

The sense in which town leaders were proprietary officers rather than settler representatives grew stronger when selectmen were nonresidents. The first selectmen for Groton, appointed by the General Court, were nonresidents. The first Medfield selectmen were Dedham residents appointed to supervise the settlement of that Dedham offshoot. Thomas Brattle and Elisha Hutchinson served as selectmen of Dunstable in 1677 and 1682, elected in town meetings held in Woburn. Both were Dunstable proprietors who lived in Boston.[64]

During the many years when the proprietors attempted to launch the town of Northfield, they met together with a committee appointed by the General Court in the town of Northampton and conducted all town

63. Burt, *Official Records of Springfield*, I, 26–32. See also Snell, "Freemanship, Officeholding, and the Town Franchise in Seventeenth-Century Springfield, Massachusetts," *NEHGR*, CXXXIII (1979), 163–179. On Manchester: Manchester, *Town Records of Manchester*, I, 93; and see Manchester discussed in Chapter 6, "Towns Launched by Other Towns."

64. Samuel Abbott Green, *Proceedings of the Centennial Celebration at Groton, Massachusetts* (Groton, Mass., 1876 [rpt. in Green, ed., *Pamphlets on History of Groton* (n.p., n.d.)]), 12; Tilden, ed., *History of Medfield*, 40; Nason, *History of Dunstable*, 26–27.

business. A similar committee, itself made up of proprietors, disposed of Worcester's business in meetings held outside Worcester for six decades, from the 1660s to the 1720s. John Pynchon acted as the leader for handling all "prudentials" for many Connecticut River Valley towns of which he was a proprietor but not a resident. A committee made up partly of nonresident proprietors governed Wrentham for its first twenty years.[65]

An "inhabitants'" meeting of Northfield chose Major John Stoddard to be their town clerk. Stoddard lived in nearby Northampton throughout his several tenures as town clerk of Northfield; he probably held this post by virtue of being a proprietor of Northfield. If all settlers had voted in the town meeting of Northfield "inhabitants," they probably would have chosen a resident clerk, for settlers outnumbered nonresident proprietors. That a nonresident served as clerk for several years suggests that the meeting of Northfield inhabitants was actually a meeting of proprietors.[66]

Hartford selectmen not only resembled proprietary officers: they represented different proprietorships. In 1635, the first settlers of Hartford settled on the north side of the Little River; in 1636, the next wave of people settled on the south side. These two "plantations" joined together during 1637–1639 to form a single town government. For many years after this union, each plantation nevertheless managed its own proprietary business, divided land solely among its own shareholders, and chose its own selectmen, constables, haywards, surveyors, and fence viewers. Selectmen who did not explicitly represent one plantation or another were not chosen until 1687, fifty years after Hartford's founding. In Providence, the two sides of a land dispute called separate town meetings and elected two different sets of town officers, each claiming to constitute the town government.[67]

65. Rice, ed., *Records of Proprietors of Worcester,* esp. 13–14; William Lincoln, *History of Worcester* . . . (Worcester, Mass., 1862), 35, 50. On Pynchon and Wrentham, see Pynchon discussion in Chapters 1 and 2; Fiore, *Wrentham,* 22, 24; Wrentham Petition, Oct. 15, 1673, Misc. Bound, MHS.

66. Temple and Sheldon, *History of Northfield,* 95, 97, 132–134, 142, 146–158. Though Northfield was launched in the 17th century, Stoddard's tenure occurred during the third settlement attempt, in the 1710s–1720s.

67. William DeLoss Love, *The Colonial History of Hartford* . . . , 2d ed. (Hartford, Conn., 1935; rpt., 1974), 52–54; Charles J. Hoadly, ed., *Hartford Town Votes,* I, *1635–1716* (Conn. Hist. Soc., *Colls.,* VI [Hartford, Conn., 1897]), 42, 123, 222; Daniels, *Dissent and Conformity,* 17.

Like selectmen, some town deputies did not live in the towns they represented. It has been said that colonial life replicated the "medieval circumstances conducive to the concept of attorneyship in representation" and that it was the custom to require town representatives to be residents of the places they represented. Attorneyship may have characterized eighteenth-century representation—colonies did pass laws in the eighteenth century requiring deputies to be residents of their constituencies—but not seventeenth-century representation. Then it was common for towns to send as deputies to the court individuals who did not live in town and who were, in fact, prominent residents of other towns, often of Boston (in the case of Massachusetts towns).[68]

John Hull, the merchant, mint-master, and land speculator, represented five different towns from the 1660s to the 1680s. Edward Hutchinson represented Kittery in 1670–1671. William Davis represented Springfield and Haverhill in the 1650s, 1660s, and 1670s. All these men lived in Boston. Humphrey Atherton of Dorchester represented Springfield in 1653. Richard Collicot of Dorchester represented Portsmouth and Saco in 1672. Rhode Island, where deputies had to be "admitted inhabitants," allowed nonresidents to represent towns; so did Connecticut.[69]

Assistants also occasionally did not live in the regions they represented. In 1663, the active town promoter Eleazer Lusher was an assistant for Maine, though he lived, of course, in Dedham. Bartholomew Gedney represented Maine as a member of the Dudley council, though he lived in Salem. Also in the Dudley council, Fitz John Winthrop represented the Narragansett, though he did not live there. Later, under governors Samuel

68. Michael Kammen, *Deputyes and Libertyes: The Origins of Representative Government in Colonial America* (New York, 1969), 6. Article 68 of the *Body of Liberties*, framed in 1641, allowed deputies to be chosen "either in their owne Townes or elsewhere." Article 62 allowed towns to choose "their Deputies whom and where they please for the General Court. So be it they be free men, and have taken there oath of fealtie, and Inhabiting in this Jurisdiction" (*The Massachusetts Body of Liberties*, in Morgan, ed., *Puritan Political Ideas*, 190–192).

69. John Hull, "The Diaries of John Hull, Mint-Master and Treasurer of the Colony of Massachusetts Bay," American Antiquarian Society, *Transactions, Collections*, III (1857), 121; Hubert Phillips, *The Development of a Residential Qualification for Representatives in Colonial Legislatures* (Cincinnati, Ohio, 1921), 24–25, 65–73, 82–85; William D. Williamson, *The History of the State of Maine . . .* , 2 vols. (Hallowell, Maine, 1832), I, 451–452n.

Shute and William Dummer, the councillors for Maine included Adam Winthrop, Edward Hutchinson, Spencer Phips, and Samuel Thaxter, none of whom lived in Maine.[70]

As time went on, this nonresidency came under attack. In Massachusetts, Governor Phips and the council led the movement to require deputies to be town residents. A bill to that effect passed the General Court in 1693. New Hampshire required the same of town deputies for the first time in 1698. In Rhode Island, no prohibition was enacted, but nonresidency of deputies died out by the end of the seventeenth century. Only in Connecticut did nonresidency remain common toward the end of the century, and the first prohibition against it did not appear until the 1818 state constitution. (Records make it impossible to tell the residency of Connecticut deputies before 1670.)[71]

The question is, Why did towns and regions choose nonresidents to represent them in the colonial capitals of New England? There are several possible answers. Some towns, like Springfield, and some regions, like Maine, were far from the seat of government, and it cost too much and was not convenient to send a deputy or assistant all that distance to join each new session of the General Court. Also, it undoubtedly helped a town get from the court what it wanted when a Hull or a Hutchinson or a Winthrop spoke for its interests. A third explanation involves landownership. Hutchinson, a nonresident deputy of Kittery, had extensive lands there. Job Lane represented Billerica and was a nonresident proprietor of that town. Daniel Allin represented the French town of Oxford and was the nephew of Joseph Dudley, one of the five proprietors who launched the town. As for assistants, Fitz John Winthrop had land in the Narragansett, and Adam Winthrop, the Hutchinson family, Spencer Phips, and Bartholomew Gedney all were owners of tracts in Maine.[72]

Nathaniel Byfield, one of the four Boston purchasers of Bristol, repre-

70. Williamson, *History of Maine*, I, 404, II, 160–161; Everett Kimball, *The Public Life of Joseph Dudley: A Study of the Colonial Policy of the Stuarts in New England, 1660–1715,* Harvard Historical Studies, XV (New York, 1911), 28–29.

71. Phillips, *Development of a Residential Qualification for Representatives,* 34–35, 51, 75, 86, 92.

72. *York Deeds,* I, 57; Hazen, *History of Billerica,* 213; Phillips, *Development of a Residential Qualification for Representatives,* 29; Daniels, *History of the Town of Oxford,* 78–79; Kimball, *Dudley,* 201–203. See Chapter 2 for Hutchinson and Fitz John Winthrop. See *York Deeds,* III, 43, 95–96, IV, 75–77, for some of Gedney's lands. Adam Winthrop was one of the purchasers of the Pejepscot Purchase (*York Deeds,* VIII, 163, 167–168).

sented Bristol to the court (and was speaker of the house). In fact, the right to send a deputy appears to have been granted to the four purchasers, at the time of their township grant, and not to the town or its settlers. John Stanley, who represented Waterbury, Connecticut, as a nonresident in 1690, was a founder and a proprietor of that town with one of the largest land shares.[73] Atherton, who represented Springfield, owned two square miles of that town's land with Roger Clap before their tract became part of the new town of Westfield. Other prominent individuals had farms at Westfield, and it may be that John Hull, who represented Westfield as a nonresident, was a landowner there, too.[74]

In a later case, in 1714, Jonathan Belcher petitioned to the Connecticut General Court asking to represent the town of Pomfret. Belcher lived elsewhere, but he owned six thousand acres of land near Pomfret. In return for joining his land with Pomfret's, he asked that he and his male heirs be allowed to serve Pomfret as representatives to the General Court, although he had no plans of becoming "actually Resident In Said Township." The upper house endorsed the request (though the lower house vetoed it).[75]

Evidently, the colonies allowed nonresidents to represent towns out of a belief that landownership gave one an interest that deserved representation. This notion was an old one, inherited from England. On the one hand, medieval thinking about representation gave the colonists the tradition of attorneyship, which would seem to require the residency of representatives. On the other, there was the medieval tradition of royal grants, in which ownership of land was thoroughly blended with lordship. Massachusetts house members had this latter tradition in mind when they objected to the Phips bill outlawing nonresident representation, saying such a ban "hindered men of the fairest estates from Representing a Town where their Estates lay, except also resident."[76] This blending of ownership with rulership perhaps not only justified the representation of towns by nonresidents

73. Munro, *History of Bristol,* 77–79; Phillips, *Development of a Residential Qualification for Representatives,* 33; Bronson, *History of Waterbury,* 31, 40; Mattatuck Petition, Oct. 9, 1673, Towns and Lands, I, 162–164, Conn. Archives. Phillips (p. 85), who did not remark upon and may not have noticed the shareholding of any of these nonresident deputies, gives Stanley's name as Staley.

74. Burt, *Official Records of Springfield,* II, 109; Woronoco Petition, 1662, CXII, 143–144, Mass. Archives; and see Westfield above, Chapter 2.

75. Belcher Petition, Oct. 14, 1714, Towns and Lands, III, 31, Conn. Archives.

76. Maitland, *Township and Borough,* 11–12; Phillips, *Development of a Residential Qualification for Representatives,* 34–35.

but also underlay the general appropriation of political power by land corporations in New England towns, to the frequent exclusion of non-shareholders.

Or, more simply, it may be that proprietors controlled the choice of town deputy, just as they controlled the town meeting, and that they chose one of their own, although nonresident, to represent their interests. It is impossible to know upon what theory colonists justified nonresident representation. But whether it was because they believed that landownership should be accompanied by rulership or because the proprietors controlled the election of deputies as they did everything else, certainly these deputies were not acting as attorneys for constituencies. A Hull or Winthrop or Atherton was not the servant of settlers; he was vastly superior in stature and wealth to town settlers. Such a deputy did not take instructions from his constituents; he probably rarely, if ever, saw his constituents. Far from being attorneys for settlers, nonresident deputies who owned shares in frontier towns were more likely attorneys for the land corporations in which they owned shares. They may have looked out for the interests of the community, but their relationship to the town they represented was, not as a neighbor or community leader, but as nonresident landowner. That latter status both equipped and entitled them to represent towns to the court.[77]

Nonresidents enjoyed a different sort of political power in those towns that permitted nonresident shareholders to vote in town meetings by proxy. In Marlborough, where nonresident shareholders were called "proprietors" and resident shareholders were called "inhabitants," the former and the latter met together in town meetings. Salem fined anyone who did not attend town meetings "either by there persons or proxies."[78] In Sud-

77. Another example, though not involving nonresidency, points to the same conclusion. In 1684, Daniel Henchman represented Worcester to the General Court, although at that time the town had few settlers and was not holding town meetings. Henchman was a principal proprietor of the town. He served on the General Court committee supervising the town and was evidently chosen by his coproprietors or co-committee members (who were also proprietors) to represent the town's interests. In this sense, Henchman was the representative and the choice of the town proprietors. Ellery Bicknell Crane, ed., *History of Worcester County, Massachusetts,* 3 vols. (New York, 1924), I, 44; and see Worcester discussed in Chapter 1.

78. Franklin P. Rice, ed., "Colonial Records of Marlborough, Mass.," *NEHGR,* LXII (1908), 226; Wm. P. Upham, ed., *Town Records of Salem, Massachusetts* (Essex Institute, *Historical Collections,* 2d Ser., I, part 1 [Salem, Mass., 1868]), 179. Whether this order of 1654 was intended to accommodate nonresidents or not, it did incorporate the principle

bury, in 1656, one man cast three votes in the town meeting on behalf of three nonresident shareholders. Some objected to this voting, saying that even if the nonresident shareholders had been present, they should not have been permitted to vote. The settlers of Ashford, Connecticut, similarly opposed an effort by absentee proprietors to vote in their town meeting. In 1712, when New London, Connecticut, split apart and Groton was formed as a new town, the latter town ordered that the proprietors Wait Winthrop and John Winthrop should have liberty to "voat in any of our towne meeetings that may bee held at any time or times hereafter . . . or in theire absences any two of theire Tenants may have the like Liberty of voating and no moor but two in theire LandLords Steads in the Severall towne meetings." A Massachusetts law of 1739 revising the town franchise clearly prohibited voting by people not present. Among the new qualifications required of voters, the court for the first time insisted that they be "Personally present at such meeting." The court would not have made this requirement if people had not previously been voting without being present.[79]

In some cases, although nonresidents may not have cast votes in town meetings, they decided who could and could not. At the end of the seventeenth century, the four purchasers of Lebanon granted to settlers the right to "be accounted inhabitants, and have the priviledg to give theire voate in all the town affaires, and in any grant of any lands, within the sd township." The Sowams proprietors, some of them nonresidents, decided in 1667 which people should be admitted as inhabitants, with rights to vote and to share lands, in the new township of Swansea. The same procedure may have been used to constitute the town meeting of Bristol.[80]

Whether voters were resident or not, they sometimes counted their votes by shares, not by hands, when voting on land matters; in this political habit as well towns resembled English joint-stock companies. The Dorchester "town meeteinge" voted in 1642 that "all Oregenale lottes In the necke of Land shall have there Voates About planteinge the Necke: and If any have bought one: two or three more or les: they shall have soe many Voates as

---

of voting by proxy, which is a device more commonly associated with business corporations than with communities.

79. Powell, *Puritan Village*, 124–125; Daniels, *Connecticut Town*, 23; Groton Items, 1712, Towns and Lands, III, 237b, Conn. Archives; Act for Regulating Townships, 1739, CXIV, 325–328, Mass. Archives.

80. Lebanon, c. 1699, Towns and Lands, II, 146d–147, Conn. Archives; Bicknell, *History of Barrington*, 139; Munro, *History of Bristol*, 77–79.

they have lottes." The General Court not only endorsed this method of counting votes; it required it. In 1643, Massachusetts ordered that, with regard to managing enclosed common lands, "those who have the greatr quantity in such feilds shall have power to order the whole." (This act also ordered commoners to maintain fences in proportion to their interests in the enclosed tract.) In 1647, the court broadened this order by requiring that those "proprietors" with the greatest part of the land shall order affairs for common fields. In 1667, the court reversed a Woburn town vote on the grounds that Woburn had failed to count votes by shares. In resolving that town's controversy, the court ordered that Woburn's land be divided solely among "those that are legally interested therein" and that all future divisions be ordered by those with the "greater" interest.[81]

Occasionally people objected to voting by shares. Proprietors and non-proprietors fought each other in Windsor, Connecticut, over this issue, the former wishing to count votes by rights represented and the latter by hands raised. The proprietors of East Greenwich, Rhode Island, declared in their founding covenant of 1677 that all decisions would be made by majority vote and that although one man might have more than one share, he should not have more than one vote "about anything relating to said land." But this prohibition merely confirms that voting by shares occurred; otherwise, the Greenwich order would not have been necessary. Certainly land companies that founded towns voted by shares. The Sowams "Company of Proprietors" decided that "in all things concerning the premises be accounted according to the number of shares and proportions which each one does injoy."[82] The Atherton shareholders frequently voted by proxy, with one individual casting the votes of several absent voters; this style of counting votes placed emphasis on the share, not on the holder of the share. So it is likely, though there is no way of telling one way or another, that the Atherton Company also cast votes according to shares. The Conihasset Partners, an association claiming a large part of Scituate, recorded the following vote on March 1, 1640: "Agreed by the Company being met together for the ordering of the said land . . . that what shalbe voted by the

81. Boston, Registry Dept., *Dorchester Town Records (Fourth Report of the Record Commissioners)* (Boston, 1880), 49; *Mass. Records,* II, 39, 195, IV, part 2, 354–356.

82. Andrews, *River Towns,* 52 n. 3; D. H. Greene, *History of the Town of East Greenwich and Adjacent Territory, from 1677 to 1877* (Providence, R.I., 1877), 29–30; Thomas W. Bicknell, *Sowams, with Ancient Records of Sowams and Parts Adjacent* (New Haven, Conn., 1908), 45.

company, the greater vote shall carry it . . . and that every thirtyeth part or share shall have one voyce and that two half shares shall have but one voyce."[83]

Towns were similar to land companies in so many other ways that it is possible, though not recorded, that some towns voted by shares on all matters, not just land matters. But even if they voted that way just when managing land, voting by shares was yet another manifestation of the business precocity of New England colonists. Not until the Restoration did English joint-stock companies switch from voting by hands to voting by shares, when only a few large enterprises, like the East India Company, made the switch.[84] In America, land corporations were counting votes by shares at least by 1640, if not before then. In this behavior, colonists did not so much borrow as pioneer corporate techniques.

From the beginning of colonization, New Englanders used shares to apportion rights and responsibilities in towns. They divided land by shares, taxed themselves by shares, and based political participation upon the holding of shares. In some places, they even voted by shares. Shares shaped the essential relations between individuals and their towns. They gave to towns a strong business character by reflecting the principle that rights were anchored by investment.

83. John Fones, *The Records of the Proprietors of the Narragansett, Otherwise Called the Fones Record,* ed. James W. Arnold (Providence, R.I., 1894), esp. 19–21, 29–30; Harvey Hunter Pratt, *The Early Planters of Scituate* (Scituate, Mass., 1929), 45.

84. Scott, *Constitution of Joint-Stock Companies,* I, 270.

6 | The Exclusiveness of Land Corporations

1. Limiting the Membership of Corporations

Sometime after each land corporation was formed, whether it was a town or a land company, the founders limited the stockholders in it. This limiting of shareholders did not mean that towns refused grants to all newcomers. Some did, and others did not; some made grants in early years, then ceased in later years. But a town's granting a piece of land to someone, without expressly admitting the grantee to rights in the land corporation, did not oblige the town to include the grantee in future divisions of the town's undivided lands. Such grants conferred only acreage upon individuals—not rights. The grant of land rights admitted the grantee to the shareholders, and this was the group that land companies and towns closely limited.

They did so not necessarily to limit the number of residents in a town. In most towns, the number of residents increased while the number of stockholders in the land corporation remained steady. Towns did, of course, screen newcomers, rejecting those they did not wish to have as neighbors because of their poverty or their heresies or their licentious behavior. But towns maintained this social control by means of a variety of laws and customs that had little to do with restricting shareholders of the corporation (see Chapter 7). The restriction of shareholders was a business measure. Shareholders carefully controlled their own numbers principally to preserve the value of their shares. They wished to divide their land among as few people as possible.[1]

Of the towns here studied, more than half either terminated or drastically reduced admissions to the land corporation within thirty years of settlement, and more than a third did so within the first ten years of settlement (see Appendix 5). These data do not count those companies that launched towns but were not towns themselves; if they did, they would be larger. The termination of admissions did not foreclose all possibility that a newcomer could become a shareholder. One could—if one bought a share or a fraction of a share of an existing proprietor. In either case, however often shares changed hands, the number of whole shares remained the same after the termination of admissions to the land corporation.

Of the land corporations that ceased admitting members in the first ten years, some closed admissions as soon as they were opened. That is, as soon as the proprietorship was formed and the grant received, no one could acquire a share in the township except by purchase from an existing shareholder. Several Merrimack Valley landowners created Dunstable by petitioning for a grant that would take in their farms as well as convey to them a much larger area than their farms encompassed. Nearly all of these individuals lived far from Dunstable: William Brenton, Thomas Brattle, Sampson Sheafe, Peter Bulkeley, Joseph Dudley, Thomas Weld, and the heirs of John Endicott and Isaac Johnson. In order to receive a share of the undivided portion of Dunstable (some two hundred square miles), one had to purchase a right or a fraction of a right from a member of this absentee proprietary association. Oxford, Massachusetts, also sealed the land corporation virtually upon its creation.[2] Most towns launched by other towns,

1. As for antecedents, English joint-stock companies, of course, restricted membership to stockholders, a fact noted by George Lee Haskins in remarking upon social solidarity in early New England (*Law and Authority in Early Massachusetts: A Study in Tradition and Design* [New York, 1960], 58). F. W. Maitland pointed out that Cambridge, England, acted to restrict pasture rights after it was incorporated, and it did so by the same standard employed by many New England towns, restricting rights to those who had been in town by a certain date (*Township and Borough* [Cambridge, 1898; rpt., 1964], 89).

2. Elias Nason, *A History of the Town of Dunstable, Massachusetts . . .* (Boston, 1877), 6–10, 16–17, 26–27. It is possible that 12 years after Dunstable was founded residents who had not bought rights or parts of rights were entitled to some small part of the common lands. Town residents entered into an agreement with the nonresident proprie-

such as New Roxbury, Milton, and Manchester, all in Massachusetts, closed admissions to the land corporation at the outset of the venture (see below, "Towns Launched by Other Towns").

Other towns admitted new shareholders after their founding but set a limit, a maximum number of shareholders they agreed ever to accept. In 1654, the year Lancaster received town liberties, the town voted that there "should not be taken into the towne" more than thirty-five families, there being twenty-five "townsmen" at the time. Settlement began in Northfield in 1673, was interrupted by war, and resumed in 1685, when the shareholders decided that new members should be admitted "until the number of forty families be settled." In 1655, when Amesbury split off from Salisbury, the settlers agreed not to admit more than twenty-six inhabitants with land rights, and they kept their word, or very nearly so. Swansea voted four years after its creation not to give land rights to more than sixty inhabitants. The Sowams Company, which launched the town of Swansea, followed an even more restrictive policy; for many years, the number of shares stood at approximately ten, and no one acquired a share except by purchase or inheritance.[3]

When towns did not set a limit at the outset for shareholders, they often simply cut off admissions within a few years of settlement. Dorchester ordered on January 18, 1635/6, "that all the hoame lots within Dorchester plantaton which have bene granted before this 'sent day shall have right to the Commons and no other lotts that are graunted hereafter to be commoners." In the fall of 1635, Watertown decided that "too many Inhabitants" were being accepted, by which the town might be "ruinated," so it ordered that "no Foreainer comming into the Towne, or any Family arising among our selves shall have any benefitt either of Commonage, or Land

tors in 1685 for dividing the common lands of the town, and it is possible that some of these residents had never purchased rights or parts of rights yet were nonetheless included in this deal (Dunstable Meeting, July 22, 1685, MSS Bound, MHS). On Oxford, see Dudley Grant, May 18, 1683, CXII, 341, Mass. Archives; George F. Daniels, *The Huguenots in the Nipmuck Country; or, Oxford Prior to 1713* (Boston, 1880), 40–48.

3. Henry S. Nourse, ed., *The Early Records of Lancaster, Massachusetts, 1643–1725* (Lancaster, Mass., 1884), 41; J. H. Temple and George Sheldon, *A History of the Town of Northfield, Massachusetts* . . . (Albany, N.Y., 1875), 97; Joseph Merrill, *History of Amesbury and Merrimac, Massachusetts* (Haverhill, Mass., 1880; rpt., 1978), 55; Thomas Williams Bicknell, *A History of Barrington, Rhode Island* (Providence, R.I., 1898), 58–66, 157–158.

undivided but what they shall purchase, except that they buy a mans right wholly in the Towne." Hartford limited its land shareholders within three years of the town's founding, Providence within perhaps a year or two, and others at an equally early stage.[4]

Other towns left no formal record of limiting their land corporations early in their history, but evidence indicates that they must have done so. When Waterbury, Connecticut, was founded, in 1674, 29 men subscribed to articles of association and were accepted as shareholders of the town's undivided land. In 1688, the town had 34 proprietors sharing land divisions. In 1722, thirty-four years later, the town had only 36 full-fledged proprietors, an increase of 6 percent. During this same thirty-four-year period, the town population grew by 94 percent (from 180 to 350). This disparity in growth rates suggests that Waterbury closed its land corporation soon after the town was founded. The proprietors arrived at the same conclusion in 1703, when they voted that only those original purchasers of the township and such as had been accepted by the grand committee that had organized the town "shall be acknowledged proprietary inhabitants."[5]

Forty-four people shared land divisions in Marlborough in 1665, soon

4. Boston, Registry Dept., *Dorchester Town Records (Fourth Report of the Record Commissioners)* (Boston, 1880), 14; Historical Society of Watertown, *Watertown Records, Comprising the First and Second Books of Town Proceedings with the Lands, Grants, and Possessions,* 5 vols. (Watertown, Mass., 1894), I, 2; Charles J. Hoadly, ed., *Hartford Town Votes,* I, 1635–1716 (Connecticut Historical Society, *Collections,* VI [Hartford, Conn., 1897]), 10, 16–20; Hartford, Conn., *Original Distribution of the Lands in Hartford among the Settlers: 1639* (Conn. Hist. Soc., *Colls.,* XIV, [Hartford, Conn., 1912]), 494–501, 549–550; William DeLoss Love, *The Colonial History of Hartford . . . ,* 2d ed. (Hartford, Conn., 1935; rpt., 1974), 52–53, 126, 152; Samuel Greene Arnold, *History of the State of Rhode Island and Providence Plantations,* 2 vols. (New York, 1859–1860), I, 99–100, 121; John Callender, *An Historical Discourse, on the Civil and Religious Affairs of the Colony of Rhode-Island and Providence Plantations . . .* (Boston, 1739 [republished in RIHS, *Collections,* IV (Providence, R.I., 1838)]), 204–205; Henry C. Dorr, "The Proprietors of Providence, and Their Controversies with the Freeholders," RIHS, *Publications,* n.s., III (1895), 143, 155–157, 201–206, 209–215; Sidney S. Rider, "The Forgeries Connected with the Deed Given by the Sachems Canonicus and Miantinomi to Roger Williams of the Land on Which the Town of Providence Was Planted," *Rhode Island Historical Tracts,* 2d Ser., no. 4 (Providence, R.I., 1896), 59–64; A. B. Patton, "The Early Land Titles of Providence," *NHR,* VIII (1890), 166–167.

5. Henry Bronson, *The History of Waterbury, Connecticut . . .* (Waterbury, Conn., 1858), 8–9, 40, 123, 566; Katharine A. Prichard, ed., *Proprietors' Records of the Town of Waterbury, Connecticut: 1677–1761,* Publications of the Mattatuck Historical Society, I (Waterbury, Conn., 1911), 57.

after the town was founded. In 1684, forty-six shareholders divided the town's land, an increase of two shareholders in twenty years. Forty-one people shared a division of Haverhill plowland in 1652. Forty-one shareholders again shared a division six years later (being the same individuals, with one change). In 1661, Haverhill had fifty proprietors. During the rest of that decade and in later years, the town refused on numerous occasions to give people land shares. In 1721, when the commoners made their fifth division, forty-six people shared the land, only five more than had done so in the early 1650s. Of these forty-six, all but seven had last names that appeared on town records within the first three years of the town's founding.[6]

Some towns delayed the closing of their corporate membership rolls. Cambridge closely regulated who was admitted to the town with land rights, but it was not until 1665, more than thirty years after founding, that the town voted that "no more proprietors shall be allowed without unanimous consent." This vote virtually sealed admissions. Having taken an account "of all the grants that had bine given and granted," Groton "did solemlie determine to take in no more but a taylear and a smith" fourteen years after the town's founding. In 1673, during its fourth decade, Scituate ordered that no one had any interest in the undivided lands "that is not allowed and approved" by the town of Scituate.[7]

Notwithstanding these slower-acting shareholders, more towns, by a margin of two to one, sealed their corporate membership early rather than late—within the first ten years of settlement—of those towns' sealing membership during the first thirty years. This restriction of shareholders provoked serious fights in several towns. In Providence, the fight was so

6. Franklin P. Rice, ed., "Colonial Records of Marlborough, Mass.," *New England Historical and Genealogical Register,* LXIII (1909), 120–121; Marlborough Petition, 1709, CXIII, 524–527, Mass. Archives. The Haverhill figures are derived by comparing land division lists given in George Wingate Chase, *The History of Haverhill, Massachusetts, from Its First Settlement, in 1640, to the Year 1860* (Haverhill, Mass., 1861), 35–47, 76–77, 87, 92–94, 129, 131, 256.

7. Cambridge, Mass., *The Register Book of the Lands and Houses in the "New Towne" and the Town of Cambridge, with the Records of the Proprietors of the Common Lands . . .* (Cambridge, Mass., 1896), 144–148 (hereafter cited as *Cambridge Proprietors Records*); Samuel A. Green, ed., *The Town Records of Groton, Massachusetts: 1662–1678* (Groton, Mass., 1879 [rpt. in Green, ed., *Pamphlets on History of Groton* (n.p., n.d.)]), 24 (hereafter cited as *Groton Town Records*); Josiah Henry Benton, *Warning Out in New England* (New York, 1911), 26.

severe that political authority broke down; in Sudbury, it was so nasty that a number of men left the town to found Marlborough. Complaints also accompanied the termination of admissions in Portsmouth.[8] In defense of their actions, shareholders argued that it was they who had started the town, who had borne the expense of developing it, and who should, therefore, benefit from the land divisions. When Groton terminated admissions to the land corporation, the town noted that it took this action "Consedering the great Charg that hath bine upon the present inhabitants." In Salisbury, years after the founding, a man sued the proprietors to be included in a land division, arguing that even though his father had moved out of the town years before, he had never surrendered his rights to the common land. The town answered that by leaving the town years before, the plaintiff's father had not helped pay for the government, the church, and other public expenses by which the town of Salisbury was built up. In the opinion of Salisbury, Richard Coy "did Nothing and therefore had Nothing."[9]

In Marlborough, resident nonproprietors petitioned the court years after the founding, asking to be included in town land divisions. The proprietors stated in rebuttal that it was the proprietors who had "borne the Charge of Settleing the town and a minister therein . . . for a Great many years to gether."[10] These proprietors were, of course, the children of the individuals (and some of them the individuals themselves) who had left Sudbury in anger over that town's refusal to let newcomers have rights in Sudbury's undivided lands. Half a century later, the Marlborough proprietors justified an identical land monopoly that they had begun to exercise soon after starting the new town.

Of course, the Marlborough, Salisbury, and Groton proprietors had a point, and so did the thirty-one other towns studied that cut off admissions

8. Adelos Gorton, *The Life and Times of Samuel Gorton* . . . (Philadelphia, 1907), 23–24, 28–29, 32–33, 98; Dorr, "Proprietors of Providence," RIHS, *Publs.,* n.s., III (1895), 143; Rider, "Forgeries Connected with the Deed Given by the Sachems Canonicus and Miantinomi to Roger Williams," *R.I. Hist. Tracts,* 2d Ser., no. 4 (1896), 50–51; Roger Williams to John Whipple, Jr., Aug. 24, 1669, in *R.I. Hist. Tracts,* 1st Ser., no. 14 (Providence, R.I., 1881), 41; Sumner Chilton Powell, *Puritan Village: The Formation of a New England Town* (Middletown, Conn., 1963), 75–77, 94, 96, 99, 118–131; Sudbury Petitions, 1708, CXIII, 441–449, Mass. Archives.

9. *Groton Town Records,* 24; Salisbury Case, 1706, CXIII, 554–565, Mass. Archives.

10. Marlborough Petition, 1709, CXIII, 524–527, Mass. Archives.

to their corporation soon after the town's founding. The first shareholders *did* bear the expense of launching the town, and by doing so, by their settling and developing the town, the lands of the town rose in value. If anyone was going to profit from this increased value, it was only natural that those whose labor and time and money had created the value should do so; and those were the members of the limited land corporation.

This logic not only armed the town founders and their children in defense of their rights; it also persuaded colonial authorities. During the 1650s, several towns had fought over the limiting of their land corporations and taken their cases to the General Court. In 1660, the Massachusetts General Court enacted legislation that, it hoped, would put an end to these difficult controversies. The court enacted that "no cottage or dwelling place shallbe admitted to the priviledg of comonage for wood, timber, and herbage, or any other the priviledges that lye in comon in any toune or peculiar, but such as already are in being or hereafter shallbe erected by the consent of the toune."[11]

With this legislation, the court seemingly struck a compromise between the two contending camps, a compromise by which all existing houses could enjoy land rights and none in the future could do so without permission of the town. The apparent balance notwithstanding, the court's action came down on the side of the shareholders. For in 1660, shareholders controlled nearly every town; and by placing this important issue within their discretion from 1660 henceforward, the court ratified the power of shareholders to restrict their own membership, a power they had been exercising on their own since the 1630s. Throughout the colonial period, the General Court disliked interfering in the affairs of town land corporations; the milestone act of 1660 was no exception.

Immediately, a number of towns took advantage of the new law to restrict their land corporations. In the same year the court passed its measure, Andover prohibited the building of houses on lands not granted for that purpose, "the town having given houselots to build on to all such as they have received as inhabitants of the town." The Ipswich selectmen ordered that "as it is found by dayly experience that the Common Lands of this Towne are overburdened by the multiplying [of] houses contrary to the true intent and meaneing of the Inhabitants in their grant of house Lotts and other Lands . . . no house henceforth erected shall have any right to the

11. *Mass. Records*, IV, part 1, 417.

common lands." In 1661, Haverhill took advantage of the court act by drawing up a list of those individuals who had built houses in the town and were not entitled to land privileges (there were twenty such people). Rowley followed the next year, voting that there should be "noe more Adission of Gates [the Rowley unit of measuring land rights] nether by Giveing leting or selling" except to accommodate teachers.[12] Across Massachusetts, towns took advantage of the new law to restrict land shareholders, if they had not already done so on their own.

II. The Nonproprietors of New England Towns

This limiting of shares, both before and after the 1660 act, had a profound consequence for New England towns: it constituted the body of shareholders as an exclusive, privileged club in each town, and it produced a shareless population in most towns. Of the towns studied, the overwhelming majority—three-quarters—had adult male residents who did not own rights to the undivided land contained within their own towns' borders (see Appendix 6).

Some of these men received small land grants, but did not participate in repeated divisions of common lands. Some may have been servants. But the preponderance of the evidence about nonshareholding relates to men who were neither servants, nor minors, nor necessarily poor men or single men. It was not just an underclass that was denied land shares. Some of those excluded were taxpayers, heads of families, and householders.

They fell into two broad categories; or, rather, they were denied land shares by one of two possible ways. There were those denied land shares by shareholders who were mostly nonresidents; and there were those denied shares by fellow residents, their own neighbors. As to the first group, nonresidents frequently denied shares to residents both when older towns started new settlements and when groups of individuals started settlements. When the General Court granted a township to a group of individuals, it usually required the grantees to settle a certain number of families and to

---

12. Benton, *Warning Out,* 37; Ipswich Town Order, 1659–60 (?), CXII, 27, Mass. Archives; Chase, *History of Haverhill,* 93; Rowley, Mass., *The Early Records of the Town of Rowley, Massachusetts, 1639–1672* (Rowley, Mass., 1894), 128–129.

procure a minister within a given time period. These grant conditions were sometimes hard to meet—whenever warfare on the frontier lowered the demand for wilderness land and whenever a proliferation of township grants increased the available land supply. At these moments, grantees came under pressure to find settlers or forfeit their grants. They responded to this pressure by drawing up plans for placing settlers on their lands. In every decade, in many towns, nonresident proprietors in all likelihood placed settlers on lots purely in order to satisfy the settlement conditions of their grant; but the actual plans stating their intent to do so have survived only in a few cases, most of those being instances when proprietors came under court pressure to fulfill the grant terms on penalty of forfeiture.

Such was the case in Northfield. The Indian war of 1675 aborted the first settlement attempt. On the second attempt, the court committee overseeing the town declared that every grantee receiving sixty acres of interval land should "settle two inhabitants" upon it. Joseph Parsons, a nonresident owner of Northfield, received ninety acres and therefore had to place three settlers in town. These settlers did not receive Parsons's rights to the undivided land, for that would have defeated his purpose in owning rights in the first place. (It would also have made it unreasonable for the court to demand of him that he place three settlers in the town.) Parsons held on to his rights for many years.[13]

Worcester also had trouble getting started. Through the several different settlement attempts, the proprietors were charged with having to "Setle an inhabitant acceptable to the comittee," having to "endevor either in their persons, or by their Relations or by their purses to Setle the Said plantation," and settling either "themselves in the said place . . . [or placing] a servant there." In the last case, any undertaker with more than one right could by placing a single servant in the town perform the settlement duty for two, three, or four rights.[14]

Many nonresident proprietary organizations put settlers who were not proprietors on the land. In 1662, the Misquamicut Company offered five pounds to every person who would "go and abide at Misquamocuk," later Westerly. Joseph Dudley and his partners gave eleven thousand acres first to the French, then to the English, settlers of Oxford, who in neither case had rights to the remaining thirty thousand acres of Oxford. Mathew Cradock

13. Temple and Sheldon, *History of Northfield,* 67–69, 95, 103–107.

14. Franklin P. Rice, ed., *Records of the Proprietors of Worcester, Massachusetts* (Worcester Society of Antiquity, *Collections,* III [Worcester, Mass., 1881]), 17, 21–31, 37, 42.

peopled Medford with his employees, who, being tenants, had no rights to the undivided lands of the town. As early as 1623, Gorges and Mason wrote to their American agent, Ambrose Gibbins, about the Piscataqua settlement. "We have not onlie each of us shipped people present to plant upon our owne landes at our own charge," they wrote, "but have given direction to invite and authoritie to receive such others as may be had to be tenants, to plant and live there for the more speedie peopleing of the countrie." By this means, initially at least, Dover was settled—by tenants, not owners of rights to undivided lands.[15]

It is possible that most tenants placed upon lands by nonresidents eventually came to own their own lots or that their children became landowners. There is evidence that some did so.[16] If many did, then the gradual passage from tenancy to freeholdship offered to early Americans an important route for economic advancement that is worth further study. That possibility, however, interesting as it is, does not speak to the constitution of the land corporations that held the undivided lands of New England towns. Nor does it alter the point that wherever nonresidents retained ownership of the corporate shares and put tenants or servants or lot purchasers on some part of their lands, there lived men in frontier towns who were not shareholders and who therefore did not participate in repeated divisions of common lands.

In addition to these shareless settlers, there was a second group of nonproprietors: those denied land shares, not by nonresidents, but by

15. Potter, *Early History of Narragansett,* 259–260; Holmes Ammidown, *Historical Collections . . .* , 2d ed., 2 vols. (New York, 1877), I, 185–187; A. Holmes, "Memoir of the French Protestants, Who Settled at Oxford, Massachusetts, *A.D.* 1686 . . . ," MHS, *Collections,* 3d Ser., II (1830), 59; George F. Daniels, *History of the Town of Oxford, Massachusetts . . .* (Oxford, Mass., 1892), 46; Charles Brooks, *History of the Town of Medford . . .* (Boston, 1855), 39, 87; Jeremy Belknap, *The History of New-Hampshire* (Dover, N.H., 1831), 3–4, 428.

16. In 1677, Philip Mattoon rented Deerfield lands from the nonresident proprietor John Pynchon. Mattoon was not included in the lists of those assessed for the purchase price of Deerfield in 1669, nor of those drawing lots in 1670 and 1671, nor of those with fence responsibility in 1687, nor of those with cow commons in 1688. His absence from these lists suggests that Mattoon was not a Deerfield proprietor during the town's first several decades. Then in 1723 an Isaac Mattoon appeared on the list of town proprietors. George Sheldon, *A History of Deerfield, Mass. . . .* , 2 vols. (Deerfield, Mass., 1895–1896), I, 14, 16–17, 19, 179–180, 196–197, 208–209, 498–499 (where these lists are reprinted).

fellow residents. Of the forty-nine towns with nonproprietor residents, thirty were towns in which those denying land shares to residents were primarily resident proprietors, not nonresident. Nonresident owners were not the only ones wishing to regulate closely their shareholder membership. The desire to preserve the value of land shares was common to resident and nonresident proprietors alike.[17]

Court petitions, settlement plans, and references to tenantry are the principal evidence pointing to the existence of nonproprietors in towns begun by nonresidents. In towns where residents excluded fellow residents from the common land, other sources provide the evidence. The comparison of tax lists with land division lists, of voting lists with proprietors' lists, and of shareholder totals with population totals; the town orders rejecting residents who applied to be shareholders; and the different steps that towns took to appease their nonshareholders—from these diverse sources, the evidence is unmistakable that thousands of New Englanders in the seventeenth century were denied land rights by their own neighbors.

The first source is the record of rejections of those seeking admission to the land corporation. To become a member of a town's land corporation, one had to be admitted by the shareholders. (This admissions procedure is explained in Chapter 7.) Towns sometimes rejected their own residents who applied for admission to the land corporation. In 1639, just five years after it was founded, Ipswich refused to give land rights to Humphrey Griffin, though Griffin lived in the town. Within a few years of its founding, in 1671, the town of Groton allowed people to become inhabitants of the town, without giving them rights to the town's land.[18] There were other such rejections (discussed below). There were also towns that neither admitted nor rejected applicants for years on end. In these towns, some of which had passed orders sealing the land corporation, it is likely that nonproprietors did not bother applying for admission because they knew the possibility was foreclosed.

17. The 30 towns were Amesbury, Andover, Boston, Cambridge, Charlestown, Dedham, Dorchester, Groton, Haverhill, Ipswich, Lancaster, Marlborough, Rowley, Roxbury, Salem, Salisbury, Springfield, Sudbury, Watertown, Woburn; Hartford, New Haven, Norwich, Stratford, Wethersfield; Portsmouth, Providence, Warwick; Falmouth, Scarborough. See Appendix 6.

18. Thomas Franklin Waters, *Ipswich in the Massachusetts Bay Colony* . . . , 2 vols. (Ipswich, Mass., 1905–1917), I, 90; *Groton Town Records*, 31.

Second, in several towns the number of adult male residents exceeded the number of people sharing in land divisions. In some towns the excess was considerable. In 1641, there were 111 commoners in Ipswich, yet there were at that time more than twice as many—250—adult male residents. In Springfield, 19 people shared a land division in 1640, 21 in 1643, and 46 in 1656. On the other hand, some 150 males came to Springfield during the years 1636–1663. In 1679, there were 132 adult males resident in Springfield, yet in 1665, only 72 males were entitled to share in the town's land division (and it is likely that the population was lower in 1679 than it had been in the ten years before King Philip's War). Other records reveal the early presence of residents, such as Richard Everett, who were not included in land divisions.[19]

In Watertown, within six years of the town's founding, in 1636, 120 grantees shared a land division. In 1644, an inventory of grants again revealed 120 grantees. In 1647, however, 150 adult males lived in Watertown, and that figure does not count the many people who left Watertown, like the founders of Sudbury, because the town excluded them from land divisions. At the same time Watertown was denying land shares to some of its residents, 94 percent of the town's land was not under cultivation. This squirreling of land suggests a land corporation determined to preserve the value of its shares, even at the cost of inequity. The inequity was only

19. In comparing population with proprietors, the author has relied on the population estimates of Robert E. Wall, Arlin I. Ginsburg, and others who have studied the population of 17th-century New England towns. Tax figures and proprietors' figures are drawn from tax lists, proprietors' lists, and division lists found in town records, proprietors' records, General Court records, and reliable town histories.

On Ipswich: Edward S. Perzel, "Landholding in Ipswich," Essex Inst., *Hist. Colls.*, CIV (1968), 325; Arlin I. Ginsburg, "The Franchise in Seventeenth-Century Massachusetts: Ipswich," *William and Mary Quarterly*, 3d Ser., XXXIV (1977), 451. In 1679, commoners represented anywhere from 36% to 50% of the adult male Ipswich population (Waters, *Ipswich in the Massachusetts Bay Colony*, I, 93–106; Ginsburg, "Franchise in Ipswich," 447–451). These authors primarily were interested in calculating the proportion of residents who were voters, but the lists they reprint and figures they present enable one to calculate the proportion of residents who were commoners.

On Springfield: Henry M. Burt, *The First Century of the History of Springfield: The Official Records from 1636 to 1736*, 2 vols. (Springfield, Mass., 1898–1899), I, 40–45, 156–158, 160–161, 164–168, 170–172, 190–191, 240–242, II, 77, 567 (hereafter cited as Burt, *Official Records of Springfield*).

enhanced by the fact that those who did have land owned average holdings of two hundred acres each and lived on homesteads that averaged twenty acres each. Some house lots even reached sixty-six acres.[20]

Third, in some towns the number of taxpayers exceeded the number of proprietors.[21] In Hartford, in 1666, 95 people were entitled to land shares. Yet twelve years before, in 1654, Hartford had had 177 ratable persons, which means that at least 82 people, or 46 percent, were excluded from shares in the land corporation (and probably more, for undoubtedly the population grew in twelve years). Other evidence points to nonproprietors living in Hartford during the first four years of settlement. In Dedham, 102 people paid taxes in 1647, yet only 83 people shared a land division in 1645. In 1653, Dedham rated 90 residents for the country rate, yet in that same year only 76 people shared a division of town lands.[22]

20. *Watertown Town Proceedings,* I, 2; *Watertown Proprietors Records,* I, 3, 8–14, 17–67, 69–113; Robert Emmett Wall, Jr., "The Massachusetts Bay Colony Franchise in 1647," *WMQ,* 3d Ser., XXVII (1970), 148; Powell, *Puritan Village,* 76–77. A later example is Salisbury, Mass. In 1650, the Salisbury town meeting took an accounting of "townsmen and Comoners" and declared that none but the officially entered names should be considered in this category. The town listed 66 people, including 2 women. In the preceding decades, however, the town had had 68 adult male residents. Salisbury Town Meeting, Mar. 3, 1650/1 [incorrectly identified as Dec. 3 owing to error in translating Old Style dates], Misc. Bound, MHS; Merrill, *History of Amesbury,* 11–12; Wall, "Massachusetts Franchise in 1647," 138.

21. Composition of taxpayers is discussed in Chapters 1 and 5.

22. Hoadly, ed., *Hartford Town Votes,* 16–20; Love, *Colonial History of Hartford,* 126, 152; Robert E. Wall, "The Franchise in Seventeenth-Century Massachusetts: Dedham and Cambridge," *WMQ,* 3d Ser., XXXIV (1977), 453–455; B. Katherine Brown, "Puritan Democracy in Dedham, Massachusetts: Another Case Study," *WMQ,* 3d Ser., XXIV (1967), 387–388; Dedham, Mass., *The Early Records of the Town . . . ,* 6 vols. (Dedham, Mass., 1886–1936), III, 109–111, 211–214. Wall and Brown were interested in the franchise, but their estimates of commoners are useful. Jackson Turner Main's findings about tax rolls are helpful. In Fairfield, Middletown, and Windsor, one-third to one-half of young men paid no tax (not to mention other men—paupers, servants, migrants, the insane—also kept off the rolls) (*Society and Economy in Colonial Connecticut* [Princeton, N.J., 1985], 88–89). Hence whenever one finds taxpayers excluded from the land corporation, one may assume that other men in addition were also excluded. Moreover, Main has found that population figures derived from tax figures are usually underestimates and that tax rolls should be multiplied by a factor of 4.5–5 rather than the usual 4 to arrive at a more accurate population total. Thus populations in towns would be larger and the proportion of people included in land corporations would be even smaller than indicated here. *Society and Economy,* 8.

Fourth, voters outnumbered shareholders in some towns. In 1639, 111 men had signed the political covenant of New Haven as burgesses (the term used for voters there), yet two years later only 86 people shared a meadow division in New Haven, including 7 women. In other words, some 32 men, or 29 percent of voters, were excluded from the land corporation of New Haven in the first year of settlement.[23]

Fifth, the existence of nonproprietors is revealed by the fights that occurred between them and proprietors. These fights, already mentioned, did much to tear apart the communities of Providence, Portsmouth, and several other towns in the first ten years of their founding. Sometimes a town made concessions to its nonproprietors, perhaps to ward off a fight, concessions that usually took the form of partial land rights granted to nonshareholders, newcomers, children, and freed servants—a sort of halfway covenant for the nonproprietors. Rarely did the concession rectify the enormous disparity in landownership between proprietors and nonproprietors. Nor did these halfway covenants prevent the impending rebellion by nonproprietors in every town. On balance, the historical significance of the concessions of proprietors is the additional evidence they supply that nonproprietors existed and were a problem in early seventeenth-century towns.

In Providence, in 1646, the proprietors created "quarter-rights," giving nonproprietors one acre for every four acres divided to the proprietors. Over the next few years, the proprietors bought up most of these quarter-rights, and, in 1663, they terminated all admissions to their ranks. By 1640, Hartford had granted lots "at the towns courtesy" to twenty-six men. These men did not have rights to town land; they merely received lots out of the generosity of the town. The town continued this practice, granting courtesy lots to forty-one people in 1666, yet still keeping the number of full shares at the 1640 level. Courtesy lots were smaller than lots received by shareholders. In 1640, the largest allotment of a nonproprietor was 3.8 percent the size of the largest allotment assigned to one of the proprietors.[24]

In 1662, Amesbury granted what it called "townships" to the children of proprietors and other nonproprietors, but these grants did not entitle the grantees to land shares. Norwalk, Connecticut, also included children in a

23. Charles J. Hoadly, ed., *Records of the Colony and Plantation of New Haven, from 1638 to 1649* (Hartford, Conn., 1857), 17, 49–51.
24. See note 4, above.

once-in-a-lifetime grant, which did not entitle the children to participate in later divisions. Waterbury, Connecticut, late in the seventeenth century, granted "bachelor rights" to the sons of proprietors, but these rights did not carry the important privilege of voting in proprietary affairs.[25] In Waterbury, as elsewhere, efforts to conciliate sons were no help to members of the community who were not children of proprietors.

Finally, nonproprietors existed wherever tenants existed, for resident as well as nonresident proprietors sometimes rented their lands to tenants. (It is likely that some tenants were also proprietors who rented additional lands to increase their arable land, in which cases tenantry is no proof of nonproprietorship.) Stephen Innes has discovered that more than one-third of the adult males in Springfield from 1652 to 1702 rented some or all of their lands or housing or livestock, mostly from John Pynchon, who also had tenants in other Connecticut Valley towns. The towns of Maine also had many tenants. Falmouth was probably first settled by tenants renting from former agents of Ferdinando Gorges.[26] Another Gorges agent and his assigns rented out lands that filled up with settlers and became the town of Scarborough. Since the patent containing Scarborough was conveyed repeatedly, from Thomas Cammock to Henry Jocelyn to Joshua Scottow, even as the town filled up with settlers renting their lands, it is likely that the land remained in one individual's hands for many years and that the tenants did not enjoy rights to its division.[27]

All the towns just discussed excluded some portion of residents from the undivided land within the first ten years of settlement. There were also towns that excluded residents later on. In this survey, thirty-three towns excluded residents within the first ten years (some of those, of course, even before settlement began), and sixteen towns did so between the tenth and thirtieth years. Cambridge, Charlestown, Dorchester, Haverhill, Lancaster, Rowley, Roxbury, Salem, Salisbury, Norwich, Stratford, Wethersfield,

25. Merrill, *History of Amesbury*, 72–73, 77–78, 153; Edwin Hall, ed., *The Ancient Historical Records of Norwalk, Conn., with a Plan of the Ancient Settlement, and of the Town in 1847* (New York, 1865), 60–62; Prichard, ed., *Proprietors' Records of Waterbury*, 44–45, 57.

26. Stephen Innes, *Labor in a New Land: Economy and Society in Seventeenth-Century Springfield* (Princeton, N.J., 1983), 38 (for further evidence of nonshareholders in early Springfield, see Burt, *Official Records of Springfield*, I, 32, 40–45, 144, 156–158, 160–161, 164–165, 167–168, 170–172, 190–191, 240–242, II, 77); William Willis, "The History of Portland . . . ," Maine Historical Society, *Collections*, 1st Ser., I (1831), 76, 79.

27. For more on land tenancy, see section on profits in Chapter 1.

and other towns fell into the latter category. These sixteen towns possibly excluded residents within the first ten years, but the first record of their doing so does not occur until after the first ten years (see Appendix 6).

The ratio of towns with shareless residents in the first ten years to towns with shareless residents in later years was two to one (thirty-three to sixteen). This ratio is similar to the ratio of towns limiting their land corporations within the first ten years (twenty-two) to those doing so after ten years (twelve). Together the ratios suggest that the husbanding of land rights did not gradually evolve. It was not the case that at the outset of settlement all settlers were proprietors and that, as time went on, as children matured and newcomers arrived, proprietors only then restricted their land corporation. Certainly, maturing children and newcomers swelled the ranks of nonproprietors in later years. But nonproprietors who were adult male residents were present from the very first years in the majority of towns. Far from being the product of time, the class of nonproprietors was the product of a deliberate and early decision by the shareholders to exclude from their own ranks a segment of the town population and to preserve thereby the value of their shares.[28]

28. In contrast with the view presented here, Roy Hidemichi Akagi implied that all first residents of towns were proprietors and that only with time did nonproprietors appear (*The Town Proprietors of the New England Colonies: A Study of Their Development, Organization, Activities, and Controversies, 1620–1770* [Philadelphia, 1924], 44–49). Anne Bush MacLear observed the presence of nonproprietors but suggested that they were constituted solely of those who came to town after settlement began and were not, therefore, present from the very beginning (*Early New England Towns: A Comparative Study of Their Development* [New York, 1908], 101–102). Other authors noted the presence of nonproprietors in passing but nonetheless spoke of the "equality" and "fairness" of town land systems (Melville Egleston, *The Land System of the New England Colonies,* Johns Hopkins University Studies in Historical and Political Science, 4th Ser., nos. 11–12 [Baltimore, 1886], 54–56; Herbert L. Osgood, *The American Colonies in the Seventeenth Century,* 3 vols. [New York, 1904–1907], I, 460–461). Kenneth A. Lockridge did not investigate the possibility of nonproprietors but nonetheless described early Dedham as "communal" and "united" in spirit (*A New England Town, the First Hundred Years: Dedham, Massachusetts, 1636–1736* [New York, 1970], 19, 76). John Fairfield Sly, also without exploring the possibility of nonproprietors' existence, stated that towns absorbed newcomers "on a basis of equality in the common property" (*Town Government in Massachusetts [1620–1930]* [Cambridge, Mass., 1930], 221). Jessica Kross suspected that "everyone" in early Newtown probably held rights to the undivided land (*Evolution of an American Town: Newtown, New York, 1642–1775* [Philadelphia, 1983], 64–65). Richard I. Melvoin found "rough equity" in land matters and "communalism" generally prevailing in early Deerfield ("Communalism in Frontier Deerfield," in

III. Towns Launched by Other Towns

Most of the settlements discussed so far were started by groups of individuals receiving township grants. Individuals did not, however, launch all new towns. As many as one-fifth of the towns established in the seventeenth century were launched by older towns. And the land corporations that held title to these townships were especially exclusive, perhaps even more exclusive than the corporations of other towns.

These towns were begun in one of two ways. Either the court made a grant of vacant land to an established town, which then undertook to develop the grant; or an established town split apart, and an offshoot of the former town received town privileges. As to the first method, when the General Court made grants to towns, it usually granted land to the selectmen or to a small group of individuals representing the town. In the grant order, the court sometimes stated that it intended to "accommodate the town." It also sometimes stated a time period (usually three to five years) during which the court expected the town to make a settlement on the premises.[29] Examining these grant orders, historians have understood that the court was acting to relieve land pressure in older towns and that older towns used land grants to provide their landless residents with homesteads.[30] They probably are correct: landless residents benefited from grants to towns.

But so did others—people who already owned land and had no intention

---

Stephen C. Innes et al., *Early Settlement in the Connecticut Valley,* ed. John W. Ifkovic and Martin Kaufman [Deerfield, Mass., 1984], 45–48). Bruce C. Daniels found that "most adult white male inhabitants were proprietors" (*The Connecticut Town: Growth and Development, 1635–1790* [Middletown, Conn., 1979], 66; for his treatment of proprietorship, see 119–127).

Alternatively, David Grayson Allen found exclusivity among the early proprietors of Newbury (*In English Ways: The Movement of Societies and the Transferal of English Local Law and Custom to Massachusetts Bay in the Seventeenth Century* [Chapel Hill, N.C., 1981], 110–111, 215–216). Stephen Innes uncovered a considerable Springfield population without rights to the undivided land (*Labor in a New Land,* esp. 38).

29. For the grants to Cambridge, Rehoboth, and Roxbury that produced the new towns of Billerica, Attleborough, and Woodstock, see Henry A. Hazen, *History of Billerica, Massachusetts . . .* (Boston, 1883), 6–8; John Daggett, *Sketch of the History of Attleborough . . .* (Dedham, Mass., 1834), 9; Roxbury Grant, Oct. 10, 1683, CXII, 342–343, Mass. Archives.

30. Egleston, *Land System of the New England Colonies,* 33.

of moving to the frontier. These people provided the capital necessary for launching new settlements, and the landless grantees provided the pool of settlers. The grants to towns demonstrated in microcosm the symbiotic relationship between investors and the landless that was so important to the land system generally, a relationship in which the former made money when the landless settled the wilderness. The town authorities who managed these grants probably understood this symbiosis, for in the constitution of new land corporations they always included wealthy individuals. Although grants were sometimes identified as being for the use of landless residents, not once did a town restrict the landholding body to the landless people in town. Landless people were never the sole grantees of these grants.

Sometimes the landless were not grantees at all. In most cases, in fact, towns used grants from the General Court to benefit the already landed, wealthy people in town. Shareholders might sell their rights or lots of land in the new town, perhaps for a cheap price, and the purchasers might well be landless people, perhaps children of shareholders, in the old town. The court in making the grant might expect the land to end up in the hands of these landless. But in these cases, where the landless were not included as initial grantees, where they had to buy or otherwise acquire land through negotiation with the town's elite, help for the landless arrived indirectly and was probably not the priority of the court in making the grant or of the town in distributing it.

In either case, whether or not a town included the landless among the grantees, the town did not leave the grant in the public domain. Even though grants were made to "the town," not once did a town admit every adult male resident to be a shareholder in the new land corporation. Nor did the selectmen hold a grant in trust for those who would later come of age or move to the town. Rather, town authorities quickly converted the grant into private property; they took immediate action to determine who had rights to the new grant, limit the number of people with rights, and make rules among these chosen people for the financing, dividing, and developing of the new tract. In other words, the first thing an older town did when it received a new grant was to create a well-defined, limited landholding body.

Towns used several methods to restrict membership in these bodies. Some towns restricted rights in the new township to those residents already owning land and houses in the established town. This was the policy of

Cambridge, Massachusetts, which in 1640 received the grant of Shawshin from the General Court. Cambridge ordered that Shawshin, which later became Billerica, should be laid out to "such as are owners of house and land in the town"; the town further declared that land shares in Shawshin should be determined by "the proportion now alloted" in Cambridge. Concord, Massachusetts, ordered in 1668 that a grant of fourteen thousand acres should be a "free common to the present householders of Concord, and such as shall hereafter be approved and allowed to be inhabitants." In 1682, Hartford ruled that its recent five-mile-long grant should belong to the "inhabitants."[31]

These methods of restricting the corporation owning the new grant were the most liberal, the most inclusive, of all the ways employed by towns receiving grants; and even they did not result in all-inclusive land corporations. Cambridge rated 135 people in 1647, yet only 113 Cambridge residents received rights in Shawshin. (In 1664, Cambridge had 198 adult male residents, but only 119 adult males shared a Cambridge land division the very next year.) Those who did receive rights in Shawshin were the wealthier individuals in town. The largest recipients of land in Shawshin were the wealthiest and most prestigious Cambridge residents: Edward Collins, Henry Dunster, Jonathan Danforth. Daniel Gookin, the landowner from Virginia and Maryland, received a grant from Cambridge in Shawshin the year he arrived in New England, but first he had to buy a house in Cambridge.[32] The rules governing who got land in Shawshin were not designed to benefit the landless residents of Cambridge.

On occasion, the wording of the court grant leaves no doubt that it was the town proprietors, not all residents, who were the intended grantees. Such was the case when Plymouth granted the Rehoboth North Purchase "unto the proprietors of the town of Rehoboth" in 1666, further stipulating that the recipients be only those proprietors "that hold there, from a

31. Hazen, *History of Billerica*, 11–12; Lemuel Shattuck, *A History of the Town of Concord* . . . (Boston, 1835), 41; Hoadly, ed., *Hartford Town Votes* (Conn. Hist. Soc., *Colls.*, VI [1897]), 201–202.

32. Cambridge, Mass., *The Records of the Town of Cambridge (Formerly Newtowne) Massachusetts, 1630–1703* . . . (Cambridge, Mass., 1901), 352–353; Hazen, *History of Billerica*, 9, 11–14, 16–17, 31; *Cambridge Proprietors Records*, 144–148, 335–338; Wall, "Franchise in Dedham and Cambridge," *WMQ*, 3d Ser., XXXIV (1977), 455–458; B. Katherine Brown, "The Controversy over the Franchise in Puritan Massachusetts, 1954 to 1974," *WMQ*, 3d Ser., XXXIII (1976), 227. On Gookin, see above, Chapter 1.

fifty pound estate and upwards." In other words, all who possessed a fifty-pound share or more of Rehoboth's land corporation automatically became shareholders in the new corporation owning the Rehoboth North Purchase. This tract later became Attleborough. Next door, two years later, the "proprietars of the town of Taunton" bought the Taunton North Purchase from Plymouth Colony for one hundred pounds. Nonshareholders, not to mention the outright landless, were denied ownership in this tract, too, which later contained the towns of Norton and Easton.[33]

Deerfield also was first owned by a restrictive land corporation created in an older town. In 1663, the court granted eight thousand acres to Dedham. Sixty-eight commoners of Dedham held this land in the same proportions by which they held the common fields of Dedham. At this same time, however, ninety-two Dedham residents paid the country rate. Thus more than a quarter of Dedham taxpayers (and an even larger proportion of residents) were excluded from this grant to the town. When the owners drew their first house lots, in 1671, only thirty-two proprietors of Deerfield participated, not all of them Dedham residents; at this time, Dedham contained more than three times that number of adult male residents.[34]

When towns did not bestow new grants on their landowners and proprietors, they apportioned grants among even more restricted groups. For instance, towns sometimes limited grants to those proprietors willing to invest in the new town and meet the considerable expenses of developing a wilderness settlement. Such may have been the case with the Hartford grant referred to above. When Hartford declared that all "inhabitants" of the town were owners of the five-mile-long grant from the General Court,

33. Daggett, Sketch of Attleborough, 5–6; Mortimer Blake, "Taunton North Purchase," Old Colony Historical Society, Collections, III (1885), 36–40, 48. The conclusion that some residents were excluded by this arrangement is drawn from the following numerical difference: there were 52 Taunton proprietors permitted shares in the Taunton North Purchase (Blake, "Taunton North Purchase," 37–39), but there were 88 Taunton "free Inhabitants" permitted shares in the Taunton South Purchase just four years later, in 1672 (Taunton Meeting, Nov. 29, 1672, Misc. Bound, MHS).

34. Sheldon, History of Deerfield, I, 9, 19. Sheldon assumes that the discrepancy between the number paying taxes and the number owning shares in Deerfield can be accounted for by sales by Dedham commoners of their shares in Deerfield. It is more likely that the discrepancy can be explained by the fact that not every Dedham taxpayer was a proprietor of Dedham. As evidence of the latter, note that whereas 90 Dedham residents were rated in 1653, only 76 shared a land division the same year (Dedham Town Records, III, 211–214).

it also ordered that they should divide this tract according to how much each one had contributed to the purchase price of the land. The contribution each made to the purchase price had been determined, in turn, by the amount each had paid in the last town rate. It is possible, but unlikely, that the town compelled all ratepayers to contribute to the purchase of a tract that very few individuals intended to settle upon; more likely is the possibility that only those "inhabitants" wishing to invest in this tract had to contribute to the purchase price according to the rate list. That the investors then divided their tract according to their purchase contributions heightened the sense in which this landholding body was a business venture.[35]

In the case of New Roxbury (later Woodstock), the business character of the landholding corporation was explicit. In the fall of 1683, Roxbury selectmen petitioned on behalf of the town for a grant; the court made the grant in the same year; and the following year, a town committee chaired by Joseph Dudley ordered that if any "do see good to withdraw from any interest in the grant of land," then was the time to do so, and they would thereafter be freed of any charges associated with the grant. Ten years later, a petition stated that the court had granted New Roxbury to the "then Proprietors of the sd Town of Roxbury." It appears that the owners of New Roxbury were those proprietors of old Roxbury who were willing to bear the charges of developing a frontier town.[36]

These charges were not trivial. In addition to purchasing the Indian title (which Dudley arranged), surveying the township, and paying the expenses of various town committees charged with overseeing the settlement, the owners of New Roxbury agreed to pay one hundred pounds to those who

35. Hoadly, ed., *Hartford Town Votes* (Conn. Hist. Soc., *Colls.*, VI [1890]), 201–202.

36. Grant to Roxbury, Oct. 10, 1683, CXII, 342–343, Mass. Archives; Ammidown, *Historical Collections*, I, 261; Roxbury Petition, 1693, CXIII, 17, Mass. Archives. Dudley used the term "inhabitants" in describing who was entitled to shares in New Roxbury, but by this term he meant "proprietors." This meaning is apparent from the list of those who turned out to be New Roxbury proprietors and from the fact that there were fewer than 113 New Roxbury proprietors living in Roxbury in 1696, yet Roxbury furnished some 129 members of the militia in 1690. Boston, Registry Dept., *Roxbury Land Records (A Report of the Record Commissioners . . . [Sixth Report])*, 2d ed. (Boston, 1884), 51–56; Evarts B. Greene and Virginia D. Harrington, *American Population before the Federal Census of 1790* (New York, 1932), 19. See also discussion of inhabitancy below, in Chapter 7.

would settle the township. Their method of raising this money was by rating themselves "according to each man's assessment per head and estate, in the country rates, by the last year's roll." They agreed to use the same assessments as a yardstick for dividing their land at New Roxbury. Again, as in Hartford's case, the proprietors gave themselves a dividend in return for the precise amount they contributed to the town's development.[37]

This method of land apportionment had, of course, nothing to do with giving land to landless residents of Roxbury. It rested upon a strictly business principle: namely, investments yield proportional dividends. Indeed, the landless of Roxbury could not have afforded to be owners of New Roxbury, for the costs associated with being an owner continued to climb during the 1680s, rising so much that owning rights in New Roxbury became a burden, and many rights traded hands in the 1680s and 1690s. The nonresident owners still had not paid half the one hundred pounds owed the settlers in 1695, ten years after they had promised to do so. When threatened with the loss of their rights, they finally paid up.[38]

Taunton created a similar corporation from among its residents to own and develop the Taunton South Purchase. In 1672, a committee of six men bought the Indian title to a four-mile-square tract south of town and then admitted as their "associates" eighty-eight "free Inhabitants of the Town of Taunton" who agreed to pay for the purchase. This association did not mirror the Taunton proprietors, though it included the Taunton proprietors, or the Taunton residents; rather, it was composed of those Taunton proprietors and residents who agreed to shoulder the cost of buying and developing the vacant land. Within two decades, they were known as the Proprietors of Taunton South Purchase.[39]

Towns disposed of new grants in still other ways. Boston granted Mount Wollaston in the mid-1630s to some of the wealthiest Bostonians, who used their lands as farms, run by servants and tenants. Such was the origin of Braintree. Later on, Braintree received its own grant of wilderness land, and it, too, used the grant as a reward for individuals who already had homesteads. Many of the Braintree grantees became absentee landlords,

37. Roxbury Petition, 1693, CXIII, 17, Mass. Archives; Ammidown, *Historical Collections*, I, 261.

38. Ammidown, *Historical Collections*, I, 270–272.

39. Taunton Meeting, Nov. 29, 1672, Misc. Bound; Proprietors of Taunton South Purchase, Jan. 4, 1699/1700, Misc. Bound, MHS.

making money off settlers in what soon became the town of Mendon, just as Bostonians had made money off the settlers of Braintree.[40] In 1643, when Charlestown received a much smaller grant (only three thousand acres), it granted the land to five or six men, giving one of them nearly half of it, which he then sold to John Hull, who bequeathed it to Samuel Sewall, who rented it out. There could have been no expectation that this General Court grant was to be used in a way that helped landless or land-hungry residents.[41]

The landless, then, were not the initial recipients of wilderness grants to established towns. The recipients were, instead, landowners, proprietors, people willing to invest in new towns, and people who wanted large farms. Many of these people had no intention of moving to the acquired wilderness tracts. The primary beneficiaries of grants made to towns were nonresident owners of wilderness lands, hoping to profit from their holdings.

These owners profited in several ways. They could sell one of the lots they drew in the distant tract and still keep their rights to undivided land there. They could lease their lots to tenants or place servants on the land; or they could do nothing with their land, simply wait for it to rise in value, and then sell it. Any one of these four ways generally required the owner to hold on to his rights to undivided land. When the chief profit in being a nonresident came from the accrual in land value, and accrual took time, it did not pay to sell one's rights immediately. So nonresident owners waited, perhaps selling a lot, renting, or placing a servant, until land values rose. In the meantime, those who purchased or rented or farmed the nonresidents' lots did not themselves always become shareholders; that is, they did not automatically own rights to the undivided land of the new town.[42] Often settlers did not own even the lots they tilled. This situation—prolonged

40. Charles Francis Adams, *History of Braintree, Massachusetts* . . . (Cambridge, Mass., 1891), 2; Braintree Petition, Oct. 11, 1666, photostats, MHS; Darrett B. Rutman, *Winthrop's Boston: Portrait of a Puritan Town, 1630–1649* (Chapel Hill, N.C., 1965), 88–90. Barely half the Braintree grantees ever moved to the new town of Mendon. This would not have been the case if the grant recipients had been men in search of homesteads. Mendon, Mass., *The Proprietors' Records of the Town of Mendon, Massachusetts* (Boston, 1899), 5–6, 11–12; Mendon Petition, Sept. 10, 1684, photostats, MHS; Ellery Bicknell Crane, *History of Worcester County, Massachusetts,* 3 vols. (New York, 1924), I, 26–29.

41. Samuel Sewall, June 5, 1701, photostats, MHS.

42. See Chapter 7, below, for mention of those towns where alienation of mere lots did convey rights to the undivided land.

nonresidency and the presence of settlers without land rights—created tension in the towns launched by older towns.

Of the 113 Cambridge grantees of Shawshin, only 1 or 2 ever lived in Billerica; the rest remained in Cambridge, holding on to their rights. For their part, the settlers of Billerica owned but a small portion of Billerica's land. They disliked this state of affairs and complained in the 1650s to the court, which acted to appease Billerica, giving the town eight thousand acres of land. Billerica then sold these eight thousand acres to William Brenton for two hundred pounds and spent the money buying out the Cambridge nonresidents in 1659. Billerica did not buy out all nonresident owners, and in 1674 the settlers had to make another purchase. By this means, the settlers finally became owners of Billerica's undivided lands. (Interestingly, even after this turning point in town history, not every adult male resident of Billerica owned rights to the undivided land. In 1685, the town made a division among 65 persons; Billerica had 73 taxpayers three years later, and taxpayers did not include all adult male residents.)[43]

Braintree residents also complained about their landless condition. In 1666, the residents of Braintree petitioned the court, saying they had never had "any Lands granted them free . . . nor commonage but what they have purchased, which is not Two thousand acres and that is very poor and barren Lands." The settlers complained of "a great part of the Towne being in farmes which consist of the best lands . . . which do belong to Gent. and friends of other Townes which severall of our Inhabitants are inforced by their rents to hire of them at dear rates." The town concluded its petition with a plea for land. The petition was granted, but in 1670 the settlers renewed their complaint about land shortage, and the controversy continued until 1700, when the Braintree residents, like Billerica residents, finally bought out en masse their nonresident landlords.[44]

Probably in response to the settlers' unhappiness, the court in 1660 granted Braintree a wilderness tract. This tract was eight miles square, located in the Nipmuck country. It soon became the town of Mendon, Massachusetts. Significantly, the town of Braintree did not behave any

43. Hazen, *History of Billerica*, 14, 42–47, 208–209, 308–309; Billerica Petitions, Sept. 20, 1658, XLV, 333, May 28, 1674, CXII, 239, Mass. Archives.

44. Braintree Petition, Oct. 11, 1666, photostats, MHS; Braintree Petition, May 13, 1670, CXII, 206, Mass. Archives; Adams, *History of Braintree*, 2; William Haller, Jr., *The Puritan Frontier: Town-Planting in New England Colonial Development, 1630–1660* (New York, 1951), 62–64.

better toward Mendon than Boston had toward Braintree. In the first twenty-five years after Braintree men received the grant of Mendon, fewer than half of the grantees settled in Mendon. The rest remained nonresident proprietors, and not very conscientious ones. In 1684, the town of Mendon complained to the court that the nonresidents were not paying their taxes and that this delinquency was unfair, since by the residents' "abiding upon the place thayer lands Regaine considerable advantage." The court granted Mendon the right to tax nonresidents' lands.[45]

Of the sixty-eight Dedham grantees of Deerfield, not one settled permanently in Deerfield. Instead, the Dedham proprietors traded land shares in Deerfield so quickly that from 1671 to 1688, only two of fifty proprietors retained an interest in the new town. One of those two, and perhaps the largest shareholder in Deerfield, was not a Dedham resident at all—John Pynchon.[46] In 1678, Deerfield settlers complained to the General Court that the "best of the Land; the best for soile; the best for situation," belonged to nonresidents. "As to quantity neare half belongs unto or proprietors, each and every of the[m] are nevr Like to come to a Settlement amongst us, which we have formerly found grevious." Nor would the nonresidents put tenants on their lands, the settlers alleged, and as a consequence the town was not growing as it should. The settlers asked for help.[47]

Deerfield was not the only Dedham satellite unhappy with its nonresident owners. Wrentham was also begun by Dedham. In 1662, the commoners of Dedham bought the Indian title to Wollomonopoag; in 1663, they drew lots for the first division of land there; and in 1669, they made rules for financing a settlement there, agreeing among other things to pay for a minister. Then these otherwise efficient town planners for some reason neglected their duty. In 1673, Wrentham settlers complained that the proprietors living in Dedham had not paid what they had engaged to pay and that, as a consequence, the town could not maintain its minister. They went on to charge that "so many that have Rights here seme onely to be willing wee should here Labour under the strayghts of a new plantation so as to bring there land to a great price, which no other can regulate."[48]

45. Mendon Selectmen's Petition, Sept. 10, 1684, photostats, MHS.
46. Sheldon, *History of Deerfield*, I, 201–202, 207–209.
47. Deerfield Petition, May 8, 1678, LXIX, 200–201, Mass. Archives.
48. Jordan D. Fiore, *Wrentham, 1673–1973: A History* (Wrentham, Mass., 1973), 8–10, 25; Wrentham Petition, Oct. 15, 1673, Misc. Bound, MHS.

These petitioners understood the situation precisely. Those who received shares in new towns did indeed expect their land to appreciate, owing to the labor and very presence of settlers. In every case of towns started by older towns, nonresidents owned some, if not all, the land, and they did so, bearing large financial burdens—paying the minister, surveying the land, petitioning the court, sometimes subsidizing settlers—because they expected to profit from their ownership.

The same group of nonresidents might be involved with more than one project. The commoners of Dedham owned and launched several towns (Deerfield, Medfield, and Wrentham), and the ones who usually led these Dedham efforts, Eleazer Lusher and Joshua Fisher, assisted in the founding of other Massachusetts towns. These leaders were land developers. Sometimes the land they developed had been granted to an established town, sometimes to an independent association; but the role of entrepreneurs—organizing and financing the venture—was the same. The only difference between a settlement venture conducted by an established town and one by a new proprietorship was that the former was more efficient.

It was more efficient because, first, the investors were already organized, as proprietors of the established town. Second, shareholder meetings were convenient, since they doubled as Roxbury or Dedham or Rehoboth town meetings. Third, the needs of the established town provided an excuse, or at least a high-minded reason, for the grant in the first place: for the petitioners could say that there were men in town who were "straitened for land." Finally, towns had landless people who, in some instances, peopled the new town.

This last point was important. The grant to Roxbury probably provided land to landless Roxbury residents. Of the forty-seven goers in 1686—men who took up rights in New Roxbury, promising to settle there—more than half were related to Roxbury residents. Many of these were sons and grandsons of Roxbury founders.[49] As the offspring of Roxbury commoners, the first Woodstock settlers may have been landless men, and if such was the case, then the southern half of Woodstock provided homesteads to needy people. The northern half of Woodstock served the uses of

49. A comparison of various Roxbury and Woodstock lists of proprietors and tax rolls shows that at least 26 Woodstock settlers were related to Roxbury families, and, unsurprisingly, these were the least-landed families in Roxbury. For this analysis, see John Frederick Martin, "Entrepreneurship and the Founding of New England Towns: The Seventeenth Century" (Ph.D. diss., Harvard University, 1985), chap. 10, n. 30.

absentee investors, and the southern half probably served the uses of landless men. In fact, for the grant to serve one cause it had to serve the other.

It would not have been easy for landless men in Roxbury to obtain the court grant; no doubt Dudley and others were helpful there. Nor could poor men have borne by themselves the tremendous costs of starting a wilderness settlement; the assessments upon shares of nonresidents financed Woodstock during its first ten years. By the same token, the nonresidents' lands would not have gone up in value, as the Wrentham petitioner put it, without the labor and proliferation of settlers "to bring there Land to a greate price."[50] Investors clearly understood this mutual dependency. That is why they taxed themselves and spent considerable amounts on developing towns. The petitions of unhappy settlers notwithstanding, nonresidents wanted to see settlement advance on the frontier just as residents there did. Settlement was the key to their profits.

Towns launched settlements not only by receiving new grants; they also did so by dividing land contained in their original grants and forming two distinct towns, each one endowed by the court with town privileges. (Towns created in this manner are here called offshoots of older towns.) There were many such towns in the eighteenth and nineteenth centuries, few in the seventeenth. But some towns did split apart in the seventeenth century. John Winthrop declared that the court included much land in township grants so that when towns "increased by their children and servants growing up," they might have "place to erect villages, where they might be planted, and so the land improved." Winthrop went on to explain that the General Court fully expected new towns to be formed in this way, multiplying the number of towns as well as the number of people given land of their own. Following Winthrop's script, Hadley granted the undivided lands on the west side of the Connecticut River to those living there, who erected the new town of Hatfield in 1670.[51]

Other towns, however, followed a different script and granted outlying lands to the well-established proprietors of the town. When the settlers on

50. Wrentham Petition, Oct. 15, 1673, Misc. Bound, MHS.

51. John Winthrop, *The History of New England from 1630 to 1649*, ed. James Savage, 2 vols. (Boston, 1825–1826; rpt., New York, 1972), II, 254; Sylvester Judd, *History of Hadley, Including the Early History of Hatfield, South Hadley, Amherst, and Granby, Massachusetts* (Springfield, Mass., 1905), 78–85.

these outlying lands (often tenants of the proprietors) received town privileges, they had little common land to divide among themselves, or none at
all. For example, in the 1630s Dorchester began making grants to its
commoners in the remote lands that would later constitute Milton. These
grants were long strips of land suitable for farming but not at all suitable for
settlement in a compact, orderly way. The recipients of the largest grants
were Richard Collicot, Israel Stoughton, Humphrey Atherton, John Ca-
pen, and Roger Clapp—men who were in no sense wanting of land. They
were the wealthiest Dorchester proprietors. By the time Milton received
town privileges, in 1662, all of its land had been granted by Dorchester and
was held in severalty by individuals who sold or rented their lands to Milton
settlers. Probably few of the Dorchester grantees ever settled in Milton. As
late as 1700, there were still not as many taxpayers in Milton as there had
been grantees in 1660.[52]

Manchester, Massachusetts, had a similar beginning. Its mother town,
Salem, began granting land just north of Salem village during the 1630s. In
1640, the grantees of this land, numbering seventeen, asked that their lands
be set off from Salem and that the court grant enough additional land to
them (to be held in common) to make up a township. In their petition to
the court, these grantees alleged they were "straitened in our accommodations." The court granted the request, and Manchester was created in 1645.
From this sequence of events, one would suppose that Salem was using its
surplus land precisely as Winthrop had said towns should use it—as land
for the landless and for making new towns—but that is not what happened
here. As it turned out, of the seventeen petitioners, at least twelve never
moved to Manchester. Some of them became selectmen, court marshals,
and other town officers in Salem after they received the Manchester grant.
Some of them, in addition to being nonresidents of Manchester, were
nonresidents of Marblehead and Beverly, which also were offshoots of
Salem. As late as the 1690s and 1710s, nonresidents from Salem were still
trading Manchester land rights.[53]

52. Edward Pierce Hamilton, *A History of Milton* (Milton, Mass., 1957), 19; A. K.
Teele, ed., *The History of Milton, Mass., 1640 to 1887* . . . (Boston, 1887), 12, 15–18,
212–215; Boston, *Dorchester Town Records*, 99, 109.

53. Sidney Perley, *The History of Salem, Massachusetts,* 3 vols. (Salem, Mass., 1924–
1928), II, 172–173; Manchester, Mass., *Town Records of Manchester,* 2 vols. (Salem,
Mass., 1889), I, 16–17, 62–64, 87–93, 129–130. The assertion that 12 Manchester
grantees were nonresidents is deduced from the fact that they were appointed to town

Not only were the Manchester commoners absentee landlords; they also formed a tightly held, restrictive land corporation. Fewer than two dozen people received Manchester grants from Salem in the 1630s. Seventeen grantees asked for town privileges in 1640. Thirty years later, the common land of Manchester was still being divided among just nineteen individuals. In 1695, there were only twenty-two proprietors of Manchester; in 1699, only twenty. The landholding body of Manchester had been sealed probably before the town was created, and through seven decades it did not expand.[54] Considering the persistence of nonresident landholding in Manchester, this extreme exclusiveness of the land corporation meant in all likelihood that the bulk of town residents were not commoners.

Like the proprietors of Salem, the proprietors of Saybrook, Connecticut, argued that they were "straitened" when they proposed creating a new town. As in Salem, the use of this term did not signify that the petitioners of Saybrook were short of land. On the contrary, thirty-seven men owned more than one hundred square miles that the township of Saybrook comprised. In 1648 these men divided their tract in three, assigning land to each proprietor in one of the three pieces (though some men owned land in more than one piece). Upon two of these offshoots soon appeared the settlements of Lyme and Westbrook. The move to divide Saybrook's extensive lands had less to do with helping the landless than with helping proprietors overcome the difficulty of owning land so spread out. "Straitened," in Saybrook, meant "inconvenient to the owners."[55]

Occasionally proprietors simply sold an older town's offshoot. In 1649, Dedham created a committee for admitting inhabitants and regulating the

offices in Salem or Marblehead or Beverly or were among the founding settlers of other Salem offshoots after they received their Manchester grants. For their names and evidence of their involvement with these other towns, see chap. 10, n. 39, and Manchester in Commentary for Table 5, Martin, "Entrepreneurship."

54. Perley, *History of Salem*, II, 172–173; Manchester, *Town Records of Manchester*, I, 16–17, 62–64, 87–93.

55. Christopher Collier, "Saybrook and Lyme: Secular Settlements in a Puritan Commonwealth," in George J. Willauer, Jr., ed., *A Lyme Miscellany, 1776–1976* (Middletown, Conn., 1977), 16–17. Saybrook had 37 proprietors, 24 of whom participated in this division of outlying lands. Significantly, the total proprietors participating in the outlying division also numbered 37, indicating that, however many shares may have changed hands, the land corporation of Saybrook was the same as the land corporation presiding over the creation of offshoots.

settlement upon a corner of Dedham land, later to be Medfield. At the same time, Dedham ordered that those admitted as grantees of the new township should pay fifty pounds to "such of the inhabitants of Dedham as do not remove to the village." In other words, though Dedham may well have accommodated its landless in Medfield, the proprietors of Dedham also made money from the deal. Some grantees also sought profits from their Medfield holdings; at least some were clearly not landless people seeking a home. Joshua Fisher had land in Medfield in the 1650s, so did Robert Keayne, and so did John Hull.[56]

In another case, Springfield made grants during the 1650s and 1660s in the area where Westfield later was erected. Some of the grantees were leading Springfield citizens (Pynchon, Thomas Cooper, Samuel Chapin, George Colton) who never moved to Westfield. Instead, these absentee owners rented and sold their lands to Westfield settlers, who complained about their treatment at the hands of the proprietors. In the 1670s, the settlers of Westfield told the court that the proprietors had failed to give them deeds to their land; the court ordered the proprietors to execute deeds. Even so, as late as 1684, Pynchon still owned rights in Westfield.[57]

Westfield was not alone. The town of Springfield encompassed 729 square miles at one time, and it spun off numerous towns: Westfield, Suffield, part of Southwick, all of West Springfield, Enfield, Somers, Wilbraham, Ludlow, and Longmeadow. The land of these towns was initially, at least, controlled by the handful of men who were proprietors of Springfield. These proprietors made grants of outlying lands until the court erected the lands into townships. In some offshoots, and perhaps all of them, the proprietors of Springfield owned rights. John Pynchon and his

56. William S. Tilden, *History of the Town of Medfield, Massachusetts, 1650–1886* . . . (Boston, 1887), 36–40, 64; Abstract of Estate Inventory of Capt. Robert Keayne, Apr. 23, 1656, Otis Papers, box 1, MHS; John Hull, "The Diaries of John Hull, Mint-Master and Treasurer of the Colony of Massachusetts Bay," American Antiquarian Society, *Transactions, Collections*, III (1857), 149.

57. Haller, *Puritan Frontier*, 99–103; Josiah Gilbert Holland, *History of Western Massachusetts*, 2 vols. (Springfield, Mass., 1855), I, 64–65; Burt, *Official Records of Springfield*, II, 88ff, 98–100, 107; Petition from Woronoco Settlers, 1662, CXII, 143–144, Mass. Archives; John Warner Barber, *Historical Collections . . . History and Antiquities of Every Town in Massachusetts . . .* (Worcester, Mass., 1848), 299–304; General Court Order re Westfield, 1679, CXII, 272, Mass. Archives; Harry Andrew Wright, Jr., *Indian Deeds of Hampden County* (Springfield, Mass., 1905), 97.

relatives not only helped found distant towns up and down the Connecticut River valley; they also helped found, and owned shares in, towns that split off from Springfield.[58]

It is possible that the landless residents of Springfield, Salem, Saybrook, Dedham, Dorchester, and other towns found land in the offshoots of older towns; indeed, it is likely that they did. Certainly the well-established proprietors with houses in the center of a large market town had no interest in moving to the outlying reaches of town. They instead could profit from renting and selling outlying lands to others. So Winthrop's plan—of towns' using their surplus to accommodate maturing men and servants—was not necessarily betrayed by seventeenth-century towns, but it was achieved in a more complicated, roundabout way than he probably foresaw. The young and landless did get their lands, but not before the proprietors of older towns got theirs, not without renting and purchasing lots from absentee landlords, and not without protesting their privations to the General Court. In the case of settlements founded by older towns, as throughout the New England town-launching experience, nonresident investors as well as wilderness settlers played each his own part in developing the wilderness. Absentee proprietors and settlers did not always agree. But their different interests nonetheless converged in a way that gave land to the landless, profits to investors, and momentum to frontier settlement.

58. Barber, *Historical Collections: Massachusetts,* 291. See Pynchon discussed above, in Chapters 1 and 2; also Holland, *Western Massachusetts,* II, 148, 155; Barber, *Historical Collections: Massachusetts,* 307–310; Petition to Court, May 1683, CXII, 338–340, Mass. Archives (wherein Pynchon is identified as one of those interested in a grant made by the town of Springfield).

7 | *The Communal Ideal*

1. The Landholding Community

[Inasmuch as the corporations holding town lands were exclusive, not fraternal, in their membership, what became of the Puritan ideal of community?]There can be no definitive answer to this question, but one can begin by exploring that most important colonial term, "the inhabitants." Inhabitancy was never defined in colonial statutes or literature.[1] But since people admitted to the body of "inhabitants" resided in and paid taxes in the town, historians have assumed that the term "inhabitants" meant simply those people permitted to be permanent residents. And since "inhabitants" were given shares in the land corporation, it logically followed that all those accepted as permanent residents were made proprietors. Thus upon the definition of "inhabitancy" rest, in part, commonly held opinions about the comprehensiveness of the landowning class. There is even more than that, however, at stake in this term; for land matters were frequently disposed of in town meetings. [If all residents were proprietors and they conducted their business in town meetings, then it has appeared inescapable that all permanent residents constituted both the political community and the land community of the town in a most communal and egalitarian arrangement.[2]

1. Charles M. Andrews, *The Beginnings of Connecticut, 1632–1662* (New Haven, Conn., 1934), 13.
2. Curiously, few writers have openly declared that "inhabitants" was a synonym for residents or discussed the term at all. But many have taken it to mean "permanent

Inhabitants were, however, more than mere residents. Colonial legislatures did not use the term "inhabitants" casually; they recognized that it signified a category of town residents with special rights. The Fundamental Orders of Connecticut, drafted in 1639, opened with the words: " . . . we the Inhabitants and Residents of Windsor, Harteford and Wethersfield." If inhabitants had been merely residents, it would have been unnecessary to use both terms. Next, the orders assigned special power to the inhabitants of towns. Governor and magistrates were to be chosen in the new government by "admitted freemen . . . having beene admitted Inhabitants by the major prt of the Towne wherein they live." Deputies were to be elected "by all that are admitted Inhabitants in the severall Townes and have taken the oath of fidellity."[3]

In later years, the Connecticut General Court clarified these franchise laws. In 1643, the court stated that "such only shall be counted admitted inhabitants, who are admitted by a generall voate of the mayor parte of the Towne that receaveth them." Fourteen years later, the court tried again, declaring: "By admitted inhabitants, specified in the 7th Fundamentall, are meant only housholders that are one and twenty yeares of age, or have bore office, or have 30 l. estate." In 1660, the court ordered that "none shalbe receaved as Inhabitant into any Towne in the Collony but such as are knowne to be of an honest conversation, and accepted by a major part of the Towne." In 1679, the court observed that people were voting in towns without permission and so ordered that "no person that is not an admitted inhabitant, a housholder, and a man of a sober conversation, and have at least fifty shillings freehold estate in the common list . . . shall adventure to vote."[4] In the opinion of Connecticut authorities, therefore, inhabitants

residents." B. Katherine Brown's casual acceptance of this sense of the term is, in this author's opinion, the important misstep that led to her errors on the colonial franchise ("The Controversy over the Franchise in Puritan Massachusetts, 1954 to 1974," *William and Mary Quarterly,* 3d Ser., XXXIII [1976], 227, 230, 239). One who did attempt a definition of inhabitants was Josiah Henry Benton, whose standard *Warning Out in New England, 1656–1817* (Boston, 1911) is a treasure of town disciplinary orders. Unfortunately, Benton lumped the orders together indistinguishably and argued that they were all aimed at assembling a town populace of moral and solvent citizens. To Benton, inhabitants meant permanent residents (pp. 5, 9, 10).

3. *Conn. Records,* I, 20–23. The editor of *Conn. Records* observed that the clause about "admitted inhabitants" where it first appears in the Fundamental Orders was interlined at a later date.

4. *Ibid.,* I, 96, 293, 351, III, 34.

were people of honest conversation who were "admitted" and "received" into towns as "inhabitants" by majority vote. To vote in town and colony elections, inhabitants had to meet additional tests, like be householders and have an estate of fifty shillings, which tests changed with time.

Other colonies also enacted legislation with special reference to "inhabitants." In 1634, the Massachusetts General Court ordered towns to take surveys of the houses and lands of "every Free inhabitant" within their jurisdictions. In 1636, the court ordered that houses built without the leave of a town could be taken down by "the inhabitants of the said towne." During this time, the General Court of Massachusetts employed other terms ("freemen," "persons," "stranger," and "man") to describe other people affected by various laws.[5] "Inhabitant" was not a catchall term meaning "person" or "colonist" or "resident."

Colonial courts did not, however, define inhabitancy; courts merely referred to a group already existing. It was, rather, for the towns to define and regulate the inhabitants. They did so with great care, lavishing particular attention on the procedure for admitting fellow inhabitants. Northfield ordered that "no inhabitant be received into the Plantation" without the approval of "the major part of the Company." Windsor ordered in 1659 that no one "shall be admitted inhabitant in this town" without approval of "the town or townsmen." Hartford ordered that no one could become an inhabitant "without it be first consented to by the orderly vote of the inhabitants." Hadley voted that no one should be accounted an inhabitant or vote in town affairs till he had been received as an inhabitant.[6] One did not become an inhabitant just by being in a new town; one had to be received.[7]

Some town residents were not. In 1639, Ipswich voted to "refuse to

5. *Mass. Records,* I, 116, 167, 168ff, 172, 196.

6. J. H. Temple and George Sheldon, *A History of the Town of Northfield, Massachusetts* . . . (Albany, N.Y., 1875), 63–64; Benton, *Warning Out,* 37, 86; Charles M. Andrews, *The River Towns of Connecticut: A Study of Wethersfield, Hartford, and Windsor,* Johns Hopkins University Studies in Historical and Political Science, 7th Ser., nos. 7–9 (Baltimore, 1889), 87, 88. Andrews appears to take the same position Benton did, that screening inhabitants was primarily a way to keep out unwholesome, poor, and heretical people. Warwick, Swansea, Bristol, Waterbury, Worcester, and other towns passed orders similar to Hadley's.

7. Usually the very first admissions to the ranks of inhabitants were made by the General Court committee charged with supervising the new town. Later, once the town was established, the admissions procedure was taken over by the town's political body.

receive Humphrey Griffin as an inhabitant, to provide for him as inhabitants formerly received, the town being full." Notwithstanding his rejection, Griffin continued living in Ipswich. When Marlborough was just a few years old, it granted to town resident Henry Axtell a parcel of land but did not give Axtell "a Towne Right" to hold as the other "Inhabitnts" held their rights. Sometimes individuals would live in towns for a number of years before being admitted as inhabitants. In 1639, Boston ordered that "John Seaborne, a Taylor, having served for the space of three years within this Towne, is granted to be an Inhabitant." In 1640, the town voted that John Palmer, "now dwelling here, is to be allowed an Inhabitant, if he can gett an house, or land to sett an house upon."[8]

In other towns, men might be residents for many years and still be refused admission to inhabitancy. In Springfield, one received the land rights of an inhabitant by purchasing a lot that the town had granted to an inhabitant, but to effect such a purchase the purchaser, or "chapman," had first to be approved by the town. Springfield authorities vetoed chapmen from time to time. On March 14, 1642/3, the inhabitant Henry Gregory proposed Richard Everett to be his chapman, and the town disallowed the sale. Everett had been in the town for at least seven years. He had witnessed the transaction in which William Pynchon bought Springfield's land from the Indians, had contributed to the fund for building the minister's house and paying the minister, and had owned a small piece of land in town; but he was not an "inhabitant," and the town would not let him become one.[9]

It was possible for women to be inhabitants even when some male residents were not. Warwick, Rhode Island, accepted a woman as inhabitant in 1647. Roxbury had female inhabitants. Springfield also had female inhabitants.[10] In these towns, the number of female inhabitants was

8. Thomas Franklin Waters, *Ipswich in the Massachusetts Bay Colony . . .* , 2 vols. (Ipswich, Mass., 1905–1917), I, 90; Franklin P. Rice, ed., "Colonial Records of Marlborough, Mass.," *New England Historical and Genealogical Register,* LXII (1908), 341–342; Benton, *Warning Out,* 21–22. These cases for some reason did not prompt Benton to wonder about his definition of inhabitancy as nothing more than permanent residency.

9. Henry M. Burt, *The First Century of the History of Springfield: The Official Records from 1636 to 1736,* 2 vols. (Springfield, Mass., 1898–1899), I, 32, 144, 156–158, 160–161, 164–165, 170–172, 190–191, II, 55, 567 (hereafter cited as Burt, *Official Records of Springfield*).

10. Warwick, R.I., Town Records, 34, LC; Boston, Registry Dept., *Roxbury Land Records (A Report of the Record Commissioners . . . [Sixth Report]),* 2d ed. (Boston, 1884),

small—but significant. If "inhabitants" had referred to all residents, male and female, then many females would have been included on these lists, not just a few. If "inhabitants" had referred to just male residents, then no females would have appeared on these lists. If "inhabitants" had been primarily a political term, designating town voters, then again no females would have appeared on these lists.

The most revealing category of inhabitants is the nonresidents: those people who were accounted inhabitants of towns where they did *not* dwell. In many towns, nearly every inhabitant was a nonresident at the beginning of town-planting. When a grant was made, a committee of either the court or the grantees "admitted inhabitants." These initial admissions took place in a settled community, far from the town site, and long before settlement began. A period of time elapsed between their admission and commencement of settlement, while the Indian title was extinguished, lots laid out, and other preliminary work accomplished. This work sometimes took several months, even a year or two, during which interval, even though they did not live in the new town, the grantees were nonetheless inhabitants of it. The grantees of Northfield, for instance, engaged to resettle their town after Indian wars, pledging "that each inhabitant shall fence, build, and actually inhabit there" in two years' time.[11] For a few years, one could be an inhabitant of Northfield without actually living there.

In some towns, the nonresidency of inhabitants had nothing to do with the unavoidable time lapse between admission and first settlement, but, rather, occurred because individuals did not live in the towns where they were accounted inhabitants. The Boston residents who had farms in Braintree, though remaining themselves in Boston, were called inhabitants and townsmen of Mount Wollaston. When the shareholders of the Atherton Company asked Connecticut to take the Narragansett under its authority, they signed a petition describing themselves as "all inhabitants," although none lived in the Narragansett.[12] Another land developer, John Saffin, was

---

4–5. In February 1664/5, the "Widdow Burt" was included in a list of "admitted Inhabitants" (Burt, *Official Records of Springfield*, I, 8).

11. Temple and Sheldon, *History of Northfield*, 134.

12. Charles Francis Adams, *History of Braintree, Massachusetts* . . . (Cambridge, Mass., 1891), 5. The Atherton petition was dated July 3, 1663 (Ray Greene Huling, "The Earliest List of Inhabitants at Narragansett," *NHR*, III [1884–1885], 170). John Fones, *The Records of the Proprietors of the Narragansett, Otherwise Called the Fones Record*, ed. James W. Arnold (Providence, R.I., 1894), 23–25, gives a different, though more complete, version of the same petition. The signatories were Edward Hutchinson, Elisha

listed as an inhabitant of Bristol in 1681, yet he did not move there until 1688. Others accounted inhabitants of Bristol were Nathaniel Paine and Major Robert Thompson, the first a resident of Rehoboth, the second of London, England.[13]

Even towns that prohibited nonresident landowning made exceptions and allowed nonresidents to enjoy the rights of inhabitants. Marlborough inhabitants granted land to Andrew Belcher during one of their first town meetings and voted that "the Towne doth graunt unto him the sd Andrew Belcher the rights and priviledges of an Inhabitnt within this Towne in all farthr devissions of Lands as well Meadows as upland."[14] Belcher was a town promoter, a land expert for the General Court, involved in several town launchings—and a resident of Cambridge. He never lived in Marlborough.

One does not have to suppose that these landowners were trying to deceive others by calling themselves inhabitants of towns they did not live in. Rather, in most towns, the term "inhabitants" referred to shareholders or town proprietors, resident or not. In his discussion of the English parish meeting of the seventeenth century, Edward Channing observed that all attended the meeting "who had benefit of the things there transacted . . . that is to say, all householders, and all who manured land within the parish. Such were technically termed inhabitants even though they dwelt in an-

---

Hutchinson, William Hudson, Wait Winthrop, George Denison, Thomas Stanton, Amos Richison, Increase Atherton, and others—men who certainly owned land in the Narragansett, some of them being shareholders in towns, others shareholders in the company. Several of these men (Richison, Stanton, and Denison) by virtue of living in Southertown could say they were residents of the Pequot country, but that was not considered part of the Narragansett.

13. Wilfred H. Munro, *History of Bristol, Rhode Island: The Story of the Mount Hope Lands* . . . (Providence, R.I., 1880), 79, 87–90; Daggett, *Sketch of Attleborough*, 10–12. Additional evidence of nonresident inhabitants is the preamble to Connecticut's Fundamental Orders, which began with the words ". . . we the Inhabitants and Residents of Windsor, Harteford and Wethersfield"—a choice of words probably meant to distinguish the signatories from those inhabitants who were not residents (*Conn. Records*, I, 20–23). William DeLoss Love made the same observation (*Colonial History of Hartford* . . . , 2d ed. [Hartford, Conn., 1935; rpt., 1974], 75.

14. Rice, ed., "Colonial Records of Marlborough," *NEHGR*, LXII (1908), 228. This town order noted that the town was acting notwithstanding its own prohibition of nonresident landowning.

other town."[15] A similar usage was in force in New England during the same century, where the "benefit" came in the form of membership in the corporation holding the town's land. Hence nonresidents and women could be inhabitants: they derived that status from their owning transferable land shares acquired through purchase or inheritance. Hence many residents were not inhabitants: they did not own those same property rights. Usually inhabitants were town-dwellers, but sometimes they were not, for inhabitancy was primarily concerned, not with residency, but with rights.

The evidence describing inhabitancy as a proprietary status is voluminous. In Waterbury, Connecticut, the founding Articles of Association provided that everyone accepted as an inhabitant should receive an eight-acre house lot and other land. In Groton, inhabitants were at first given acre-rights upon admission (acre-rights being the denomination of land shares there). In Ipswich, one had to be accepted as an inhabitant before being granted land. Amesbury declared in one of its first meetings that only certain people should be "Inhabitants and Commoners," and no more without the consent "of every Inhabitant of the plantation." Boston, Andover, Watertown, Dedham, Lancaster, and numerous other towns automatically gave commonage rights to all admitted inhabitants (until, that is, these towns terminated admissions to their land corporations). No wonder towns regulated admission of inhabitants with great care: inhabitancy bestowed the most important right there was in a town, the right to share the undivided lands.[16]

15. Edward Channing, *Town and County Government in the English Colonies of North America,* Johns Hopkins University Studies in Historical and Political Science, 2d Ser., no. 10 (Baltimore, 1884), 12. For this interpretation, Channing cites Sir Edward Coke.

16. Bronson, *History of Waterbury,* 4–9; Samuel A. Green, ed., *The Town Records of Groton, Massachusetts: 1662–1678* (Groton, Mass., 1879 [rpt. in Green, ed., *Pamphlets on History of Groton* (n.p., n.d.)]), 24 (hereafter cited as *Groton Town Records*); Green, ed., *An Account of the Early Land-Grants of Groton, Massachusetts* (Groton, Mass., 1879 [rpt. in Green, ed., *Pamphlets on History of Groton* (n.p., n.d.)]), 5–6 (hereafter cited as *Groton Land Grants*); Edward S. Perzel, "Landholding in Ipswich," Essex Institute, *Historical Collections,* CIV (1968), 306; Joseph Merrill, *History of Amesbury and Merrimac, Massachusetts* (Haverhill, Mass., 1880; rpt., 1978), 53–55. See also Benton, *Warning Out,* 10 (Boston); Darrett B. Rutman, *Winthrop's Boston: Portrait of a Puritan Town, 1630–1649* (Chapel Hill, N.C., 1965), 87–88; Philip J. Greven, Jr., *Four Generations: Population, Land, and Family in Colonial Andover, Massachusetts* (Ithaca, N.Y., 1970), 45;

One could also acquire the status of an inhabitant by purchasing land rights. This backdoor entrance to the land corporation was the result of the transferability of land rights, which inhabitants liked, of course; but inhabitants did not like the idea that merely by purchasing shares one could become an inhabitant, with rights and responsibilities in the land corporation, without being approved by the existing inhabitants. In some towns, the purchase of mere lots of land, not even shares, earned one the right to participate in future divisions and become an inhabitant. (In other towns, land purchases did not convey this all-important right.)[17] Towns therefore not only closely regulated the institution of inhabitancy; they also regulated those alienations that conveyed rights to the land corporation. Windsor prohibited the sale or lease of "any house or land so as to bring in any to be inhabitant into the town without the approbation of the townsmen."[18] Cambridge ordered in 1644 that one could not let his house to a stranger "to settle him or her self as an Inhabitant in or Towne, without the consent of the major prt of the Townsmen." In Springfield, if the selectmen did not

Historical Society of Watertown, *Watertown Records, Comprising the First and Second Books of Town Proceedings with the Lands, Grants, and Possessions,* 5 vols. (Watertown, Mass., 1894), I, 2; Dedham, Mass., *The Early Records of the Town* . . . , 6 vols. (Dedham, Mass., 1886–1936), III, 2–5, 18, 24; Henry S. Nourse, ed., *The Early Records of Lancaster, Massachusetts, 1643–1725* (Lancaster, Mass., 1884), 27–29.

The wording of town orders confirms the proprietary nature of inhabitancy. On Jan. 10, 1669/70, Taunton chose a committee to draw up a list of "the Purchasers or free Inhabitants here in Town" (Taunton Proprietors Vote, Jan. 10, 1669/70, Misc. Bound, MHS). In Springfield, in 1660, the town referred to "the severall Inhabitants or proprietors of the meddows." Again, in 1663, Springfield ordered there be three days' warning given "to all the Inhabitants or proprietors of land in the Town" (Burt, *Official Records of Springfield,* I, 275, 305).

17. In Salisbury, a deponent in a land action observed that "it hath been the Generall Custome and the practice of the towne of Salsbury to Lay out their Severall devisions of Lands to the Name of him [who] was the originall proprietor of the town not Minding who may have bought it" (Salisbury Deposition, Sept. 24, 1695, Misc. Bound, MHS). This would seem to suggest that the original shareholder retained his land rights to the undivided land, irrespective of any conveyances of parcels he might make over the years. In a slightly different but related matter, David Thomas Konig found that in 17th-century Essex County it was not always clear whether the purchaser of a commonage share also obtained the right to future land allotments, unless the deed said so (*Law and Society in Puritan Massachusetts: Essex County, 1628–1692* [Chapel Hill, N.C., 1979], 51). In the cases cited below, such uncertainty did not exist, nor did the rule invoked by the Salisbury man seem to apply.

18. This order was in 1659. Benton, *Warning Out,* 87–88 n. 3.

buy a seller's lot or provide him with a chapman of their choosing, then the seller was to "have his Liberty to take his Chapman, and Such Chapman or Stranger shalbe esteemed as entertayned and allowed of by the Towne as an Inhabitant." Rowley declared in 1662 that there should be no further divisions, "nor noe more Adission of Gates [the term for shares in that town] nether by Giveing leting or selling." This order implied that not only could one acquire land rights in the Rowley undivided lands by renting and purchasing lands; new rights could actually be created by these transactions.[19]

In some places, just the possession of a house lot bestowed the rights of inhabitancy upon the owner. In Boston, in 1638, George Barrill bought a house from Thomas Painter with the consent of the townsmen, "and soe is admitted a Townesman upon Condition of Inoffensive Carryage." ("Townsman" was frequently used instead of "inhabitant" with the same apparent meaning.) In 1639, the selectmen noted that "John Seaberry, a Seaman hath with leave bought our brother Water Merrye's house, and half an Acre under it in the Mylne feild, and so is allwed for an Inhabitant." In December 1638, William Teffe was "allowed to bee an Inhabitant, and hath this day fully agreed with Jacob Wilson of his house, and the ground under it, in this town."[20] In other towns, purchasing the "accommodations," a term for land acquired by divisions, conveyed the rights of inhabitant. Whichever kind of land had the magical effect, in Boston, Springfield, Cambridge, Windsor, and many other towns, certain land sales conveyed rights to the undivided land, so the existing landholders exercised a veto over buyers.

If all residents had been inhabitants, this close regulation of conveyances would have been, as some historians have assumed, a way of screening town residents, restricting the common land to those people permitted to be permanent residents, and reinforcing communalism.[21] But residents

19. *Ibid.*, 30–31; Burt, *Official Records of Springfield*, II, 55; Rowley, Mass., *The Early Records of the Town of Rowley, Massachusetts, 1639–1672* (Rowley, Mass., 1894), 128–129.

20. Benton, *Warning Out*, 21, 22.

21. Looking at the intrusive municipal legislation, Charles M. Andrews said, "No one can study the history of the Connecticut towns during the seventeenth century without realizing how at every point the freedom of the individual was under restraint whenever the needs of the community at large were involved" (*Beginnings of Connecticut*, 51). Elsewhere Andrews said that restraints upon alienation were "a widely recognized principle of community life" in America and other places (*River Towns*, 72, 72 n. 1).

were not all inhabitants and owners of land rights. The regulation of land conveyances did not have as its primary goal to keep out licentious, heretical, and unfriendly people.]

Some towns passed alienation restraints that even superficially bore no relation to community control. In 1677, Derby, Connecticut, ordered that no one could "admitt entertain or countenanc any parson or parsons directly or indirectly to sett upon or joyn in with the trade of fishing." In Exeter, New Hampshire, the staple was lumber. When someone was admitted an inhabitant there, the important right he obtained was, not land, but the right to make a thousand white oak pipe staves each year (three thousand per family). In 1644, Exeter ordered that "none but seteled inhabitantes shall make use of wode or common." In 1650, the town repeated the order and barred newcomers from timber privileges. In 1654, the town repeated the order again, adding the making of lumber to the list of proscribed activities for noninhabitants. Significantly, the town forbade the sale of one's oak stave privilege, though an inhabitant might hire men to help him fill his quota. Exeter was not screening residents or regulating the morality of neighbors by prohibiting the sale of lumber privileges—nor was Derby when it regulated fishing, nor Rowley when it forbade the renting of gates.[22] The purpose of these alienation laws was economic, not spiritual or communal.]

If their purpose had been communal, one would not expect nonresident proprietors, whose communal interest in towns is not self-evident, to have passed identical bylaws; but they did. The Deerfield proprietors, who were mostly nonresident commoners of Dedham during the 1660s, prohibited land sales unless approved by the proprietary body. Far from contributing to a communal spirit there, these proprietors entered into a vituperative dispute with the eventual settlers of Deerfield. The proprietors of Bristol, some of whom were nonresidents, also inserted the right of first refusal in

---

Melville Egleston described the restraints upon alienation as bylaws with which early towns preserved the character of the community and sought "the greatest safety and prosperity of all" (*The Land System of the New England Colonies,* Johns Hopkins University Studies in Historical and Political Science, 4th Ser., nos. 11–12 [Baltimore, 1886], 26–27, 48–49). William B. Weeden also emphasized the communal spirit of early towns (*Economic and Social History of New England, 1620–1789* [Boston, 1891], I, 50–55). So did Turner, Akagi, Lockridge, and others.

22. Derby Town Order, May 3, 1677, Towns and Lands, I, 168a, Conn. Archives; Charles H. Bell, *History of the Town of Exeter, New Hampshire* (Exeter, N.H., 1889), 52, 53, 447.

their Grand Articles of 1680. In 1660, the shareholders of the Atherton Company "all mutually agree not to sell their share before tendering it to the company." The Pettaquamscut Company declared in 1668 that "no Person shall be accepted or granted by any of us to become Partner with[out] the consent of all the Partners." The one hundred individuals who bought Conanicut Island pledged not to sell either lots or shares to anyone not a proprietor unless the company approved the sale.[23] When Joseph Dudley, Richard Wharton, William Stoughton, Samuel Shrimpton, and others framed an agreement for developing a large tract in the Nipmuck country, they stipulated that the partners should have the first refusal of lands in case one of them decided to sell. The shareholders of the Sowams Company in Plymouth declared in 1660 that none of them would let or sell "any of the said Lands" to "any stranger that is not allready a proprietor with us without the Joynt Consent of us all." Twenty years later, the company altered this rule to make it a first refusal rather than a blanket veto power that the company possessed.[24]

[Whether it was a town or company, whether the asset was land or lumber, land corporations tightly controlled admissions and distributed assets with extraordinary vigilance.[25] They did so for several reasons. Wherever the alienation of property gave the purchaser a claim on the undivided

23. George Sheldon, *A History of Deerfield, Mass.* . . . , 2 vols., (Deerfield, Mass., 1895–1896), I, 9; Munro, *History of Bristol,* 94–96; Richard A. Wheeler, "Major Atherton's Company," *NHR,* II (1883–1884), 106–107; Pettaquamscut Meeting, Newport, June 4, 1668, "Narragansett lands," 27–29, Prince Collection, BPL. Conanicut Island was largely a speculative venture for the benefit of Newport merchants (Bruce C. Daniels, *Dissent and Conformity on Narragansett Bay: The Colonial Rhode Island Town* [Middletown, Conn., 1983], 31–32).

24. New Plantation Indenture between William Stoughton, Samuel Shrimpton, *et al.,* May 23, 1686, photostats, MHS; Thomas Williams Bicknell, *A History of Barrington, Rhode Island* (Providence, R.I., 1898), 66; Thomas W. Bicknell, *Sowams, with Ancient Records of Sowams and Parts Adjacent* (New Haven, Conn., 1908), 40, 48.

25. There were other kinds of restraints imposed besides simple prohibitions on sales and rents without the inhabitants' (or proprietors') approval. Some towns prohibited the nonresident ownership of lands, but these laws were often either ignored or waived, as in the Marlborough example given above. Other towns prohibited multiple holdings until either the purchaser had resided in town for five years (as in Springfield) or the town had grown to 50 families (as in Worcester) (Franklin P. Rice, ed., *Records of the Proprietors of Worcester, Massachusetts* [Worcester Society of Antiquity, *Collections,* III (Worcester, Mass., 1881)], 37; Burt, *Official Records of Springfield,* I, 164–165). The reason for these bylaws—both the bar against nonresidency and against multiple holdings—was, not to prevent speculation, but to promote settlement.

lands, the transaction had the effect of watering the stock, as if the town had granted a new land right, instead of merely sanctioning the conveyance of a parcel; and no shareholder welcomed unregulated dilution. Even when there was no stock watering, inhabitants wanted to be sure that every candidate for inhabitancy could bear the expenses that inhabitants had to bear. When founders framed the articles of association that launched towns, they usually declared that all wishing to become "inhabitants" had to pay their "proportion of common charges." This financial burden grew more onerous for all inhabitants whenever any one inhabitant could not meet his share of the costs. Inhabitants wanted to be sure that their fellows were good financial risks.

Finally, inhabitants wished to have business partners with whom they could get along. They wished to have associates who would do nothing to compromise the delicate relations that the corporation had with Indians, nonproprietors, and the assembly. Above all, inhabitants wished to maintain control over their own organizations, which could be accomplished only by maintaining strict control over the admission of new shareholders. Business ventures no less than tribes have a drive for exclusivity. The English trading companies of the seventeenth century were exclusive organizations; so it was with land corporations in New England towns.[26]

Inhabitancy created a club, the ruling club in most towns, in which members jointly controlled the politics, the lawmaking, the land, and the admission of future inhabitants. In this sense, the various restraints on alienation and rigorous admissions process did support a kind of communalism—a strong feeling of belonging. But the community being bolstered was coterminous with the land corporation, not the town population. The group being maintained was shareholders, not town-dwellers; the purpose was to control rights, not residency.[27]

26. For the parallel between exclusiveness in towns and English trading companies, see George Lee Haskins, *Law and Authority in Early Massachusetts: A Study in Tradition and Design* (New York, 1960), 58.

27. Ironically, the business purpose of these alienation restraints stemmed in part from the fact that land was valued not solely for its commercial nature. If land had been solely a commercial asset and inhabitants purely shareholders in a business corporation, it would not have been possible for the purchase of mere lots (as opposed to shares) to earn one the right to participate in future divisions and become an inhabitant. But land also gave the purchaser a new home; and the institution of inhabitancy was, in addition to being a business institution, also a sort of town citizenship, conferring political and economic rights upon its beneficiaries. Hence the custom arose that a self-sufficient newcomer

11. The Social Community

⌈This is not to say that towns exercised no social con-
trol. On the contrary, towns paid close attention to the moral and religious
inclinations of their residents, screened candidates for residency, and in-
truded considerably into the private lives of residents. But they did not
accomplish this social control by regulating the inhabitants. They accomplished it with the church and with bylaws aimed specifically at the noninhabitants, who were usually called "sojourners," sometimes "strangers."⌉

The term "sojourner," like "inhabitants," did not mean in seventeenth-
century New England what it means today. Far from being visitors, or
temporary lodgers, sojourners could be permanent members of town communities. A petition from Wallingford in 1677 complained about the many
nonresident "planters" who were "absent and sojourne in other townes." In
1679, the Connecticut General Court observed that "there are in most of
the plantations a number of sojurners or inmates that doe take it upon them
to deale, vote or intermedle with the publique occasions of the towne and
places where they doe live, to the dissattisfaction of theire neighbours,
which to prvent, this Court doe order that no person that is not an admitted
inhabitant, a housholder, and a man of a sober conversation" should be
allowed to vote. The clause "where they doe live" suggests that sojourners
were, not transients, but town-dwellers.[28]

New Haven in 1645 ordered that "noe planter, inhabitant or sojourner"
could purchase lands from the Indians. Another order of the same year referred to "planters, farmers sojourners, or others belonging to this towne."
In this last phrase, the words "belonging to" signified that sojourners were
permanent residents. New Haven also required "every male from 16 to 60
yeares of age who shall dwell or sojourne" there to bear arms. A Warwick
town order applied to everyone in town, "either stranger or Inhabitant."
Another order referred to "neither Inhabitant or Sojourner."[29] An order

---

arriving in town, buying a home lot, and becoming a resident had claims to being an
inhabitant, with all the economic and political rights that that position bestowed. To
guard against the resulting unregulated distribution of those rights, alienation restraints
were passed.

28. Wallingford Petition, May 9, 1677, Towns and Lands, I, 170, Conn. Archives;
Conn. Records, III, 34.

29. Charles J. Hoadly, ed., *Records of the Colony and Plantation of New Haven, from
1638 to 1649* (Hartford, Conn.), 200, 201, 213; Warwick, R.I., Town Records, 120,

from Rowley enjoined "any man Inhabitant servant or sojoyner" from cutting trees on the common.[30]

[Sojourners in all likelihood constituted a class of permanent town residents. Precisely which rights sojourners possessed is not clear. As the Connecticut order observed, they did not enjoy political rights. Nor did they have proprietary rights. It appears they possessed no more than the right of residing in town.] But this was an important right, for which sojourners had to apply, just as others applied to be inhabitants. In 1643, two men applied to New Haven and were "admitted to sojourne in this plantatio[n] upon their good behavior." Windsor, Wallingford, and other towns also formally allowed people to "sojourne" within their precincts.[31]

Towns had authority to accept or exclude sojourners, thanks to several laws that prohibited the "entertaining," or acceptance and dwelling, of strangers for more than a period of weeks or months without the allowance of magistrates, selectmen, or inhabitants. No master of a family should "give habitacon of interteinment to any yonge man to sojourne in his family," declared an early order of the Connecticut Court, "but by the allowance of the inhabitants of the saide Towne where he dwelles under the like penalty of 20s. per weeke." Boston in 1647 ordered that no one could entertain a stranger who had an "intent to reside here" without the selectmen's permission. Selectmen fined many people for violating this order. Connecticut prohibited giving habitation to anyone without the allowance of the town inhabitants.[32]

Towns used this power to exclude people as a tool with which to assemble an acceptable community of residents. The law forbidding the entertaining of strangers for more than three weeks without the magistrates' approval was, in John Winthrop's words, "made in Mrs. Hutchinson's time," when the threat of heresy was on people's minds. Or as a Hartford town order put it in 1659, the inhabitants' veto on newcomers was necessary to prevent "many persons ushering in themselves among us who are strangers to us, through whose poverty, evil manners or opinions, the town

LC. Yet another Warwick order declared that "no man of this towne whether Inhabitant or other" should sell liquor to Indians. Note the phrase "of this towne" (Warwick Town Records, 103).

30. Rowley, *Early Records of Rowley*, 165.

31. Hoadly, ed., *Records of the Colony of New Haven*, 84; Benton, *Warning Out*, 85–86.

32. *Conn. Records*, I, 8, 538–539; Benton, *Warning Out*, 22–24. Benton equates this regulation of strangers with the regulation of inhabitants.

is subject to be much prejudiced endangered." In the next decade, the Connecticut court prohibited towns from letting "unmeet" men sojourn and required that sojourners live with families and worship God.[33]

Town-dwellers took a great interest in the character of the men and women who came to live with them and acted also to prevent poor transients from becoming a charge to the town. With laws aimed at sojourners, towns kept the riffraff out. In the course of regulating the land corporation, inhabitants may also have furthered these sumptuary goals, for inhabitants wanted sober, responsible, upstanding business partners. But when inhabitants prohibited people already living in town from purchasing certain pieces of land, they did nothing to improve the moral fiber of the community. The main work of policing morality was accomplished by the sojourner laws and by the deacons and elders of the church.

There were, then, two sets of laws—those controlling inhabitants, who held certain economic rights, and those controlling sojourners, who had the right of residency—and two distinct classes of people. In some towns, a minority of New England towns in the early years of colonization, the social structure was even more layered than that, for in some towns inhabitancy did not confer land rights upon its beneficiaries, even during the towns' first years. Inhabitants were admitted to town citizenship and usually given the right to vote, but another group, called "proprietors" or "purchasers," made up the land corporation. Sometimes inhabitants of these towns received partial land rights, sometimes they could purchase land from the proprietors; but in either case the bulk of the undivided land remained with the proprietors.

Such was the situation in Warwick. When that Rhode Island town was founded, in the early 1640s, the "purchasers" framed the foundation orders for organizing town life. Among the rules they made was one that kept "the disposall of Lands in o[u]r o[w]ne hands." Another rule provided that one could gain admission to the purchasers by paying ten pounds to the town treasury. So far, Warwick was developing no differently from other towns, with the exception that here the shareholders called themselves "purchasers," but elsewhere called themselves "inhabitants." As it turned out, however, Warwick also had its "inhabitants," twenty-two of them, who were

33. Winthrop, *History of New England,* ed. Savage, II, 250; Andrews, *River Towns,* 87–88 n. 3; *Conn. Records,* II, 281. There were many other such laws, taking various forms, all designed to keep unsavory types out of town.

not purchasers at the time of the founding and whose acts the recorder noted separately from the purchasers' acts in town minutes. The purchasers of Warwick continued for many years to receive divisions of land not accorded to the inhabitants, though inhabitants, too, owned small land rights by virtue of their inhabitancy. As of 1660, the town ceased the practice of automatically granting even these small land rights to all admitted inhabitants. Like other New England towns, Warwick also had sojourners, who apparently never had land rights.[34]

In the town of Windsor, the proprietors met separately from the town meeting and controlled the land themselves from the very beginning. In New Haven, from the outset the "planters" owned the land, "burgesses" possessed the franchise, and "inhabitants" and "sojourners" had the right to live there. In 1643, the New Haven General Court reaffirmed the independent status of the planters, stipulating that they, unlike burgesses, did not have to be church members.[35]

Wherever nonresidents owned the bulk of town land, there, too, inhabitants had diminished land rights. Joseph Dudley and his partners gave eleven thousand acres to the "inhabitants" they admitted to the township of Oxford, but the inhabitants of Oxford had no rights to the rest of the township, comprising thirty thousand acres, owned by Dudley and his partners. The first settlement plan for Worcester empowered the court committee "to Setle inhabitants therrupon forr lives orr time upon a smal Rente." It is not clear whether the inhabitants so placed were to enjoy rights to the undivided lands, but the wording of this plan suggests that they were tenants, not proprietors. Moreover, the ownership of land rights was the incentive that kept nonresident grantees involved over a fifty-year period in trying to develop the town, an incentive that would not have existed if land rights had automatically passed to residents.[36]

These towns were different in two ways from most seventeenth-century towns. First, it was easier to become an inhabitant of Worcester or Oxford or New Haven precisely because inhabitants there did not enjoy the valuable land rights held by inhabitants elsewhere. In fact, it was more than easy; the Oxford and Worcester proprietors sought out people and induced

34. Warwick Town Records, 42, 65–74, 103, 108, 139, 161, LC.

35. Andrews, *River Towns,* 48; Hoadly, ed., *Records of the Colony of New Haven,* 13–15, 112.

36. George F. Daniels, *The Huguenots in the Nipmuck Country; or, Oxford Prior to 1713* (Boston, 1880), 46–48; Rice, ed., *Records of Worcester Proprietors,* 14.

them to become inhabitants. Second, in these towns a larger number of people, or at least a larger number of classifications, separated those at the bottom from those at the top of the social structure. In New Haven, Warwick, Oxford, and perhaps in Providence and other towns, purchasers owned the bulk of the undivided land, "inhabitants" possessed small land rights or none at all, and "sojourners" lived in town without land rights.

Another way to imagine the structure of these towns is as a series of circles. The largest one was made up of all town-dwellers. The middle one included the inhabitants allowed to vote and perhaps receive parcels of land, at least until the curtain was brought down on land grants. The smallest, inner circle constituted just the proprietors, resident and nonresident, who owned the bulk of the town's undivided land and, sometimes, controlled political power as well (see "Voting," in Chapter 5, above).

All New England towns had exclusive land corporations that kept out some portion of the resident population. The question was, How many circles of town-dwellers were excluded? In most towns, at the outset, land corporations excluded just one circle, the sojourners. But as time went on, most New England towns changed and imitated the Windsors, the New Havens, and other towns just described. Their populations expanded, children matured, servants gained their freedom, and newcomers arrived. As this growth in eligible landowners took place, towns added a third ring to their societies. They distinguished those inhabitants with land rights from all other people and began calling them "commoners" or "proprietors." They continued admitting "inhabitants" but without granting land rights, so that gradually the chief benefit conferred upon admitted inhabitants became the right to vote in town affairs. And they continued to permit sojourners who were not inhabitants to live in town.[37]

The moment when a town underwent this fundamental reordering of its structure varied from town to town. In some cases, there were three orders

37. Early in a town's life, the reason not to admit sojourners to inhabitancy was to limit the number of land shareholders. Once towns stopped granting land shares to inhabitants, they still continued, nevertheless, to deny sojourners admission to inhabitancy into the 18th century in order to save themselves from supporting indigents. Colonial laws required all towns to be responsible for their inhabitants should the latter fall ill or become indigent (Benton, *Warning Out*, 38–43, 49–50, 55ff, 65). Benton helpfully gives many examples of towns' warning out sojourners in the later 17th and the 18th centuries, but he fails to see the difference between these actions, which towns took when they were mature settlements, and the rejection of inhabitants when towns were young. In other words, he does not see any change in the character of inhabitancy.

234 | Towns

from the very beginning of the town's life. In other towns, the third circle emerged only gradually. Groton began admitting inhabitants without land rights fifteen years after settlement began. Salem received men as inhabitants without giving them land rights in 1638. In Boston, inhabitants without land rights were accepted in the 1640s. Norwich, Connecticut, began distinguishing "purchasers" from "inhabitants" in 1679, approximately twenty years after its founding. In Dorchester, initially the "inhabitants" were proprietors, but by the end of the 1650s the "Commoners" were meeting separately from the town; and by 1661, they were making provisions for "non-commoners." As this change transformed the town, it became easier to become an inhabitant of Dorchester, the chief requirement being that one not become a charge to the town.[38] So it went throughout the seventeenth century and into the eighteenth, each town following the rhythm of its own development, gradually becoming more stratified, more layered, except for a few towns, which were heavily layered from their outset.]

Whenever the change occurred, landholding in all towns was stratified to some degree from the first years of their settlement. All towns had exclusive land corporations, all had residents who were not stockholders, all had residents who were not inhabitants, and some even had inhabitants who were not stockholders. No matter how many rings a town had, it had more than one. No matter how many gradations of landowners it had, it had nonlandowners, too.

An uneven social structure is no bar to communalism, if by communalism one means the spirit of belonging and loyalty that binds people to the community of which they are members. For people can be treated unequally but not feel they are treated unfairly or, if they do, not protest the unfairness, out of deference to the social system they accept.[39] The present study, however, has described, not an uneven social structure—which was surely one of the results of landholding patterns—so much as a splintered

38. *Groton Town Records*, 31; Richard P. Gildrie, *Salem, Massachusetts, 1626–1683: A Covenant Community* (Charlottesville, Va., 1975), 72–73; Rutman, *Winthrop's Boston*, 87–88; Frances Manwaring Caulkins, *History of Norwich, Connecticut* . . . (Hartford, Conn., 1874), 101; Boston, Registry Dept., *Dorchester Town Records (Fourth Report of the Record Commissioners)* (Boston, 1880), 91, 98, 99, 108–109, 130.

39. There is ample evidence that town-dwellers both thought the land system was unfair and did not accept their treatment at the hands of proprietors and nonresidents. Land fights occurred in many towns (see Chapter 8 and Appendix 12). If harmony is a condition of communalism, communalism did not reign in many towns.

society. Not one single community, but, rather, several different communities existed within each town: the town residents, some of whom might be proprietors, inhabitants, or voters; the inhabitants, most of whom would be proprietors and voters; and the proprietors, some of whom would be residents and others nonresidents. There was in addition the church congregation, different in composition from the proprietorship on the one hand and the body of town residents on the other.[40]

It is difficult to imagine feelings of harmony and fraternalism transcending these separate universes. On what could they have been based? These groups undoubtedly overlapped. Many people participated in all four and were residents, inhabitants, proprietors, and church members. But each group had its own membership and its own purpose, each policed its membership vigorously, each managed its own business discretely, and each assiduously kept all nonmembers at arms' length. The record is replete with denial and rejection.

Some laws, like the 1679 franchise law in Connecticut, specifically prohibited sojourners from voting in the public affairs of towns because they were not "admitted inhabitant[s]." Others, like Hartford's order of 1659, gave town inhabitants veto power over a sojourner's attempting to become

40. The constitution of congregations is beyond the scope of this study. It is therefore only a hypothesis that church membership differed from proprietors on the one hand and residents on the other, a hypothesis, however, with considerable circumstantial support. Land corporations included many nonresidents and excluded many residents: there are two bases for differences between their membership and church rolls (see Chapter 4, "The Separation of Church and Corporation," above). As to the relationship of church membership and resident population, growth in church membership began to fall behind population growth already in the 1640s (David D. Hall, *The Faithful Shepherd: A History of the New England Ministry in the Seventeenth Century* [Chapel Hill, N.C., 1972], 97–98). This is not to say that there were not individual churches that experienced surges and others with cycles in church membership throughout the century (David D. Hall, "On Common Ground: The Coherence of American Puritan Studies," *WMQ*, 3d Ser., XLIV [1987], 223–225). Nevertheless, figures from certain towns evidence a lack of correspondence between church membership and residents. In Salem only one-fifth of the adult population signed the church covenant of 1636, and between 1638 and 1650, some 80 families, or one-third of the total, were not represented in Salem's church (Gildrie, *Salem*, 51–54, 85). B. Katherine Brown found that of 84 townsmen in Dedham in 1651, 27 were not church members in full communion ("Puritan Democracy in Dedham, Massachusetts: Another Case Study," *WMQ*, 3d Ser., XXIV [1967], 390). One suspects that a systematic comparison of church membership and town population across New England towns would yield similar disparities.

"an inmate" of someone's house. Colony laws specifically empowered inhabitants, towns, and prudential men to expel any noninhabitants they wished.[41] Shareholders in most towns barred the possibility of new shareholders soon after the founding. Restrictions on property sales everywhere had the effect of maintaining the gulf between proprietors and nonproprietors, not of binding the community together.[42]

Ironically, this pervasive negativism owed something to the strong communal feelings present in towns. For community derives some of its substance from exclusivity, from the sense people have of being alone, together, against the world. The refusal of candidates for inhabitancy, the ejectment of sojourners, the limitation of shareholders—these restrictive acts occurred because townsmen considered vital the integrity of their different organizations, the very unity and strength of which ran like fault lines beneath each town, jeopardizing strong communal ties throughout the town.

This paradox had its parallel, perhaps its source, in Puritanism. Covenants, upon which Puritans based all their organizations, gathered people into units, then erected barriers between the units. There were civil covenants—that is, town covenants and corporate covenants—and religious ones: the social covenant, the national covenant, church covenants, and the covenant of baptism. A covenant of works bound (and blessed) the whole nation, but only the elect were allowed the covenant of grace. These various covenants not only bound people to each other but also roped them off from others; indeed, that was a main purpose of them. Just as the church covenant protected members from the unregenerate, so the town covenant

41. *Conn. Records,* I, 8, 538–539, III, 34; Andrews, *River Towns,* 87–88 n. 3; Benton, *Warning Out,* 48.

42. Interestingly, the towns most sundered by inequity and public disputes had stiff laws regulating the sale of property. Springfield prohibited land sales without approval of the selectmen, and that town, with perhaps the most uneven social structure in the 17th century, had few inhabitants and many residents excluded from inhabitancy (Burt, *Official Records of Springfield,* II, 55). The Deerfield proprietors also barred sales without permission; that town was torn between nonresident proprietors and struggling settlers (Sheldon, *History of Deerfield,* I, 9). Providence, in 1637, prohibited sales without consent of the town meeting. There, as in Springfield, a few men controlling the town meeting perpetuated their land monopoly, which in the 1640s was the source of town division and turmoil, not town comity (Henry C. Dorr, "The Proprietors of Providence, and Their Controversies with the Freeholders," RIHS, *Publications,* n.s., III [1895], 222).

was a shield against unwelcome intruders. Puritans were in the habit of sorting people into their own inviolable compartments.[43]

[To a striking degree, Puritans compartmentalized not only people but also each person's life. Carefully segmenting one's activities was one way the orthodox mind could deal with complexity and contradiction.] It was the Puritan penchant for compartmentalizing human behavior that commanded "Diligence in worldly business, and yet deadnesse to the world"; that enabled John Saffin and John Hull to have disdain for the fruits of commerce while deeply engaged in commerce; that permitted William Bradford to lament the land engrossers while calling for large farms for nonresident owners; and that explains how the same individuals could regard a town as a business venture one moment, a community the next, and a religious refuge the next.[44] [This ability to act on several stages at once enabled townsmen to sort themselves into a congeries of communities, to erect barriers among themselves, not in combat with, but, instead, out of loyalty to Winthrop's communal ideal.]

43. Perry Miller, *The New England Mind: The Seventeenth Century* (Cambridge, Mass., 1939), 478; Michael McGiffert, "Grace and Works: The Rise and Division of Covenant Divinity in Elizabethan Puritanism," *Harvard Theological Review*, LXXV (1982), 501. In finding a clash between covenants and communalism, Miller focused on the individualism implicit in contractualism, which was antithetical to the communal, organic spirit (pp. 416, 429–431). F. W. Maitland also suggested, for the same reason, an opposition between community and borough corporation in Cambridge, England (*Township and Borough* [Cambridge, 1898; rpt., 1964], 36, 83–85). Edmund S. Morgan said that the early manner of gathering churches in New England, with only saints admitted, amounted to a "spiritual withdrawal from the world" (*Visible Saints: The History of a Puritan Idea* [Ithaca, N.Y., 1965], 120). According to McGiffert, the covenant of works was necessary to preserve uncontaminated, to rope off, the covenant of grace (p. 501).

The predisposition to compartmentalize was no doubt fortified by the Puritan habit of classifying nearly everything: of making categories, rules, lists; and fixing status, rights, and duties. "Method is the parent of intelligence," went a Puritan refrain. The New England mind was rule-conscious, order-bound, and legalistic (Miller, *New England Mind: Seventeenth Century*, 20, 104, 139). It is likely that this cast of mind contributed to the importance that townsmen attached to fixing the status of people, defining their rights, admitting them to this group, barring them from that, and erecting innumerable barriers between the various people affiliated with town life.

44. Sydney V. James has described Roger Williams's ability to act on more than one stage at a time in "The Worlds of Roger Williams," *Rhode Island History*, XXXVII (1978), 99–109.

8 | *The Ambiguous Character of Town Institutions*

1. Towns as Private Enterprises

Having been first created, then controlled, by land corporations, town institutions were to a considerable extent dedicated to the private, exclusive aims of town proprietors in the seventeenth century. In most towns, decisions about fencing and other matters relating to the common fields were taken in the town meeting and implemented by selectmen, even though these decisions benefited just the commoners. Connecticut formally required towns to take care of proprietary business. In February 1643/4, the court ordered that, inasmuch as the cultivation of land was an important public goal, each town should choose five men to decide in what way the "Common Lands" might best be improved, and the orders these five promulgated were to be attended by "all such persons that have any propriety or interest in any such Lands." The clear understanding of the legislators was that not everyone had an interest in such lands; nonetheless, it was the "town's" responsibility to choose officers for regulating common lands.[1]

1. Anne Bush MacLear, *Early New England Towns: A Comparative Study of Their Development* (New York, 1908), 88; Warwick, R.I., Town Records, 72–73, 77, 189, LC; Cambridge, Mass., *The Records of the Town of Cambridge (Formerly Newtowne) Mas-*

[Town officers regulated affairs for the sole benefit of proprietors both in the early and in the later years of town settlement.]The "Ten Men" who supervised Dorchester in the 1630s admitted men as commoners of the town, though the body of commoners was restricted and separate from the body of settlers. In Haverhill, in 1661, the selectmen kept a list of all householders who did not own land rights; by 1681, they had added seventy-two Haverhill householders to this noncommoner list. As late as 1700, the constables of Cambridge collected assessments that proprietors levied on themselves.[2] [Some selectmen and deputies were creatures of the land corporation, representing shareholders more than settlers.]

Especially when existing towns disposed of new land grants from the court did they reveal how much they identified with land corporations, how devoted towns were to the exclusive interests of shareholders. Not certain individuals, but the *town* of Dedham received the court grant of land that became the town of Deerfield. It was Dedham selectmen who called meetings of the Deerfield grantees, Dedham constables who collected Deerfield proprietors' assessments, the Dedham town meeting that ordered men to lay out the new grant and to admit new purchasers, and Dedham selectmen who decided in 1671, eight years into the settlement project, which men could buy rights in the Deerfield land corporation. One would suppose, then, that the town of Dedham or the residents of Dedham benefited from this grant of land. But, as we have seen, only sixty-eight of more than ninety Dedham taxpayers received rights in the Deerfield grant in the 1660s. Within a few years, an even smaller proportion of Dedham residents had an interest there. By 1671, only thirty-two people drew house lots in Deerfield, and not all of them were Dedham residents. The Deerfield

sachusetts, *1630–1703* . . . (Cambridge, Mass., 1901), 8ff, 136; *Conn. Records,* I, 100–101, 517. Charles Francis Adams likened the selectmen to boards of directors in early New England towns, and the evidence presented here coincides with Adams's view. Adams, however, said that soon after towns were founded, the directors gave way to town meetings, which represented the rise of a "political community" (Adams *et al., The Genesis of the Massachusetts Town, and the Development of Town-Meeting Government* [Cambridge, Mass., 1892], 9–20). It has been argued above that even after the rise of town meetings, the political community frequently was in the exclusive hands of shareholders.

2. Boston, Registry Dept., *Dorchester Town Records (Fourth Report of the Record Commissioners)* (Boston, 1880), 14, 40; George Wingate Chase, *The History of Haverhill, Massachusetts, from Its First Settlement, in 1640, to the Year 1860* (Haverhill, Mass., 1861), 93–94; *Records of the Town of Cambridge,* 333.

grant benefited solely its owners, who were but a fraction of Dedham commoners and an even smaller fraction of Dedham residents. Still, it was a grant to the town of Dedham, managed by Dedham.[3]

In 1666, the Plymouth Court granted the North Purchase to the town of Rehoboth in order "to accommodate the town of Rehoboth respecting an enlargement of their town." At the same time, the court restricted the grantees to those "proprietors of the town of Rehoboth (viz.) unto all that hold there, from a fifty pound estate and upwards." Later, not only were some proprietors of Rehoboth excluded from this grant, but some North Purchase proprietors were not even Rehoboth residents. Nevertheless, this was a grant to the "town," managed by the town meeting for several years.[4]

Nearby, in the town of Taunton, in 1672, the "Town doth agree" that a certain body of individuals should pay Indians for the South Purchase tract. The purchasers declared "the now liveing free Inhabitants of the Town of Taunton" to be their associates in this land. Over the next thirty years, the affairs of the South Purchase were handled sometimes in Taunton town meetings and sometimes in meetings of South Purchase proprietors. This close relationship between the town of Taunton and the South Purchase tract would suggest that the town owned the tract, or that its residents were the beneficiaries of it; but, in fact, the owners of the South Purchase were restricted to those that paid their share of the purchase money. They numbered eighty-eight men. They declared that any of the associates who failed to pay his share of the purchase price would forfeit his right, not to the town of Taunton, but to "the Assotiats." [In other words, the owners of the South Purchase formed a self-regulating, private corporation, even as they disposed of their affairs in town meetings and even though they owed their origin to the actions of the town.[5]]

On October 10, 1683, the Massachusetts General Court answered the petition of the selectmen of Roxbury and granted a township to the town. Ten years later, in a confirmation of this action, the court recalled that it

3. George Sheldon, *A History of Deerfield* . . . , 2 vols. (Deerfield, Mass., 1895–1896), I, 6, 13, 14, 15, 19, 36–37. In 1653, Dedham had 90 taxpayers in the country rate. Dedham, Mass., *The Early Records of the Town* . . . , 6 vols. (Dedham, Mass., 1886–1936), III, 213–214 (hereafter cited as *Dedham Town Records*).

4. John Daggett, *Sketch of the History of Attleborough* . . . (Dedham, Mass., 1834), 5–21.

5. Taunton Items, Jan. 10, 1669/70, Nov. 29, 1672, Oct. 21, 1674, July 5, 1695, February 1696/7, Jan. 4, 1699/1700, June 28, 1710, Misc. Bound, MHS.

originally had made the grant "in behalfe of the Inhabitants of" Roxbury. In 1684 and 1685, it was the town meeting of Roxbury that organized the settlement effort in the new township, and a committee appointed by the town meeting that drew up the rules for taking up rights and financing the settlement there. The selectmen of Roxbury assessed the New Roxbury proprietors, and the constable of Roxbury collected the assessments. Not until 1690 did the town and officers of Roxbury cease management of this frontier settlement.

Notwithstanding this public involvement, only those individuals who took up rights and contributed to the launching of the new town were proprietors of New Roxbury. These did not encompass all residents of Roxbury by any means. (By 1713, the nonresident proprietors of New Roxbury numbered 113; in 1690, Roxbury had probably furnished 129 militia.) Rather, the grantees of New Roxbury included people who led development efforts throughout the Nipmuck country and were the owners of Pomfret, Hardwick, Oxford, and Leicester, among other towns. When the court granted New Roxbury to the "town" of Roxbury, it actually made the grant to a group of investors, led by very active land speculators.[6] The point here is, not to belabor the inequity, but to stress that inequity was guaranteed by the fact that the town was identified with, and acting for, a privileged society of shareholders.

Some towns sold town land and then divided the proceeds solely among shareholders. In Providence, each person admitted to the proprietorship had during the early years to purchase a "proprietor's right," which entitled him to a certain amount of meadow and a house lot. The existing proprietors divided the purchase money according to their shares. In Manchester, the town meeting voted to sell so much common land as earned seven pounds in order to cover the country rate of the proprietors. After receiving five pounds from one man, the selectmen gave him a deed for "a sertain comon right . . . with the rest of the comon rights belonging to the proprietors." In 1657, "the Town" of Hartford decided to build a gristmill and

6. Grant to Roxbury, Oct. 10, 1683, CXII, 342–343; and Court Confirmation, Nov. 8, 1693, CXIII, 14–16, Mass. Archives; Holmes Ammidown, *Historical Collections . . .* , 2d ed., 2 vols. (New York, 1877), I, 261–268; Boston, Registry Dept., *Roxbury Land Records (A Report of the Record Commissioners . . . [Sixth Report])*, 2d ed. (Boston, 1884), 51–56 (hereafter cited as *Roxbury Land Records*); Evarts B. Greene and Virginia D. Harrington, *American Population before the Federal Census of 1790* (New York, 1932), 19; see Nipmuck country discussed in Part 1.

to divide the "profits" from the mill among the inhabitants according to their "proportions."[7]

Springfield entered into a complex transaction in which town inhabitants clearly functioned as a private organization. In 1641, John Cable left Springfield and sold his lot and "all his right in future dividents" to "the inhabitants," who paid Cable forty pounds for this conveyance. Not every inhabitant joined this purchase; some excepted themselves from it. Two years later, the inhabitants sold Cable's land and house to Thomas Cooper for twenty-five pounds. William Pynchon and Henry Smith signed the deed in behalf of the "inhabitants."[8] The inhabitants of Springfield, who held title to the seven hundred square miles of town land and controlled the town meeting, thus bought and sold Springfield's land; and they evidently incurred personal liabilities and earned personal profits from doing so, for otherwise some inhabitants would not have exempted themselves from this transaction.

In these cases, commoners earned dividends on shares by the sale of town property and services. In other cases, the earning of dividends was not explicitly recorded by the town, but it may have occurred. The Braintree settlers paid a fee of one shilling per acre to the Boston treasury; who benefited from the treasury is not certain. Though the town of Haverhill terminated land grants early in its history, it did sell land to newcomers. Groton sold land to pay for the building of its first meetinghouse. Both Springfield and Hartford rented land to settlers in the seventeenth century. In one of the most interesting proposals, the purchasers of Warwick offered

7. Henry C. Dorr, "The Proprietors of Providence, and Their Controversies with the Freeholders," RIHS, *Publications,* n.s., III (1895), 205–206; Manchester, Mass., *Town Records of Manchester . . . ,* 2 vols. (Salem, Mass., 1889–1891), I, 60, 64; Hartford, Conn., *Original Distribution of the Lands in Hartford among the Settlers: 1639* (Connecticut Historical Society, *Collections,* XIV [Hartford, Conn., 1912]), 484–485. In Manchester, it is not clear whether the country rate was that of the proprietors or that of the town, but it is highly likely that the proprietors considered themselves as making up the town and there was consequently no difference between the two. That absence of difference is, in fact, the point here: by selling town land, the town meeting was chiefly and probably only profiting the shareholders. In the case of Hartford, the town ordered that after the inhabitants had been repaid for their investment in building the mill, all mill profits should go to the common use of the town.

8. Henry M. Burt, *The First Century of the History of Springfield: The Official Records from 1636 to 1736,* 2 vols. (Springfield, Mass., 1898–1899), I, 153–155 (hereafter cited as Burt, *Official Records of Springfield*).

to sell their entire town, with all lots and rights, in 1652. Many people in Warwick were not purchasers; nevertheless, the purchasers put the town up for sale.⁹

No one took the offer, so it is not clear who would have profited from the sale of Warwick. Nor can we know how the towns of Boston, Haverhill, and Groton used their land proceeds. However they used their profits, these towns joined the land business, selling and renting wilderness land to settlers, functioning as miniature land companies. Meanwhile, in Providence, Manchester, Hartford, and Springfield these miniature land companies paid dividends in cash to shareholders.

The similarities between towns and land companies were numerous, extending beyond the mere sale of land to settlers. Both began with articles of association laying down the rules for division and financing. Both reserved land for the shareholders and other land for sale, rent, or gift. Both apportioned rights and liabilities according to shares, however shares were determined. Both used land as a dividend payable upon shares. Both elected clerks to keep track of land business and hired surveyors to survey the land. Both prohibited the purchase of land shares without permission of the shareholders.

Unsurprisingly, towns, like companies, often employed the language of business enterprises. Dedham, Watertown, Dunstable, Fairfield, and other towns laid land out in "dividends" and "genrall devidents." In so doing, they were no doubt imitating the Massachusetts Bay Company practice of distributing "devidents of Land" to stockholders.¹⁰ As investors would describe themselves, the grantees of Northfield called themselves "under-

---

9. Charles Francis Adams, *History of Braintree, Massachusetts* . . . (Cambridge, Mass., 1891), 8–9; Chase, *History of Haverhill*, 204; Samuel A. Green, ed., *An Account of the Early Land-Grants of Groton, Massachusetts* (Groton, Mass., 1879 [rpt. in Green, ed., *Pamphlets on History of Groton* (n.p., n.d.)]), 6; Burt, *Official Records of Springfield*, I, 415; Charles J. Hoadly, ed., *Hartford Town Votes*, I, *1635–1716* (Conn. Hist. Soc., *Colls.*, VI [Hartford, Conn., 1897]), 120; Ray Greene Huling, "An Offer of Sale by the Proprietors of Warwick in 1652," *NHR*, II (1883–1884), 237–238.

10. *Dedham Town Records*, III, 13; Watertown, 1650s, CXII, 67, Mass. Archives; Dunstable, July 22, 1685, MSS Bound, MHS; Fairfield, July 30, 1670, Towns and Lands, I, 94, Conn. Archives; Letter of Instruction to Endicott, May 28, 1629, in Massachusetts, *Records of the Company of the Massachusetts Bay, to the Embarkation of Winthrop and His Associates for New England as Contained in the First Volume of the Archives of the Commonwealth of Massachusetts* (AAS, *Transactions, Collections*, III [Boston, 1857]), 96–107.

takers" and the "company" in the 1670s. So did the Nashaway founders in the 1640s, the Worcester proprietors in the 1680s, and even the religious founders of Hadley in 1663. The founders of Worcester spoke of pooling their proprietary assessments into a "comon stock" for the financing of public expenditures, just as the Bay Company had created a "common stock" to transport families and bear the public charges of the new plantation. John Winthrop referred to taxation as the "raising of a publick stock."[11]

[By far the most intriguing use of language concerned the word "town" itself. Often town founders used this term to signify the private association of land shareholders, even when many nonshareholders lived in the settlement.]In 1694, a man bought a right in Manchester from "the towne or proprietors." In Hartford, some men held lots "onely at The Townes Courtesie," which meant in actuality at the "shareholders' courtesy," for those who decided this matter were the shareholders. In Wethersfield, the commons was reserved "for the use of the Town, viz the inhabitants-proprietors," a group that did not include all settlers in Wethersfield.[12] [It was because of this identification of "town" with shareholding inhabitants that the possessive pronoun for "town" was sometimes given as "their," indicating, not an institution, but a group of individuals, the proprietors.[13]]

The clerk of Amesbury referred to a "right in the new town," not a right in the common lands, or a right in the common field, or a right in the

11. J. H. Temple and George Sheldon, *A History of the Town of Northfield, Massachusetts* . . . (Albany, N.Y., 1875), 62–64; Nashaway Company, Oct. 3, 1645, photostats, MHS; Franklin P. Rice, ed., *Records of the Proprietors of Worcester, Massachusetts* (Worcester Society of Antiquity, *Collections,* III [Worcester, Mass., 1881]), 16–17, 33; Hadley, May 1663, photostats, MHS; *Mass. Records,* I, 68; John Winthrop, *The History of New England from 1630 to 1649,* ed. James Savage, 2 vols. (Boston, 1825–1826; rpt., New York, 1972), I, 76.

12. Manchester, *Town Records of Manchester,* I, 64; Hartford, *Original Distribution in Hartford* (Conn. Hist. Soc., *Colls.,* XIV [1912]), 501; Charles M. Andrews, *River Towns of Connecticut: A Study of Wethersfield, Hartford, and Windsor,* Johns Hopkins University Studies in Historical and Political Science, 7th Ser., nos. 7–9 (Baltimore, 1889), 65 n. 4, 66.

13. In 1657, in Hartford, "the Town" decided to build a mill "at their own pp charge . . . to be raised of the Sewall Inhabitants according to their just proportions." Hartford, *Original Distribution in Hartford* (Conn. Hist. Soc., *Colls.,* XIV [1912]), 484–485.

proprietorship; yet the right referred to was very much a private property right. For the clerk's purposes, the "town" was the proprietorship.[14] Other towns called shares "privileges" and "rights." Often clerks inserted the word "town" before these words; when they did so, the combination "town rights" said more about the conception of "towns" than it did about "rights."

What it said was that towns were to some degree private associations, or land corporations, in which one purchased or was granted property rights. Paradoxically, because of this private character of towns, it was sometimes left to individual settlers to shoulder public duties. In 1669, Groton, Massachusetts, decided "to take in no more" but a tailor and a blacksmith, considering "the great charg that hath bine upon the present inhabitants." This vote did not, however, stop Groton from admitting new settlers; it merely terminated the granting of new town rights. Thus in the same year, Groton accepted Robert Parish as townsman without giving him a town right. Two years later the town admitted Samuel Scriptur as an inhabitant without giving him a town grant. Since these men needed land and the town would not give it to them, eight individuals gave Scriptur "some Small grants of upland" out of their own holdings for "his Incoridgment"; and Parish's admission was described as not "a towne act but out of everie mans owne petikuler Right." In other words, individual settlers gave their land away as an enticement to badly needed settlers because the "town"—a corporation of land shareholders—wished to restrict the number of land shares and thus preserve the value of stock. The "town" had assumed such a private, business character that it was left to individuals to perform a public service.[15]

II. The Clash of Public and Private Interpretations of Towns

This is not to say that towns were wholly private organizations, merely devoted to the interests of stockholders—far from it.

14. Joseph Merrill, *History of Amesbury and Merrimac, Massachusetts* (Haverhill, Mass., 1880; rpt., 1978), 72–73.

15. Samuel A. Green, ed., *The Town Records of Groton, Massachusetts: 1662–1678* (Groton, Mass., 1879 [rpt. in Green, ed., *Pamphlets on History of Groton* (n.p., n.d.)]), 11,

Frontier towns had many public duties. They were defense posts, communities, and centers of local political authority, carrying out numerous colony mandates to educate, tax, and discipline New England settlers.

Even the corporateness of early towns had a public-spirited purpose behind it. A town would make a grant to an individual promising to build a mill, then rescind the grant if the individual failed to finish or maintain the mill. This power to rescind grants would not have been possible if grantees had been mere tenants in common; it was, rather, a result of towns' corporate character.[16] The exercise of corporate power to advance public aims has led historians to conclude that a communal, as opposed to individualistic, ethic ruled in seventeenth-century towns. In fact, the power of towns could be used to further different aims, some public and others private, and to benefit different people, sometimes all settlers and other times just shareholders. This dual personality to towns was fundamental to their nature. The line between public and private was never clear. There was an ambiguity about town institutions.[17]

Because of it, towns were scenes of great conflict. People fought throughout the seventeenth century precisely because rights as well as the towns that bestowed them were open to various interpretations. In more than a third of the towns, fights broke out during the seventeenth century (see Appendix 12). This figure does not count the religious fights, just the disputes over land, taxes, and the franchise. Nor is it reasonable to suppose that where

---

24, 31. A more complicated but apparently similar granting of lands by eight individuals accompanied the admission of Thomas Dewey as an inhabitant in Springfield in 1687 (Burt, *Official Records of Springfield*, II, 190, 268–269).

16. Dorr, "Proprietors of Providence," RIHS, *Publs.*, n.s., III (1895), 156; James Sullivan, *The History of Land Titles in Massachusetts* (Boston, 1801), 171–172; David Thomas Konig, "Community Custom and the Common Law: Social Change and the Development of Land Law in Seventeenth-Century Massachusetts," *American Journal of Legal History*, XVIII (1974), 166–167n, 167–168.

17. The ambiguity recalls F. W. Maitland's comment that it is hard to "disengage those elements of property and rulership which are blent in the medieval *dominium*" (*Township and Borough* [Cambridge, 1898; rpt., 1964], 98). Note that the ambiguity was not confined to towns in New England. New York City, owing to its charter of 1730, which was a "throwback" to earlier practices in the words of Hendrik Hartog, combined the features of both a public and private entity well into the 18th century. A clear distinction in law between public and private corporations did not emerge until the 1830s. Hendrik Hartog, *Public Property and Private Power: The Corporation of the City of New York in American Law, 1730–1870* (Chapel Hill, N.C., 1983), 21, 210.

there were no fights, the calm was maintained by the "voluntary restraint" of town-dwellers and the "organic" unity of the community, as some have said.[18] When noninhabitants were excluded from voting in the town meeting, they could not express their grievances in votes. When shareholders refused to share their land with nonshareholders, it was not "voluntary" restraint that kept noncommoners from owning land rights. When colony law ratified the shareholders in their refusal, it was probably because nonshareholders knew the futility of petitioning that they did not protest to the courts more often than they did. As it was, more than one of three towns lodged some protest in the seventeenth century.

Modern work on Springfield, Massachusetts, reveals a highly stratified social order in that town, yet town records contain little evidence of discord in Springfield.[19] If shareholders and nonshareholders did not fight it out in Springfield—where so many of the adult males were tenants, few residents were inhabitants, and a handful of individuals controlled the board of selectmen and land grant committee for years—then one cannot assume that the absence of recorded discord anywhere affirms the fairness, organicism, or harmony of New England towns. One should not deduce the existence of a one-class society wherever there was no conflict. Gross inequity of rights and wealth did not always produce outbursts and struggles.

There was more than "one class, one interest, one mind" in seventeenth-century towns.[20] There was inequality, not just between individuals, but between groups of individuals. In most towns, shareholders in the land

18. Kenneth A. Lockridge, *A New England Town, the First Hundred Years: Dedham, Massachusetts, 1636–1736* (New York, 1970), 55. For an account of extensive religious dissension, see Paul R. Lucas, *Valley of Discord: Church and Society along the Connecticut River, 1636–1725* (Hanover, N.H., 1976), 43–57, 204, 206. Lucas's conclusion is that the early Puritans' legacy was one of "drift, dissension, and institutional instability . . . [and] a growing argument over the locus of authority in church and society." See also David D. Hall, *The Faithful Shepherd: A History of the New England Ministry in the Seventeenth Century* (Chapel Hill, N.C., 1972), 108ff.

19. Ronald K. Snell, "Freemanship, Officeholding, and the Town Franchise in Seventeenth-Century Springfield, Massachusetts," *New England Historical and Genealogical Register,* CXXXIII (1979), 163–179; Stephen Innes, "Land Tenancy and Social Order in Springfield, Massachusetts, 1652 to 1702," *William and Mary Quarterly,* 3d Ser., XXXV (1978), 33–56; Stephen Innes, *Labor in a New Land: Economy and Society in Seventeenth-Century Springfield* (Princeton, N.J., 1983), chap. 3. The absence of discord is deduced from an examination of the town records.

20. The phrase is Lockridge's (*A New England Town,* 76).

corporation could vote, and nonshareholders could not; and shareholders held title to the undivided land while nonshareholders were excluded from land divisions. In many towns, shareholders bore the initial settlement expenses, and others did not. So far as rights were concerned, there were at least two major classes in each town, and in some towns there were three.

Having said that, one must guard against describing town struggles as simply a matter of class conflict. Frederick Jackson Turner and his disciples portrayed town struggles as a ceaseless and heroic combat between the pioneer settlers on the one hand and the eastern men of capital on the other. Several things are wrong with this portrait. Progressives spoke only of the eighteenth century, in the belief that before then capitalists had no part in the New England land system. But land speculators operated, and settlers fought with them, throughout the colonial period, including the seventeenth century. Moreover, town struggles in both centuries were more than simply a contest between wealthy nonresidents and indigent pioneers. Pioneers were not always poor men combatting big speculators; sometimes they were speculators themselves. In Bristol, the leader against the nonresident proprietors was none other than John Saffin, himself a prosperous merchant and nonresident landowner of other towns. John Pynchon on occasion helped settlers appeal to the General Court when nonresidents would not place settlers on their lands or pay their dues. The Sudbury faction that lost the land fight in that town and left to found Marlborough included some founders and large proprietors of Sudbury. In many town fights of the seventeenth century, it is impossible to draw a class line between the parties to conflict. There was more to the controversies of seventeenth-century towns than class struggle.[21]

 [The fights that disrupted town life in the seventeenth century were not caused by class conflict, but by the ambiguity of town institutions.] There had been no such thing as a town before New Englanders invented it, no English precedent, no guide to instruct the colonists. In creating the town,

21. Wilfred H. Munro, *History of Bristol, Rhode Island: The Story of the Mount Hope Lands* . . . (Providence, R.I., 1880), 89–90; see Marlborough discussed in Chapter 1. As to Pynchon, in 1692 he signed a Brookfield petition to the General Court complaining about the unwillingness of absentee proprietors to move to the town and bear their share of town charges (Brookfield Petition, Oct. 25, 1692, CXII, 425–427, Mass. Archives). And he appealed to the court on behalf of Suffield, arguing for tax remission for that town (Pynchon Report, May 20, 1674, photostats, MHS).

colonists came up with a wholly new institution. [It was part land company and part borough, part joint-stock company and part village. The entrepreneurial aspect of towns helped overcome the tremendous organizational and financial difficulties presented by settling the wilderness. The borough qualities helped establish public order in the wilderness. These twin aspects of towns fitted uneasily together within a single institution, a single town meeting, a single framework of rights. Conflict inevitably resulted.]

[The first and most important fight centered upon land. If the town were essentially a borough or municipal corporation, then land should have been available to newcomers. If it were essentially a private land corporation, then land belonged to the existing shareholders.] These opposing conclusions provoked fights in Portsmouth, Dorchester, Salem, Haverhill, Sudbury, Simsbury, Stratford, Wethersfield, and elsewhere; but the first towns to grapple with this critical issue were Boston and Providence.[22]

In 1634, when the inhabitants of Boston wished to divide land immediately among themselves, John Winthrop wished to save land "for new comers and for common." In essence, what Winthrop called for was the holding of Boston's land in trust for future generations. Roger Williams had the same idea in Providence. In 1637 and again in 1638, Williams conveyed to the first settlers the land of Providence, which he had earlier bought from the Indians. In doing so, he was careful to make the deed out to the settlers "and such others as the major part of us shall admit," for his intention was that the settlers of Providence should hold the land in trust, as a corporate body perpetually expanding with each new settler. William Harris and the first twelve settlers of Providence thought differently. They

---

22. Adelos Gorton, *The Life and Times of Samuel Gorton* . . . (Philadelphia, 1907), 23–24, 28–29, 32, 33; Boston, *Dorchester Town Records,* 129; Dorchester Town Meeting, Dec. 10, 1665, CXIII, 644, Mass. Archives; Sidney Perley, *The History of Salem, Massachusetts,* 3 vols. (Salem, Mass., 1924–1928), III, 130–131; MacLear, *Early New England Towns,* 102–103; Chase, *History of Haverhill,* 204–206; Sumner Chilton Powell, *Puritan Village: The Formation of a New England Town* (Middletown, Conn., 1963), 94, 96, 99, 118–131; Sudbury Petitions, 1708, CXIII, 441–449, Mass. Archives; Noah A. Phelps, *History of Simsbury, Granby, and Canton, from 1642 to 1845* (Hartford, Conn., 1845), 28–29, 80–81; Stratford Items, 1685, Towns and Lands, I, 213–221, Conn. Archives; Andrews, *River Towns,* 52; and see discussion of these and other towns in Commentary for Table 10, John Frederick Martin, "Entrepreneurship and the Founding of New England Towns: The Seventeenth Century" (Ph.D. diss., Harvard University, 1985).

held that Williams had conveyed the land to them as individuals, not as a corporate body, and that if they did form a corporate body, it was a private corporation that had no duty to admit new shareholders.[23]

There was, therefore, a fundamental disagreement over the kind of corporation that held town land. Some thought that landholders formed a public or municipal corporation, which held town land for future settlers and used it to pursue other public purposes. Others thought that landholders formed a private corporation, which held town land purely on behalf of the current shareholders, their heirs, and their assigns.

As things turned out, Winthrop and Williams lost this argument. Both Boston and Providence as well as most other towns severely restricted land rights and divided town land among the early shareholders and their assigns. Moreover, in Massachusetts the General Court ratified these closings with its act of 1660 giving the then-inhabitants of each town exclusive control over common rights. This act, and the decision by each town to terminate commoner admissions, answered for the seventeenth century the most important question arising out of the ambiguous character of town institutions: land corporations were to be private associations.

Considering this outcome, it would have been better for nonshareholders if Williams had simply let the first twelve settlers take a large piece of Providence and divide it among themselves, and better for nonshareholders everywhere if land corporations had ceased existing after launching towns. For if William Harris and his colleagues had been permitted to take the land of Providence and divide it immediately among themselves, they might never have sought control over that town's political machinery. They might never have formed a corporation that called itself the "town" and that controlled town meetings for most of the seventeenth century. Providence proprietors did not tax their own lands, but heavily taxed shipbuilding and other industries, and, as a result, Providence never developed the maritime business that by its size and wealth and position it should have, so that in the eighteenth century this town fell behind other New England seaports in wealth and population.[24] When a town carried out the actions

23. Winthrop, *History of New England,* ed. Savage, I, 151–152; Dorr, "Proprietors of Providence," RIHS, *Publs.,* n.s., III (1895), 155–157, 201–202.

24. Dorr, "Proprietors of Providence," RIHS, *Publs.,* n.s., III (1895), 203–206, 214–218, 222, 224–225; Sidney S. Rider, "The Forgeries Connected with the Deed Given by the Sachems Canonicus and Miantinomi to Roger Williams, of the Land on Which the Town of Providence Was Planted," *Rhode Island Historical Tracts,* 2d Ser., no. 4 (Providence, R.I., 1896), 59–64.

of a private land association, the shareholders' interest was clothed with all the force of public authority. It was possible to argue with landowners, but harder to quarrel with the town, especially when nonshareholders could not vote and when colony courts backed up town decisions.⌉When shareholders called themselves "inhabitants," when the land they kept to themselves was called "town" land, and when their land corporation was sometimes known as "the town," their monopoly of land and political power enjoyed the authority of public institutions.⌉Ironically, the creation of land trusts, proposed by Williams and Winthrop as an antidote to land greed, ended up enhancing the power of exclusive groups, not serving the interests of the disenfranchised.

⌈The composition of land corporations was just one of the issues underlying town fights. After it was resolved, the basic ambiguity about towns— were they private, or public entities?—persisted; and so did town fights.⌉If the town were essentially a public institution, then town-dwellers should have been allowed to vote in its meetings. If it were essentially a private corporation, then only shareholders should have voted. Those were the two sides to the franchise conflict that sundered Portsmouth and Providence. If only shareholders could vote, then should not votes have been counted by shares? That was the issue dividing residents of Windsor and Woburn. If the rights of shareholders came to them as citizens of the town, then they had an obligation to support the town financially. If these rights were merely property rights, then they were not liable for more taxation than colony laws allowed. That was the contest that unsettled Wrentham, Mendon, and Wallingford.[25]

⌈In Deerfield, Lancaster, Simsbury, Wallingford, Wrentham, Braintree, and Bristol, the issue was nonresident proprietors.⌉If land shares were property rights, then it did not matter whether one were resident or not, or helpful or not; a right was a right. On the other hand, if shares were held at town sufferance and carried with them a public duty, then nonresidents had better support the town or risk forfeiting their rights.[26]

25. Andrews, *River Towns*, 52 n. 3 (re Windsor); Woburn Petition, Oct. 1667, photostats, MHS; *Mass. Records*, IV, part 2, 354–356; Wrentham Petition, Oct. 15, 1673, Misc. Bound, MHS; Mendon Petition, Sept. 10, 1684, photostats, MHS; Wallingford Petition, May 9, 1677, Towns and Lands, I, 170, Conn. Archives.

26. Deerfield Petition, May 8, 1678, LXIX, 200–201, Mass. Archives; Sheldon, *History of Deerfield*, I, 496–497; Henry S. Nourse, ed., *The Early Records of Lancaster, Massachusetts, 1643–1725* (Lancaster, Mass., 1884), 49–52; Lancaster Petition, May 28, 1684, photostats, MHS; Lancaster Item, May 28, 1684, CXII, 366–366a,

Did one surrender his right to future divisions by moving out of town or selling a house lot, or were land rights absolute? This was a hot issue in several towns. In Salisbury, an original grantee (or his heir) got into a fight with a purchaser over ownership of land divisions. The issue was whether land divisions accrued to the original owner of a right, or to his purchaser. The town ruled in favor of the original owner. Other towns grappled with a similar problem.[27]

In another Salisbury dispute, Robert King moved out of town in the 1640s, then protested his exclusion from a land division of 1651. The position of Salisbury was simply to "deny any land to be due to him devided in the time he removed himselfe." King, on the other hand, maintained that he was an inhabitant and property owner, whether resident or not. Similarly, in 1639, the court ordered that those residents of Lynn who planned to move to the new land granted to that town must surrender their accommodations in Lynn within two years. The Lynn residents objected to this order, which was rescinded in the following year.[28]

These different disputes involving nonresidents centered upon a single question. If towns granted land with a public or communal purpose in mind, such as orderly settlement and development of wilderness land, then those grants should have reverted to the towns when grantees moved out of town or failed in some other way to carry out their duty. By this same logic, grants made to millers reverted to towns when grantees failed to build or keep up their mills as promised. On the other hand, if landowners held the rights of freeholders in the eyes of the common law, then one could move out of town, sell his lots, and behave in any other way he pleased with no ill consequence for his land rights. This question was never fully resolved in the seventeenth century. Disputes continued precisely because landowners had a public responsibility even as they possessed powerful private rights.

Above all, through all these fights, disputants were arguing over the definition of the New England town. Was it principally a business venture,

---

Mass. Archives; Phelps, *History of Simsbury,* 28–29; Wallingford Petition, May 9, 1677, Towns and Lands, I, 170, Conn. Archives; Wrentham Petition, Oct. 15, 1673, Misc. Bound, MHS; Braintree Petition, Oct. 11, 1666, photostats, MHS; Munro, *History of Bristol,* 89–90.

27. Salisbury, Sept. 24, 1695, Misc. Bound, MHS; Konig, "Community Custom and the Common Law," *Am. Jour. Leg. Hist.,* XVIII (1974), 165.

28. Salisbury, 1657, photostats, MHS; *Mass. Records,* I, 272, 302. The ultimate disposition of the Salisbury case, after several trials, is not clear.

or a community? Towns had corporate powers certainly, but was the corporation a private one dedicated to maintaining the property rights of investors, or was it a public corporation, whose powers were to be used for promoting the well-being of settlers?

This was the central question, from which flowed the other questions about land division, voting, taxation, and nonresidency that disrupted town peace. What was the New England town? The answer was not given in the seventeenth century; or, rather, contradictory answers were given. On the one hand, the land corporation existed to restrict land shares and benefit existing shareholders; on the other, it existed to develop the town land for the better health of the settlement. On occasion, shareholders were made to forfeit their rights for failing to do their public duty; but often the court bent over backwards to keep from dispossessing noncomplying non-residents. In some towns, only shareholders in the land corporation voted in town meetings; in other towns, nonshareholders voted, too. The great variety in town practices from town to town is surely owing in part to the ambiguity at the heart of a town's purpose. Towns were both business and municipal corporations, both private and public bodies. Those two con-flicting identities were not reconciled before the seventeenth century was out.

III | *Towns Transformed*

9

The Separation of Proprietorships from Towns

There was nothing predestined about the resolution of the basic contradiction inherent in New England towns. Just because towns embodied both public and private characteristics, it was not inevitable that towns would decide which set of characteristics should predominate. Nor was it inevitable that the conflicts arising from this contradiction should eventually clear up the ambiguity about town institutions. After all, by the 1680s colonists had argued and fought over the purpose and nature of town institutions for half a century, and the outcome of their fights had solidified the power of private corporations over public institutions, which confirmed the mixed identity of towns. Not until the nineteenth century did American law take on the task of distinguishing the different rights and immunities of public and private corporations, and then much dispute accompanied the drawing of the lines.[1] It was possible that towns could continue indefinitely without clearly becoming either public or private institutions.

But that did not happen. The confusion of town identity came to an end around the turn of the eighteenth century, when the commoners holding

1. Hendrik Hartog, *Public Property and Private Power: The Corporation of the City of New York in American Law, 1730–1870* (Chapel Hill, N.C., 1983), 192–193, 210; U.S., Congress, Senate, *The Constitution of the United States of America: Analysis and Interpretation,* 92d Cong., 2d sess., S. Doc. 92-82 (Washington, D.C., 1973), 388–389, 395–399.

title to town lands formed independent organizations, separate from town institutions. Historians have ably described this creation of town proprietorships, pointing out that the landless in each town increased in number, eventually seized control of town meetings, and challenged the monopoly of the landowners. They have correctly said that, to protect their land rights, commoners created independent proprietorships.[2]

These events nevertheless bear reexamination, for they have been construed as a sign of the growing commercialization of land transactions in the eighteenth century. As Part I of this study illustrates, colonists throughout the seventeenth century put wilderness land to commercial uses. Moreover, historians have said that when individuals erected these new proprietorships, they barred others from sharing in common lands, and that from this point onward New England towns were divided between proprietors and nonproprietors. Certainly proprietors in the eighteenth century excluded nonproprietors, but so did commoners in the seventeenth century. Shareholders did not have to create separate proprietary organizations to exclude fellow town residents from the common lands: operating through regular town institutions, they had been excluding their brethren for decades and had done so with the full support of the general courts.[3] There was no presumption that land rights were available to all in seventeenth-century towns: just the reverse.

The question is, then, if commoners already prevented some town residents from owning land rights and if the courts backed them up in their monopoly, what was the point of creating new proprietorships around the turn of the century? It appears that the point was to make land titles conform to new directions in colonial land law, law that would have dispossessed commoners if they had not separated from towns. In this sense, commoners did indeed form proprietorships to protect their land rights; and there is no doubt that these rights were threatened by noncom-

2. Roy Hidemichi Akagi, *The Town Proprietors of the New England Colonies: A Study of Their Development, Organization, Activities, and Controversies, 1620–1770* (Philadelphia, 1924), 55–60; Shaw Livermore, *Early American Land Companies: Their Influence on Corporate Development* (New York, 1939), 27. Others have followed the lead of Akagi and Livermore.

3. Typical of the official attitude was the General Court's reply to those in Lancaster protesting the shareholders' monopoly. "Only such as have beene first orderly admited and accepted . . . to the enjoyment theirof" could hold land and voting rights, ordered the court in 1657. Henry S. Nourse, ed., *The Early Records of Lancaster, Massachusetts, 1643–1725* (Lancaster, Mass., 1884), 52.

moners' gaining control of town meetings. But commoners' rights would not—could not—have been threatened if the legal basis of ownership of town lands had not changed toward the end of the seventeenth century. [And the reason it changed is that New England landholding customs came under attack from royal envoys, principally Sir Edmund Andros and Edward Randolph, to whom the institutions of New England towns were anomalous, without precedent, and unlawful.]

[What is interesting about the Andros assault is not that it curbed the liberties of colonists—which it certainly did—but that by examining town institutions in the light of the common law, Andros exposed the incongruities, the ambiguities, the strange mixture of public and private functions that existed within the New England town.\He pointed out these incongruities, objected to them, and caused New Englanders to rethink town structure. He made them clarify the functions of town institutions.[His actions, combined with the growing internal tensions between commoners and noncommoners, led to the separation of public and private spheres of activity in towns.]

It has been said that land companies made their appearance in New England at the dawn of the eighteenth century and changed the land system. What was new in 1700 was not land companies: colonists had formed quasi-corporations throughout the seventeenth century, even though they lacked authority to do so. It was indeed the unauthorized assumption of corporate powers by towns that Randolph and Andros attacked, and in response to that attack colonists rethought their institutions. *That* was new.

So the creation of proprietorships was significant, but not in the ways usually described.[The reason commoners created new proprietorships was, not to exclude the already excluded, but to conform to new law and to a new understanding of town structure, so that they could *continue* excluding noncommoners.]The effect of erecting these proprietorships was not to create a class of landholders separate from town residents—commoners were already separate from noncommoners—but to define town institutions anew and set them upon a more rational, firmer basis. It was a time of institutional, but not social, transformation. This transformation was accompanied by great confusion, reflected in the sudden uncertainty about terms referring to town matters, and by great conflict, which was not surprising. After all, colonists were redefining their most important local institution, crystallizing for the first time an institution that until then had been amorphous.

1. The Land Policy of Sir Edmund Andros

⸢The administration of Sir Edmund Andros as governor general of the Dominion of New England was the most disliked government of the colonial period up to the crisis of the 1760s. There were many reasons for Andros's unpopularity.⸣ As an Anglican, he offended Puritans; as royal governor, he symbolized the end of the colonists' self-rule; and as an autocrat, he did away with representative government.

It has also been said that colonists hated the quitrents charged by Andros, "feudal dues from which [colonists] had always been free." Quitrents, however, probably were not what most rankled colonists about the Andros land policy, inasmuch as New Englanders had imposed quitrents upon themselves before Andros arrived. When Massachusetts bought the province of Maine from Gorges, in 1679, it assumed for itself the title "Lord proprietor" of Maine with all the prerogatives that Gorges once had held, including the exaction of quitrents from landholders in Maine. In conveying the townships in Maine to boards of trustees, Thomas Danforth reserved a small quitrent as a token of the land tenure of the lord proprietor, Massachusetts. (The royal governor of the duke of York's domains in America, Governor Thomas Dongan, remitted quitrents in Maine during the same years that Danforth imposed them.) Moreover, at least 129 men who applied for land warrants were willing to pay quitrents to Andros: quitrents were probably not the chief reason Andros lost favor with his land policy.[4]

The opposition to Andros's land policy was practical, not ideological. Just before Andros arrived, the Dudley council, firmly in the hands of land speculators, had confirmed the land claims of the largest land entrepreneurs (see Chapter 2). Speculators hoped that these confirmations would guaran-

4. Akagi, *Town Proprietors of New England*, 118–120 (for the statement about feudal dues); William D. Williamson, *The History of the State of Maine . . .*, 2 vols. (Hallowell, Maine, 1832), I, 561–562, 567–568, 574–575; William S. Southegate, "The History of Scarborough, from 1633 to 1783," Maine Historical Society, *Collections,* 1st Ser., III (1853), 232–234; James Phinney Baxter, ed., *Documentary History of the State of Maine,* IV–VI, IX–XXIV, *The Baxter Manuscripts* (Portland, Maine, 1889–1916), IV, 405–407; Franklin B. Hough, "Pemaquid Papers," Maine Hist. Soc., *Colls.,* V (1857), 80. The Dongan remission of quitrents applied only to the areas between the Kennebec and the St. Croix. In September 1684, Dongan, too, was collecting quitrents at Pemaquid (Hough, "Pemaquid Papers," 105). As to Andros's land warrants, see below, n. 10.

tee their title and that they would not have to submit their claims to Andros, who might not be so partial to their interests.[5] Andros took it upon himself to review the speculators' claims. In 1687 and 1688, he sent out surveyors, and himself journeyed, to distant lands to consider the claims of the Atherton Company in the Narragansett, of Wharton in Maine, and of others elsewhere. With a few exceptions, he rejected these claims. On October 31, 1687, Andros informed Whitehall that Wharton's pretensions to Pejepscot presented "a great hindrance to settlement" there. On the same date, he rejected the Atherton mortgage lands, saying that the "grant was extorted by a troop of horse . . . and that the debt was fictitious." Andros did confirm a modest parcel of 1,712 acres to Wharton, saying the latter "had improved" it. Improvement, the cultivating and settlement of wilderness land, was equally a land goal of Andros as it had been of the General Court. (Why Andros confirmed several large tracts to Joseph Dudley in the Nipmuck, in Sherburn, and elsewhere is not clear.)[6]

The owners of large tracts loathed Andros for his punctilious rejection of their claims. It is not surprising to find them among the leaders of the rebellion that overthrew Andros in 1689. As early as June 1687, Richard Wharton went to England to reverse the Andros land policy and, if failing in that goal, to have Andros removed. That fall, Elisha Hutchinson joined Wharton to fight for confirmation of the Atherton claims. Wait Winthrop remained in America but contributed money to the lobbying effort. In the summer of 1688, these men with Increase Mather petitioned the king for, among other things, confirmation of all property held before May 1686.[7]

5. On Feb. 3, 1686/7, Randolph informed Blathwayt that there was a fight between "Landed men" and the merchants, for the latter wanted to raise public money on land, "but Mr Dudley Stoughton and others who have gott very larg tracts of Land are for Laying all upon the trading party and hope by their former Lawes relating to their possession: to have all their Lands assured to them without obtaining Grants from his excellence for their Confirmation." Robert Noxon Toppan and Alfred Thomas Scrope Goodrick, eds., *Edward Randolph, Including His Letters and Official Papers . . .* , 7 vols., Prince Society, XXIV–XXVIII, XXX–XXXI (Boston, 1898–1909; rpt., 1967), VI, 210–213.

6. King's Province Report, CXXVI, 203, Mass. Archives; Toppan and Goodrick, eds., *Randolph Letters*, IV, 224; *Cal. S.P.*, Col., XII, 423–424, XIII, 255; Andros Confirmations of Dudley Lands, Jan. 11, 1687/8, July 5, 20, 1688, all in Misc. Large, MHS.

7. Richard S. Dunn, *Puritans and Yankees: The Winthrop Dynasty of New England, 1630–1717* (New York, 1971), 245; Wait Winthrop, "Correspondence of Wait Winthrop," in *The Winthrop Papers* (Massachusetts Historical Society, *Collections*, 6th Ser., V

On the morning of the revolution itself, April 18, 1689, Wait Winthrop took command of the rebel troops. William Stoughton told Andros he had only himself to blame for his predicament. A committee of leading citizens asked Andros to surrender; on it sat (besides Winthrop and Stoughton) Samuel Shrimpton and Bartholomew Gedney, both of them substantial landholders. One of the reasons they gave for the revolt was Andros's rejection of Indian deeds. Others, however, put it differently; it was said that Andros was overthrown to safeguard "acres of other men's lands . . . begged by councillors."[8] Speculators, therefore, played a special role in the deposition of Sir Edmund Andros. They wanted him out of the way because he had disrupted their speculative activities, which, once he was gone, the Atherton and Pejepscot partners promptly resumed.

The large landholders were not the only colonists opposed to the Andros land policy. For Andros attacked not just the big speculators who failed to improve their lands; he overturned the land system itself. Under Andros, the New England land system was thoroughly examined for the first time ever by an envoy of Whitehall and found to be extraordinary, unprecedented, beyond the pale of the common law. Rigorously evaluating the land system by legal standards, Andros exposed its incongruities and challenged its premises. The clash between Andros and the colonists over land was really a conflict between English law and the strange New England land system.

The principal objection Andros raised to titles was that the colonists did not in their conveyances recognize or uphold the king's right to the land. Indian purchases were worthless, since, Andros said, the land was the king's to convey, not the Indians'. All grants that did not come from the Massachusetts Bay Company were worthless, for only that entity had received

[Boston, 1892]), 9–10, 12, 12n. In their petition to the crown, received on Aug. 10, 1688, Increase Mather, Elisha Hutchinson, and Samuel Nowell asked in behalf of their fellow colonists that all property, including commons, owned before May 24, 1686, be confirmed (*Cal. S.P.,* Col., XII, 580).

8. Nathaniel Byfield, "An Account of the Late Revolution in New-England . . . ," in W. H. Whitmore, ed., *The Andros Tracts: Being a Collection of Pamphlets and Official Papers* . . . , 3 vols., Prince Society, V–VII (Boston, 1868–1874; rpt., 1971), I, 6, 20; "A Narrative of the Proceedings of Sir Edmund Andros and his Complices . . . ," in *Andros Tracts,* I, 142–143; "Extracts from Cotton Mather's 'Parentator' . . . ," in *Andros Tracts,* III, 145n; "An Appeal to the Men of New England . . . ," in *Andros Tracts,* III, 197; Dunn, *Puritans and Yankees,* 254; Charges against Andros, Jan. 27, 1689/90, XXXV, 189–190, Mass. Archives.

the king's right to grant lands. All grants not bearing the corporate seal did not conform with law. Since very few land titles rested upon grants from the Bay Company, executed with the corporate seal, most titles were, in the eyes of Andros, spurious.[9]

Having reached this judgment, Andros ordered all who wished to retain ownership of their lands to apply to him for confirmation of their titles. Before he was overthrown in April 1689, at least 129 people had applied to Andros for land patents, paid quitrents, and had their titles confirmed.[10] A great many others did not apply for warrants, and across New England there was a general anxiety about land titles while the Dominion lasted.

Owners did not ask for patents, because they objected vehemently to the assertion of the king's tenure. For fifty years, the colonists had invented land policy as they went along, granting land according to their own lights, and suddenly to be reminded that the land that they had surveyed and fought for and cultivated did not after all belong to them struck the colonists as a severe injustice. To be made to petition for something that was by all right theirs seemed tyrannous.

"The generality of People are very averse," Samuel Sewall wrote to Increase Mather in the summer of 1688, "from complying with any thing that may alter the Tenure of their Lands." Sewall reported that he himself was regarded with opprobrium for applying for patents for some of his lands. When Andros ordered the secretary of Plymouth Colony to hand over the public records, Thomas Hinckley complained to William Blath-wayt: "almost every one I meet wth upon the Road or in Townes earnestly Desiring mee to do wt I can that they [that is, the records] may be kept within the Colony," for the records contained people's only proof of grants and titles. After Andros was overthrown, his assault on titles was listed prominently among the grievances drawn up justifying the revolution. Just

9. Viola Florence Barnes, *The Dominion of New England: A Study in British Colonial Policy* (New Haven, Conn., 1923; rpt., 1960), 177ff; Akagi, *Town Proprietors of New England*, 118; James Sullivan, *The History of Land Titles in Massachusetts* (Boston, 1801), 121ff; Melville Egleston, *The Land System of the New England Colonies*, Johns Hopkins University Studies in Historical and Political Science, 4th Ser., nos. 11–12 (Baltimore, 1886), 6–7.

10. Barnes, *Dominion of New England*, 184; Julius Herbert Tuttle, "Land Warrants Issued under Andros, 1687–1688," Colonial Society of Massachusetts, *Publications, Transactions*, XXI (1919), 292–363; unnumbered volume labeled Sir Edmund Andros Land Warrants, 1687–1688, Mass. Archives. The issuing of a land warrant was one step short of, and tantamount to, confirming a claimant's title.

land rights had been denied, the colonists wrote, purely because of "some Defects and wants of Forme and due manner alledged to be in the way of the disposing and conveying of all Lands from the patentees to the townships and People here."[11]

[By far the most threatening step Andros took was his decision that town grants, divisions, and the holding of undivided lands were all illegal methods of disposing of land and that, therefore, the titles derived from these acts were worthless.[12]] No one was unaffected by this sweeping policy. When Joseph Lynde told Andros that his lands in Charlestown derived from a town grant to his father-in-law, Andros replied that such a title had no value and that Lynde must take out a new land patent. On another occasion, Andros granted some of the Charlestown commons to Charles Lidgett. The town objected, but Andros held that, since inhabitants could not show proof of legal grants giving them the common lands, the lands were nothing more than ungranted waste lands and thus ripe for granting.[13]

In a similar controversy, Randolph requested seven hundred acres of "vacant and unappropriated land" between Cambridge and Watertown. Representatives of these two towns appeared before the council and said that the lands were not unappropriated, that they were fenced and used by some eighty families for wood and pasture. Randolph thereupon demanded that Cambridge show by what royal grant the town possessed these lands and by what right Cambridge conveyed these lands. Cambridge conceded that it had not "exactly observed" the "formallity of the Law." In the "infancy" of the colony, people could not have been expected to follow the letter of the law in all its details. Such was the town's defense, but Andros was unmoved. In June 1688, the council ordered a survey made of the lands and a draft returned to the secretary's office. Andros was about to

11. Samuel Sewall, *Diary of Samuel Sewall, 1674–1729,* 3 vols. (MHS, *Colls.,* 5th Ser., V–VII [Boston, 1878–1882]), I, 231n (the letter to Increase Mather was dated July 24, 1688); Hinckley Papers, II, 18, Prince Collection, BPL; Charges against Andros, Jan. 27, 1689/90, XXXV, 189–190, Mass. Archives.

12. Assaults upon undivided lands were the most hated actions Andros undertook. See Barnes, *Dominion of New England,* 203; Thomas Hutchinson, *The History of the Colony and Province of Massachusetts-Bay,* ed. Lawrence Shaw Mayo, 3 vols. (Cambridge, Mass., 1936), I, 305–307.

13. Barnes, *Dominion of New England,* 193–195 (for which the original source is *Andros Tracts,* I, 91, 152–153).

give Randolph possession of these common lands when the rebellion occurred.[14]

[Implicit in this attack on common land was a far-reaching attack on the colonists' most important local institution, the New England town.]In the Charlestown and Cambridge cases, Andros and Randolph had made several arguments: that towns lacked authority to grant lands, that individuals could not hold lands in common simply by virtue of being inhabitants and grantees of a town, and that all so-called common lands were therefore waste lands. The implication of these propositions was that towns had assumed powers that by law were not theirs, that towns were themselves illegal institutions. This ominous idea, latent in all the challenges Andros and Randolph brought against the owners of common lands, was made explicit in the fight between Andros and the town of Lynn.

On October 1, 1687, Edward Randolph petitioned the Andros council for a grant of five hundred acres of "undivided and unfenced" lands on Nahant Neck in Lynn. The petition was read February 3, 1687/8. Naturally, the Lynn inhabitants objected to the request. In March, they presented a paper to the council with extracts of town records showing that as early as 1635 the town of Lynn had exercised jurisdiction over Nahant Neck by granting lots to individuals. In 1657, the town had converted the Neck into pasture land and had "the whole fenced as a common field." Randolph replied that Lynn could not have granted titles to land there, for Lynn was not an "incorporated" town. Lynn was not "invested with a power of receiving or disposing such lands." It was "equall to a village in England," nothing more, said Randolph. Those who had voted land divisions in the past were freemen of the colony, perhaps, but not freemen or authorized voters of any legal town corporation.[15]

From the legal point of view, Randolph was right.[Towns were institutions without precedent in the common law. They were not legal corporations, as Randolph said. They were nothing more than villages. As such, there was no established way that a "town" could hold land, grant land, or restrict the number of landowners.] For that matter, there were no legal grounds for the holding of town meetings, which, consequently, Andros banned. [On March 17, 1687/8, the Andros council barred towns from

14. Toppan and Goodrick, eds., *Randolph Letters,* II, 60–69, IV, 211–213; Barnes, *Dominion of New England,* 197–198.

15. Toppan and Goodrick, eds., *Randolph Letters,* II, 56–57, 58, IV, 205–206.

meeting to manage their lands and order other business. Under Andros, towns were permitted only a single annual meeting for the choosing of town officers. When Lynn inhabitants asked permission to hold a town meeting to discuss Randolph's challenge to their commons, Andros prohibited the town from meeting. "Neither should we have Liberty so to meet, neither were our Antient Town Records (as he said) which we produced for the vindication of our Titles to said Lands worth a Rush," the Lynn residents later reported. "There was no such thing as a *Town* in the Country," Andros "angrily" told the Lynn residents.[16]

"There was no such thing as a town"—that was the sobering verdict when the imperial administration passed judgment on the jury-rigged land system of New England. It made the colonists ponder. If the towns that granted land were illegally assuming corporate powers, then land had better be conveyed to new, legal bodies. If commons were nothing more than waste land in the eyes of the law, then they ought to be granted to individuals. If land titles were weak, then they must be strengthened. These were the new directions in which the colonists struck out after their collision with Andros. Forthwith there began a movement to divest towns of landownership, for towns had become poor guarantors of colonists' titles.

II. The Reaction of the Towns

In fact, the colonists had begun strengthening their titles even before Andros arrived, in anticipation of the challenge to their unorthodox land system. As early as 1676, Edward Randolph reported to the Committee on Trade and Plantations that Massachusetts land practices did not conform to English law.[17] Then in 1683 the quo warranto issued against the Massachusetts charter prepared all colonies for the worst. Without their charters, colonists feared for their land titles. Beginning in the early 1680s, colonies began taking steps to strengthen land titles.

In 1685, Plymouth Colony declared that all lands formerly granted by the court to towns or persons should remain to the towns or persons and

16. *Conn. Records,* III, 429; Barnes, *Dominion of New England,* 96; Charges against Andros, Jan. 27, 1689/90, XXXV, 189, Mass. Archives; testimony of town residents in "The Revolution in New England Justified, and the People There Vindicated . . . ," in Whitmore, ed., *Andros Tracts,* I, 95–96.

17. Toppan and Goodrick, eds., *Randolph Letters,* I, 66.

their heirs and that the colony seal should be affixed to any grants not yet bearing the seal. Massachusetts passed a similar act, confirming all court and town grants. On May 22, 1685, the Connecticut General Court, to prevent "future trouble," ordered that every township should take out a patent for its grant and that these patents should be made out to the "proprietors inhabitants of the Towne." The following January, the Connecticut court granted lands in the northwest part of the colony to the towns of Hartford and Windsor, hoping thereby to keep the coming royal government from confiscating this vast, vacant territory. Rhode Island confirmed the titles of its proprietors in 1682.[18]

Town-dwellers also acted to strengthen titles during this unsettled period, mainly by transferring titles from towns to inhabitants. In 1685, the inhabitants of Springfield voted to grant large portions of the common lands to "each present Inhabitant and proprietor." New owners were not created with this act; the inhabitants were as much owners of Springfield Mountains before the vote as after it. But as a result of this act a group of individuals, rather than the town, formally held title to the land, and it was hoped this formality would strengthen their title. Springfield backdated this vote to 1684, so as to precede the charter revocation. In 1686, the selectmen of Salem procured an Indian deed conveying the town land to the "Purchasers and Proprietors" in the hopes of reinforcing the title of town commoners.[19] Other towns took similar action.

Such was the pre-Andros resolve to safeguard titles. After Andros had come and gone, colonists were more assiduous than ever in transferring titles from towns to individuals. The new Massachusetts charter of 1692 confirmed all previous colony grants to towns as well as to individuals despite "any want or defect of Form."[20] Nevertheless, the colonists were taking no chances; they placed titles with people, not towns. In one of the

18. Sullivan, *Land Titles in Massachusetts*, 376; Hutchinson, *History of the Colony of Massachusetts-Bay*, ed. Mayo, I, 289; *Conn. Records*, III, 177–178; Theron Wilmot Crissey, comp., *History of Norfolk, Litchfield County, Connecticut, 1744–1900* (Everett, Mass., 1900), 12; Akagi, *Town Proprietors of New England*, 59.

19. Henry M. Burt, *The First Century of the History of Springfield: The Official Records from 1636 to 1736*, 2 vols. (Springfield, Mass., 1898–1899), II, 171; Josiah Gilbert Holland, *History of Western Massachusetts*, 2 vols. (Springfield, Mass., 1855), II, 155–156; Joseph B. Felt, *Annals of Salem*, 2 vols. (Salem, Mass., 1845–1849), I, 28–33. Simultaneously Springfield confirmed all town grants.

20. *Mass. Acts and Resolves*, I, 10.

first acts passed by the new provincial General Court, in 1692, Massachusetts ordered that "the proprietors of the undivided or common lands within each town and precinct in this province . . . shall and hereby are impowered to order, improve or divide in such way and manner as shall be concluded and agreed upon by the major part of the interested, the voices to be collected and accounted according to the interests." The tradition of voting by shares was hereby confirmed, and the term "proprietors," previously used to identify tenants in common of a single field, was used for the first time in Massachusetts law to identify the owners of a town's undivided land. Those who were not proprietors were to have no part of town lands: "No cottage or dwelling-place in any town shall be admitted to the priviledges which lie in common in any town . . . other than such as were erected or priviledged by the grant of such town . . . before the year one thousand six hundred sixty-one, or that have been since . . . granted by the consent of any town."[21]

Other colonies followed Massachusetts, confirming the titles of town proprietors either in that decade or in succeeding years. In 1703, Connecticut listed the twenty-seven towns the "proprietors" of which had been confirmed in their land titles. In 1712, Rhode Island passed an act quieting all possessions.[22] In 1701, the New Hampshire assembly confirmed all grants made within townships. The lord proprietor of New Hampshire, Samuel Allen (who had purchased the province from the Mason heirs), had this act disallowed in England and then embarked upon a land policy identical to the Andros policy of fifteen years earlier. Before a hearing in London, Allen's agent staked a claim to the "waste lands" of New Hampshire. Defendants argued that these lands were town lands, not "waste" lands. But the crown attorney general ruled for Allen and stated that "all lands unenclosed and unoccupied were to be reputed waste." Allen thereupon entered and took possession of the common land of each town in New Hampshire.[23]

Although Allen died soon after this verdict and his heirs did not win the

21. *Ibid.*, I, 64–65. A manuscript version of this act, dated Nov. 14, 1692, is available in CXII, 428–434, Mass. Archives.

22. Connecticut Patents, 1703, Towns and Lands, II, 111, Conn. Archives; Elisha R. Potter, Jr., *The Early History of Narragansett* (RIHS, *Collections* [Providence, R.I., 1835]), III, 370. The Connecticut measure referred to the 1685 court act giving the governor power to confer patents upon the proprietors of towns.

23. Jeremy Belknap, *The History of New-Hampshire* (Dover, N.H., 1831), 158–161.

bulk of the towns' common lands, the effect of Allen's challenge on New Hampshire residents was similar to the effect earlier produced by Andros upon the residents of southern New England. New Hampshire townsmen conveyed titles from towns to individuals, whom they called proprietors. In 1718 and 1719, New Hampshire recognized the right of town proprietors to control and dispose of town common lands and to hold proprietary meetings.[24] In later township grants, whether by the Masonian Proprietors or by Benning Wentworth, the undivided lands of new townships were bestowed upon grantees, who were named in the grant orders, and no one else.

[After initial acts confirming the titles of those who increasingly were called town "proprietors," provincial legislatures enacted a series of laws laying down procedures for proprietorships and conferring broad powers upon them.] In 1694, Massachusetts empowered proprietors of common and undivided lands to sue others in the defense of their lands. In 1713, the court ordered "how meetings of Proprietors of Lands Lying in Common may be called" and authorized proprietors to choose clerks, who were to be sworn "as the law directs for the swearing of town officers." Next the court allowed proprietorships to raise money to defend their lands, then to pass bylaws and impose penalties on their members. These powers were to help proprietorships discipline those proprietors who did not pay their assessments or perform other tasks voted by the proprietorship.[25] When any town proprietor neglected to pay his share of proprietary assessments, the court ordered in 1739, it should be lawful to sell the delinquent proprietor's lands. In 1753, the court gave proprietors the power to tax themselves for carrying out activities other than defending lawsuits and improving common fields. Such other activities might include paying bounties to settlers.[26] Other jurisdictions passed similar laws during the first half of the eighteenth century. In short order, Connecticut authorized the calling of proprietary meetings, enabled proprietors to manage common fields, "computing according to their interests in the field," gave them the power

24. Livermore, *Early American Land Companies*, 26–27; Akagi, *Town Proprietors of New England*, 59; Florence May Woodard, *The Town Proprietors in Vermont: The New England Town Proprietorship in Decline* (New York, 1936), 57.

25. *Mass. Acts and Resolves*, I, 182–183, 704, II, 30, 407–408, 425–426. The original of the 1694 act is found in CXIII, 98–99, Mass. Archives.

26. Act in Addition to 1726 Act, January 1738/9, CXIV, 317, Mass. Archives; *Mass. Acts and Resolves*, III, 669–670.

to sue, fine delinquent members, choose their own clerk, make "rates," appoint collectors with the same power as town collectors, and be under the same penalties for nonpayment of proprietary assessments as town inhabitants were for the nonpayment of town rates.[27]

[The purpose of these several acts was to designate the "proprietors" as owners of common lands, empower them to conduct business, and bar any claim that towns had upon these same lands.]An exception was made for "sequestered land," also called the "town commons," which usually amounted to a small parcel of land near the house lots and of which the town retained ownership. Sometimes sequestered lands were larger, outly-ing lands that the town wrested from the proprietors, but in nearly every case the bulk of the town's undivided lands, which formerly the town had controlled, passed into the hands of private, autonomous proprietorships. [Indeed, in distinguishing trespass upon undivided lands from trespass upon sequestered lands, the Connecticut assembly underscored the new separation of proprietorships and towns.]In 1726, the trespass act ordered that "the proprietors of the common and undivided lands in the several townships are the persons trespassed upon by cutting . . . any timber . . . lying on the common undivided lands in said towns; and that the inhabit-ants of the respective towns are the persons trespassed upon by all such trespasses as aforesaid done in sequestered lands for town commons."[28]

[Thus by statutes the colonies formally distinguished town and township, the one a political entity, the other a geographic one.] This distinction was not, however, immediately grasped in each individual town. For genera-tions, the "inhabitants" of towns had owned town land, and now, even after statutes bestowed title upon certain designated "proprietors," town inhabitants who were not among the designated proprietors attempted to claim undivided lands by virtue of their status as "inhabitants." These inhabitants argued that ancient lands originally had been granted to the whole town, or to "the inhabitants" generally; and since they, the peti-tioners, were "inhabitants" and residents of the town they had a right (so they said) to participate in land divisions. The answer to this argument was that while it was true that inhabitants as a class formerly had been com-

27. Act concerning proprietary meetings, n.d., Towns and Lands, III, 231, Conn. Archives; *Conn. Records,* IV, 346, 500–501, 544, V, 234, VI, 25, VII, 137–138. The original of this last act is found in Oct. 27, 1727, Towns and Lands, V, 2, Conn. Archives.

28. *Conn. Records,* VII, 80.

moners, now they were not, and unless one could show that an ancestor had been an inhabitant and that his land rights had been passed down intact to the present petitioner, the proprietors were under no obligation to honor the claims of mere town inhabitants.

This dispute and these arguments were repeated in town after town, always with the same result: the proprietors won. On May 14, 1719, the newly created "proprietors" of New London petitioned the court, saying that some years before, in 1703, the "inhabitants" of the town had asked for a confirmation of their ownership of town land, and the court had granted the request. Since then, the petitioners alleged, others not included in the patent of 1704 had made claims to the town land, and now the question was:

> Whether when a Town has been Setled after the customary manner, with a considerable number of Persons, and they Petition this Assembly that the Land allowed them in their Township, may be by Patent, or Deed granted and confirmed to them and their Heirs forever; and their Petition is granted; and a Deed of it accordingly executed, for each of them to hold his Lot or Farm Severally, and all of them the undivided Land in Common. . . . They and they only are not the just and lawfull Proprietors of the same? Or whether any persons, who shall come afterwards into Such Town, and become Inhabitants thereof; have thereby any Title in the sd undivided or common Land; and may lawfully dispose of it in a Town Meeting, by voting therein?

In the opinion of the petitioners, the answer was clear: the land belonged only to the patentees, and "the sd Town in their Town meeting, or otherwise, have nothing to do, in dividing, or disposing of the same." The General Court agreed, and the following year it ruled that no person merely "by becoming an Inhabitant afterwards Could have any Right to dispose of any Land in sd Town by Voting In a Town Meeting."[29]

The patentees of Groton, Connecticut, which was a spur of New London, pressed a similar claim before the Connecticut assembly. They protested the dividing of the common land by the town meeting of Groton. (In May 1719, the upper house ruled in this case that those who came after the

29. Petition of New London Proprietors, May 14, 1719, Towns and Lands, III, 174, Conn. Archives; Assembly Resolution, May 1720, Towns and Lands, III, 184–185, Conn. Archives. A version of this same resolution is found in *Conn. Records,* VI, 189.

execution of the town patent could not be parties to the patent, even if they did become town residents.)[30] Other towns fell to fighting over this same issue—in fact, so many others that Connecticut, in 1723, enacted that the owners of town lands were the "Severall Proprietors" to whom the assembly had granted patents. These "Lawfull owners" had power to dispose of common lands without suffering "any other persons who Should afterwards become Inhabitants of the Said Towns to be Concerned and act with them." Henceforward no one merely "by becoming an inhabitant" of a town was to have "any Estate title right or Interest" in common lands without the consent of the proprietors. This act put an end to the dispute in Connecticut.[31]

30. Groton Petitions, May 1719, Towns and Lands, III, 240–242b, Conn. Archives. In another case, the following year, when the court incorporated the new town of Bolton, Conn., the incorporating legislation specifically withheld power from the inhabitants to dispose of any lands within the township (Bolton Item, October 1720, Towns and Lands, III, 194, Conn. Archives). Increasingly, assemblies were distinguishing between conferring land title upon proprietors and conferring town privileges upon inhabitants.

31. Act concerning Land Titles, May 1723, Towns and Lands, IV, 74–75, Conn. Archives. This act began with the accurate observation that by ancient custom some land was divided "by the Inhabitants of the said Towns in Town Meeting," and other lands were retained "in Comon." In a veiled reference to the events surrounding the Andros regime, the assembly noted that it was "afterwards thought needfull" to confirm estates obtained in this manner "to the Severall Proprietors" and give deeds under the seal of the colony. The persons whose lands were thus confirmed became thereby the "True and Lawfull owners" of both their lands in severalty and their lands in common. The assembly further observed that previously proprietors had sometimes allowed non-proprietors to vote with them and had conducted their business in town meetings. As a result, some people were holding grants that had not been granted, as they should have been, by the town proprietors. But it would be a severe injustice, the assembly averred, at that date to take away their lands because of this technical deficiency in their titles. All previous town grants were therefore confirmed, so long as the lawful proprietors had given their consent to the same. But (the assembly emphasized) henceforward no one, "by becoming an inhabitant" of a town, should be "Esteemed to have any Estates title right or Interest" in common lands without the consent of the proprietors. And proprietors were "to have their Meetings . . . to Choose their Clerk to Enter and record their votes," and were to have "full power . . . by their Maj[ority] Vote in Such their Meetings (to be reckoned According to their Interest in Such Comon Land) to regulate Improve Manage and divide Such Comon Land . . . as they Shall See good." This important act of 1723 finally put to rest the long-running conflicts over land titles that had roiled Connecticut towns, after several previous, unsuccessful attempts at a resolution. See

[There, and across New England, assemblies stripped towns and their inhabitants of land titles and bestowed ownership upon proprietors.] Proprietors were so clearly favored over towns that some towns, in the attempt to maintain control over common lands, called meetings that they called "proprietors' meetings," even though the meetings were actually town meetings. Suffield, Massachusetts, was forbidden to meddle with the common land of that town in 1715, so the town called "Proprietors Meetings, At which they have continued all the Town Grants Gifts and Sales of Land which were condemn'd and made void." The court ordered Suffield to desist. Ashford, Connecticut, engaged in a drawn-out battle with the original purchasers of the township (who themselves had bought the land from speculator James Fitch). In 1719, the town asked the assembly for a patent to the township. Since a patent could no longer be made out to anything so vague as "the town," the town meeting drew up a list of men whom the "Town has a Lowed to be proprietars" and asked that these become the patentees.[32]

Stoutly resisted by towns, the transference of property was unstoppable. It occurred, however, at a different pace within each community. In some towns, proprietors had held meetings separate from the town meeting since the mid-seventeenth century. The proprietors of Dorchester held their own meetings as of the 1650s; on occasion, they met in the house of Humphrey Atherton. The proprietors of different fields of Boston and Cambridge held their own meetings, too, long before Edmund Andros appeared in New England. Hartford proprietors held their own meetings, separate from the town meeting, in the 1670s.

In other communities, the town and the proprietorship continued to mingle their affairs long after Andros had come and gone, long after colonial legislatures granted authority to proprietors to act alone. Overseeing the resettlement of North Yarmouth, during the 1720s, a committee of nonresident proprietors wielded both governmental and proprietary authority. Another eastern seacoast town, Falmouth, also perpetuated the old forms of landholding. There, as late as 1727, the town meeting was selling lots to newcomers and granting rights to the common land.[Not until 1732

---

various acts and petitions, Towns and Lands, III, 60, 134, 146–149, 231–232, Conn. Archives.

32. *Mass. Acts and Resolves,* IX, 565; Ashford Town Petition, May 14, 1719, Towns and Lands, V, 135, Conn. Archives.

did a self-contained group of proprietors separate themselves from the town and wrest control of the land from the town meeting.[33]

Similarly, Londonderry, New Hampshire, continued the old ways far into the eighteenth century. This town, settled by Scotch-Irish immigrants in the 1720s, held hybrid "town meetings" that disposed of both proprietary and public business. Sometimes "the town" took action at "proprietors' meetings." There seems to have been an almost complete identification of the town with the proprietors, even though nonproprietors were living in the town. Just as in towns of the seventeenth century, the proprietors of Londonderry paid taxes in proportion to their land draw. In 1727, the town meeting ruled that "no proprietor nor any man that have any share of a propriety [shall] have any land laid out, nor an Equall Lott with the rest of the proprietor's untill they pay their Equall share of all the town." Town and proprietary affairs were so mingled in Londonderry that on one occasion the "town" chose a moderator at a "proprietors" meeting.[34]

Then, in 1727, the hint of a dispute appeared between the town and the proprietors over land. Thereafter, although the proprietorship and the town continued to mix their affairs, with meetings of each handling the business of both, slowly the two entities segregated their activities. For the first time, the town began convening meetings of "proprietors[,] Inhabitants and freeholders" in 1729, distinct from meetings solely of "proprietors." In 1730, the town held meetings of inhabitants and freeholders, without giving the proprietors special mention in the meeting call. Increasingly in the 1730s the proprietors held separate meetings to dispose of land. By 1742, the proprietors and the town meeting each elected their own clerk, though they chose the same individual to fill the two jobs. By the late 1740s, all town business not related to land was handled by meetings of "inhabitants and freeholders," and all land business was handled exclusively by the proprietors. Thus did Londonderry follow the same path of development as other towns, half a century behind most other towns.[35]

33. Charles E. Clark, *The Eastern Frontier: The Settlement of Northern New England, 1610–1763* (New York, 1970), 124–129, 144–145.

34. Londonderry, N.H., *Early Records of Londonderry, Windham, and Derry, N.H.: 1719–1762* (Manchester Historic Association, *Collections*, V [1908] [vol. I of the printed town records]), 21–22, 25, 58, 60, 62, 63. The record read thus: "At a proprietory meeting held at Londonderry July the 3d 1727, the town Chuse for Moderator John Blair."

35. *Ibid.*, 64–65, 103, 108, 137, 158–159, 246, 300ff. See also Londonderry, N.H.,

Similarly, the thirty individuals who bought the village of Oxford from Joseph Dudley and his partners exercised both proprietary and public powers in the 1710s. In 1713, for instance, they held a meeting and voted that "Peter Shumway shal com in as an inhabatent into Oxford upon the rites of Joshua Chandler." (Chandler had been one of the grantees of Dudley and his partners.) That same year, these same men convened a "town meeting" in which they laid out lots for a minister and burying place.[36] The acceptance of an inhabitant who thereupon assumed rights in the town land corporation was, of course, common in the seventeenth century; and so was the granting of lots by the town meeting. But by 1713 these were the very practices that elsewhere proprietors labored to terminate, as they asserted their independence from towns. In Northfield, the anachronisms were even more striking than in Oxford. There, in the 1710s, "inhabitants" were the shareholders in the town's land corporation; the town meeting was in reality the shareholders' meeting, not open to all residents; and town grants were the grants of a proprietorship. As late as the 1720s, Northfield elected as town clerk a nonresident proprietor. The Northfield proprietorship was not organized until November 12, 1750, thirty to fifty years after other proprietorships were formed. Northfield went through the same cycle that seventeenth-century towns went through, only it did so in the eighteenth century.[37]

The reason for this odd perpetuation of seventeenth-century customs probably lies in the prolonged founding that Northfield went through. Northfield had been launched during the 1670s upon seventeenth-century principles that mixed public and private spheres and invested great authority in the corporation of shareholders. Then Indian wars forced settlers to abandon Northfield twice, and the town did not get on its feet until the 1710s, forty years after it was first launched. This same phenomenon of aborted settlement may account for the similar anachronisms found in Falmouth, North Yarmouth, Oxford, and other towns disrupted by Indian warfare. All these towns were launched in the seventeenth century, aban-

---

Early Records of Londonderry, Windham, and Derry, N.H.: 1719–1745 (Manchester Hist. Ass., *Colls.*, VI [1911] [vol. II of the printed town records]), 330ff.

36. George F. Daniels, *History of the Town of Oxford, Massachusetts* . . . (Oxford, Mass., 1892), 37; Holmes Ammidown, *Historical Collections* . . . , 2d ed., 2 vols. (New York, 1877), I, 187–188.

37. J. H. Temple and George Sheldon, *A History of the Town of Northfield, Massachusetts* . . . (Albany, N.Y., 1875), 132–134, 150, 157, 222.

doned at least twice during Indian wars, and finally established after 1713. With a prolonged founding, these towns lived in a time warp, carrying seventeenth-century ideas about rights and institutions far into the eighteenth century.

But these were a minority of towns. In the vast majority, the land corporation separated from the town during the period from 1685 to 1720, the era of dramatic change for New England towns. Hartford proprietors held their first separate meeting in 1672 and confirmed for the first time a land grant made by the town in 1683. In 1687, selectmen were for the first time elected who did not represent either one of the two proprietorships existing in town. In Taunton, the town and proprietors split apart during a period of twenty-five years. In 1670, the town drew up a list of "the Purchasers or free Inhabitants here in Town"; in 1688, it referred only to "purchasers," with no mention of "free inhabitants"; and in 1695, the "proprietors" of Taunton held their own separate meeting, independent of the town. Many other towns—Billerica, Deerfield, Haverhill, Medfield, Lancaster, and others—went through the identical transformation during the last two decades of the seventeenth century and the first two of the eighteenth.[38]

In most towns, the break between town and proprietorship was not a clean one, and the change was seldom rapid. It took time to sort out the new roles intended for town inhabitants and town proprietors. For a period of years, while people adjusted to the new organization of town institutions, the town and proprietary activities, despite being the activities of two

38. Hartford, Conn., *Original Distribution of the Lands in Hartford among the Settlers: 1639* (Connecticut Historical Society, *Collections,* XIV [Hartford, Conn., 1912]), 364, 551; Charles J. Hoadly, ed., *Hartford Town Votes,* I, *1635–1716* (Conn. Hist. Soc., *Colls.,* VI [Hartford, Conn., 1897]), 222; Taunton Items, Jan. 10, 1669/70, Feb. 27, 1687/8, Jan. 8, 1694/5, Misc. Bound, MHS; Billerica Petitions, 1705, XLV, 315–318, 325–326, 330, 335–337, 339, 340, Mass. Archives; George Sheldon, *A History of Deerfield . . . ,* 2 vols. (Deerfield, Mass., 1895–1896), I, 496–499; George Wingate Chase, *The History of Haverhill, Massachusetts, from Its First Settlement, in 1640, to the Year 1860* (Haverhill, Mass., 1861), 204–206, 215–216, 232, 250–257, 266–269; William S. Tilden, ed., *History of the Town of Medfield, Massachusetts, 1650–1886 . . .* (Boston, 1887), 121–123; Clark, *Eastern Frontier,* 144–145; Nourse, ed., *Early Records of Lancaster,* 176–180, 188, 198, 206. For further analysis, see discussion of these towns in Commentary for Tables 10, 11, and 11a in John Frederick Martin, "Entrepreneurship and the Founding of New England Towns: The Seventeenth Century" (Ph.D. diss., Harvard University, 1985).

distinct organizations, were nonetheless still mingled in curious ways. This transition period from 1685 to 1720 was one of confusion for town-dwellers, marked by overlapping jurisdictions, imprecise terminology, and fuzzy thinking about town institutions.

In Haverhill, the proprietors held their first meeting separate from the town meeting in 1700, but in 1706, it was the town moderator who called the proprietors' meeting. For several years thereafter, the town clerk doubled as proprietors' clerk. The Amesbury commoners met to transact town business at noon one day in 1710, in keeping with the time-honored practice of proprietary domination of town affairs; but then they officially turned the meeting into a commoners' meeting to dispose of land matters, in keeping with the new idea of strictly segregating town and proprietary business. Benjamin Rolfe served as clerk both to the proprietors and to the town of Rumford (later Concord), New Hampshire, in 1734. Ebenezer Eastman served as town moderator and proprietors' moderator simultaneously.[39]

Terminology gave colonists perhaps the most difficulty: what should be the new name for shareholders of land corporations? In 1683, the General Court of Massachusetts granted a township to the town of Roxbury for the use of the "inhabitants," in the manner of many seventeenth-century grants. In confirming this grant ten years later, the court recalled that it had made the initial grant to the selectmen, "in behalfe of the Inhabitants of" Roxbury. But in the petition seeking the same confirmation, the owners of Woodstock stated that the court grant of 1683 was made to the "then proprietors of the sd town of Roxbury," in keeping with the new usage. In the confirmation itself the court confirmed the land to the "Inhabets and Proprietors" of Roxbury and Woodstock. Perhaps unsure precisely which of the two terms, or classes of people, was the correct one, the court took refuge in both. For several years, the owners of Woodstock continued using both terms in referring to themselves, omitting, however, the conjunction between the words. In 1695, it was "the Inhabitants proprietors" of Wood-stock who chose a committee to lay out lots there. These inhabitants-proprietors were nonresident owners, conducting their proprietary business in the town meeting of Roxbury. Only later, sometime between 1696

39. Chase, *History of Haverhill*, 204–206, 215–216, 232, 250–253, 256–257; Joseph Merrill, *History of Amesbury and Merrimac, Massachusetts* (Haverhill, Mass., 1800; rpt., 1978), 160; Nathaniel Bouton, *The History of Concord from Its First Grant in 1725 to the Organization of City Government in 1853* . . . (Concord, N.H., 1856), 142–143.

and 1713, did these owners quit acting through the town meeting, form their own proprietorship, and begin calling themselves "proprietors," dropping entirely the term "inhabitants" from their name.[40]

[The practice of using both terms to indicate the single group of shareholders was widespread during the years from 1685 to 1720.] The owners of Waterbury, Connecticut, began to refer to themselves as "propriator: inhabetants" or "propriatory inhabitanc" in the 1690s. In 1697, the "Proprietors and Inhabitants of the towne called Freetowne" sent a petition to the General Court about the bounds of the township. Those who had formerly called themselves the "inhabitants" of Marlborough in 1702 called themselves "the Inhabitants and Proprietors of the Towne."[41]

Often the authors of public documents altered the phrase "proprietors inhabitants" with revealing interlineations. In the bitter New London controversy, in which the patentees of the township came into conflict with the inhabitants of the town, the assembly ordered that the town's undivided lands belonged to "the sd Proprietrs Inhabitants." In drafting the document, however, the draftsman crossed out the word "Inhabitants," thereby having the resolve confirm the common lands solely to the "proprietors." The resolve concluded with the decree that no one by becoming an inhabitant could have any say in the disposition of common lands. Thus in the space of this short measure, the legislators or draftsmen started out using "proprietors inhabitants," a phrase which referred to both the new and the old basis of land rights, and ended up conferring full title upon the proprietors and excluding inhabitants from participation in the land corporation.[42]

In 1700, the four purchasers of Lebanon, Connecticut, granted the township to "the present proprietors Inhabitants of the Town," then added the conjunction "and" to the conveyance document, making the grantees the "proprietors and Inhabitants" of the town. Voluntown sent a petition

40. Court Grants to Roxbury, CXII, 14–17, 342–343, Mass. Archives; Boston, Registry Dept., *Roxbury Land Records (A Report of the Record Commissioners . . . [Sixth Report])*, 2d ed. (Boston, 1884), 51–56, 67. The first minutes of a full-fledged "proprietors" meeting of nonresident Woodstock owners took place in 1713.

41. Henry Bronson, *The History of Waterbury, Connecticut . . .* (Waterbury, Conn., 1858), 41; Katharine A. Prichard, ed., *Proprietors' Records of the Town of Waterbury, Connecticut: 1677–1761,* Publications of the Mattatuck Historical Society, I (Waterbury, Conn., 1911), 50; Tiverton Item, Sept. 8, 1697, CXIII, 157; Marlborough Item, 1702, CXIII, 312, Mass. Archives.

42. New London Items, May 1720, Towns and Lands, III, 184–185, Conn. Archives.

to the General Assembly in 1729 signed by the "In Habitants and propra-
tors" of the town—with the last two words added by a caret as an after-
thought. In 1732, when the upper house of the Connecticut legislature
ruled that the owners of Union township should be apprised of a recent
petition, the clerk of the house first referred to the owners as the "principall
proprietors," then added the word "inhabitants" to the phrase. The defense
of Wethersfield's land was undertaken in 1696 by the "inhabitants &
proprietors of this Town," with the ampersand added later. In 1705, when
the Connecticut assembly granted a tract to the "present Proprietors and
Inhabitants of Killinworth," yet again the draftsman inserted the "and"
with a caret after the order was drawn up.[43]

One cannot be sure what these interlineations mean. The most frequently interlined word was the article "and," inserted between "inhabitants" and "proprietors," thereby creating yet another term in the pro-
cession of terms by which owners of common lands were known. First
"inhabitants" had been the term used to indicate owners of town lands;
then it was "inhabitants proprietors"; finally it was simply "proprietors."
The interlineation of the word "and" was perhaps a stepping-stone for
draftsmen as they hopped from the second usage to the third. It suggested a
difference between "proprietors" who were commoners and "inhabitants"
who were merely residents of towns, and was therefore a verbal companion
to the relegation of "inhabitants" to a nonproprietary status, a relegation
complete when "proprietors" stood alone as the term designating landowners. The interlined "and" is, possibly, an artifact left over from the
period of reconceiving New England towns.

In any case, through most of the seventeenth century, no similar interlineations appeared in phrases describing landowners, nor did inserts reap-
pear later in the eighteenth century. They appeared with frequency only
during this transition period from 1685 to 1720. Similarly, the use of two
terms to refer to one class of people did not occur in any other but this same
period. In the seventeenth century, the shareholders of the land corporation
were "inhabitants"; by the 1720s and 1730s, they were called "proprietors"
nearly everywhere. Only during this middle period were commoners called
"inhabitants and proprietors" or "inhabitants proprietors." It would appear
that this combined phrase was a sort of catchall phrase, a deliberate ambigu-

43. In Towns and Lands, Conn. Archives: Lebanon Item, January 1699/1700, II,
150; Voluntown Item, 1729, VI, 293; Union Item, 1732, VI, 69; Wethersfield Item,
Mar. 19, 1695/6, II, 258; Killingworth Item, October 1705, II, 159.

ity used until the questions concerning land corporations and towns were cleared up.]With it, colonists could hedge their bets, perhaps not knowing precisely who were the lawful owners of common lands or by what name to call the owners. Interlineations of whatever sort reflected the same uncertainty. This was a period of great change for town institutions. The language to describe these institutions also changed, and for a while it captured the uncertainty with which colonists greeted the transformation of town institutions.

Eventually, the uncertainty ceased, and terms became unambiguous. Laws spelled out in detail the power of private proprietorships over town land, and New Englanders adjusted to the new regime of land ownership. [By the 1720s, in most towns, proprietors were invested with title to common lands, not by virtue of their identity as town founders, residents, or citizens, but because they held the deeds, patents, and inherited rights. They took charge of undivided lands, not because of any relationship they had to the town, but because of their relationship to the land.]This change had far-reaching consequences, not just for the proprietors, who created new landholding organizations, but also for town institutions, from which they had separated.

10 | The Emergence of Public Institutions

[The turn of the century was a period of transition not only for land corporations throughout New England but also for the towns from which the corporations separated.]When commoners created autonomous, private proprietorships, they ceased their vigilance of the town meeting. No longer did they have to restrict membership in town meetings in order to protect their land monopoly: now proprietors had their own meetings. Far from leading to a new age of denial for nonproprietors, the separation of the proprietors from towns liberated the New England town meeting from the control of anxious proprietors. The creation of separate proprietorships also caused town institutions to address more public, rather than private, business; for, stripped of their responsibility for most land matters, town forums concentrated on matters that concerned all residents, not just landowners. [Thus the separation of proprietors from towns not only strengthened the privateness of land corporations; it also strengthened the public identity of town institutions. In the first decades of the eighteenth century, for the first time ever, towns emerged as fully public institutions.]

It was not a coincidence that in the very same acts that awarded common lands to private proprietors the assemblies also spelled out new procedures for the governing of towns. For immediately upon the separation of proprietorships, the need arose to define towns anew. In 1692, Massachusetts passed "An Act for Regulating of Townships, Choice of Town Officers, and

Setting Forth their Power," section 3 of which gave the proprietors of undivided lands power to order their own affairs. Section 4 provided for annual town meetings, in which the "freeholders and other inhabitants" with twenty pounds estate were to choose selectmen, constables, and other town officers. The next sections empowered town meetings to make by-laws, empowered selectmen and assessors to make and levy assessments, provided for the employment of the poor, imposed a penalty for not serving as constable, permitted people to become inhabitants if not warned out of town, and laid down rules for warning town meetings—all in greater detail than had ever before been done.[1]

This act was just the beginning. In the next year, the Massachusetts assembly passed an "Act for Highways," which provided for the choosing of two freeholders each year in each town to be surveyors of highways and take care that all highways and bridges be kept in repair at town expense. An act of 1699 required towns to choose treasurers, in addition to clerks, selectmen, constables, and other officers, at their annual town meetings. The following year another act provided for the election of town assessors and collectors to assist the collection of country rates. In 1723, the Massachusetts court provided a method for calling the first town meeting in a town set off from another town.[2]

[The definition of town institutions proceeded, and as it did, the assembly gave towns new powers over the proprietors. In 1730, the Massachusetts General Court provided a method for collecting taxes from owners who did not live in town and had no stock in town.](The remedy was to distrain their goods.) The next year the court subjected unimproved lands of non-resident proprietors to sale by the town for payment of taxes.[3]

Connecticut enacted a parallel set of laws from the 1720s onward. One provided for the calling of town meetings in new towns, another for the

1. *Mass. Acts and Resolves*, I, 64–68.

2. *Mass. Acts and Resolves*, I, 136–138; Act in addition to the Act Regulating Townships, June 27, 1699, CXIII, 214, Mass. Archives (also found in *Mass. Acts and Resolves*, I, 384); *Mass. Acts and Resolves*, I, 406–412, II, 306. Additional acts defining town procedures are found in the franchise laws of the 18th century and in the laws defining the status of town inhabitants. See below for discussion of this legislation.

3. *Mass. Acts and Resolves*, II, 544, 616–617. See John Frederick Martin, "Entrepreneurship and the Founding of New England Towns: The Seventeenth Century" (Ph.D. diss., Harvard University, 1985), chaps. 16 and 17, for additional discussion of taxation and the complicated relationship between proprietorships and towns in the 18th century.

creation of the treasurer's office, another for the creation of societies with nearly all the powers of towns; and many laws set the franchise qualifications of town voters. These were but a few of many measures.[4] In both colonies, towns received new powers, and town procedures were spelled out in detail.

Many of these procedures were notably similar to the procedures that assemblies during these same decades were laying down for town proprietorships. Both towns and proprietorships were authorized to elect clerks, moderators, treasurers, assessors, collectors, and other officers. Massachusetts ordered that proprietors' clerks be sworn "as the law directs for the swearing of town officers." Both organizations had taxing power. Both warned meetings in advance and only upon a warrant issued by the justice of the peace. Both could sell the lands of delinquent ratepayers. When confusion arose in Massachusetts whether the assembly had meant to authorize town assessors or proprietors' assessors to sell delinquent lands, the assembly clarified the law by saying that the law applied equally to both.[5] Side by side, town and proprietorship emerged in the eighteenth century with parallel powers and procedures but each with its own jurisdiction, one public, the other private. This emergence of parallel organizations was a breakthrough for town residents, including nonproprietors, who at last had town institutions devoted to their interests and not solely, or mainly, at the disposal of commoners. Proprietors had their proprietorships, and "inhabitants" had their town institutions.

The latter term, by which shareholders had been called in the seventeenth century, had changed in meaning as a result of the separation of proprietors from towns. When assemblies bestowed title to commons upon proprietors and barred town "inhabitants" from the same, the seventeenth-century right associated with being an "inhabitant"—the right to share in the commons—was destroyed. If an inhabitant was no longer equivalent to a commoner, what did it mean to be a town inhabitant in the eighteenth century?

Inhabitants were, first of all, town residents, which had not always been their status in the seventeenth century. Even in the eighteenth century, every now and then some petitioner or legislative draftsman still used the term "inhabitant" while referring to a nonresident. When the settlers of

4. *Conn. Records,* VII, 74, 211, 466, 554, XII, 298.
5. *Mass. Acts and Resolves,* I, 704, II, 759–760. This latter act was in 1735.

Coventry complained to the assembly in 1723 about nonresident proprietors, the lower house responded by ordering the "Non Settled Inhabitants" of the town to pay a certain amount of tax per right. But this usage
was an anachronism; it was more common in the eighteenth century for
"inhabitant" to stand as a synonym for "resident." In a 1700 Massachusetts
act concerning taxation of nonresident landowners, the court included in
this class anyone who was not "an inhabitant of the town." In a later
petition from Bolton, Connecticut, the settlers complained that "a Considerable part of the proprietors of said allotments are not Inhabitants In said
town."6

To be an inhabitant, however, was to be something more than a mere
town resident, even in the eighteenth century. For one still had to be
admitted as an inhabitant by the town meeting, or, if not, one at least had to
gain the tacit approval of the town to become an inhabitant. This tacit
approval was given when someone moved to a town and was permitted to
live there three months or more without being warned out of town by the
constable.7 If he was warned out, he might be forced to leave. Or he might
be permitted to continue living in the town, but without being an inhabitant. Many people, warned out of towns, continued living in those same
towns as noninhabitants.8

The point of preventing them from becoming inhabitants, but permit-
ting them to live in town, was to save the town from bearing financial
responsibility for sick or indigent people who happened to come to town.9
Laws specifically bound towns to care for their own inhabitants, should the
latter be unable to care for themselves.10 Sometimes towns asked for addi-

6. Coventry Petition and Lower House Action, May 1723, Towns and Lands, V, 39,
Conn. Archives; *Mass. Acts and Resolves*, I, 406–412; Bolton Petition, c. 1721, Towns
and Lands, III, 195d, Conn. Archives.

7. The 1692 Massachusetts act regulating townships ordered that all people not
warned out within three months should be reputed inhabitants of the towns where they
lived (*Mass. Acts and Resolves*, I, 67–68). There were many such acts in the 18th century,
some providing different time periods during which a newcomer had to be warned out
before becoming an inhabitant.

8. Josiah Henry Benton, *Warning Out in New England, 1656–1817* (Boston, 1911),
55, 59–60.

9. This is Benton's main point about inhabitancy (*Warning Out*, esp. 52, 55). It
appears he is correct insofar as the 18th century is concerned, but incorrect with regard
to the 17th century, when so much evidence exists to indicate that inhabitancy was more
than just a town welfare system.

10. *Mass. Acts and Resolves*, I, 67.

tional powers to keep poor people from becoming inhabitants. Boston sent a petition to the court in 1698 alleging that the town was "at a very Great Charge in the Continual maintenance of the poor" and asking that the law be revised so that people should "not be accounted Inhabitants without Having Liberty first from the Selectmen." Towns frequently fought with each other over which one had to accept a particular poor person as an inhabitant. In 1756, Wrentham petitioned the court, saying that although Dedham had persuaded the court to make Wrentham support a pauper named Samuel Davis, Wrentham could now prove that Davis was indeed an "inhabitant" of Dedham and so should be maintained by that town.[11]

Towns were trying to fob "inhabitants" onto one another to avoid supporting them: to such a low station had inhabitants fallen from their seventeenth-century privileged status. That it became easier as time wore on for anyone to become an inhabitant was another sign of this same decline. In most seventeenth-century towns, one became an inhabitant only by vote of the existing shareholders. In 1692, however, when inhabitants enjoyed no proprietary rights, anyone in Massachusetts automatically became an inhabitant who was not warned out of town after three months' residence. In 1718 the Rhode Island General Assembly ruled that a town could not refuse anyone as an inhabitant who owned real estate there worth at least fifty pounds. By the end of the colonial period, in Vermont nearly everyone was an automatic inhabitant, even former apprentices, even bastards who lived in towns where their mothers last resided. In 1821 Maine extended town inhabitancy to apprentices who set up trade and to anyone over twenty-one who had lived in town for five years without receiving charity.[12] These easy admissions tests were a far cry from the elaborate procedures that had kept town residents from becoming inhabitants in the seventeenth century. [Practically anyone who was not a pauper could become a town inhabitant in the eighteenth century.]

The nearly open admissions policy for inhabitants meant that the franchise was, presumably, open to more people than it had been in earlier times—presumably, we say, because the property requirement shifted throughout the colonial period, and because we have not compared the numbers of residents who voted in seventeenth- and eighteenth-century

11. Boston Petition, May 31, 1698, CXIII, 190, Mass. Archives; Wrentham Petition, 1756, CXVII, 178–180, Mass. Archives (this was one of dozens of such controversies).
12. *Mass. Acts and Resolves,* I, 64–68; Sydney V. James, *Colonial Rhode Island: A History* (New York, 1975), 147; Benton, *Warning Out,* 102–103, 106–107.

towns. What we do know would nevertheless support the proposition that more people were eligible than before. In the seventeenth century, when inhabitancy was a condition of the town franchise, many town residents were excluded from inhabitancy and, therefore, from the franchise. By the end of that century, the class of eligible voters began to change, as "free-holders"—those merely possessing a certain amount of property—were automatically permitted to vote in town meetings. In 1692, Massachusetts opened town meetings to the "freeholders and other inhabitants of each town," ratable at twenty pounds estate in a single rate. New Hampshire passed a similar law.[13] Soon the composition of town meetings across New England reflected the participation of freeholders. Where once the Spring-field, Amesbury, and Lancaster town meetings had been restricted to "ad-mitted inhabitants," in the eighteenth century they were composed of "Freeholders and Inhabitants . . . qualifyed for Voters."[14]

This change in the franchise was significant, for although the property test kept many people from voting in the eighteenth century, it was none-theless an arithmetical test, imposed upon all men equally by the colony—not a subjective admissions test, in which each applicant had to win the approval of a self-interested land corporation. As of 1692, the mere posses-sion of property worth a certain amount qualified one to vote. That stan-dard was a major political gain for ordinary town residents who did not happen to own shares in the land corporation.

This gain was the result of the general transformation of town institu-tions that occurred at the end of the seventeenth century. The first time "freeholders" were mentioned as town voters, without reference to their being inhabitants or commoners as well, was in 1688, when Elisha Hutch-

13. *Mass. Acts and Resolves,* I, 65. New Hampshire, in 1718, opened town meetings to "freeholders and proprietors of land in such town, or those born, or that have served an apprentice-ship there, and have not remov'd and become inhabitants elsewhere" (Ben-ton, *Warning Out,* 90).

14. Henry M. Burt, *The First Century of the History of Springfield: The Official Records from 1636 to 1736,* 2 vols. (Springfield, Mass., 1898–1899), II, 74; Joseph Merrill, *History of Amesbury and Merrimac, Massachusetts* (Haverhill, Mass., 1880; rpt., 1978), 146; Henry S. Nourse, ed., *The Early Records of Lancaster, Massachusetts, 1643–1725* (Lancaster, Mass., 1884), 202. Freeholders also voted in those towns founded in the 18th century. See Londonderry, N.H., *Early Records of Londonderry, Windham, and Derry, N.H.: 1719–1745* (Manchester Historic Association, *Collections,* VI [1911] [vol. II of the printed town records]), 79; Dudley, Mass., *Town Records of Dudley, Mas-sachusetts, 1732–1754* (Pawtucket, R.I., 1893), 87.

inson, Increase Mather, and Samuel Nowell sent a petition to the king on behalf of their fellow colonists, in which they asked that titles be confirmed and "that townships may decide on questions as to commons and other business by vote of the majority of the freeholders."[15] This petition was written at a time when Sir Edmund Andros attacked not only common lands but also the holding of town meetings, saying there "was no such thing as a town." New Englanders quickly moved, just as they had in the matter of their lands, to define town meetings in a legally acceptable way. Freeholders were a recognizable category to the English legal mind, a group to which one gained admittance not by privilege or corporate membership, but by the simple possession of property. Mentioned by Hutchinson and company in their ingratiating petition to the king, freeholders were designated town voters in the Massachusetts act of 1692.

The admission to the franchise of freeholders who were potentially nonproprietors would have been a severe threat to proprietors if proprietors had not been, just then, taking steps to see that town meetings no longer had a say in disposing of common lands. But proprietors were doing precisely that by creating their own organizations. The rise of autonomous proprietorships had therefore a liberating effect on town meetings. In charge of their own meetings, commoners no longer needed to control town meetings in order to control town land, no longer needed to fear the admission of nonproprietors as voters.[16]

This opening up of the town meeting had occurred every now and then before, in those few seventeenth-century towns (such as Watertown) where proprietors early on had separated from the town and had held their own meetings. In those towns, too, the town meeting had been open to nonproprietors.[17] Now, at the dawn of the eighteenth century, across New

15. *Cal. S.P.*, Col., XII, 580. This petition was received at Whitehall Aug. 10, 1688.

16. One must not exaggerate the importance of proprietors' feelings of security in the emergence of independent town meetings. Even though 18th-century proprietors argued that town meetings had no claim on their lands, proprietors were not invulnerable; in many towns, they lost these arguments and ceded lands to nonproprietors (see below). To a considerable extent, the emergence of freeholder town meetings flowed from the acts of Sir Edmund Andros, the charter of 1692, the formal separation of proprietorships from towns, and proprietors' reaction to these events. It owed a great deal to the proprietors' search for security, less to their feelings of security.

17. Historical Society of Watertown, *Watertown Records, Comprising the First and Second Books of Town Proceedings with the Lands, Grants, and Possessions,* 5 vols. (Watertown, Mass., 1894), I, 35–37, 74.

England, as proprietors formed their own organizations and as freeholders became voters, town meetings became the forum of nonproprietors as well as proprietors.

This is not to say that all fighting over the town franchise ceased. People who disagreed about the placement of the church or the selection of town officers tried, as they always had, to get what they wanted by calling into question the voting qualifications of their opponents. But the precise objections—the qualifications being called into question—were different from what they had been in the seventeenth century. In the early period, in Sudbury and Lancaster and other towns, inhabitants had alleged that people were voting who had not been formally admitted to town privileges; and the court had backed up the inhabitants and prohibited voting by nonshareholders.[18] In the eighteenth century, towns had no such power. If a resident met the property test, he could vote. Franchise disputes pivoted on narrow, technical issues concerning the interpretation of the law—how to evaluate estates, for example—not larger issues, such as the basis of the franchise itself.

In 1727, for example, Massachusetts passed an act to clear up the "many Doubts and Controversys" surrounding the town franchise. One clause of this act permitted men with twenty pounds ratable estate to vote in parish and district meetings as well as town meetings. Another clause permitted men with the requisite freehold property to vote in all town meetings, not just the annual meetings, which chose town officers.[19] An act of 1735, evidently passed in response to disagreements about the manner of evaluating estates, spelled out precisely what the assembly meant by "twenty pounds ratable estate." A further act clarified the property requirement in 1743. Yet another bill dealt with this subject in 1751; in this act, the lower house mentioned that men continued to be confused about the proper method of valuating estates.[20]

18. Sumner Chilton Powell, *Puritan Village: The Formation of a New England Town* (Middletown, Conn., 1963), 119–125, 129; Nourse, ed., *Early Records of Lancaster*, 49–52. In Lancaster, the court order of 1657 restricting voting rights to admitted inhabitants probably was issued to end a franchise dispute between inhabitants and noninhabitants.

19. Act in Addition to the Act for Regulating Townships, June 20, 1727 (?), CXIII, 710–712, Mass. Archives. This document is a draft of an act; it may well not have become law. It also was a heavily revised document; the freehold requirement in the second clause was changed more than once.

20. *Mass. Acts and Resolves,* II, 761, III, 47–48; Lower House action on town voting, Feb. 21, 1750/1, CXV, 826, Mass. Archives.

Even when a franchise dispute pitted a town against the town proprietors, the issue was not a substantive one: that is, it did not take up the question of which classes of people were entitled by law to vote or whether the town had the authority to bar otherwise eligible voters. Disputes centered, rather, on a technical question. Around 1720, the town of Ashford, Connecticut, which for several years had engaged in a property dispute with the town proprietors, complained to the court that "young persons and others that have not one peney in the Lyst" were voting, whereas other residents were omitted from the voting list. The town asked the court to help in "puting a Stop to all the worlds voting in ashford." The opposing side in this argument told the court that when the town was incorporated there were very few men in town who met the franchise law's property qualification; so the town permitted men to vote "without strict regard to the quallefications of the Law respecting the voaters." Now (the petition continued), if the court should decide that the letter of the law must be followed, the town would comply, but the court should know that business will be "managed by a verry few hands."[21] Franchise fights had changed since the seventeenth century. No more was voting a flash point of controversy between proprietors and nonproprietors—because no longer was voting a proprietary privilege.

[Once the makeup of town meetings changed, everything that had given to seventeenth-century towns their peculiar mixed identity was transformed. Formerly taxes had often been borne in relation to one's shares in the land corporation, but as of 1706 Massachusetts shifted the tax on lands and housing from the proprietors thereof to "the Tenants or Occupants of houseing or Lands."] Formerly deputies had sometimes been nonresident proprietors of the towns they represented, but in 1693 Massachusetts required that deputies be town residents, and other colonies did the same.[22] Formerly nonresident proprietors sometimes had cast votes in town meetings by proxy, but Massachusetts passed a law in 1739 that restricted voters to those "Who are Personally present at such meeting."[23] Formerly the

21. Ashford Petitions, 1722, Towns and Lands, V, 141–143, Conn. Archives.

22. Order in Council re Tax Law, Nov. 6, 1706, CXIII, 401, Mass. Archives; Hubert Phillips, *The Development of a Residential Qualification for Representatives in Colonial Legislatures* (Cincinnati, Ohio, 1921), 34–35, 51, 75, 86, 92.

23. At least three Massachusetts franchise acts contained this requirement. The first was passed in 1735, the second was drafted (and perhaps passed) in 1739, and the third was passed in 1743. The quotation given in the text is from the second of these, found in CXIV, 325–328, Mass. Archives. The other two are found in *Mass. Acts and Resolves,* II, 761, III, 47–48.

term "town" had often meant "grantees" or "commoners," but in the eighteenth century there was seldom such melding of public and private categories.[24] Formerly only "admitted inhabitants," the commoners of the township, could vote in town meetings; but now, in the eighteenth century, "freeholders and inhabitants," whose presence in the town meeting room had nothing to do with the ownership of shares in the proprietorship, ruled the town meeting. With all these changes, towns became public institutions at last, dedicated to the interests of the people who lived there.

Out of this critical passage in the development of towns, nonproprietors emerged with their first political leverage over town proprietors. They used that leverage. In the new towns founded in the eighteenth century, nonproprietors taxed, dispossessed, and pressured proprietors with an authority unparalleled in the seventeenth century.[25] Also in the old towns, in those founded in the seventeenth century, nonproprietors won new gains in the eighteenth century that would never have been possible before the transformation of town institutions. The most significant gain was land. Armed with new political power, nonproprietors forced proprietorships in older towns to expand and take in great numbers of nonproprietors in the space of a few years. Land corporations that had been restricted throughout most of the seventeenth century suddenly opened their doors to town residents.

Information is lacking for some of the towns covered in this survey, but in at least twenty towns founded in the seventeenth century, proprietors opened their ranks to significant numbers of nonproprietors during the eighteenth century. In most of these cases, they did so after maintaining a tight lid on proprietary membership during most of the seventeenth century. In only five towns did the proprietorship remain as tightly restricted in

24. One of many examples of the new awareness that the "town" encompassed more than one or another group of individuals is this: on Mar. 2, 1743/4, the court directed Joseph Buckminster to call the first meeting of the proprietors of the new township of Lanesborough, which had just been "Granted to the Town of Framingham." In this document, the words "Sundry Inhabitants of" were inserted after the words "Granted to"—making it clear that the grant of the township was not to the town of Framingham (in the manner of 17th-century grants) but rather to certain residents of Framingham. It was a small but significant alteration of form. Lanesborough Grant, Mar. 2, 1743/4, CXV, 210, Mass. Archives.

25. See Martin, "Entrepreneurship," chaps. 16, 17.

the eighteenth century as it had been in the seventeenth (see Appendix 13).[26]

In many of the twenty towns, the expansion of the proprietorship occurred in the course of a fight between the town meeting and the proprietors. In Billerica, in 1705, 30 men protested their exclusion from a division of town lands. They said that they had paid taxes in town for years and that the law should "Treat all the Inhabitants of the sd Town alike." The proprietors replied that the petitioners had not contributed to the purchase of town lands and in any case owned no "rights." The court resolved the dispute by giving proportional rights to all who had paid taxes for at least seven years, excluding from this arrangement certain portions of common lands.[27] The heirs and assigns of Hartford's original proprietors carefully protected their land rights for most of the seventeenth century; then, under pressure, they granted all taxpayers rights in the mid-eighteenth century. In other towns, the people sharing common lands were greatly augmented when all "inhabitants," or permanent residents, were included in divisions. Such was the case in Charlestown, where 104 people shared a division (and many were excluded) in 1681 and where by contrast every inhabitant shared a division in 1700. In other towns, the land-sharing community expanded when the town suddenly included all freeholders, that is, all people owning land and a house. Such was the case in Salem, where the proprietorship expanded in 1702. In many towns, land shares were given out to people on the basis of how long they had resided or paid taxes in town. Such was the case in Concord, Massachusetts, where as of 1725 all those whose ancestors had had a freehold in town as of 1661 received three-acre rights, those with a freehold in 1684 received two-acre rights, and those with a freehold in 1715 received half-acre rights.[28]

---

26. The opening of land corporations to nonproprietors during the 18th century in towns where land corporations had theretofore remained solidly closed can only be explained by the new-found political power of nonproprietors and the proprietors' consequent need to propitiate the town meeting. This shift of political power in favor of nonproprietors is also—even more—evident in new towns founded in the 18th century. For new towns, see Martin, "Entrepreneurship," chaps. 16, 17.

27. Billerica Petitions, 1705, XLV, 315–318, 325–326, 330, 335–337, 339, 340, Mass. Archives.

28. Charles J. Hoadly, ed., *Hartford Town Votes*, I, *1635–1716* (Connecticut Historical Society, *Collections*, VI [Hartford, Conn., 1897]), 16–20, 201–202; Hartford,

The results of these measures were dramatic. Andover had 102 proprietors in 1702, representing only about half the heads of families. Twelve years later, Andover added 120 people to the proprietors' list, leaving out only about 11 heads of families. In Dorchester, there were roughly 104 proprietors in 1637, 124 in 1698—and 227 in 1713. Salem had 225 grantees in 1637, many shareless residents during the rest of the seventeenth century, and then 1,738 shares in 1722. Through most of the seventeenth century, New Haven had anywhere from 86 to 123 proprietors of common lands, but in 1711, under a new expansion, 418 people held shares to the town's land. Hartford had 95 proprietors through most of the seventeenth century, but in 1754 a land division was shared by 477 people, apparently all taxpayers in town.[29] Not every adult free male had belonged to the proprietorship even at the founding of some of these towns; but now, seven and eight decades later, for the first time ever in some places, the proprietorship nearly mirrored the free population.

So the separation of proprietors from towns transformed towns in several ways. By the second and third decades of the eighteenth century, town meetings were the forums for the whole eligible populace, not just the commoners. Town officers represented town residents, not the landholding corporation. And in many older towns, nonproprietors finally cracked

Conn., *Original Distribution of the Lands in Hartford among the Settlers: 1639* (Conn. Hist. Soc., *Colls.,* XIV [Hartford, Conn., 1912]), 499–501, 549–550; William DeLoss Love, *The Colonial History of Hartford* . . . , 2d ed. (Hartford, Conn., 1935; rpt., 1974), 117; Charles M. Andrews, *The River Towns of Connecticut: A Study of Wethersfield, Hartford, and Windsor,* Johns Hopkins University Studies in Historical and Political Science, 7th Ser., nos. 7–9 (Baltimore, 1889), 60–61n, 61; Boston, Registry Dept., *Charlestown Land Records (Third Report of the Record Commissioners of the City of Boston)* (Boston, 1878), 75–81, 189–191; Charles Brooks, *History of the Town of Medford* . . . (Boston, 1855), 483; Charlestown Items, May 27, 1685, CXII, 386–393, Mass. Archives; Sidney Perley, *The History of Salem, Massachusetts,* 3 vols. (Salem, Mass., 1924–1928), I, 454–459, 460–465, III, 131, 132; Joseph B. Felt, *Annals of Salem,* 2 vols. (Salem, Mass., 1845–1849), I, 189, 199; Lemuel Shattuck, *A History of the Town of Concord* . . . (Boston, 1835), 275–279.

29. Philip J. Greven, Jr., *Four Generations: Population, Land, and Family in Colonial Andover, Massachusetts* (Ithaca, N.Y., 1970), 48, 128, 176; Dorchester Items, 1719 and 1698, CXIII, 641, 645–646; 1713, XLV, 418–425, Mass. Archives; Boston, *Dorchester Town Records,* 29–31; Charles J. Hoadly, ed., *Records of the Colony and Plantation of New Haven, from 1638 to 1649* (Hartford, Conn., 1857), 17, 49–51, 91–93; *New Haven Town Records,* II, 333–335, III, viii, ix, 296–308. For Salem and Hartford, see citations in preceding note.

open the sealed membership of land corporations. Nonproprietors during the eighteenth century possessed both more power and more access to the common lands than they had had during the seventeenth century. In their battle with proprietors and in their dealings with the provincial govern-ment, nonproprietors had for the first time a powerful institution to serve their needs and extend their influence: the New England town.

Conclusion.
The New England
Town Reconsidered

In reviewing this history, several facts stand out. Prominent individuals played a crucial role in the town-founding system: it was they who obtained the grant, negotiated with Indians, created the landholding corporation in town, admitted shareholders, apportioned rights, financed costs, and lured settlers. People sought profits from owning wilderness land during the seventeenth century. Multiple and absentee landholding was common.

[Yet perhaps more interesting than this enterprise was how strongly towns and general courts relied upon entrepreneurs as agents in the town-founding process.] Under the supervision of general courts, town-founding routinely drew wealthy easterners into an embrace with frontier settlers, making each dependent on the other: the nonresidents needing settlement to proceed in order for their property to appreciate in value, the settlers needing capital and other assistance that prominent nonresidents contributed to launching their town. This productive symbiosis was most evident in those many towns where proprietors contracted out the settlement duty, placing tenants or purchasers in frontier towns and even recruiting settlers with financial inducements. But it was evident also when nonresidents were barely involved, for towns needed the contribution of shareholders, and shareholders insisted on maintaining their land monopoly. [Whether nonresidents were involved or not, and more often they were, the land system married a hard-nosed business interest to the larger interest of creating towns.]

As to towns, the finished products reflected the methods of their manufacture. Most towns closed admissions to the land corporation, had residents without rights to the undivided lands, turned the town meeting into essentially a shareholders' meeting, divided land according to fixed shares of interest, and regarded taxes in early years as a kind of stock subscription—all because to a remarkable (though not complete) extent towns continued to bear the character of the businesses that launched them.

On the other hand, towns had many nonbusiness characteristics, many communal and religious pursuits. Perhaps there is no better way to capture the complexity of town life than to look in detail at the progress of one single town from launching early in the seventeenth century to maturation in the eighteenth. The town of Dedham, Massachusetts, is a good study because it contained precisely that mixture of mentalités both communal and commercial, both religious and business, that makes New England towns so unyielding of simple, one-dimensional description.

In 1635 or 1636 a group of individuals petitioned the General Court for a township, which the court granted on September 10, 1636. Soon thereafter the founders would sign a covenant in which they pledged to practice "that most perfect rule. the foundacion where of is Everlasting Love," to keep out of their community the "contrarye minded" and accept only those of "peaceable conversation," to arbitrate all differences, to require all men that should receive lots to bear their fair share of charges and obey all orders for the purpose of creating a "Loveing and comfortable societie." One hundred twenty-five men signed this founding covenant. A higher-minded, more fraternal beginning cannot be imagined.[1]

Nor can one fail to be struck by the commitment of the church founders. Dedham's first pastor, John Allin, left an account of the church-founding, wherein he tells how few of Dedham's first families knew each other before becoming neighbors in Dedham's precincts. For that reason, when they began to discuss the foundations of their church, the first thing they did was to make professions and acquaint themselves with one another, "opening their hearts." The founders decided that "only visible saints or believers were to be received" into the church, people who could prove themselves not only by baptism (for Papists could be baptized) and not only by leading a civil life (for that too was a deceptive test) but by "a p'fession of an inward

1. Dedham, Mass., *The Early Records of the Town* . . . , 6 vols. (Dedham, Mass., 1886–1936), III, 2–3.

worke of faith and grace declared by an holy life sutable therto [which] may p'suade the [church] to imbrace them wth such a brotherly love as ought to be amongst sfs in so neere a covenant." Only the pure would be members of Dedham's church.

Next the founders set aside a day for fasting and prayer, followed by a day to "open ev'ry one his spirituall condicion to the rest, relating the manner of our conversion to god." This event, in which strangers related to one another their most important experience and which they knew was a building block for starting a new life, new town, and new church in the wilderness, could only have been profoundly moving. On November 8, 1638, then, the founders entered into a solemn covenant with God and one another, and Dedham's church was born.[2]

Judging from this portrait, the motives of Dedham's founders appear straightforwardly communal and religious. And undoubtedly they were. But one cannot stop there; Dedham's founders undertook a great many other activities at the same time as—and even earlier than—these events, which also must be accounted for. Before the church was founded, Dedham's founders had framed a quite different set of orders that created Dedham's land corporation, set the terms of shareholders' interest, and organized the town's finances. The first order held that everyone receiving land should "beare all equall charges with other men according to his proportion." Another provided that meadow land should be apportioned according to the size of first upland lots. Another provided that no one could sell his lot to a stranger, the reason being that the town needed to be certain that all landholders would "pay equall share of charges with other men of the same proportion of grownd" and obey all orders. Alienation restrictions are sometimes described solely as communal instruments. But they were also used to assure land shareholders that new shareholders were able and committed to bearing their share of costs, for in the early years no one else bore public charges but the shareholders, who were rated according to their lot size.[3] These early orders prove, not that Dedham's founders were profit-minded individuals, but that they had many preoccupations in the early months, primary among them the need to create a system for financing the town and dividing the town land, a system they put in place probably before they framed the town covenant and two years before they founded the church.

2. *Ibid.*, II, 1–8.
3. *Ibid.*, III, 4–5, 21, 23–24.

The system they created was, moreover, anything but communal; it excluded a great many people from sharing land and power. Barely one year after the court bestowed the township grant, the Dedham town meeting closed the land corporation to newcomers. "Noe more Lotts shalbe graunted out," the founders declared, until they could acquire new lands. Those people who had land requests pending "shall have a negative Answer given them."[4] In time, Dedham found new lands and land grants resumed, but the number of land shareholders always remained considerably smaller than the number of town residents. By February 1643, just six years after the founding, Dedham's commoners had reached the number (roughly 70) that they were to maintain for the rest of the century, regardless of the fact that Dedham both grew in population and acquired new land mass. In that year, Dedham had 68 commoners, yet 112 church members; in 1653, 76 people shared a division, yet 90 people paid taxes; in 1663, it had 69 commoners, yet 96 residents paid the country rate the year before; in 1685, there were 75 proprietors, but 120 taxpayers. Throughout the century, anywhere from one-sixth to one-third of Dedham's taxpayers were excluded from the association that owned and divided Dedham's land.[5]

Nor did all people share political power. In the beginning, voters included anyone "of our Towne that is admitted a Townesman with us." Not everyone was admitted, however. The town gave permission to sojourners to live in Dedham without, however, making them "townsmen." In 1656, the town ruled that a townsman who left Dedham and later returned might not be granted the "privileges" of a townsman. Who precisely the townsmen were is not clear, but it seems that they were members of the land corporation. In 1651 the question was raised whether a person merely by purchasing or inheriting land acquired "Towne privilidges and right of voateing in all cases with other Townsmen."[6] The question suggests that landownership carried with it the right to vote, for the issue raised was whether all landowners could vote, or only those who received their grants

4. *Ibid.*, III, 34–35.

5. *Ibid.*, II, 13–33, III, 94–96, 211–214, IV, 63–64, 68–69, V, 170–171, 178–179. It is likely that the proportion of excluded male residents was higher than these figures indicate, because not all commoners were town residents—after 1656, shareholders who moved out of town continued to participate in land divisions in proportion to the number of "Common rights" they owned (III, 141–142)—and because the lists of taxpayers included several women.

6. *Ibid.*, III, 18, 135.

from the town and were admitted to "townsmanship" by formal process. Town records do not report the answer, but numbers indicate that Dedham had roughly the same number of voters as land shareholders. In 1645, eighty-three people shared a division of woodland; six years later, eighty-six townsmen were called to town meeting. In 1666, eighty-four people were town voters; at the same time, seventy-one people shared a land division near Medfield. More or less, the numbers of shareholders matched the numbers of town voters. And in both cases, voters and shareholders were fewer than taxpayers, not to mention male residents. One hundred twenty-five men signed Dedham's covenant in 1636, but fewer than twenty persons attended town meetings that year. Fourteen men were present when the town passed its alienation restriction in 1636, barring any "inhabitant" from selling his lot without permission of the "company."[7]

Dedham, then, had at least three communities during its early decades. There was the community of town residents, best represented by the 125 people who signed the town covenant, including servants, single men, and individuals financially incapable of becoming members of the land corporation as well as the three to four score people who were land shareholders and voting townsmen. Male and female sojourners were added to this community of residents with great care; the selectmen or town meeting passed on each person proposed for sojourner status who, if he was accepted and then behaved himself, became a permanent member of the residential community.[8] Next, there was the church, which started with 8 members in 1638 and grew by 1653 to have 171 members (not to mention an additional 199 baptisms between 1638 and 1653), at a time when Dedham had 76 commoners and 90 taxpayers. Dedham's church screened its applicants with vigilance; although the church clearly included many servants and wives and others not included in the land corporation, it also formally rejected some of Dedham's leading shareholders for "rash carriage" and being "too much addicted to the world."[9] Finally, there was the land corporation, the most restricted of Dedham's organizations, excluding many members of the church and the resident population and containing roughly 70 members from the 1640s to the 1680s. Thus Dedham's three distinct communities overlapped but, nevertheless, sustained

7. *Ibid.*, III, 21–22, 24, 109–111, 190, IV, 124–126.
8. *Ibid.*, IV, 11.
9. *Ibid.*, II, 6, 13–33.

discrete memberships, each policing itself, screening applicants, and protecting its integrity against the outside world.

With time, this organization of Dedham's life changed. The first thing to change was the tax base, for Dedham's shareholders were eager to move their financial burden from land shares to other units. In 1639, three years after the founding, Dedham began rating acres and cattle instead of just acres. The next year the town rated the visible estate "of every man in our towne," in a move that shifted the tax not only away from shares but also, significantly, away from shareholders. Then in 1651 the town rated the present possessors of houses, land, and cattle; this change meant that where tenants existed, they, instead of owners, bore the tax liability. Thus in fifteen years did the shareholders gradually shift financial responsibility from themselves alone to those who lived in houses and worked the land.[10]

The control of political power also was to change over time. In 1685 Dedham's proprietors held their first separate meeting, independent of the town meeting.[11] This bifurcation of the town meeting occurred at the same time in a great many New England towns, principally because the quo warranto against the Massachusetts charter in 1683, together with Whitehall's increasingly vocal skepticism of New England's land system, compelled the colonists to take action to safeguard their land titles. The New England town, as Sir Edmund Andros was to declare, was a legal fiction, and since towns created most land titles, most land titles were in jeopardy. The surest way to protect titles was to separate the landholding body from the town and erect it into a recognizable proprietorship. Hence proprietors began meeting separately from the town meeting.

An ancillary result of this separation was the liberation of the town meeting from the proprietors' thrall. No longer did Dedham residents have to be admitted to the small group of "townsmen" in order to vote in town meetings. No longer could the townsmen at their own discretion refuse someone voting privileges just because he had moved out of town and then moved back, or just because he purchased his land instead of receiving it as a grant—both of which denials Dedham bylaws contemplated. After the new provincial charter of 1692, Dedham voters were simply the "Free Houlder and others of the Towne qualified as the law require it."[12] With

10. *Ibid.*, III, 53, 64, 177.
11. *Ibid.*, V, 167.
12. *Ibid.*, V, 222.

this change, Dedham's political structure represented the eligible qualified residents and not, as during most of the seventeenth century, just the land shareholders. Property still was the basis of the town franchise (just as it would remain the basis of suffrage until the mid-nineteenth century), but property was itself no longer the thing deserving representation. The ancient connection between rulership and ownership was beginning to break up when proprietors separated from towns and towns enfranchised all voters who reached a fixed level of estate.

Forthwith Dedham's nonproprietors gained new power against the proprietors. In 1703, in an act unimaginable during the preceding decades, the town meeting ordered the proprietors not to lay out a certain piece of land, as it fell within the town's "Common land." The new exercise of power by nonproprietors may also have something to do with the expansion of the proprietors' ranks that soon occurred (as indeed it did in many New England towns at the dawn of the eighteenth century). For at least five decades the number of Dedham commoners had hovered around 70; then in 1707 Dedham suddenly had 102 proprietors, an increase of almost 50 percent.[13]

Looking back on Dedham's seventeenth-century life, one does not find an obvious profit-mindedness ruling the residents' passions. But neither was Dedham a sleepy backwater, oblivious of the world of commerce. Early on, the town gave encouragement to individuals who built mills, giving them land and other assistance, so much encouragement that during the seventeenth century Dedham had altogether eleven mills, producing far more goods than Dedham could consume, so that Dedham produced for larger markets, most likely Boston's. One of the earliest acts of the town was to grant mineral rights to whoever should discover a mine, reserving for the town one-tenth of the mine's profits. In addition to mineral rights, the town agreed to furnish "such necessary helps and accomodacions as may be necessary in any such worke that may be helpfull for private and publike good." With their land and ability to grant solitary franchises, the Dedham land shareholders fostered enterprise within the town.[14]

They also engaged in considerable enterprise themselves. The Dedham commoners acting through the town meeting both acquired and divided a great deal of land during the seventeenth century, and although these transactions were made in the name of the "town of Dedham," in fact

13. *Ibid.*, V, 308, VI, 7–8.
14. *Ibid.*, III, 9–10.

ownership was restricted to members of the land corporation. Medfield, Natick, Wrentham, and Deerfield were all launched by the Dedham share-holders. In 1660 the town meeting voted to buy Wollomonopoag (later Wrentham) from the Indians, "that the place might be planted wth meet Inhabitants." Dedham gave six hundred acres to a group of screened settlers as encouragement for their settlement, reserving the rest of Wrentham's lands for itself. Sixty-nine Dedham commoners drew lots in Wrentham in 1663; in that same year ninety-six Dedham residents were rated in the country rate. Seventy commoners drew lots "near Medfield" in 1665; the next year, ninety-two people were rated in the country rate. Sixty-six Dedham commoners owned Deerfield in 1667; the next year ninety-four people were rated in the country rate.[15]

The Dedham shareholders acted as a kind of real estate development company. They taxed only themselves, not all taxpayers, for the costs of purchasing, surveying, and laying out these new plantations. Dedham made contracts with Indians and other towns for the purchase of new lands. In 1651 the town ordered a committee "in the behalfe of the Towne to conclude a firme Contract with whomesoever of Roxbery shall be enabled with the like power" for the purchase of Roxbury land. The town even sold lands to settlers on remote lands. In 1652 Dedham sold to the town of Medfield part of Medfield's own meadow for £100. Ten years later Dedham agreed to cede certain Wrentham lands if the Wrentham settlers paid to Dedham £160 over four years. Collectively the Dedham shareholders made money from ownership of distant lands, and also individually. Nearly all the Dedham owners of Deerfield common rights sold their rights within the first ten years. When they did not sell, Dedham leaders, such as Eleazer Lusher and Joshua Fisher, accumulated large, absentee landholdings (see Appendix 1).[16]

It is more than likely that landless people received house lots in Natick, Medfield, Wrentham, and Deerfield, but only as the tenants, purchasers, and grantees of Dedham's commoners. Unsurprisingly, friction occurred between these dependent settlers and their absentee Dedham landlords. "So many that heve Rights here," wrote the Wrentham settlers, "seme onely to be willing wee shouyld here Labour under the strayghts of a new plantation so as to bring there Land to a greate price, whyich no other can regulate." Deerfield's residents held a similar point of view. Nonresidents

15. *Ibid.*, IV, 28–29, 34, 63–64, 68–69, 111, 119–120, 136–137, 158–159.
16. *Ibid.*, III, 133, 199, IV, 43.

monopolized the "best of the Land; the best for soile; the best for situation, as Lying" in the town's center, they wrote. "As long as the maine of the plantation Lies in mens hands that Cant improve it themselves," the settlers continued, nor "are ever Like to putt such tenents on to it as shall be Likly to advance the good of the place," Deerfield's residents would be "much discouraged."[17]

The explanation for the system's giving rise to such grievances is no mystery. Lands had to be purchased, surveyed, and laid out; a system had to be created for owning and dividing the land; and applicants had to be screened. Some authority had to negotiate with the Indians, and, after the new town was launched, some authority had to govern the new plantation until settlers were sufficient to govern themselves (whereupon, as happened in 1651 in Medfield's case, Dedham formally handed over Medfield's government to the settlers there). All these tasks were performed by the already existing, functioning organization of Dedham proprietors, which, operating through the Dedham town meeting, performed both public and private roles. On the one hand, the Dedham town meeting was advancing the cause of settlement and creating plantations of like-minded settlers; on the other, the Dedham shareholders were operating as a real estate development company, acquiring, developing, and selling land for the financial gain of its shareholders. The landless got their land, but that was only one result (never, incidentally, mentioned as a goal in Dedham town records) of a complex public sponsorship of private enterprise, in which a land corporation undertook the organizational and financial responsibilities for starting new towns in return for substantial land ownership, apportioned among its shareholders according to their shares.

One is struck, then, by the variety of motives and purposes of Dedham's seventeenth-century residents. There is no greater record of idealism and bravery than that of Dedham's Puritans starting a new life in the New England wilderness, opening their hearts to one another and facing up to both their frailties and their enormous responsibilities. Dedham's founders were visionaries. At the same time, perhaps driven by their vision, they were extraordinarily industrious, creative, and acquisitive. The pious and the commercial existed alongside each other in Dedham, and the most

17. Wrentham Petition, Oct. 15, 1673, Misc. Bound, MHS; Deerfield Petition, May 8, 1678, LXIX, 200–201, Mass. Archives.

striking thing is the absence of conflict between them, the harmonious coexistence of institutions with radically different purposes and outcomes. New Englanders were no less capable than we of complexity: of being devout, sincere, idealistic, and fraternal; of being exclusive, acquisitive, and unjust at the same time. They did not become commercially minded by gradual steps. With time, the economic scale grew, technology changed, markets expanded, and wealth increased, but the tension in New England culture was not chronological; it was intellectual. The New England mind was divided from the outset of colonization.

Dedham cannot stand for all towns: there was no typical New England town. For one thing, nonresident entrepreneurs played a smaller role in launching Dedham than in most seventeenth-century towns, including Dedham's own satellites. But across towns a common structure did exist, within whose bounds deviations were large but nevertheless contained in a single pattern. On the extreme perimeters were Springfield, dominated by a single family, and Dedham, where many families shared the land and franchise; but one need not choose one of these two towns as the model New England town. For their similarities were greater than their differences. Both Springfield and Dedham (and nearly every other town) restricted land rights to shareholders and excluded some residents and taxpayers from shareholder status. Some towns were founded with little help from entrepreneurs, some with much; but questions of numbers aside, the organizational and financial problems of starting a town were so huge and at the same time so conspicuously remediable by resort to business organizations (examples of which abounded in the very joint-stock companies bringing the English to America) that every town reflected the character of a business in either the structure of its institutions or the apportionment of rights.

Nor is it necessary to take sides in the old dispute over whether towns were communal. Everyone cherished community. The record of self-sacrifice, subordination of personal to communal interests, and intrusiveness in the economic and personal lives of townsmen is prodigious. But one habit of community is exclusiveness, and it was practiced to circumscribe at least three different groups in a given town—the shareholders, the church, and the residents—each group guarding the gate against unwelcome intruders, controlling membership, and deriving internal strength from its sense of uniqueness, of being united against the outside world. As it happened, the several communities in each town, while overlapping, were not coterminous. Often the people being excluded from this or that membership were fellow residents and neighbors. People spent a good deal of time saying no to each other in New England towns. While the record of communal behavior is prodigious, so also is the record of rejections. This persistent negativism should be taken not merely as a sign of divisions in towns (which surely it was) but as a sign also of the zeal with which people protected their organizations, as an ironic token of their own devotion to the communal ideal.

A town was not one big happy family, but several families, some happier than others. Indeed, what most catches one's eye about the Puritan town builders is that they harnessed people's appetite for gain to achieve a preeminent social goal, the building of strong communities, which were not, however, shared in, owned by, or of equal benefit to all.

Appendixes, Part I

APPENDIX 1. *Real Estate of Town Promoters*

	Acres Owned	No. of Parcels	No. of Towns[a]	Proportion of Estate
Benedict Arnold[b]	5,000	13	4	—
Simon Bradstreet[b]	1,556	18	5	—
Thomas Brattle[b]	444	4	2	—
William Brenton	11,000	12	12	88%
Francis Brinley[b]	270	4	4	—
John Chandler	472	10	2	70
John Clarke[b]	—	6–7	4	—
John Coggeshall[b]	—	5–6	3	—
Richard Collacott[b]	950	6	4	—
Richard Davis	—	—	1	60
Daniel Denison	—	6	4	50
Joseph Dudley[b]	7,150	8	7	—
John Endicott	1,000	8	7	70
Joshua Fisher	600	16	3–4	51
Andrew Gardiner	350	7	3	86
Daniel Gookin	406	5	5	77
William Harris[b]	1,100	—	2	—
Daniel Henchman	—	6	2	80
Edward Hutchinson	600	6	6	64
Joshua Lamb	74	—	—	87
John Leverett[b]	17,000	—	—	—
Eleazer Lusher	—	15	3–4	67
Stephen Paine	—	—	2	64
Joseph Parker	775	14	4	100[c]
Joseph Parsons	—	9	4	77
William Phillips[b]	11,040	6	5	—
John Prescott	442	9	—	66
Samuel Ruggles	—	12	5	79
Samuel Ruggles, Jr.	—	9	5	88
Peleg Sanford[b]	2,949	17	8	—
Philip Sherman[b]	—	4	3	—
Richard Smith[b]	—	5–6	1–2	—
Benjamin Tucker	—	7	4	73
William Tyng	801	8	1	53
Stukeley Westcote[b]	—	6	5	—
Samuel Wilbore[b]	—	4	3	—
Simon Willard	1,501	15	5–6	—
Samuel Wilson[b]	1,480	5	3	—

ªRegions as well as towns are included, since some lands fell in areas not bounded by township borders.

ᵇWills are the source. (For all others, the source is inventories, except for Thomas Brattle, where a court division is the source.)

ᶜThe probate court reported finding no personal property in Parker's estate; all was in real property.

Comment. Town promoters were selected here in the same manner they were selected for this study—by culling the names that appear repeatedly in the multiple records of town-founding. Roughly 100 such people are discussed in this study, though, no doubt, there were more than that operating in New England during the seventeenth century (perhaps as many as 200). Sufficient information was gathered to justify placing 38 of those individuals here. Probate records are incomplete. Some repositories have been lost in their entirety. Newport, which had perhaps the largest concentration, per capita, of real estate speculators in the seventeenth century, lost its probate records when the British evacuated in 1779. Many individual records have been lost or are inadequate. For example, Humphrey Atherton of Dorchester, one of the great land entrepreneurs of the century, left a valuable estate in Narragansett (£461 in lands and stock) when he died in 1661, but we do not have an inventory of his whole estate; so Atherton has been omitted here (Humphrey Atherton Inventory of Estate at Narragansett, Nov. 7, 1661, IV, 192–193, SCPR). William Arnold amassed great quantities of land in and around Providence, but probate records for Arnold were not found (though his son, Benedict, is included here) (Elisha Stephen Arnold, comp., *The Arnold Memorial: William Arnold of Providence and Pawtuxet, 1587–1675, and a Genealogy of His Descendants* [Rutland, Vt., 1935], 47). Incomplete records have kept Bartholomew Gedney, John Hull, John Saffin, Simon Lynde, William Hudson, John Tinker, John Paine, and other important individuals off the list.

Where they do remain, probate records buttress the assertion that town promoters tended to accumulate more land than the average colonist, and in greater numbers of parcels, more spread out, amounting to a larger proportion of their wealth. But for several reasons probate records are a tricky source, not so reliable for this study as the records of towns, land companies, and general courts. Inventories often failed to appraise distant lands, and thus real property as a proportion of estate value was higher in actuality than given here. Inventories also often failed to count the acres of distant lands, so the total acreage and number of parcels owned were also higher than shown in probate records. These omissions occurred more often with town promoters' lands than ordinary settlers' lands, because the lands of the former were often spread out, sometimes far away, sometimes in other colonies, and therefore harder to discover, let alone enumerate and appraise. For example, Thomas Brattle's inventory mentions his lands in Narragansett, Quebaug, and the Kennebec but does not appraise them or give the acreage. John Endicott's appraisers state that they omitted from the appraisal the 10-acre lots Endicott bought from others, 250 acres he had in Topsfield, two other farms he purchased, and an island. Daniel Denison's inventory mentions but does not give a value or size for his Narragansett lands. Edward Hutchinson's inventory mentions but does not appraise his farm in Narragansett, a farm in Newport, and a grant from the General Court. Hardly any inventory of a town promoter counted or appraised all his lands. So one should use the data given here only for comparison with other men's probate records and not as definitive information about the extent of these individuals' real estate holdings at death, which were more substantial than given here.

Moreover, sometimes the key to profits was in selling land. In those cases, probate records do not give an accurate picture of a speculator's interest in lands, for the simple reason that he had sold them (or some of them) by the time of death. William Phillips, while listing his real estate in his will, stated that this list did not count the lands he had already sold. Daniel Gookin's estate inventory failed to mention his lands in Sherburn; either he sold them before dying or the appraisers simply missed them. William Arnold sold off many of his extensive holdings around Providence in the twelve years before he died (see Phillips and Gookin below, and Arnold, comp., *Arnold Memorial*, 47). So for this reason as well probate records must be used with caution.

Sources. Thomas Brattle Estate Division, Mar. 13, 1683/4, n.s., II, 393–395; William Tyng Inventory, May 25, 1653, II, 138–147; Eleazer Lusher Inventory, Dec. 5, 1672, I, 107; Richard Davis Inventory, Mar. 6, 1662/3, IV, 129–130; Edward Hutchinson Inventory, Aug. 24, 1675, V, 287–289; Edward Hutchinson Will, Aug. 19, 1675, VI, 95; John Endicott Inventory, Apr. 27, 1665, V, 149–150; John Leverett Will, Mar. 15, 1678/9, VI, 259–261; William Phillips Will, Feb. 1682, VI, 526; Daniel Gookin Inventory, Mar. 31, 1687, IX, 341–343; Daniel Henchman Inventory, Apr. 29, 1686, IX, 279; Joshua Fisher Inventory, Aug. 20, 1672, VII, 239–243; Simon Bradstreet Will, Dec. 23, 1689, XI, 276–282; Richard Collacott Will, Apr. 23, 1686, XI, 17–18, SCPR. Simon Willard Inventory, 1676, box 1878, docket 24955, MCPR. Peleg Sanford Will, Feb. 28, 1700/1 (summarized), *New England Historical and Genealogical Register,* CIII (1949), 274. Samuel Wilson Will, Apr. 29, 1670; Richard Smith Will, 1666 (summarized), in P. F. Pierce, "Descendants of Richard Smith," RIHS. "Philip Sherman Will," July 31, 1681, in Roy V. Sherman, *Some of the Descendants of Philip Sherman, The First Secretary of Rhode Island* (Akron, Ohio, 1968), 26–28; William Brenton Will, Feb. 9, 1673, and Inventory, 1674 (summarized), in John O. Austin, *Genealogical Dictionary of Rhode Island . . .* (Albany, N.Y., 1887; rpt., 1969), 254; Samuel Wilbore Will, Apr. 30, 1656, transcribed in *Ye Wildbore,* I, no. 2 (February 1929), 1, 4 (family newsletter, copy in RIHS); John Coggeshall Will, June 22, 1708, in Charles Pierce Coggeshall and Thellwell Russell Coggeshall, comps., *The Coggeshalls in America . . .* (Boston, 1930), 355–362; John Clarke Will, Apr. 20, 1676, in *Rhode Island Historical Magazine,* VII (1886–1887), 128–133; Benedict Arnold Will, Dec. 24, 1677, in Elisha Stephen Arnold, comp., *The Arnold Memorial: William Arnold of Providence and Pawtuxet, 1587–1675, and a Genealogy of His Descendants* (Rutland, Vt., 1935), 54–56; William Harris Will, Dec. 4, 1678, in Providence,

R.I., Record Commissioners, *Early Records of the Town of Providence,* 21 vols. (Providence, R.I., 1892–1915), VI, 48–56; Stukeley Westcote Will, Jan. 12, 1676/7, in J. Russell Bullock, *Incidents in the Life and Times of Stukeley Westcote, with Some of His Descendants* (n.p., 1886 [privately printed, copy in RIHS]), 23–24. Stephen Paine Inventory, Mar. 18, 1709/10, BCPR. Joseph Parsons Inventory, 1683 (summarized), in Henry M. Burt, *Cornet Joseph Parsons: One of the Founders of Springfield and Northampton, Massachusetts . . .* (Garden City, N.Y., 1898), 66–68. Daniel Denison Inventory, 1690, photostats, MHS. Samuel Ruggles Inventory, Nov. 11, 1692, XIII, 103–104; Samuel Ruggles Inventory, April 1716, XIX, 149–150; John Chandler Inventory, Apr. 15, 1703, XV, 152–153; Andrew Gardiner Inventory, Apr. 16, 1694, XIII, 584–585; Joshua Lamb Inventory, Mar. 13, 1700, XIV, 316–317; Joseph Dudley Will, Oct. 27, 1719, XXI, 708–710; Francis Brinley Will, Oct. 19, 1719, XXI, 526–529; Benjamin Tucker Inventory, Aug. 9, 1714, XVIII, 351, and Appraisal, Jan. 31, 1714/5, n.s., VIII, 52, SCPR. Joseph Parker Inventory, Dec. 25, 1697, box 1801, docket 16680; John Prescott Inventory, 1682, box 1814, docket 18076, MCPR.

APPENDIX 2. *Timing of Church Formations*

A. Towns with Churches from the Beginning of Settlement (12)

Massachusetts

Andover	Hadley	Roxbury
Boston	Rowley	

Connecticut

Guilford	Milford	Windsor
Hartford	New Haven	

Plymouth Colony
Plymouth

New Hampshire
Exeter

B. Towns without Churches at the Outset of Launching (41)

Massachusetts

Billerica. Grants were made in 1637, 1648, 1649, and 1652 by the General Court and by Cambridge, settlement began in 1653, a land corporation was formed in 1658, and the first mention of a minister occurred in 1659. Henry A. Hazen, *History of Billerica, Massachusetts* . . . (Boston, 1883), 2–3, 9, 11–14, 48, 54–55.

Braintree. Settlement occurred by 1635, and the church was formed after 1639. Charles Francis Adams, *History of Braintree, Massachusetts* . . . (Cambridge, Mass., 1891), 3–7; John Winthrop, *The History of New England from 1630 to 1649,* ed. James Savage, 2 vols. (Boston, 1825–1826; rpt., 1972), I, 313.

Dedham. Settlement occurred in 1636, and the church was formed in 1638. Dedham, Mass., *The Early Records of the Town* . . . , 6 vols. (Dedham, Mass., 1886–1936), II, 1–8, III, 2–3.

Deerfield. The land corporation was formed in 1666, settlement began in 1669, land was divided in 1670, and the first church was organized in 1686. George Sheldon, *A History of Deerfield* . . . , 2 vols. (Deerfield, Mass., 1895–1896), I, 5, 7, 12–13, 17; Josiah Gilbert Holland, *History of Western Massachusetts,* 2 vols. (Springfield, Mass., 1855), II, 355.

Dunstable. The land corporation was formed in 1673, and the first church of six members was organized in 1685. Elias Nason, *A History of the Town of Dunstable, Massachusetts* . . . (Boston, 1877), 28.

Groton. The township grant was made in 1655, and Simon Willard's son accepted the offer of minister in 1663. Samuel A. Green, ed., *The Town Records of Groton, Massachusetts, 1662–1678* (Groton, 1879 [rpt. in Green, ed., *Pamphlets on History of Groton* (n.p., n.d.)]), 7.

Haverhill. The first land division was in 1643, the church was gathered in 1644, and the minister ordained in 1645. George Wingate Chase, *The History of Haverhill, Massachusetts, from Its First Settlement, in 1640, to the Year 1860* (Haverhill, Mass., 1861), 58.

Ipswich. Settlement began in 1633, during which year the town "had yet no minister." Thomas Franklin Waters, *Ipswich in the Massachusetts Bay Colony* . . . , 2 vols. (Ipswich, Mass., 1905–1917), I, 9–10, 11.

Lancaster. The church was gathered fifteen years after settlement commenced. Samuel Eliot Morison, "The Plantation of Nashaway—an Industrial Experiment," Colonial Society of Massachusetts, *Transactions*, XXVII (1927–1930), 205.

Marblehead. Settlers were present in 1630, it became a town in 1648 (whose residents attended church in Salem), and it formed its own church in 1684. Richard P. Gildrie, *Salem, Massachusetts, 1626–1683: A Covenant Community* (Charlottesville, Va., 1975), 68.

Marlborough. The land corporation was formed in 1656, settlement began in 1660, and the church was organized in 1660 or later. Franklin P. Rice, ed., "Colonial Records of Marlborough, Mass.," *New England Historical and Genealogical Register*, LXII (1908), 220–225, 226–228.

Medfield. The grant was made in 1649, lots were laid out in 1650, a town meeting was held in January 1650/1, and the first minister arrived the following December. William S. Tilden, *History of the Town of Medfield, Massachusetts, 1650–1866* . . . (Boston, 1887), 34–48.

Medford. Settlement began by September 1630, and the first minister was ordained in 1712. John Winthrop, *The History of New England from 1630 to 1649*, ed. James Savage, 2 vols. (Boston, 1825–1826; rpt., 1972), II, 161–162n.

Milton. First grants were made in the 1630s, town privileges were granted in 1662, and the church was established in 1678. Edward Pierce Hamilton, *A History of Milton* (Milton, Mass., 1857), 27.

Northfield. Settlement began in 1673, and the first church was organized in 1718. Josiah Gilbert Holland, *History of Western Massachusetts*, 2 vols. (Springfield, Mass., 1855), II, 407.

Northampton. Purchasers received the grant in 1653, settlement began in 1654, and the first minister arrived in 1661. Josiah Gilbert Holland, *History of Western Massachusetts*, 2 vols. (Springfield, Mass., 1855), II, 245.

Reading. Settlement began in 1644, and the church was formed in 1645. Wilson Waters, *History of Chelmsford, Massachusetts* . . . (Lowell, Mass., 1917), 1; John Winthrop, *The History of New England from 1630 to 1649,* ed. James Savage, 2 vols. (Boston, 1825–1826; rpt., 1972), II, 252–253.

Springfield. Settlement began in 1636, and the first minister arrived two years later. Henry M. Burt, *The First Century of the History of Springfield: The Official Records from 1636 to 1736,* 2 vols. (Springfield, Mass., 1898–1899), I, 23.

Wenham. Salem men were given the right to start a village in 1638, a meeting-house was built in 1641, the town recognized by the court in 1643, and a church formed in 1644. Richard P. Gildrie, *Salem, Massachusetts, 1626–1683: A Covenant Community* (Charlottesville, Va., 1975), 69.

Westfield. Traders were present in the 1630s, the township was granted in 1662, the first preacher arrived in 1667, and the first church was organized in 1679. Josiah Gilbert Holland, *History of Western Massachusetts,* 2 vols. (Springfield, Mass., 1855), II, 141.

Weymouth. Settlement occurred in the 1620s, the town was named in 1635, and the church was formed in 1638. John Winthrop, *The History of New England from 1630 to 1649,* ed. James Savage, 2 vols. (Boston, 1825–1826; rpt., 1972), I, 287.

Woburn. The grant was made and the clerk was chosen in 1640, inhabitants were admitted and building began in 1641, the church was gathered in August 1642, and the first minister ordained in November 1642. Samuel Sewall, *The History of Woburn, Middlesex County, Mass.* . . . (Boston, 1868), 10–22.

Woodstock. The grant was made in 1683, the business agreement was made in 1685, settlement began in 1686, and a committee was appointed to supervise the building of the first minister's house in 1690. General Court Grant to Roxbury, Oct. 10, 1683, CXII, 342–343, Mass. Archives; Holmes Ammidown, *Historical Collections* . . . , 2d ed., 2 vols. (New York, 1877), I, 259–281. (This town was granted by Massachusetts and later fell under Connecticut jurisdiction.)

Worcester. The grant was requested in 1665, town orders were framed in 1669, the proprietors met in Cambridge through the 1670s and 1680s, and a church was probably not gathered until the permanent settlement of the 1720s. Franklin P. Rice, ed., *Records of the Proprietors of Worcester, Massachusetts* (Worcester Society of Antiquity, *Collections,* III [Worcester, Mass., 1881]), 11–19, 21–31, 37, 42; William Lincoln, *History of Worcester* . . . (Worcester, Mass., 1862), 9–20, 36, 42.

Wrentham. The first land division was in 1663, town privileges were granted in 1673, the first preacher was present circa 1673, and the first church was gathered in 1692. Jordan D. Fiore, *Wrentham, 1673–1973: A History* (Wrentham, Mass., 1973), 28.

Connecticut

Durham. The grant was made in 1699, and the first church of fourteen males was formed in 1711. "Extracts of Letters to Rev. Thomas Prince," Connecticut Historical Society, *Collections,* III (1895), 309.

Haddam. Purchasers bought the township in 1662, and the church was gathered in 1700. "Extracts of Letters to Rev. Thomas Prince," Connecticut Historical Society, *Collections,* III (1895), 280.

Lyme. The grant was made to Saybrook in 1663, preaching began in 1666, a petition to form an ecclesiastical society was drawn up in 1676, and a society was formed in 1693. Christopher Collier, "Saybrook and Lyme: Secular Settlements in a Puritan Commonwealth," in George J. Willauer, Jr., ed., *A Lyme Miscellany, 1776–1976* (Middletown, Conn., 1977), 12–14.

Middletown. The grant was made in 1651, settlers arrived in the 1650s, and the first church of ten members was gathered in 1668. "Extracts of Letters to Rev. Thomas Prince," Connecticut Historical Society, *Collections,* III (1895), 278–279.

New London. The grant was made in 1644, the site was explored in 1645, the town was established in 1646, house lots were laid out in 1647, and the church was begun in 1650. William J. Haller, *The Puritan Frontier: Town-Planting in New England Colonial Development, 1630–1660* (New York, 1951), 97–99.

Norwalk. Land was purchased in 1640, a land corporation was formed in 1650, settlement began in 1651, and a preacher arrived in 1652. Edwin Hall, ed., *The Ancient Historical Records of Norwalk, Connecticut* (New York, 1865), 13, 14, 32–33.

Saybrook. A fort was erected in 1635, a chaplain was present the following year, and a church was formed in 1646. Christopher Collier, "Saybrook and Lyme: Secular Settlements in a Puritan Commonwealth," in George J. Willauer, Jr., ed., *A Lyme Miscellany, 1776–1976* (Middletown, Conn., 1977), 13.

Simsbury. The manufacture of pitch and tar began in 1643, grants were made in 1653, settlement began in 1664, town privileges were granted in 1670, and a church was gathered in 1670 or later. Noah A. Phelps, *History of Simsbury, Granby, and Canton, from 1642 to 1845* (Hartford, Conn., 1845), 11, 12, 16.

Stonington. Land was divided in 1668, and the first church was formed in 1674. Richard Anson Wheeler, *History of the Town of Stonington . . .* (New London, Conn., 1900), 18–19.

Waterbury. The grant was made in 1673, the land corporation was formed in 1674, settlement began in 1677, and a church was formed sometime thereafter. Henry Bronson, *The History of Waterbury, Connecticut . . .* (Waterbury, Conn., 1858), 4–5, 8–9, 16.

Rhode Island

Little Compton. Nonresident purchasers bought the tract in 1659, settlement began sometime before 1675, the town was incorporated (initially by the Plymouth General Court) in 1682, and settlers were subsequently fined for failing to maintain a minister. Samuel Greene Arnold, *History of the State of Rhode Island and Providence Plantations,* 2 vols. (New York, 1859–1860), II, 165–166.

Providence. Settlement began in 1636, the first religious society was created in 1638, and church attendance was so low that a meetinghouse was not required until 1700. Henry C. Dorr, "The Proprietors of Providence, and Their Controversies with the Freeholders," Rhode Island Historical Society, *Publications,* n.s., III (1895–1896), 152–153.

Tiverton. Eight purchasers bought the land from Plymouth Colony, the town was incorporated in 1694, and the first church was organized in 1746. Samuel Greene Arnold, *History of the State of Rhode Island and Providence Plantations,* 2 vols. (New York, 1859–1860), II, 164–165.

Westerly. Settlement began in 1661, and the first church was formed in 1708. Frederic Denison, *Westerly (Rhode Island), and Its Witnesses . . . 1626–1876 . . .* (Providence, R.I., 1878), 60.

Plymouth Colony

Attleborough. The purchasers of the Rehoboth North Purchase formed a distinct proprietorship in the 1660s, and the town had its first minister in 1711. John Daggett, *Sketch of the History of Attleborough . . .* (Dedham, Mass., 1834), 52.

Scituate. Settlement occurred by 1633, land was sold to English businessmen in 1639, and the first minister arrived in 1641. John Fairfield Sly, *Town Government in Massachusetts (1620–1930)* (Cambridge, Mass., 1930), 24; William Bradford, *Bradford's History "Of Plimoth Plantation"* (Boston, 1898), 438–439, 458.

Note. This sample is different from the one in following appendixes because for many of the towns appearing here there was no reliable information about the structure of town rights, and for some of the towns appearing in the following appendixes there was no reliable information about the date of church formation. The list here by no means exhausts the possibilities for comparing the chronology of land corporations and churches. But the above towns represent more than one-third of all towns established in the seventeenth century. They include both inland and coastal towns, located in four different colonies, founded in all decades from the 1630s to the 1690s.

Appendixes, Part II

A Note on Sources and the Sample

Sources. The analysis of the data that justifies placing towns on these tables (as well as the citations therefore) is too voluminous to print here (see Commentary for the Tables, in John Frederick Martin, "Entrepreneurship and the Founding of New England Towns: The Seventeenth Century" [Ph.D. diss., Harvard University, 1985], Appendix, 30–287), though much of it appears in the present text and notes. For some towns, principal sources are printed proprietors' records or town meeting records; for others, petitions and other documents found in one of several archives of colonial governments; and for still others, town histories. These sources have occasionally been supplemented by probate records. Where a town's original records have been lost, it has not been possible to include that town in this study, unless random archival documents tell something about its land system. I have searched for such documents in the Massachusetts Archives, the Connecticut State Library, the Massachusetts Historical Society, the American Antiquarian Society, the Library of Congress, and the Boston Public Library. Where towns' original records are available only in town or county offices, such towns have been excluded from this study, unless duplicates of these records found their way to one or another of the central archives or unless there exist reliable town histories. Some secondary works have been used to determine the number of taxpayers, residents, and land-holders in certain towns when it is apparent that the historian himself consulted the original records. In some cases, collateral evidence in colonial archives has given support to these numbers. All other numbers are derived from town records, proprietors' records, and petitions filed with the general courts.

Sample. The following appendixes categorize towns according to various criteria—towns that excluded residents from land shares within the first ten years, towns that restricted the town meeting to shareholders, towns with nonresident landowners, and so forth. Some towns fall in as many as six or eight appendixes; others fall in just three or four. Included in the sample are only those towns about which enough could be learned to place the town in two or more of the following appendixes (not counting the first). Sixty-three towns met this condition. They are the sample. (Some towns, not included for want of adequate information, are nevertheless discussed in the text and thus bring the total number of towns whose histories contribute to the conclusions of this work to about eighty.) In selecting this sample, therefore, the first principle was arbitrary: towns were included when enough information was available to justify assertions about the origin and early history of their land systems.

The other principles were geographical and chronological. Roughly half the towns founded in New England during the seventeenth century are included in this sample. (By 1700, there were between 120 and 140 towns in New England; this sample concerns 63 of them.) They include the major towns of each colony (Hartford, New Haven, Plymouth, Boston, Portsmouth, Providence, and Falmouth) as well as rural settlements that remained bare hamlets throughout the century, such as Worcester and Oxford in Massachusetts, Scarborough in Maine, Lebanon and Wallingford in Connecticut, and Attleborough in Plymouth. Certain regional biases deserve mentioning. Of the 63 towns, 39 are Massachusetts towns, 10 Connecticut, 6 Plymouth, 4 Rhode Island, 2 Maine, and 2 New Hampshire. While Massachusetts towns make up a disproportionate part of this sample, they made up a disproportionate part of New England towns in the seventeenth century. By one count, there were in 1665 4 towns in Rhode Island, 12 in Plymouth, 22 in Connecticut, and 52 in Massachusetts (John Gorham Palfrey, *History of New England during the Stuart Dynasty,* 3 vols. [Boston, 1865; rpt., 1966], III, 36). These proportions did not change substantially through the rest of the century. Maine and New Hampshire were the least-settled jurisdictions of New England. They contained few towns, and the records of what towns there were are mostly lost. It is difficult to reconstruct the development of town land systems in those two colonies. This is a pity, for we know from other evidence, mainly deeds, that Maine and New Hampshire were the scene of considerable land speculation during both the seventeenth and eighteenth centuries.

The sample includes towns founded during every decade of the seventeenth century, though it emphasizes the early decades. (It also includes towns founded by each of the four principal methods employed in town-founding; see Appendix 3.) Of sixty-three towns, twenty-nine, or nearly half, were founded before 1640. (Of the towns covered, 70 percent were founded before 1660, and 86 percent before 1670.) So many towns from the first few decades were chosen for two reasons. First, the conventional interpretation holds that, in the early years of colonization, business activity played a negligible role in the founding of New England's settlements and that, when land speculation came upon the scene late in the seventeenth century, it disrupted or transformed the established method of starting towns. The key test of the conventional interpretation is, therefore, not to find business activity in the later towns, but to find it in early towns. Hence, the preponderance of early towns in this sample. Second, town-planting dropped off sharply after 1675 as a result of three decades of warfare between the colonists and the French and Indians.

APPENDIX 3. *The Town Sample (63 Towns)*

A. *Towns Launched by English Ventures* (3 Towns)

Salem, Massachusetts
Plymouth, Plymouth Colony
Dover, New Hampshire

B. *Towns Launched by Individuals* (47 Towns)

1630s	1640s	1650s	1660s
Massachusetts			
Boston	Andover	Chelmsford	Marlborough
Cambridge	Haverhill	Groton	Mendon
Charlestown	Lancaster	Hadley	
Concord		Northampton	
Dedham			
Dorchester			
Ipswich			
Medford			
Rowley			
Roxbury			
Salisbury			
Springfield			
Sudbury			
Watertown			
Connecticut			
Hartford		Norwalk	Simsbury
New Haven		Norwich	
Wethersfield			
Windsor			
Plymouth			
Marshfield			Swansea
Scituate			
Rhode Island			
Portsmouth	Warwick		Westerly
Providence			
Maine			
Falmouth[a]			
Scarborough			
New Hampshire			
Exeter			

1670s	1680s	1690s

Massachusetts
Dunstable   Oxford
Northfield
Worcester
Connecticut
Waterbury   Lebanon
Plymouth
             Bristol[b]

C. *Towns Launched by Other Towns* (8 Towns)

Massachusetts
  Billerica (by Cambridge, 1650s)
  Braintree (by Boston, 1630s)
  Deerfield (by Dedham, 1660s)
  Woburn (by Charlestown, 1640s)
  Woodstock (by Roxbury, 1680s)[c]
  Wrentham (by Dedham, 1660s)

Connecticut
  Wallingford (by New Haven, 1670s)

Plymouth
  Attleborough (by Rehoboth, 1660s)

D. *Towns Begun as Offshoots of Established Towns* (5 Towns)

Massachusetts
  Amesbury (of Salisbury, 1650s)
  Manchester (of Salem, 1640s)
  Medfield (of Dedham, 1650s)
  Milton (of Dorchester, 1660s)
  Westfield (of Springfield, 1660s)

[a]Falmouth later became Portland, Maine.
[b]Bristol began under Plymouth jurisdiction and later fell to Rhode Island.
[c]Woodstock began under Massachusetts jurisdiction and later fell to Connecticut.

APPENDIX 4. *Covenants Creating Land Corporations*

These towns (twenty-seven) began with covenants or articles of association or other evidence pointing to the creation of corporations for holding town land and financing town affairs.

Massachusetts

Andover	Dunstable	Sudbury
Amesbury	Hadley	Woburn
Billerica	Lancaster	Woodstock
Cambridge	Medfield	Worcester
Dedham	Northfield	Wrentham
Deerfield	Springfield	

Connecticut

New Haven	Norwalk	Waterbury

Plymouth

Attleborough	Plymouth	Swansea
Bristol		

Rhode Island

Portsmouth	Warwick	Westerly

APPENDIX 5. *Reduction of Admissions to Land Corporations*

A. These towns (twenty-two) terminated or drastically reduced admissions to the land corporation within the first ten years of settlement.

Massachusetts

Amesbury	Manchester	Oxford
Dorchester	Marlborough	Sudbury
Dunstable	Milton	Watertown
Groton	Northfield	Woodstock
Lancaster		

Connecticut

Hartford	Lebanon

Plymouth

Plymouth	Swansea

Rhode Island

Portsmouth	Providence	Warwick

Maine

Falmouth

New Hampshire

Exeter

B. These towns (twelve) terminated or drastically reduced corporate admissions between the tenth and thirty-first year of settlement.

Massachusetts

Andover	Dedham	Roxbury
Boston	Haverhill	Salem
Cambridge	Rowley	Woburn

Connecticut

Norwalk	Waterbury

Plymouth

Marshfield

APPENDIX 6. *Town Residents without Land Shares*

A. These towns (thirty-three) had adult male residents who did not possess shares in the town land corporation or did not share in town land divisions within the first ten years of settlement.

Massachusetts

Amesbury	Groton	Springfield
Billerica	Ipswich	Sudbury
Boston	Marlborough	Watertown
Braintree	Medford	Westfield
Dedham	Milton	Woodstock
Deerfield	Northfield	Worcester
Dunstable	Oxford	Wrentham

Connecticut

Hartford	New Haven

Plymouth

Marshfield	Scituate	Swansea

Rhode Island

Portsmouth	Warwick	Westerly
Providence		

Maine

Falmouth	Scarborough

New Hampshire

Dover

Note. Nonshareholders might receive small parcels of land as gifts, but they did not participate in repeated divisions.

B. These towns (sixteen) had nonshareholders between the tenth and thirty-first year of settlement.

Massachusetts

Andover	Lancaster	Roxbury
Cambridge	Manchester[a]	Salem
Charlestown	Mendon	Salisbury
Dorchester	Rowley	Woburn
Haverhill		

Connecticut
Norwich   Stratford[a]   Wethersfield[a]

[a]Evidence is for forty years, but extrapolating from this evidence suggests that nonshareholders lived in town before the thirty-first year.

APPENDIX 7. *Nonresident Owners of Land Shares*

These towns (forty-three) had nonresident shareholders or nonresidents who shared in town land divisions.

Massachusetts

Billerica	Manchester	Oxford
Braintree	Marlborough	Salisbury
Brookfield	Medfield	Sudbury
Charlestown	Medford	Westfield
Chelmsford	Mendon	Woburn
Deerfield	Milton	Woodstock
Dunstable	Northfield	Worcester
Groton	Northampton	Wrentham
Lancaster		

Connecticut

Hartford	Norwalk	Waterbury
Lebanon	Simsbury	Windsor
New Haven	Wallingford	

Plymouth

Attleborough	Marshfield	Swansea
Bristol	Scituate	

Rhode Island

Warwick	Westerly

Maine

Falmouth	Scarborough

New Hampshire

Dover

APPENDIX 8. *Land Division*

A. These towns (forty-one) divided land by fixed shares.

Massachusetts

Amesbury	Groton	Oxford
Andover	Hadley	Rowley
Billerica	Haverhill	Roxbury
Cambridge	Ipswich	Salem
Charlestown	Lancaster	Salisbury
Dedham	Manchester	Sudbury
Deerfield	Marlborough	Woodstock
Dorchester	Mendon	Worcester
Dunstable	Northfield	

Connecticut

Hartford	Norwalk	Wethersfield
Lebanon	Norwich	Windsor
New Haven	Waterbury	

Plymouth

Attleborough	Plymouth	Swansea
Bristol		

Rhode Island

Providence	Warwick	Westerly

B. These towns (thirteen) divided land by some method other than fixed shares.

Massachusetts

Dedham	Northampton	Watertown
Dorchester	Salem	Woburn
Groton	Springfield	Worcester
Medfield		

Connecticut

New Haven	Wallingford

New Hampshire

Exeter

Note. Some of these towns appear on 8A as well because some towns employed varying methods for dividing land.

APPENDIX 9. *Tax Assessment of Shares*

These towns (twenty-one) raised revenue by assessing shares.

Massachusetts

Billerica	Lancaster	Springfield
Dedham	Marlborough	Sudbury
Deerfield	Medfield	Woodstock
Groton	Northfield	Worcester
Haverhill	Oxford	Wrentham

Connecticut

| New Haven | Wallingford | Waterbury |

Plymouth

| Bristol | Swansea |

Rhode Island

Westerly

Note. These towns, for some period, usually the early years of settlement, raised taxes on shares; but after a while (the lapse varied from town to town) every town did tax assets other than shares. In some of the towns appearing here, the minister's rate fell upon all persons, not just shareholders, even while shares were assessed to finance other town expenditures.

A. In these towns (thirty-two) "inhabitants" voted in the town meeting.

Massachusetts

Amesbury	Groton	Medford
Boston	Haverhill	Northfield
Braintree	Ipswich	Salem
Cambridge	Lancaster	Springfield
Charlestown	Manchester	Sudbury
Dedham	Marlborough	Watertown
Dorchester	Medfield	Woburn
Dunstable		

Connecticut

Hartford	Norwalk	Wethersfield
Lebanon	Simsbury	Windsor

Plymouth

Bristol	Plymouth

Rhode Island

Warwick

New Hampshire

Exeter

B. In these towns (twenty-eight) the town meeting (or other decision-making body) was restricted to men with shares in the land corporation.

Massachusetts

Amesbury	Ipswich	Springfield
Boston	Lancaster	Sudbury
Cambridge	Manchester	Watertown
Dedham	Marlborough	Woburn
Dunstable	Medfield	Worcester
Groton	Northfield	Wrentham
Haverhill		

Connecticut

Lebanon	Norwich	Stratford
Norwalk		

Rhode Island

Portsmouth	Warwick	Westerly
Providence		

New Hampshire
  Exeter

Note. Twenty-one towns on this table also appear in 10A, listing towns where inhabitants were voters, and eleven towns on this table appear in 10C, listing towns that excluded nonproprietors from political participation. Obviously, if meetings were restricted to land shareholders, as in 10B towns, nonshareholders must have been excluded from meetings in these same towns. This deduction is probably accurate, but is still a deduction: thus 10C lists those towns where direct evidence points to the exclusion of nonproprietors from town meetings.

C. In these towns (eleven) adult male residents who were nonproprietors were excluded from voting in town meetings.

Massachusetts

Boston	Ipswich	Springfield
Cambridge	Lancaster	Sudbury
Dedham	Northfield	

Connecticut
  Norwich

Rhode Island
  Portsmouth   Providence

Note. In these eleven towns, explicit evidence (such as town orders, disparities between voting lists and tax lists, and other evidence) points to the exclusion of nonproprietors from the town franchise. It is likely that in many additional towns, especially those listed in 10B, nonproprietors were prevented from voting.

APPENDIX 11. *Town Voting by Shares*

In these towns (four) shares, not people, cast votes.

Massachusetts
  Dorchester   Woburn

Connecticut
  Simsbury   Windsor

APPENDIX 12. *Town Land Fights*

In these towns (twenty-three) shareholders and nonshareholders fought in the seventeenth century.

Massachusetts

Andover	Deerfield	Mendon
Billerica	Dorchester	Salem
Boston	Haverhill	Sudbury
Braintree	Lancaster	Woburn
Charlestown	Marlborough	Wrentham

Connecticut

Simsbury	Wallingford	Windsor
Stratford	Wethersfield	

Plymouth

Bristol

Rhode Island

Portsmouth	Providence

APPENDIX 13. *Expansion of Land Corporations*

A. In these towns (twenty) the number of people sharing town land divisions sharply increased during the provincial period.

Massachusetts

Andover	Hadley	Manchester
Billerica	Haverhill	Medfield
Charlestown	Ipswich	Northfield
Concord	Lancaster	Salem
Dorchester		

Connecticut

Hartford	Norwich	Wethersfield
New Haven	Stratford	

Maine

Falmouth

New Hampshire

Exeter

B. In these towns (five) land shares did not increase during the provincial period.

Massachusetts

Cambridge	Haverhill	Worcester
Deerfield	Lancaster	

Bibliography of Works Cited

Manuscript Collections

American Antiquarian Society, Worcester, Mass.
  Hull, John, Letterbook, 1670–1685 (microfilm)
Boston Public Library
  Prince Collection
Bristol County Probate Registry, Taunton, Mass.
  Colonial Probate Records
Connecticut Archives, Connecticut State Library, Hartford
  Towns and Lands Collection (microfilm)
Library of Congress, Washington, D.C.
  Warwick, R.I., Town Records: First Book, 1647–1677 (1911, typescript of
    original)
Massachusetts Archives, Boston
  Andros, Sir Edmund, Land Warrants, 1687–1688
  Book of Eastern Claims, 1674–1720
  Volumes II, XXXV, XLI, XLV, LVII, LXI, LXIX, CXII–CXV, CXXVI
Massachusetts Historical Society, Boston
  Misc. Bound
  Misc. Large
  MSS Bound
  Otis, James, Sr., Papers, 1642–1823
  Pettaquamscut Purchase: Sewall School Land
  Photostats
  Prescott, William H., Legal and Business Papers, 1665–1683
  Saffin, John, Note-Book, 1665–1708, transcribed MS
  Shrimpton Family Papers, 1635–1714
  Washburn Manuscripts, 1649–1795
  Winthrop Papers
Middlesex County Probate Registry, Old Courthouse, Cambridge, Mass.
  Colonial Probate Records
Rhode Island Historical Society, Providence
  Pierce, P. F., "Descendants of Richard Smith"
  Wilson, Samuel, Will, Apr. 29, 1670
Suffolk County Probate Registry, Old Courthouse, Boston
  Colonial Probate Records

Published Sources

Adams, Charles Francis. *History of Braintree, Massachusetts.* . . . Cambridge,
  Mass., 1891.

————, et al. *The Genesis of the Massachusetts Town, and the Development of Town-Meeting Government.* Cambridge, Mass., 1892.

Akagi, Roy Hidemichi. *The Town Proprietors of the New England Colonies: A Study of Their Development, Organization, Activities, and Controversies, 1620–1770.* Philadelphia, 1924.

Allen, David Grayson. *In English Ways: The Movement of Societies and the Transferal of English Local Law and Custom to Massachusetts Bay in the Seventeenth Century.* Chapel Hill, N.C., 1981.

Ammidown, Holmes. *Historical Collections.* . . . 2d ed. 2 vols. New York, 1877.

Andrews, Charles M. *The Beginnings of Connecticut, 1632–1662.* New Haven, Conn., 1934.

————. *The River Towns of Connecticut: A Study of Wethersfield, Hartford, and Windsor.* Johns Hopkins University Studies in Historical and Political Science, 7th Ser., nos. 7–9. Baltimore, 1889.

Appleby, Joyce Oldham. *Economic Thought and Ideology in Seventeenth-Century England.* Princeton, N.J., 1978.

Arnold, Elisha Stephen, comp. *The Arnold Memorial: William Arnold of Providence and Pawtuxet, 1587–1675, and a Genealogy of His Descendants.* Rutland, Vt., 1935.

Arnold, Samuel Greene. *History of the State of Rhode Island and Providence Plantations.* 2 vols. New York, 1859–1860.

Austin, John Osborne. *Genealogical Dictionary of Rhode Island.* . . . Albany, N.Y., 1887. Reprint. 1969.

Bailyn, Bernard. *The New England Merchants in the Seventeenth Century.* Cambridge, Mass., 1955.

————. *Voyagers to the West: A Passage in the Peopling of America on the Eve of the Revolution.* New York, 1986.

Baker, Darius. "The Coddington Portrait." *Bulletin of the Newport Historical Society,* no. 25 (April 1918), 1–23.

Barber, John Warner. *Connecticut Historical Collections . . . History and Antiquities of Every Town in Connecticut.* . . . New Haven, Conn., 1846.

————. *Historical Collections . . . History and Antiquities of Every Town in Massachusetts.* . . . Worcester, Mass., 1848.

Barber, Thomas. "Contributions to the History of Westerly." *Narragansett Historical Register,* II (1883–1884), 34–61.

————. "The Settlement of Westerly." *Narragansett Historical Register,* I (1882–1883), 125–214.

Barnes, Viola Florence. *The Dominion of New England: A Study in British Colonial Policy.* New Haven, Conn., 1923. Reprint. 1960.

————. "Richard Wharton, a Seventeenth-Century New England Colonial." Colonial Society of Massachusetts, *Publications, Transactions,* XXVI (1924–1926), 238–270.

Baxter, James Phinney, ed. *Documentary History of the State of Maine,* III, *The Trelawny Papers.* Portland, Maine, 1884.

————, ed. *Documentary History of the State of Maine,* IV–VI, IX–XXIV, *The Baxter Manuscripts.* Portland, Maine, 1889–1916.

Belknap, Jeremy. *The History of New-Hampshire.* Dover, N.H., 1831.

Bell, Charles H. *History of the Town of Exeter, New Hampshire.* Exeter, N.H., 1889.

Benton, Josiah Henry. *Warning Out in New England, 1656–1817.* Boston, 1911.

Bercovitch, Sacvan. "The Image of America: From Hermeneutics to Symbolism." In Michael T. Gilmore, ed., *Early American Literature: A Collection of Critical Essays,* 158–167. Englewood Cliffs, N.J., 1980.

Berman, Harold J. *Law and Revolution: The Formation of the Western Legal Tradition.* Cambridge, Mass., 1983.

Bicknell, Thomas Williams. *A History of Barrington, Rhode Island.* Providence, R.I., 1898.

————. *Sowams, with Ancient Records of Sowams and Parts Adjacent.* New Haven, Conn., 1908.

Blake, Mortimer. "Taunton North Purchase." Old Colony Historical Society, *Collections,* no. 3 (1885), 31–53.

Boston, Registry Dept. *Charlestown Land Records (Third Report of the Record Commissioners of the City of Boston).* Boston, 1878.

————. *Dorchester Town Records (Fourth Report of the Record Commissioners).* Boston, 1880.

————. *Roxbury Land Records (A Report of the Record Commissioners . . . [Sixth Report]).* 2d ed. Boston, 1884.

Bottigheimer, Karl S. *English Money and Irish Land: The "Adventurers" in the Cromwellian Settlement of Ireland.* Oxford, 1971.

Bouton, Nathaniel. *The History of Concord from Its First Grant in 1725 to the Organization of City Government in 1853. . . .* Concord, N.H., 1856.

Bozeman, Theodore Dwight. *To Live Ancient Lives: The Primitivist Dimension in Puritanism.* Chapel Hill, N.C., 1988.

Bradford, William. *Bradford's History "Of Plimoth Plantation."* Boston, 1898.

Bradstreet, Anne. "Meditations Diuine and Morall." In Joseph R. McElrath, Jr., and Allan P. Robb, eds., *The Complete Works of Anne Bradstreet.* Boston, 1981.

————. "Upon the Burning of Our House, July 10th 1666." In Robert Hutchinson, ed., *Poems of Anne Bradstreet,* 54–56. New York, 1969.

Breen, Timothy H. "Who Governs: The Town Franchise in Seventeenth-Century Massachusetts." *William and Mary Quarterly,* 3d Ser., XXVII (1970), 460–474.

Bronson, Henry. *The History of Waterbury, Connecticut. . . .* Waterbury, Conn., 1858.

Brooks, Charles. *History of the Town of Medford. . . .* Boston, 1855.

Brown, B. Katherine. "The Controversy over the Franchise in Puritan Massachusetts, 1954 to 1974." *William and Mary Quarterly,* 3d Ser., XXXIII (1976), 212–241.

———. "Puritan Democracy in Dedham, Massachusetts: Another Case Study," *William and Mary Quarterly,* 3d Ser., XXIV (1967), 378–396.

Bulkeley, Gershom. *Will and Doom; or, The Miseries of Connecticut by and under an Usurped and Arbitrary Power* (1692). Connecticut Historical Society, *Collections,* III (1895), 69–260.

Bullock, Charles J. *Essays on the Monetary History of the United States.* New York, 1900. Reprint. 1969.

Bullock, Russell. *Incidents in the Life and Times of Stukeley Westcote, with Some of His Descendants.* N.p., 1886. Copy in RIHS.

Burt, Henry M. *Cornet Joseph Parsons: One of the Founders of Springfield and Northampton, Massachusetts.* . . . Garden City, N.Y., 1898.

———. *The First Century of the History of Springfield: The Official Records from 1636 to 1736.* 2 vols. Springfield, Mass., 1898–1899.

Byfield, Nathaniel. "An Account of the Late Revolution in New-England. . . ." In W. H. Whitmore, ed., *The Andros Tracts: Being a Collection of Pamphlets and Official Papers* . . . , I, 1–10. Prince Society, V. Boston, 1868. Reprint. 1971.

Callender, John. *An Historical Discourse, on the Civil and Religious Affairs of the Colony of Rhode-Island and Providence Plantations.* . . . Boston, 1739. Republished in Rhode Island Historical Society, *Collections,* IV (Providence, R.I., 1838).

Cambridge, Mass. *The Records of the Town of Cambridge (Formerly Newtowne) Massachusetts, 1630–1703.* . . . Cambridge, Mass., 1901.

———. *The Register Book of the Lands and Houses in the "New Towne" and the Town of Cambridge, with the Records of the Proprietors of the Common Lands.* . . . Cambridge, Mass., 1896.

Campbell, Mildred. *The English Yeoman under Elizabeth and the Early Stuarts.* New Haven, Conn., 1942.

Carroll, Peter N. *Puritanism and the Wilderness: The Intellectual Significance of the New England Frontier, 1629–1700.* New York, 1969.

Casey, Thos. Lincoln. "The Hutchinson Family." *Narragansett Historical Register,* II (1883–1884), 177–179.

Caulkins, Frances Manwaring. *History of Norwich, Connecticut.* . . . Hartford, Conn., 1874.

Channing, Edward. *The Narragansett Planters: A Study of Causes.* Johns Hopkins University Studies in Historical and Political Science, 4th Ser., no. 3. Baltimore, 1886.

———. *Town and County Government in the English Colonies of North America.* Johns Hopkins University Studies in Historical and Political Science, 2d Ser., no. 10. Baltimore, 1884.

Chase, George Wingate. *The History of Haverhill, Massachusetts, from Its First Settlement, in 1640, to the Year 1860.* Haverhill, Mass., 1861.

Clark, Charles E. *The Eastern Frontier: The Settlement of Northern New England, 1610–1763.* New York, 1970.

Clarke, Dr. John. Will. *Rhode Island Historical Magazine,* VII (1886–1887), 128–134.

Coggeshall, John. "Copy of the Will of Major John Coggeshall." In Charles Pierce Coggeshall and Thellwell Russell Coggeshall, comps., *The Coggeshalls in America.* . . . Boston, 1930.

Collier, Christopher. "Saybrook and Lyme: Secular Settlements in a Puritan Commonwealth." In George J. Willauer, Jr., ed., *A Lyme Miscellany, 1776–1976,* 9–29. Middletown, Conn., 1977.

Cotton, John. *Christ the Fountaine of Life.* . . . London, 1651.

———. *God's Promise to His Plantations.* London, 1634.

Crandall, Ruth, comp. *Tax and Valuation Lists of Massachusetts Towns before 1776: Finding List for the Microfilm Edition.* Cambridge, Mass., 1971.

Crane, Ellery Bicknell, ed. *History of Worcester County, Massachusetts.* 3 vols. New York, 1924.

Crissey, Theron Wilmot, comp. *History of Norfolk, Litchfield County, Connecticut, 1744–1900.* Everett, Mass., 1900.

Cronon, William. *Changes in the Land: Indians, Colonists, and the Ecology of New England.* New York, 1983.

Daggett, John. *Sketch of the History of Attleborough.* . . . Dedham, Mass., 1834.

Daniels, Bruce C. *The Connecticut Town: Growth and Development, 1635–1790.* Middletown, Conn., 1979.

———. *Dissent and Conformity on Narragansett Bay: The Colonial Rhode Island Town.* Middletown, Conn., 1983.

———, ed. *Town and County: Essays on the Structure of Local Government in the American Colonies.* Middletown, Conn., 1978.

Daniels, George F. *History of the Town of Oxford, Massachusetts.* . . . Oxford, Mass., 1892.

———. *The Huguenots in the Nipmuck Country; or, Oxford Prior to 1713.* Boston, 1880.

Davies, Godfrey. *The Early Stuarts, 1603–1660.* 2d ed. Oxford, 1959.

Davis, Andrew McFarland. *Currency and Banking in the Province of the Massachusetts-Bay.* 2 vols. New York, 1901.

———. "Corporations in the Days of the Colony." In *American Colonial History.* Cambridge, Mass., 1894.

Davis, Charles Thornton. "Some Thoughts on Early Colonial Development." Massachusetts Historical Society, *Proceedings,* LXIV (1930–1932), 507–515.

Davis, William T. *History of the Town of Plymouth.* . . . Philadelphia, 1885.

Dedham, Mass. *The Early Records of the Town.* . . . 6 vols. Dedham, Mass., 1886–1936.

Delbanco, Andrew. "The Puritan Errand Re-Viewed." *Journal of American Studies,* XVIII (1984), 343–360.

———. *The Puritan Ordeal.* Cambridge, Mass., 1989.

Deming, Dorothy. *The Settlement of Connecticut Towns*. New Haven, Conn., 1933.

Denison, Frederick. *Westerly (Rhode Island), and Its Witnesses . . . 1626–1876. . . .* Providence, R.I., 1878.

Dorr, Henry C. "The Proprietors of Providence, and Their Controversies with the Freeholders." Rhode Island Historical Society, *Publications*, n.s., III (1895), 143–158, 199–230, IV (1896), 75–106, 139–170, 203–226.

Dudley, Mass. *Town Records of Dudley, Massachusetts, 1732–1754*. Pawtucket, R.I., 1893.

Dunn, Richard S. *Puritans and Yankees: The Winthrop Dynasty of New England, 1630–1717*. New York, 1971.

Egleston, Melville. *The Land System of the New England Colonies*. Johns Hopkins University Studies in Historical and Political Science, 4th Ser., nos. 11–12. Baltimore, 1886.

Ellis, Charles Mayo. *The History of Roxbury Town*. Boston, 1847.

"Extracts of Letters to Rev. Thomas Prince." Connecticut Historical Society, *Collections*, III (1895), 271–320.

Felt, Joseph B. *Annals of Salem*. 2 vols. Salem, Mass., 1845–1849.

Fiore, Jordan D. *Wrentham, 1673–1973: A History*. Wrentham, Mass., 1973.

Fones, John. *The Records of the Proprietors of the Narragansett, Otherwise Called the Fones Record*. Edited by James W. Arnold. Providence, R.I., 1894.

Ford, Worthington Chauncy, ed. *Broadsides, Ballads, etc., Printed in Massachusetts, 1639–1800*. Massachusetts Historical Society, *Collections*, LXXV. Boston, 1922.

Gardiner, J. Warren. "The Pioneers of Narragansett." *Narragansett Historical Register*, II (1883–1884), 112–115.

———. "Roger Williams, the Pioneer of Narragansett." *Narragansett Historical Register*, II (1883–1884), 25–34.

Gildrie, Richard P. *Salem, Massachusetts, 1626–1683: A Covenant Community*. Charlottesville, Va., 1975.

Ginsburg, Arlin I. "The Franchise in Seventeenth-Century Massachusetts: Ipswich." *William and Mary Quarterly*, 3d Ser., XXXIV (1977), 446–452.

Gookin, Frederick William. *Daniel Gookin, 1612–1687. . . .* Chicago, 1912.

Gordon, George Augustus. *The Early Grants of Land in the Wilderness North of Merrimack*. Lowell, Mass., 1892.

Gorges, Sir Ferdinando. *A Briefe Narration of the Originall Undertakings of the Advancement of Plantations. . . .* London, 1658. Reprinted in Maine Historical Society, *Collections*, 1st Ser., II (1847), 1–75.

Gorton, Adelos. *The Life and Times of Samuel Gorton. . . .* Philadelphia, 1907.

"Grant to Richard Wharton, June 10, 1686." Maine Historical Society, *Collections*, 1st Ser., III (1853), 325–329.

Great Britain. *Calendar of State Papers*. Colonial Series. 44 vols. London, 1860–1969.

Green, Samuel Abbott. *Proceedings of the Centennial Celebration at Groton*,

Massachusetts. . . . Groton, Mass., 1876. Reprinted in Green, ed., *Pamphlets on History of Groton* (n.p., n.d.).

———. *Remarks on Nonacoicus, the Indian Name of Major Willard's Farm at Groton, Mass*. . . . Cambridge, Mass., 1893.

———, ed. *An Account of the Early Land-Grants of Groton, Massachusetts*. Groton, Mass., 1879. Reprinted in Green, ed., *Pamphlets on History of Groton* (n.p., n.d.).

———, ed. *The Town Records of Groton, Massachusetts: 1662–1678*. Groton, Mass., 1879. Reprinted in Green, ed., *Pamphlets on History of Groton* (n.p., n.d.).

Greene, D. H. *History of the Town of East Greenwich and Adjacent Territory, from 1677 to 1877*. Providence, R.I., 1877.

Greene, Evarts B., and Virginia D. Harrington. *American Population before the Federal Census of 1790*. New York, 1932.

Greven, Philip J., Jr. *Four Generations: Population, Land, and Family in Colonial Andover, Massachusetts*. Ithaca, N.Y., 1970.

Hall, David D. *The Faithful Shepherd: A History of the New England Ministry in the Seventeenth Century*. Chapel Hill, N.C., 1972.

———. "The Mental World of Samuel Sewall." In Hall, John M. Murrin, and Thad W. Tate, eds., *Saints and Revolutionaries: Essays on Early American History*, 75–95. New York, 1984.

———. "On Common Ground: The Coherence of American Puritan Studies." *William and Mary Quarterly*, 3d Ser., XLIV (1987), 193–229.

Hall, Edwin, ed. *The Ancient Historical Records of Norwalk, Conn., with a Plan of the Ancient Settlement, and of the Town in 1847*. New York, 1865.

Hall, Michael G. "Randolph, Dudley, and the Massachusetts Moderates in 1683." *New England Quarterly*, XXIX (1956), 513–516.

Haller, William, Jr. *The Puritan Frontier: Town-Planting in New England Colonial Development, 1630–1660*. New York, 1951.

Hamilton, Edward Pierce. *A History of Milton*. Milton, Mass., 1957.

Hammond, Otis Grant. "The Mason Title and Its Relations to New Hampshire and Massachusetts." American Antiquarian Society, *Proceedings*, n.s., XXVI (1916), 245–263.

Hartford, Conn. *Original Distribution of the Lands in Hartford among the Settlers: 1639*. Connecticut Historical Society, *Collections*, XIV. Hartford, Conn., 1912.

Hartog, Hendrik. *Public Property and Private Power: The Corporation of the City of New York in American Law, 1730–1870*. Chapel Hill, N.C., 1983.

Haskins, George Lee. *Law and Authority in Early Massachusetts: A Study in Tradition and Design*. New York, 1960.

Hazen, Henry A. *History of Billerica, Massachusetts*. . . . Boston, 1883.

Heimert, Alan. "Puritanism, the Wilderness, and the Frontier." *New England Quarterly*, XXVI (1953), 361–382.

Heimert, Alan, and Andrew Delbanco, eds. *The Puritans in America: A Narrative Anthology*. Cambridge, Mass., 1985.

Heyrman, Christine Leigh. *Commerce and Culture: The Maritime Communities of Colonial Massachusetts, 1690–1750*. New York, 1984.

Hill, Christopher. *The Century of Revolution, 1603–1714*. New York, 1966.

Hoadly, Charles J., ed. *Hartford Town Votes*, I, *1635–1716*. Connecticut Historical Society, *Collections*, VI. Hartford, Conn., 1897.

———, ed. *Records of the Colony and Plantation of New Haven, from 1638 to 1649*. Hartford, Conn., 1857.

Holland, Josiah Gilbert. *History of Western Massachusetts*. 2 vols. Springfield, Mass., 1855.

Holmes, A. "Memoir of the French Protestants, Who Settled at Oxford, Massachusetts, *A.D.* 1686. . . ." Massachusetts Historical Society, *Collections*, 3d Ser., II (1830), 1–83.

Hooker, Thomas. *The Application of Redemption . . . The Ninth and Tenth Books*. 2d ed. London, 1659.

Hough, Franklin B. "Pemaquid Papers." Maine Historical Society, *Collections*, V (1857).

Huling, Ray Greene. "The Earliest List of Inhabitants at Narragansett." *Narragansett Historical Register*, III (1884–1885), 170.

———. "An Offer of Sale by the Proprietors of Warwick in 1652." *Narragansett Historical Register*, II (1883–1884), 233–238.

Hull, John. "The Diaries of John Hull, Mint-Master and Treasurer of the Colony of Massachusetts Bay." American Antiquarian Society, *Transactions, Collections*, III (1857), 117–281.

Hutchinson, Thomas. *The History of the Colony and Province of Massachusetts-Bay*. Edited by Lawrence Shaw Mayo. 3 vols. Cambridge, Mass., 1936.

Innes, Stephen. *Labor in a New Land: Economy and Society in Seventeenth-Century Springfield*. Princeton, N.J., 1983.

———. "Land Tenancy and Social Order in Springfield, Massachusetts, 1652 to 1702." *William and Mary Quarterly*, 3d Ser., XXXV (1978), 33–56.

Isham, Norman M. "Preliminary Report . . . on . . . Jireh Bull Garrison House. . . ." Rhode Island Historical Society, *Collections*, XI (1918), 3.

Isham, Norman M., *et al.*, eds. *Rhode Island Land Evidences*, I, *1648–1696: Abstracts*. Providence, R.I., 1921.

James, Sydney V. *Colonial Rhode Island: A History*. New York, 1975.

———. "The Worlds of Roger Williams." *Rhode Island History*, XXXVII (1978), 99–109.

Jillson, David. "John Viall, of Swansey, Mass., and Some of His Descendants." *Narragansett Historical Register*, III (1884–1885), 97–112.

Johnson, Edward. *Johnson's Wonder-Working Providence, 1628–1651*. Edited by J. Franklin Jameson. New York, 1910.

Judd, Sylvester. *History of Hadley, Including the Early History of Hatfield, South Hadley, Amherst, and Granby, Massachusetts*. Springfield, Mass., 1905.

Kammen, Michael. *Deputyes and Libertyes: The Origins of Representative Government in Colonial America*. New York, 1969.

Keayne, Robert. *The Apologia of Robert Keayne . . . The Self-Portrait of a Puritan Merchant.* Edited by Bernard Bailyn. New York, 1965.

Kimball, Everett. *The Public Life of Joseph Dudley: A Study of the Colonial Policy of the Stuarts in New England, 1660–1715.* Harvard Historical Studies, XV. New York, 1911.

Knight, Richard. "The Six Principle Baptists in the Narragansett Country." *Narragansett Historical Register,* I (1882–1883), 203–208.

Konig, David Thomas. "Community Custom and the Common Law: Social Change and the Development of Land Law in Seventeenth-Century Massachusetts." *American Journal of Legal History,* XVIII (1974), 137–177.

———. *Law and Society In Puritan Massachusetts: Essex County, 1628–1692.* Chapel Hill, N.C., 1979.

Kross, Jessica. *The Evolution of an American Town: Newtown, New York, 1642–1775.* Philadelphia, 1983.

Kulikoff, Allan. "The Transition to Capitalism in Rural America." *William and Mary Quarterly,* 3d Ser., XLVI (1989), 120–144.

Labaree, Leonard W. *Milford, Connecticut: The Early Development of a Town as Shown in Its Land Records.* Connecticut Tercentenary Commission, no. 13. New Haven, Conn., 1933.

Levett, Christopher. *A Voyage into New England, Begun in 1623, and Ended in 1624.* London, 1628. Reprinted in Maine Historical Society, *Collections,* 1st Ser., II (1847), 73–109.

Lewis, Theodore B. "Land Speculation and the Dudley Council of 1686." *William and Mary Quarterly,* 3d Ser., XXXI (1974), 255–272.

Lincoln, William. *History of Worcester. . . .* Worcester, Mass., 1862.

Livermore, Shaw. *Early American Land Companies: Their Influence on Corporate Development.* New York, 1939.

Locke, John. *The Second Treatise of Government.* 1690. Edited by Thomas P. Peardon. New York, 1952.

Lockridge, Kenneth A. *A New England Town, the First Hundred Years: Dedham, Massachusetts, 1636–1736.* New York, 1970.

Londonderry, N.H. *Early Records of Londonderry, Windham, and Derry, N.H.: 1719–1762.* Manchester Historic Association, *Collections,* V (1908). Vol. I of the printed town records.

———. *Early Records of Londonderry, Windham, and Derry, N.H.: 1719–1745.* Manchester Historic Association, *Collections,* VI (1911). Vol. II of the printed town records.

Love, William DeLoss. *The Colonial History of Hartford. . . .* 2d ed. Hartford, Conn., 1935. Reprint. 1974.

Lucas, Paul R. *Valley of Discord: Church and Society along the Connecticut River, 1636–1725.* Hanover, N.H., 1976.

McGiffert, Michael. "Grace and Works: The Rise and Division of Covenant Divinity in Elizabethan Puritanism." *Harvard Theological Review,* LXXV (1982), 463–502.

———. "The Problem of the Covenant in Puritan Thought: Peter Bulkeley's *Gospel-Covenant.*" *New England Historical and Genealogical Register,* CXXX (1976), 107–129.

———, ed. *God's Plot: The Paradoxes of Puritan Piety, Being the Autobiography and Journal of Thomas Shepard.* [Amherst], Mass., 1972.

MacLear, Anne Bush. *Early New England Towns: A Comparative Study of Their Development.* New York, 1908.

Main, Jackson Turner. *Society and Economy in Colonial Connecticut.* Princeton, N.J., 1985.

Maitland, F. W. *Township and Borough.* Cambridge, 1898. Reprint. 1964.

Manchester, Mass. *Town Records of Manchester.* . . . 2 vols. Salem, Mass., 1889–1891.

Martin, John Frederick. "Entrepreneurship and the Founding of New England Towns: The Seventeenth Century." Ph.D. diss., Harvard University, 1985.

Mason, Major John. "History of the Pequot War, 1637." *Narragansett Historical Register,* VIII (1890), 121–156.

Massachusetts. *Records of the Company of the Massachusetts Bay, to the Embarkation of Winthrop and His Associates for New England as Contained in the First Volume of the Archives of the Commonwealth of Massachusetts.* American Antiquarian Society, *Transactions, Collections,* III. Boston, 1857.

Massachusetts, General Courts. *The Acts and Resolves, Public and Private, of the Province of the Massachusetts Bay.* . . . 21 vols. Boston, 1869–1922.

Massachusetts Body of Liberties, The / A Coppie of the Liberties of the Massachusets Colonie in New England. In Edmund S. Morgan, ed., *Puritan Political Ideas, 1558–1794,* 178–203. New York, 1965.

Mathews, Lois Kimball. *The Expansion of New England: The Spread of New England Settlements and Institutions to the Mississippi River, 1620–1865.* Boston, 1909.

Melvoin, Richard I. "Communalism in Frontier Deerfield." In Stephen C. Innes *et al., Early Settlement in the Connecticut Valley,* 36–61. Edited by John W. Ifkovic and Martin Kaufman. Deerfield, Mass., 1984.

Mendon, Mass. *The Proprietors' Records of the Town of Mendon, Massachusetts.* Boston, 1899.

Merrill, Joseph. *History of Amesbury and Merrimac, Massachusetts.* Haverhill, Mass., 1880. Reprint. 1978.

Miller, Perry. *Errand into the Wilderness.* Cambridge, Mass., 1956.

———. *The New England Mind: From Colony to Province.* Cambridge, Mass., 1953.

———. *The New England Mind: The Seventeenth Century.* Cambridge, Mass., 1939.

Miller, William Davis. *A Brief Account of the William Withington Plat of Boston Neck, with a Description of the Shares of the Proprietors.* Providence, R.I., 1924.

———. "The Narragansett Planters." American Antiquarian Society, *Proceedings,* n.s., XLIII (1933), 49–115.

Morgan, Edmund S. *The Puritan Dilemma: The Story of John Winthrop.* Boston, 1958.

———. *Visible Saints: The History of a Puritan Idea.* New York, 1963.

Moriarty, G. Andrews. "President John Sanford of Portsmouth, R.I., and His Family." *New England Historical and Genealogical Register,* CIII (1942), 208–216, 271–277.

Morison, Samuel Eliot. "The Plantation of Nashaway—an Industrial Experiment." Colonial Society of Massachusetts, *Transactions,* XXVII (1927–1930), 204–222.

———. "William Pynchon, the Founder of Springfield." Massachusetts Historical Society, *Proceedings,* LXIV (1930–1932), 67–107.

Munro, Wilfred H. *History of Bristol, Rhode Island: The Story of the Mount Hope Lands.* . . . Providence, R.I., 1880.

Nason, Elias. *A History of the Town of Dunstable, Massachusetts.* . . . Boston, 1877.

New Hampshire. *Town Charters Granted within the Present Limits of New Hampshire.* Vol. II of Albert Stillman Batchellor, ed., *Town Charters,* vol. XXV of *State Papers.* Concord, N.H., 1895.

Notestein, Wallace. *The English People on the Eve of Colonization, 1603–1630.* New York, 1954.

Nourse, Henry S., ed. *The Early Records of Lancaster, Massachusetts, 1643–1725.* Lancaster, Mass., 1884.

"Original Proprietors of Sudbury, Mass." *New England Historical and Genealogical Register,* XIII (1859).

Osgood, Herbert L. *The American Colonies in the Seventeenth Century.* 3 vols. New York, 1904–1907.

Owen, Henry Wilson. *The Edward Clarence Plummer History of Bath, Maine.* Bath, Maine, 1936.

Paige, Lucius R. *History of Cambridge, Massachusetts, 1630–1877.* 2 vols. Cambridge, Mass., 1877.

Palfrey, John Gorham. *History of New England during the Stuart Dynasty.* 3 vols. Boston, 1865. Reprint. 1966.

Patton, A. B. "The Early Land Titles of Providence." *Narragansett Historical Register,* VIII (1890), 156–175.

Perkins, Edwin J. *The Economy of Colonial America.* 2d ed. New York, 1988.

Perley, Sidney. *The History of Salem, Massachusetts.* 3 vols. Salem, Mass., 1924–1928.

———. *The Indian Land Titles of Essex County, Massachusetts.* Salem, Mass., 1912.

Perzel, Edward S. "Landholding in Ipswich." Essex Institute, *Historical Collections,* CIV (1968), 303–328.

Phelps, Noah A. *History of Simsbury, Granby, and Canton, from 1642 to 1845.* Hartford, Conn., 1845.

Phillips, Hubert. *The Development of a Residential Qualification for Representatives in Colonial Legislatures.* Cincinnati, Ohio, 1921.

Pierce, John B. "One Line of the Haszard Family." *Narragansett Historical Register*, II (1883–1884), 45–51.

———. "A Sketch of the Cole Family." *Narragansett Historical Register*, II (1883–1884), 179–192.

Plymouth, Mass. *Records of the Town of Plymouth*. 3 vols. Plymouth, Mass., 1889–1903.

Poteet, James M. "More Yankee than Puritan: James Fitch of Connecticut." *New England Historical and Genealogical Register*, CXXXIII (1979), 102–117.

Potter, Elisha R., Jr. *The Early History of Narragansett*. Rhode Island Historical Society, *Collections*, III. Providence, R.I., 1835.

———. "Memoir concerning the French Settlements and French Settlers in the Colony of Rhode Island." *Rhode Island Historical Tracts*, 1st Ser., no. 5. Providence, R.I., 1879.

Powell, Sumner Chilton. *Puritan Village: The Formation of a New England Town*. Middletown, Conn., 1963.

Pratt, Harvey Hunter. *The Early Planters of Scituate*. Scituate, Mass., 1929.

Prichard, Katharine A., ed. *Proprietors' Records of the Town of Waterbury, Connecticut: 1677–1761*. Publications of the Mattatuck Historical Society, I. Waterbury, Conn., 1911.

Providence, R.I., Record Commissioners. *The Early Records of the Town of Providence*. 21 vols. Providence, R.I., 1892–1915.

Quidnesset. "Notes on Quidnesset." *Narragansett Historical Register*, I (1882–1883), 305–311.

Rabb, Theodore K. *Enterprise and Empire: Merchant and Gentry Investment in the Expansion of England, 1575–1630*. Cambridge, Mass., 1967.

Rice, Franklin P., ed. "Colonial Records of Marlborough, Mass." *New England Historical and Genealogical Register*, LXII (1908), 220–229, 336–344, LXIII (1909), 59–67, 117–126, 217–226.

———. *Records of the Proprietors of Worcester, Massachusetts*. Worcester Society of Antiquity, *Collections*, III. Worcester, Mass., 1881.

Rider, Sidney S. "The Forgeries Connected with the Deed Given by the Sachems Canonicus and Miantinomi to Roger Williams of the Land on Which the Town of Providence Was Planted." *Rhode Island Historical Tracts*, 2d Ser., no. 4. Providence, R.I., 1896.

Rose-Troup, Frances. *The Massachusetts Bay Company and Its Predecessors*. New York, 1930.

Rothenberg, Winifred B. "The Market and Massachusetts Farmers, 1750–1855." *Journal of Economic History*, XLI (1981), 283–314.

Rowley, Mass. *The Early Records of the Town of Rowley, Massachusetts, 1639–1672*. Rowley, Mass., 1894.

Russell, Edward. "History of North Yarmouth." Maine Historical Society, *Collections*, 1st Ser., II (1847), 165–188.

Rutman, Darrett B. *Winthrop's Boston: Portrait of a Puritan Town, 1630–1649*. Chapel Hill, N.C., 1965.

Sanford, Peleg. *The Letterbook of Peleg Sanford of Newport, Merchant.* . . . Edited by Howard W. Preston *et al.* Providence, R.I., 1928.

———. Will, Feb. 28, 1700/1 (summarized). *New England Historical and Genealogical Register,* CIII (1949), 274.

Sargent, William M. "The Division of the 12,000 Acres among the Patentees at Agamenticus." Maine Historical Society, *Collections,* 2d Ser., II (1891), 319–327.

Savage, James. *A Genealogical Dictionary of the First Settlers of New England, Showing Three Generations of Those Who Came before May, 1692, on the Basis of Farmer's Register.* 4 vols. Boston, 1860–1862. Reprint. 1965.

Scott, William Robert. *The Constitution and Finance of English, Scottish, and Irish Joint-Stock Companies to 1720.* 3 vols. New York, 1951.

Seaver, Paul. "The Puritan Work Ethic Revisited." *Journal of British Studies,* XIX, no. 2 (Spring 1980), 35–53.

Sewall, Samuel. *Diary of Samuel Sewall, 1674–1729.* 3 vols. Massachusetts Historical Society, *Collections,* 5th Ser., V–VII. Boston, 1878–1882.

Sewall, Samuel. *The History of Woburn, Middlesex County, Mass.* . . . Boston, 1868.

Shattuck, Lemuel. *A History of the Town of Concord.* . . . Boston, 1835.

Sheldon, George. *A History of Deerfield.* . . . 2 vols. Deerfield, Mass., 1895–1896.

Shepard, Thomas. *The Works.* Edited by John Adams Albro. Boston, 1853. Reprint. 1971.

Sherman, David. "The Sherman Family." *Narragansett Historical Register,* II (1883–1884), 226–232.

Sherman, Philip. "Philip Sherman Will," July 31, 1681. In Roy V. Sherman, *Some of the Descendants of Philip Sherman, the First Secretary of Rhode Island.* Akron, Ohio, 1968, 26–29.

Shurtleff, Nathaniel B., ed. *Records of the Governor and Company of the Massachusetts Bay in New England.* 5 vols. Boston, 1853–1854.

Simmons, Richard C. "Godliness, Property, and the Franchise in Puritan Massachusetts: An Interpretation." *Journal of American History,* LV (1968–1969), 495–511.

Sly, John Fairfield. *Town Government in Massachusetts (1620–1930).* Cambridge, Mass., 1930.

Snell, Ronald K. "Freemanship, Officeholding, and the Town Franchise in Seventeenth-Century Springfield, Massachusetts." *New England Historical and Genealogical Register,* CXXXIII (1979), 163–179.

Southegate, William S. "The History of Scarborough, from 1633 to 1783." Maine Historical Society, *Collections,* 1st Ser., III (1853), 10–237.

Stearns, Ezra S. *Early Generations of the Founders of Old Dunstable: Thirty Families.* Boston, 1911.

Sullivan, James. *The History of Land Titles in Massachusetts.* Boston, 1801.

Teele, A. K. *The History of Milton, Mass., 1640 to 1887.* . . . Boston, 1887.

Temple, J. H., and George Sheldon. *A History of the Town of Northfield, Massachusetts.* . . . Albany, N.Y., 1875.

Thornton, J. Wingate. "Ancient Pemaquid: An Historical Review." Maine Historical Society, *Collections,* 1st Ser., V (1857), 139–305.

Tilden, William S., ed. *History of the Town of Medfield, Massachusetts, 1650–1886.* . . . Boston, 1887.

Tolles, Frederick B. *Meeting House and Counting House: The Quaker Merchants of Colonial Philadelphia, 1682–1763.* Chapel Hill, N.C., 1948.

Toppan, Robert N., ed. "Records of the Council of Massachusetts, under Joseph Dudley." Massachusetts Historical Society, *Proceedings,* 2d Ser., XIII (1899–1900), 222–286.

Toppan, Robert Noxon, and Alfred Thomas Scrope Goodrick, eds. *Edward Randolph, Including His Letters and Official Papers.* . . . 7 vols. Prince Society, XXIV–XXVIII, XXX–XXXI. Boston, 1898–1909. Reprint. 1967.

Trumbull, Benjamin. *A Complete History of Connecticut.* . . . 2 vols. New Haven, Conn., 1818.

Trumbull, J. Hammond, and Charles J. Hoadly, eds. *Public Records of the Colony of Connecticut.* . . . 15 vols. Hartford, Conn., 1850–1890.

Turner, Frederick Jackson. "The First Official Frontier of the Massachusetts Bay." In Turner, *The Frontier in American History,* 39–66. New York, 1920.

Turner, Henry E. "William Coddington in Rhode Island Colonial Affairs." *Rhode Island Historical Tracts,* 1st Ser., no. 4. Providence, R.I., 1878.

Tuttle, Julius Herbert. "Land Warrants Issued under Andros, 1687–1688." Colonial Society of Massachusetts, *Publications, Transactions,* XXI (1919), 292–363.

U.S., Congress. Senate. *The Constitution of the United States: Analysis and Interpretation.* 92d Cong., 2d sess., 1973. S. Doc. 92-82. Washington, D.C., 1973.

Updike, Daniel Berkeley. *Richard Smith: First English Settler of the Narragansett Country, Rhode Island.* . . . Boston, 1937.

Upham, Wm. P., ed. *Town Records of Salem, 1634–1659.* Essex Institute, *Historical Collections,* 2d Ser., I, part 1. Salem, Mass., 1868.

Vaughan, Alden T. *New England Frontier: Puritans and Indians, 1620–1675.* Boston, 1965.

Vickers, Daniel. "Competency and Competition: Economic Culture in Early America." *William and Mary Quarterly,* 3d Ser., XLVII (1990), 3–29.

Wall, Robert E. "The Franchise in Seventeenth-Century Massachusetts: Dedham and Cambridge." *William and Mary Quarterly,* 3d Ser., XXXIV (1977), 453–458.

———. "The Massachusetts Bay Colony Franchise in 1647." *William and Mary Quarterly,* 3d Ser., XXVII (1970), 136–144.

Watertown, Historical Society of. *Watertown Records, Comprising the First and Second Books of Town Proceedings with the Lands, Grants, and Possessions.* 5 vols. Watertown, Mass., 1894.

Waters, Thomas Franklin. *Ipswich in the Massachusetts Bay Colony.* . . . 2 vols. Ipswich, Mass., 1905–1917.

Waters, Wilson. *History of Chelmsford, Massachusetts.* . . . Lowell, Mass., 1917.

Weeden, William B. *Economic and Social History of New England, 1620–1789.* 2 vols. Boston, 1891.

Wheeler, George Augustus, and Henry Wheeler. *History of Brunswick, Topsham, and Harpswell, Maine.* . . . Boston, 1878.

Wheeler, Richard A. "Major Atherton's Company." *Narragansett Historical Register,* II (1883–1884), 106–107.

Wheeler, Richard Anson. *History of the Town of Stonington.* . . . New London, Conn., 1900.

Wilbore, Samuel. Will, Apr. 30, 1656. In *Ye Wildbore,* I, no. 2 (February 1929). Copy in RIHS.

Willauer, George J., Jr., ed. *A Lyme Miscellany, 1776–1976.* Middletown, Conn., 1977.

Williams, Roger. *The Letters of Roger Williams.* . . . Edited by John Russell Bartlett. Narragansett Club, *Publications,* 1st Ser., VI. Providence, R.I., 1874.

———. To John Whipple, Jr., Aug. 24, 1669. *Rhode Island Historical Tracts,* 1st Ser., no. 14 (Providence, R.I., 1881), 25–46.

Williamson, William D. *The History of the State of Maine.* . . . 2 vols. Hallowell, Maine, 1832.

Willis, William. "The History of Portland. . . ." Maine Historical Society, *Collections,* 1st Ser., I (1831), 19–325.

Winthrop, John. *A Model of Christian Charity / Christian Charitie: A Model Hereof.* In Edmund S. Morgan, ed., *Puritan Political Ideas, 1558–1794,* 76–93. Indianapolis, Ind., 1965.

———. *The History of New England from 1630 to 1649.* Edited by James Savage. 2 vols. Boston, 1825–1826. Reprint. 1972.

Winthrop, Wait. "Correspondence of Wait Winthrop." In *The Winthrop Papers,* 3–371. Massachusetts Historical Society, *Collections,* 6th Ser., V. Boston, 1928.

Woodard, Florence May. *The Town Proprietors in Vermont: The New England Town Proprietorship in Decline.* New York, 1936.

Wright, Harry Andrew, ed. *Indian Deeds of Hampden County.* Springfield, Mass., 1905.

York County, Maine, Register of Deeds. *York Deeds, 1642.* . . . 17 vols. Portland, Bethel, Maine, 1887–.

Index

Adams, Charles Francis: on towns as corporations, 133–134n. 4; on towns as enterprises, 239n. 1

Alienation restraints, 224; in regulating inhabitancy, 224–225; and not screening residents, 225–226; upon other than real property, 226; as employed by land companies, 227; as coincident with inequity, 236n. 42; in Dedham, 296

Alienations: implications of, 252

Allen, David Grayson: on land rights, 31–32nn. 42, 43

Allen, Samuel: on land rents, 103; and seizure of common lands, 268

Allin, John, 295

Andros, Sir Edmund: and confirmation of Tyng's lands, 21; and changes in tax system, 41; and confirmation of Dudley's lands, 94; and rejection of big claims, 100n. 130, 261; removal of, sought, 108; and rejection of Wharton's claim, 109; on ambiguities of towns, 259; as autocrat, 260; overthrow of, 262; and declaration on spurious titles, 263; and assault on towns, 264–266

Arnold, Benedict, 74; and Westerly, 60

Ashford, Conn.: and franchise dispute, 289

Atherton, Hope: as minister, 126

Atherton, Humphrey, 88; as political and military leader, 62–63; landholdings of, 63–64; and signing of church covenant, 125

Atherton Company, 82–83; and tenantry, 33; shareholders of, 33, 64, 66–70; and conspiracy with John Winthrop, Jr., 54–55; designs of,

upon Narragansett, 62; first land distribution of, 68–69; corporateness of, 70–73; and advertising of land, 83; as helped by Dudley Council, 89–90; Dudley's support of, 91; and preaching, 124–125; and alienation restraints, 227; claims of, and Andros, 261

Belcher, Andrew, Sr., 11; as typical town founder, 16–17; as nonresident inhabitant, 222

Belcher, Jonathan: on representation and ownership, 181

Bellingham, Richard: bequest of land rents by, 33

Benton, Josiah Henry: on warning out, 233n. 37, 284n. 9

Bernon, Gabriel, 94

Billerica (Shawshin): founders of, 12; and Daniel Gookin, 23–24; agreement of, 141–142; owners of, 204; and fight with Cambridge, 209

Blackwell, John, 93

Blathwayt, William, 263; and approval of Wharton's claim, 109; and Randolph, 261n. 5

Blood, Richard, 12

Bolton, Conn.: and inhabitants' diminishing rights, 272n. 30

Bonython, Richard, 102

Boston: land controversy in, 249–250; proprietors of, 273

Boston Neck (Namcook), 62, 67, 70, 76, 80, 82, 84; lands of, and Winthrops, 55

Boyes, Antipas: and Kennebec Purchase, 106

Bozeman, T. D., 148

289; by shares, 183–184; conflicts over, 251

Waldo, Cornelius, 14; as typical town founder, 11–12
Wall, Robert E., 197n. 19
Wallingford: tax dispute in, 40
Wamesit Purchase, 11, 12, 99–100
Ward, Nathaniel: on wilderness experience, 113
Warfare: in thwarting land development, 110
Warning out, 284
Warwick, 142; divisions within, 231–233; offer of, for sale, 242–243
Waterbury: distributions of, 155; shareholders of, 189
Watertown: nonproprietors of, 197–198
Wentworth, Benning, 269
Westerly (Misquamicut): nonresidents of, 60, 176; agreement of, 141
Westfield (Woronoco): and Pynchon, 44, 50–51; and Springfield, 215
Westford, 12
Wharton, Richard, 70; and profits, 31; and Pejepscot, 90; lands of, 108–109; and Andros, 261
Wilbore, Samuel, 73–74; church membership of, 125
Wilderness: Israelites in, 113; struggle in, 114; as idle, 115–116
Willard, Simon: as town founder, 19–20; as father, 126
Willett, Thomas, 69, 83; career and lands of, 80
Williams, Roger: on "God Land," 118; and Providence lands, 249–251
Wilson, Samuel, 73–74
Windsor: in conflict with Simsbury, 42

Winslow, John: and Kennebec Purchase, 106
Winslow, Josias, 69
Winthrop, Fitz John: and Rhode Island lands, 55
Winthrop, John: on requirements of town-founding, 9–10; and land improvement, 37–38; on quality of land, 112; against idle land, 116; and Boston land, 118, 249–251; expounding by, of social theory, 121; and ideal town-planting, 212; on regulating strangers, 230
Winthrop, John, Jr.: and Ipswich, 10, 52–53; and Saybrook, 53–54; and New London, 54; and Atherton Company, 54–55, 62, 65; and various Connecticut claims, 55–56; estate of, 56; on improvement, 113–114
Winthrop, Wait: and Quinebaug lands, 56; and Dudley council, 90; and fight for land claims, 261; and command of rebels, 262
Woburn, 12
Woodstock (New Roxbury): origins of, 57, 96–97; owners of, 206; charges of, 207; as home to Roxbury landless, 211–212; and towns as enterprises, 240–241; and changing language, 277–278
Worcester, 15, 17; founding of, 25–28; land distribution in, 25; nonresidents of, 25–26, 140; profits in, 37; and Ephraim Curtis, 43; divisions within, 232–233
Wrentham: and fight with Dedham, 210, 301

York (Agamenticus, Gorgeana), 104